ELLEN GLASGOW
and THE IRONIC
ART OF FICTION

ELLEN GLASGOW
and THE IRONIC
ART OF FICTION

by Frederick P. W. McDowell

The University of Wisconsin Press ⋄ Madison ⋄ 1963

Published by
THE. UNIVERSITY OF WISCONSIN PRESS
430 Sterling Court
Madison 6, Wisconsin

Copyright © 1960 by the Regents of
the University of Wisconsin

Paperback Edition, 1963

Printed in the United States of America

Library of Congress Catalog Number 60-9551

To

HOWARD MUMFORD JONES

Acknowledgments

For assistance I am indebted to Mrs. Irita Van Doren, Professor Howard Mumford Jones, and Bessie Zaban Jones. Mrs. Van Doren and Mr. Frank Morley have given me permission to quote from the collected and uncollected works of Miss Glasgow. Professors W. R. Irwin, John C. Gerber, and Curt A. Zimansky, my colleagues at the State University of Iowa, criticized the manuscript in detail. Over the years, Professor Baldwin Maxwell, Head of the Department of English at the State University of Iowa, has also encouraged me with this study. I am grateful to the State University of Iowa for the use of a research assistant, a semester's leave of absence in 1956–57, secretarial help, and a generous subvention for the publication of this project. I also wish to acknowledge the generosity of the Ford Foundation with whose assistance this book has been published. To my wife, who has worked with me continually, my debt cannot be stated.

The quotations from Miss Glasgow's books and from *Letters of Ellen Glasgow,* edited by Blair Rouse, are used by permission of Harcourt, Brace & Co., Inc.

For permission to quote material from other copyrighted volumes, acknowledgment is made to the following:

Alfred A. Knopf for *A History of the South* by Francis B. Simkins and *The Mind of the South* by W. J. Cash.

Appleton-Century-Crofts for *The Age of Innocence* by Edith Wharton.

Paul H. Buck and Little, Brown & Co. for *The Road to Reunion 1865–1900* by Paul H. Buck.

Margaret F. Cabell and the McBride Co. for *As I Remember It* by James Branch Cabell.

Chilton Co. for *Thomas Hardy, Life and Art,* edited by Ernest Brennecke.

Dodd, Mead & Co., Inc., for *Before I Forget: A Pilgrimage to the Past* by Isaac Marcosson and *The Women Who Make Our Novels* by Grant H. Overton.

Doubleday & Co. and Rinehart & Co. for *McTeague* by Frank Norris.

Constance Garland Doyle, Isabel Garland Lord, and The Macmillan Co. for *Roadside Meetings* by Hamlin Garland.

Harper & Brothers for *Literature in the Making* by Joyce Kilmer and *Virginia: A New Look at the Old Dominion* by Marshall W. Fishwick.

Houghton Mifflin Co. for *An American Memoir* by Henry Seidel Canby and *Rebels and Ancestors* by Maxwell Geismar.

Little, Brown & Co. for *Letters of Sherwood Anderson,* edited by Howard Mumford Jones and Walter Rideout.

Longwood College, Virginia, for *Virginia in History and Tradition,* edited by R. C. Simonini, Jr. (C. Hugh Holman, "Ellen Glasgow and the Southern Literary Tradition").

Louisiana State University Press for *The South During Reconstruction 1865–1877* by E. Merton Coulter and *Origins of the New South* by C. Vann Woodward.

The Macmillan Co. for *Hugh Walpole* by Rupert Hart-Davis.

Arthur W. Page and Houghton Mifflin Co. for *The Training of an American: The Earlier Life and Letters of Walter H. Page 1855–1913* by Burton J. Hendrick.

Princeton University Press for *Anatomy of Criticism* by Northrop Frye.

Public Affairs Press for *The Virginia Tradition* by Marshall W. Fishwick.

Random House, Inc., for *Absalom, Absalom!* by William Faulkner.

Simon & Schuster, Inc. for *I Believe: The Personal Philosophies of Certain Eminent Men and Women of Our Time,* edited by Clifton Fadiman.

University of North Carolina Press for *Culture in the South,* edited by W. T. Couch.

Carl Van Vechten and Yale University Library for *Fragments from an Unwritten Autobiography* by Carl Van Vechten.

Acknowledgment is made to the following periodicals and their editors for material that appeared in their pages:

ALA Booklist for comment on *The Miller of Old Church* (1911).

Good Housekeeping for "Can Children Be Taught to Write?" by Albert F. Wilson (July, 1915).

Nation for comment on *Life and Gabriella* (Feb. 17, 1916), and for "What I Believe" by Ellen Glasgow (Apr. 12, 1933).

New Republic for "Barren Ground" by Carl Van Doren (Apr. 29,

1925), and "Ellen Glasgow's New Book" by Stark Young (Sept. 11, 1935).

New York Herald Tribune and *New York Herald Tribune Books* for excerpts from the following articles by Ellen Glasgow: "Impressions of the Novel" (May 20, 1928), "Portrait of a Much Loved Dog" (July 22, 1934), and "George Santayana Writes a Novel" (Feb. 2, 1936).

New York Herald Tribune Magazine for "A Prophet of the New South" by Virginius Dabney (Aug. 25, 1929).

New York Times for "Feminism" by Ellen Glasgow, *Book Review* (Nov. 30, 1913); "Ellen Glasgow's Literary Credo" by Hamilton Basso, *Book Review* (Oct. 17, 1943); and "No Valid Reason Against Giving Votes to Women," *Magazine* (Mar. 23, 1913).

Saturday Review for "Heroes and Monsters" by Ellen Glasgow (May 4, 1935).

Sewanee Review for "Fiction and Social Ethics" by Archibald Henderson (Oct., 1904).

Virginia Quarterly Review for "Ellen Glasgow's Autobiography" by James Southall Wilson (Spring, 1955).

Philological Quarterly for "Ellen Glasgow and the Art of the Novel" by Frederick P. W. McDowell (July, 1951).

Twentieth Century Literature for " 'The Old Pagan Scorn of Everlasting Mercy'—Ellen Glasgow's *The Deliverance*" by Frederick P. W. McDowell (Jan., 1959).

Texas Studies in Literature and Language for "Theme and Artistry in Ellen Glasgow's *The Sheltered Life*" by Frederick P. W. McDowell (Winter, 1960).

Frederick P. W. McDowell

Iowa City, Iowa
Winter, 1960

Contents

ELLEN GLASGOW
and THE IRONIC
ART OF FICTION

Introduction

A versatile and fastidious writer, Ellen Glasgow is possibly the most neglected novelist in her generation. There has been no previous book about her, nor has less extended commentary been abundant. Varying estimates, moreover, have recently been made of her work. In literary histories and critical surveys [1] and in most of the reviews of Ellen Glasgow's autobiography, *The Woman Within* (1954), her importance as a Southern writer, social historian, and literary artist has been recognized. At the same time, her artistic inadequacies have been emphatically discussed by John Edward Hardy in *Southern Renascence* (1953) and more tentatively suggested by Alfred Kazin in *The Inmost Leaf* (1955), who revises downward his estimate in *On Native Grounds* (1942).

This present disagreement among Ellen Glasgow's critics may be partly explained, I think, in terms of the history of her reputation.

Throughout her career, Ellen Glasgow was, on the whole, a better "seller" than either Willa Cather or Edith Wharton. In *Fifty Years of Best Sellers* Alice Payne Hackett finds Ellen Glasgow in second place in 1904 with *The Deliverance,* in tenth place in 1906 with *The Wheel of Life,* in fifth place for 1932 with *The Sheltered Life,* and in second place for 1935 with *Vein of Iron.*[2] Miss Glasgow's realistic appraisal of experience sometimes shocked her audience: in 1911, for example, the *ALA Booklist* complained that in *The Miller of Old Church* "there is a disagreeable situation throughout the story that will displease many and should perhaps bar it from immature readers." But in the main her books were well received and widely read. In 1904 Archibald Henderson praised *The Deliverance* as "notable and important in the literature not

3

only today but of the decade"; in 1908 a reviewer of *The Ancient Law* said that "from Ellen Glasgow we may always expect thoroughly well written fiction"; in 1913 a newspaper reporter, recounting an interview with Miss Glasgow, spoke of her "more than National renown"; and in 1916 another reviewer mentioned that she had "acquired an audience . . . considerable in numbers." [3] Whereas Miss Glasgow soon achieved a popular following, the sale of her work was never astronomical, and relatively inferior books such as *The Wheel of Life* and *Life and Gabriella* often sold the best.

In spite of her repute before 1925, Ellen Glasgow received little serious attention. During the early twentieth century Frederic Taber Cooper wrote the only comprehensive, if but moderately perceptive, essay upon her work.[4] With reason, then, she could complain in 1934 of the "neglect, abuse, wilful misrepresentation" which she had experienced in her career.[5] The vogue of James Lane Allen's Kentucky idylls in the 1890's and the huge sales of Mary Johnston's romances in the early 1900's established these authors, in popular opinion before the first World War, as the most important in the South.

Miss Glasgow's career illustrates the absence in America of any discerning criticism vitally and constructively interested in contemporaneous literature between Howells's championship during the 1880's and early 1890's of Crane, Norris, and Garland and Mencken's emergence during the first World War as spokesman in *The Smart Set* for a new generation of writers. The neohumanists, Babbitt, More, and Sherman—who became influential in the first decades of the century—were either indifferent or hostile toward modern literature: see Stuart P. Sherman's virulent attacks on Dreiser and other moderns in *On Contemporary Literature* (1917). W. C. Brownell had helped Edith Wharton get a start, but his interest in the contemporary seemed to cease there. In "The National Letters" Mencken himself imperceptively lumped Ellen Glasgow with Margaret Deland, Mary Johnston, James Lane Allen, and Owen Wister as genteel "academicians" (Mencken was later to write with insight on Ellen Glasgow, praising in 1929 *They Stooped to Folly* and finding in 1933 the iconoclasm and the "amiable skepticism" which he had earlier overlooked in her work [6]). When after 1914 the twentieth-century renaissance in American letters was under way, Miss Glasgow, having already written excellent novels, was unable to do as well in her books published after 1913 and before 1925. Neglect by critics during this period can in part be explained by the nature of her work itself. With the appearance of *Barren Ground* in 1925, Ellen Glasgow began to secure a recognition commensurate with her present —and past—accomplishment. Discerning reviews of this novel by Stuart

P. Sherman, Carl Van Doren, James Branch Cabell, Cameron Rogers, and Archibald Henderson now established Miss Glasgow's stature as literary artist.[7]

The absence of earlier intelligent criticism had unfavorable results on Miss Glasgow and her work. Most obviously, the delayed recognition was frustrating to an artist proud of her achievement. Of more serious consequence, Ellen Glasgow received little encouragement to go on writing in an age unsympathetic to her vigorous realism in the novel: she later was to wonder "why I did not entirely lose heart when I so often lost hope." [8] Judicious discussion of her work might possibly have alleviated some of its defects: its didacticism, its prolixity, its auctorial stridency, its sometimes facile philosophic formulations. Such sophisticated consideration of her work might also have enabled her to emerge sooner from a transitional phase of her career, the years 1913–25, and to write better books than *Life and Gabriella* (1916), *The Builders* (1919), *One Man in His Time* (1922), and *The Shadowy Third* (1923).

After 1925 serious treatment of her work had salutary effects upon it. Sherman's sympathetic review of *Barren Ground,* "The Fighting Edge of Romance," led her, she said, to continue writing when in a depressed state she had decided that she could not begin another book. She seems to have followed his advice to write in a mood less grave than that expressed in *Barren Ground;* and she also seems to have acted upon Carl Van Doren's hint to "try a sparer plot of the difficult but rewarding length of *Ethan Frome, Miss Lulu Bett,* or *A Lost Lady.*" [9] The result was her lively comedy of manners, *The Romantic Comedians* (1926), in which her wit and satiric vivacity had fuller scope than in any of her previous novels. Wit and satire became more ominous in *They Stooped to Folly* (1929) and in her best book, *The Sheltered Life* (1932).

To compensate in a measure for earlier disregard of her work, Miss Glasgow herself seems to have devoted much energy after 1925 to consolidating the reputation that she had finally won among serious readers and critics. James Branch Cabell's reminiscences are, with some reservations, illuminating at this point.[10] He asserted that he knew her better as writer and *grande dame* than anyone else had during her last twenty years; and he verified some of the impressions conveyed by Ellen Glasgow herself and by others. Since she felt cut off by incurable deafness from an independently active life, her central motivation in her last years, according to Cabell, became devotion to her writing. This absorption in her work resulted not only in her conscientious craftsmanship but also in her evident compulsion to further her general reputation. She entertained frequently and was especially cordial to journalists and critics who either reviewed her books or else wrote articles about her as woman and author. Cabell's statements are in part confirmed by Ellen Glasgow's enumeration in *The Woman Within* of her close friends in later years, who were mainly critics rather than novelists or poets. In the *Letters* she repeatedly asserted that "my work is the only thing in the world that makes life endurable." [11] Her letters during these years also reveal her solicitude about her reputation. She seems to have been at times excessively grateful for favorable comment upon her work, and at one point she quite specifically instructed her friend Stark Young what he was to say in his review of *Vein of Iron*.[12]

With her American contemporaries in the novel Ellen Glasgow evidently experienced some sense of rivalry. She was not humble when she thought of herself in relation to them, nor was she in all respects just to them. In *American Memoir* Henry Seidel Canby mentions her "brilliant sallies at successful contemporaries whom she regarded as incompetent writers or able charlatans"; and in *As I Remember It* Cabell recalled how satirically she could discourse upon "the exact literary merits of Willa Cather." [13]

She seems never to have been in doubt about the merit of her own work from the time that she wrote to Walter Hines Page concerning *Phases of an Inferior Planet* (1898): "It is going to be worth my while and worth your while and if I send it to you and you do not want it for the *Atlantic* you will be very blind and I shall be very wrathful." [14] When she described her late novels in *The Woman Within* as representing "some of the best work that has been done in American fiction," [15] we may with some diffidence agree, but recognize also a somewhat too confident assurance about her achievement.

Acting upon this compulsion to bring her work to public attention, Miss Glasgow seems to have been especially sensitive to unfavorable press notices and to have sometimes interpreted even judicious comment as a personal affront. James Branch Cabell told, for example, of her resentment toward the critic whose "adulation" had not been "vociferous" in reviewing *Vein of Iron* (1935), after she had been at pains previously to cultivate him.[16] Following a visit to "Elizabeth" (Countess Mary Annette Russell) in Switzerland in 1927, Hugh Walpole wrote that in his hostess he noticed "a fierce clutching of her literary reputation, as I saw in Ellen Glasgow." [17] In reviewing *The Woman Within* James Southall Wilson, Miss Glasgow's good friend and sympathetic critic for many years, has described the slight hiatus in friendship produced when he expressed in print some reservation about her work. She later admitted that his observation was true, but thought that he ought not to have made it since she was, she was certain, a "very much neglected author. I have not received the recognition that I feel I deserve and I think I have the right to expect my friends to say only good things about me." [18]

Along with James Branch Cabell one can be reasonably tolerant of all this, since Ellen Glasgow was, in this way, compensating for long neglect by competent critics. We can agree in part with Cabell that Ellen Glasgow's exertions on her own behalf were justified since they secured for her a wider general recognition, since they impelled her to an intensified creative activity, and since they made available to a wide circle her charm and magnetism. Except for her anxiety about her books, dignity and aloofness also characterized her actions. Her friends were, moreover, as devoted to her as she seems to have been to them. They would all apparently have agreed with Mr. Wilson when in a recent article he said: "When I left her it was always with an inner glow." [19]

The essays written in the late 1920's and after by Ellen Glasgow's friends, in some part controlled by her, were descriptive and laudatory rather than discriminatory. With the publication of the elaborate Virginia Edition of her work in 1938, she came to be accepted more as a literary institution than as an artist whose work, in being worthy of criticism, had also to be approached dispassionately. The reviews and essays of Henry Seidel Canby, Howard Mumford Jones, James Southall Wilson, Alfred Kazin, N. Elizabeth Monroe (*The Novel and Society,* 1941), and James Branch Cabell are illuminating but, for the most part, brief and appreciative. Little else written on Ellen Glasgow in the 1930's and in the 1940's has much substance.

Possibly because she was too much praised after 1925 or praised for the wrong reasons, some critics have overlooked her in the 1950's and some others, notably John Edward Hardy, have concentrated upon her weaknesses as a writer. Mr. Hardy's predominantly formalist approach to the novels, I feel, obscures their scope and vigor, and he often fails to discuss her best work. Still we must recognize with him that criticism rather than appreciation will now best serve Miss Glasgow.[20]

Some well-balanced studies of Miss Glasgow's work have also been written recently. Among them Maxwell Geismar's is the most extensive. In *Rebels and Ancestors* he has adopted a modified sociological approach, which, in the case of a professed social historian like Ellen Glasgow, has yielded good results. This method, however, has led sometimes to a misjudging of the relative aesthetic worth of the novels. In an otherwise discerning treatment of her work, this chief defect of Mr. Geismar's method is not altogether absent. He prefers, for instance, *The Wheel of Life*—since it presents deracinated New York sophisticates anticipating those of Fitzgerald and Hemingway—to a much better work, *The Miller of Old Church,* in his judgment only a "romance" and therefore among the "weakest" of Miss Glasgow's books. N. Elizabeth Monroe in *Fifty Years of the American Novel* has revised perceptively her earlier essay even if she utilizes Christian standards too insistently in discussing the novels. The best treatment in the 1950's, though brief, which judges Ellen Glasgow primarily by aesthetic canons is Frederick J. Hoffman's in *The Modern Novel in America*. Of the most recent discussions, that by Barbara Giles in 1956, "Character and Fate: The Novels of Ellen Glasgow," is one of the most stimulating and comprehensive. Louis D. Rubin, Jr.'s study of Ellen Glasgow and James Branch Cabell, "No Place on Earth," appeared in 1959; the section on Miss Glasgow provides an example of that informed, judicious criticism which she has too rarely received. Mr. Rubin's work was published too late for me to make use of his interpretations, while in some instances we both appear to have reached similar conclusions.

The critic of Miss Glasgow's work must consider her aim of presenting with fidelity and understanding a social history of Virginia from 1850 to 1939 "in the more freely interpretative form of fiction," wherein the South would be seen "not sentimentally, as a conquered province, but truthfully, as part of a larger world." [21] In writing of Virginia, she professed that she could not render what she did not know well.[22] For this reason she did not present in detail the urban laborers and the most depressed tenant farmers in her fiction. Her treatment of the Negro problem in the South, especially in *Virginia* (1913) and *In This Our Life* (1941), is frank but not exhaustive. Except for these omissions her record of coverage is virtually complete, as the thematic discussions of her separate novels in this book may demonstrate. More important, Miss Glasgow attempted, sometimes with indifferent success, sometimes with notable results, to fuse individual dramas of fruition or of frustration with social scene. Like Balzac, her ambition was to form works of art by envisaging her characters against the milieu with which she was herself so closely identified.

In any study of Ellen Glasgow's work, the social history of Virginia, as she assimilated it, becomes an inescapable consideration.[23] The critic must be thoroughly aware of the tradition reflected in Miss Glasgow's novels and of her complex relation to it, but he should be concerned primarily, I think, with defining how she represented this relationship in literary art. He is justified, then, in focussing more upon the use to which Miss Glasgow put her materials than upon their objective validity. Granted that Virginia life from 1850 to 1939 is recreated with immediacy in her fiction, Miss Glasgow herself emphasized that the regional, to be artistically effective, must go beyond the notation of local realities to provide a far-reaching commentary upon human life. Her consistent purpose as a novelist, as she expressed it in the Preface to *Barren Ground,* was "to touch, or at least feel for, the universal chords beneath the regional variations of character." [24] Miss Glasgow almost instinctively viewed in its wider aspects the life she was depicting and characteristically thought of it as "Victorian" or "modern," as the case might be, rather than as Virginian or even as Southern. Miss Glasgow was, moreover, enthusiastic about Hamilton Basso's review of *A Certain Measure* which expressed virtually this view of her work:

It is wrong, however, to think of Miss Glasgow as a "Southern" novelist. The adjective, with its implication of provincialism, has always done her a great injustice. For the theme with which she has concerned herself—the rise of the middle class as a dominant force in the life of the South—is likewise the major theme in the historical chronicle of life in America since the close of the Civil War.[25]

While regionalist loyalties remained strong in her, she tended to view Virginia culture as more typically American than that of many other regions: "But Virginia is not really Southern as the Deep South is Southern; and after all Virginians are (or were) a people within themselves and a border between two alien or hostile cultures." [26] The fact remains that Miss Glasgow was a sophisticated artist and only incidentally a regionalist. The books, moreover, which are most authentic as social history are invariably the best as novels: *The Deliverance, Virginia,* and *The Sheltered Life* are superior both as social history and literary art to *The Voice of the People, Life and Gabriella,* and *Vein of Iron.* The conclusion is inescapable that Ellen Glasgow's books can be as cogently discussed in aesthetic terms as in any other.

The bulk of Miss Glasgow's work may account in part for present neglect of it; this study, it is hoped, will among other things accomplish a tentative sorting of it. Even at their best her novels are characterized by unevenness: convincing characters, moving scenes, and a fine restraint in tone and style alternate with sentimentality of conception and ineptness of execution—again a similarity to Balzac suggests itself. Each one of Miss Glasgow's works, however, merits some consideration for two reasons: her career represents an evolution of sorts in that her best novels were scattered at intervals of many years and were often anticipated by the less distinguished books which intervened, and every novel—even the least important—has some excellences. Since I wish to determine the relative aesthetic value of her separate novels rather than to discuss her work thematically in the most general sense, I am studying each book in turn, in an attempt to assess its intrinsic worth and to establish its place in her development as an artist.

For my purposes in this study, sufficient biographical information is available from the numerous interviews which Miss Glasgow granted after 1925 (apparently reversing an earlier decision never to allow the publishing of personal information [27]), from *A Certain Measure* (1943), from *The Woman Within* (1954), and from the *Letters of Ellen Glasgow* (1958). In the main I have accepted the facts as Miss Glasgow and her admirers have presented them, although subsequent research may cause them to be somewhat modified.

One may agree with James Branch Cabell that some care must be exercised in using that fascinating document, *The Woman Within*. In retrospect, one begins to feel that Miss Glasgow may have augmented some aspects of her story for greater aesthetic effectiveness. If we compare her disillusioned reactions to the first World War expressed in *The Woman Within* with her militant support of the Allied cause expressed in other sources, we can conclude that in the autobiography Miss Glasgow may have somewhat embellished the plain facts. Thus, it is just possible that Miss Glasgow in the 1930's felt that she ought to have been disturbed to nightmare by the war, since disillusionment with it had become extreme in the 1920's and 1930's. After dispelling a certain amount of romantic haze, one can accept her version of her earlier love affair with Gerald B——; but too transparent an irony intrudes in her presentation of the affair with Harold S—— for me to be quite willing to accept all that she wrote about this episode, amusing and distressing as the experience must have been to her. I have not attempted any exhaustive investigation into the facts of Miss Glasgow's private life, because that inquiry seems apart from my main purpose in this book and because Professor Blair Rouse has fuller access to unpublished letters than I have and is preparing a study of Miss Glasgow's career.

The Woman Within does give us insights into Ellen Glasgow's life and temperament which can be found in nothing else she wrote. It is possibly most important in providing us with clues for interpreting the novels: the ever-present sense of dislocation in her personal life found expression in the bitter undercurrents of meaning in many of her books; the religious righteousness of her father is satirized vehemently in a number of characters; and the ironic cynicism characteristic of *The Romantic Comedians* (1926) and *They Stooped to Folly* (1929) may have developed from her disillusionment with Harold S——.

I have used the text in the Virginia Edition (1938)—which was, in turn, taken from the earlier Old Dominion Edition—when the same novels appear in both editions. These texts were revised from those in the first editions of the novels. Since Ellen Glasgow wrote Bessie Zaban Jones that the style in the Virginia Edition is the one she would be judged by,[28] it is, I think, fitting to use that text, even in a study like this which is to some degree developmental and which would, if space were available, consider in detail some of her textual variants. I have collated the texts, however, and in the notes and elsewhere I have occasionally referred to the original books when they differ from the final versions. The changes made in the Old Dominion and Virginia editions have been in the direction of a more supple, flexible prose, while practically nothing has been added in bulk to the novels. Generalities in descriptive statements have been made concrete; nonessential phrases or sentences have been discarded; and some descriptive passages, some sections of dialogue (often humorous), and some adventitious interpretative comments have been deleted. At times, the earlier text aids in the interpretation of a given novel; occasionally, Miss Glasgow's deletions, as in *Virginia,* change somewhat the dimensions of meaning in the novel. Because Miss Glasgow's fiction is so voluminous, because she has discussed at length her work and ideas in the prefaces to her novels and in her uncollected essays, and because the printed *Letters* are in themselves a substantial collection, I have not attempted to locate unpublished material.

The publication of *The Woman Within* in 1954 and of the *Letters* in 1958 has stimulated curiosity about Ellen Glasgow's work, although only one of her novels, the relatively inferior *Vein of Iron,* was still in print in early 1957. Since then the Sagamore Press has reprinted *Barren Ground.* It is to be hoped that more novels of an artist who perceptively reoriented in America the traditions of Jane Austen and Thomas Hardy, of Balzac and Henry James, will once again be made available and that her place in American letters will soon be more fully recognized. After all adverse comment has been made, the elusive excellence of Ellen Glasgow's best work and her contribution to "the ironic art of fiction" [29] still emerge conclusively.

❖ I ❖

The Artist
and Her Time*

In a Richmond still lethargic from defeat in war but already responding
to energies let loose by an expanding industrialism, Ellen Glasgow was
born April 22, 1873. Since her mother traced her ancestry to aristocratic
Tidewater colonists from England and her father to the Scotch-Irish
settlers in the Great Valley of Virginia, she was from the first influenced
by contrasting heritages. She reflected, she was certain, "some tragic
conflict of types." [1] Even as a child, her innermost self became "a battle-
ground for hostile forces of character, for obscure mental and emotional antagonisms." Such tensions, only partially resolved, produced
in her work an impression sometimes of richness and depth, sometimes
of spiritual confusion. She was never able to transcend completely a
sense that the self within was split between conflicting allegiances.

From her mother Ellen Glasgow inherited an appreciation for the
gracious culture of the Cavalier and a pervading humanity. A woman
bestowing light, Anne Jane Glasgow dominated the lives of her
youngest children through her affection and kindness. Some of Anne
Glasgow's sweetness and goodness were infused into the portrait of
Virginia Pendleton in *Virginia* (1913), at least in that portion of the
book completed after Ellen's ironic view of her heroine changed to a
compassionate identification with her. If her own mother was the
"loveliest" spirit Ellen was ever to know, she had also one of the

* In this chapter, otherwise undocumented facts or quotations are drawn
from *The Woman Within*.

"saddest" lives: her energies had been depleted by hardships in the Civil War and the Reconstruction and by rearing a family of ten children. She afterwards surrendered to a despondency from which she never fully recovered. The youngest children were, in particular, depressed by the mother's illness; even when they played, they could not escape "from the pressure of anxiety, from the sense of foreboding." The essence of kindness in everything else, Anne Glasgow unaccountably kept her two youngest girls in her room to suffer with her through her nights of nervous insomnia. Psychically distressed because of her mother's illness, Ellen nevertheless felt her love for her, through pity and sympathy, intensify. When Anne Glasgow died in 1893 from typhoid after only a week's illness, Ellen experienced ungovernable anguish. Part of her identity, some vital part of herself, was split from her, she felt, and held by her mother in death. In the years that followed, this part of herself never seemed to move from her mother's side. From Miss Glasgow's profound sense of the deprivations in her mother's life undoubtedly derived her preoccupation in the novels with the theme of unappreciated goodness.

After the Civil War Francis T. Glasgow, Ellen's father, became one of the managing directors of the Tredegar Iron Works with which he had been associated since 1849. This Richmond plant had been the principal source of supply for Confederate munitions and ordnance and had outfitted the Merrimac. Through her father Miss Glasgow was strongly affected by the ethical conscience of Presbyterianism, though she soon came to loathe its doctrine. If anything, the Calvinist heritage was to dominate her, although Miss Glasgow declared that she owed nothing to her father except the color of her eyes and a share in a trust fund. But the "Puritan" traits found in her most admirable characters—their insistent sense of responsibility and their disillusioned withdrawal from sensuous experience—provide some evidence that Miss Glasgow had absorbed more of her father's view of life than she might have been willing to admit. The independence which led her to reject her father's religion was, moreover, a product of the Calvinism she inherited from him. When as a child she heard her first sermon and was asked how she liked it, she revealed a characteristic resistance to authority by saying, "Well, father, he wouldn't let me answer back!" [2] A little later, she refused to go to church and to cease reading "dangerous" authors like Gibbon, Darwin, and Lecky. Miss Glasgow also came to feel that her brother Frank, who in 1909 committed suicide, had been sacrificed to their father's formidable nature. Although she instinctively withdrew from a man who imposed his will rather than his love upon his children, she came to admire his unselfishness and his "stern fortitude."

Judged to be too nervous to undergo systematic schooling, Ellen was, for the most part, privately educated. Before she had received any formal instruction, she had picked out her letters from *Old Mortality,* after hearing her Aunt Rebecca relate the plots of Scott's novels. Imaginative and precocious, Ellen at three began to invent stories, for her own delight and her mammy's, about a character named Willie and his wonderful adventures. At seven or eight, besides Scott, she had discovered Hans Christian Anderson and *Grimms' Fairy Tales.* Willie left her forever, she says, when at twelve she entered the world of Dickens, but he seemed, in retrospect, to have been the first to teach her how saturated with his material the novelist must be if he is to write at all.[3] Through the softening outlines of memory and through a perhaps exaggerated sense in maturity of the malignity of the cosmos toward her, she came to value these early years of spontaneous imaginative activity as her happiest. She was also grateful for having been "left free to browse at will in an excellent, unweeded library." [4]

At seven, fascinated by the sound of words, Ellen became a writer, jotting down verses as they came to her under the old elm tree at Jerdone Castle, the farm in the Virginia Blue Ridge Hills where the family spent the summers when she was a girl. She hoped that in the future she might write books but received no encouragement from others. As a result of the indifference or antagonism of family and friends toward her ambition, she knew even then "that strange sense of exile which visits the subjective mind when it is unhappily placed." [5] After the humiliation of hearing her sister Emily one day reading her verses to amuse some guests, Ellen felt forced to do all her writing in secret until the publication of her first book. Her first remembered story, "Only a Daisy in a Garden of Roses," written at the age of seven in "a kind of childish prose-poetry," portrayed an outcast. Even as a child she felt that she belonged among the "disinherited," a conviction which deepened with the years into a pained sense of alienation.

Except for the summers she spent at Jerdone Castle and her delight in her awakening imagination, she had had an unhappy childhood, she felt, especially after the age of seven and the loss of her mammy. It was overclouded by general poor health and morbid shyness, by memory of the death of her brother Joseph and Anne Glasgow's mental depression, by separation from her favorite brother Frank, by antagonism toward the older members of her family, and by feelings of guilt for the suffering she could not prevent. A sense of the oppressive evil at the heart of things was conveyed to her susceptible temperament by a sinister, bloated face which she had seen leering at her in the sunset when she was a young child. This recurring image in childhood seems later to have epitomized for Miss Glasgow the nightmare aspect of these years.[6]

In her early maturity the divergent pressures exerted by an anti-intellectual society and by her inquiring mind basically disturbed Miss Glasgow. The frustrations resulting from her life among the Virginia aristocrats were similar to those experienced in New York by Edith Wharton, who complained of the vast gulf between the fashionable classes, fearful of innovation, and the intellectuals.[7] Outwardly Ellen Glasgow was identified with her family in its leading position in Southern society. She attended a Saint Cecilia ball in Charleston when she was sixteen; in the following year at the University of Virginia, she experienced "all the glorified sensations of a Southern belle in the Victorian age." But she soon became more interested in the inner life than in the usual "coming out party" and the "formal presentation to Richmond society." Lacking sympathy with both the harsh religion of her father and the discreet amenity of Southern social life, Ellen, through her will and persistence, found personal liberty and intellectual self-reliance in "the life of the solitary spirit." In her studies she was guided both by her own ranging curiosity and by her sister Cary's husband, George Walter McCormack. He was a serious intellectual who was still a young man when he died alone in New York in 1894. His influence upon her was great, and she came to feel that his "fidelity to truth in an age of pompous pretense left . . . an indestructible standard" with her. Her mother's death also made her anxious to find in life some richer value than fortitude.

In solitude she studied "radicals" like Darwin (a "benign and powerful inspiration" [8]), Spencer, Romanes, Huxley, Nietzsche, Schopenhauer, and Ibsen. She also read widely in political economy, in Adam Smith, Malthus, Ricardo, John Stuart Mill, Buckle, Saint-Simon, Marx, Bagehot, Sir Henry Maine, William Morris, and—at the instigation of Mc-Cormack—Henry George.[9] In later life she described to Carl Van Vechten her activity during this period: "In the Nineties, while young men of the period were attempting to write like Henry James and to behave like Oscar Wilde, I was reading Karl Marx." [10] Despite the warnings of friends and family that she was "too attractive to be strong-minded," she so completely mastered political economy that she was able to pass an examination in it, set privately by her friend Professor George Frederick Holmes when she visited the University of Virginia. At this point, however, she did not know "what we call, euphemistically, 'the facts of life' " until a woman friend counselled her on this visit. She resented exclusion from the University of Virginia because she was a woman, but was grateful to Dr. Holmes for indicating the authors she should read.[11]

By virtue of her studies Miss Glasgow became skeptical of those self-contained conventions in the South which tended to discourage independent thinking, as in itself subversive, upon political and social subjects. Ellen was daring enough to proclaim herself a Socialist, though she was less drawn to direct agitation for reform than to a protest against man's general inhumanity. The reformer who concentrated upon immediate measures often lost through his partial vision, she thought, a sense of the true causes, inherent in a self-centered human nature, for continuing injustice: "the approach to a fairer order lies, not without but within; and . . . the only way to make a civilized world is to begin and end with the civilizing of man." [12] As an indication of her divided life during this period, Miss Glasgow at seventeen gave her first party and joined for a time the City Mission where she was shocked by the squalor and shiftlessness of the poor—by the society which permitted such suffering to exist and by the poor who would do nothing to help themselves. After her mother's death, McCormack sent her a subscription to the New York Mercantile Library; as a result, speculative natural science, especially the ideas of Germans like Weismann and Haeckel, supplemented political theory. After McCormack's death she and Cary achieved some degree of relief by studying economics, ethnology, and biology, and Ellen further escaped the "intolerable" by turning once more to her writing.

By now Miss Glasgow had entered "that strange exile to which all writers who are born and not made are condemned," and had begun to feel herself subject to forces that sometimes took her in directions contrary to those which her society clearly understood. When she was eighteen, she destroyed the manuscript of her first book, *Sharp Realities,* in her revulsion from a literary agent in New York who had shocked her by his amorous crudeness. Despite her resolve after this to give up a literary career, the same impulse which had led her to write this first book—her rejection of "the formal, the false, the affected, the sentimental, and the pretentious, in Southern writing" [13]—prompted her to write *The Descendant.*

With her mother's death in 1893, Ellen Glasgow at twenty "suffered an agonized recoil from life and death" [14] and renounced, for a time, literary ambition. If we may judge by the characters and themes recurring in Miss Glasgow's fiction, the traumatic effects of this experience and of others as painful seem never to have entirely disappeared. Thus Gabriella Carr and Dorinda Oakley, who are to some degree autobiographical projections, develop after being deserted an aversion to the senses somewhat too agonized and absolute to have resulted from their situations. With possibly too much urgency, Miss Glasgow also insisted through her characters—from Anna Allard in this first book to Asa Timberlake in her last—upon the need to renounce happiness in order to find it. Though Ellen destroyed most of the manuscript of *The Descendant* after her mother's death, it became a more mature book, she felt, when after two years she rewrote it from memory except for the salvaged first six chapters.

Although the Macmillan reader rejected the book unread, a Mr. Patton of the University Publishing Company persuaded Harper and Brothers to publish it. At Harpers the reader attributed the unsigned manuscript, because of its realism, to Harold Frederic. One of the few moments of real joy in her life, Miss Glasgow said, came in 1896 when she received word in Paris that her novel was to be published. But her summer in London and Paris was an unhappy one. The anxieties, illnesses, and frustrations of previous years now became associated in her mind with the new terror of approaching deafness. Upon her arrival in New York in the autumn, her fears were confirmed. Her hearing grew worse, although she did not become completely deaf until she was between thirty-five and forty.

Written in secret and published anonymously in 1897, *The Descendant* in Miss Glasgow's view resisted current literary fashion in the South which sentimentally extolled antebellum life and the survival of its influence after the war. Typical writers were Thomas Nelson Page whose *Red Rock* (1898) portrayed with little real penetration the hardships of an upper-class Virginia family under Reconstruction (a situation much more expertly analyzed in Ellen Glasgow's *The Deliverance,* 1904) and Francis Hopkinson Smith whose *Colonel Carter of Cartersville* (1891) made jaunty and picturesque what could only have been tragic, the impoverished exile of a Virginia gentleman in New York City.

Ellen Glasgow may have owed something to these and other writers of the "New South." [15] She may have received some hints for her own realistic approach to Southern life from Richard Malcolm Johnston's and Joel Chandler Harris's sketches of the Georgia poor whites; she may have responded to Mary N. Murfree's somewhat similar treatment of the Tennessee mountain folk; and she may have been moved by Page's preoccupation with the fallen glory of the planter caste after the war. She was doubtless impressed by George Washington Cable's psychological perceptiveness and sense of social milieu in his Creole stories and by the moral courage he later displayed in his forthright social criticism of the South. Yet her debt to these writers was, I think, minimal. All of them (Cable is in large part an exception) were retrospective, turning away from the vexatious problems of the present to celebrate an idyllic prewar culture; or else they were self-consciously regional, exploiting the colorful aspects of their materials rather than their full moral, psychological, and social implications. Neither does she seem to have been influenced by those Northern commentators upon the Southern scene after the Civil War, such as Constance Fenimore Woolson, Albion W. Tourgée, and John William de Forest, whose faithful transcriptions of experience anticipated Miss Glasgow's own more sustained interpretations of Southern life and manners.

Despite some perhaps inevitable concessions to established literary modes, Ellen Glasgow was the first self-conscious and consistent realist in the New South. In the opening pages of *The Descendant,* for example, she presented the squalid life of rural farmers in tones more somber than it had generally been painted in Southern literature. For a woman to write at all in the Richmond of this period was daring, but for her to mention illegitimacy and Bohemian free love in an age which demanded "moonlight and magnolia" sentiment in its fiction was clearly reprehensible. The book revealed Miss Glasgow's youthful eclecticism: a story of a political radical and social outcast, it has undertones of Nietzschean and Ibsenian rebellion ("at twenty, I was attracted by imprudence and hazard," [16] she said), of Spencerian optimism, and paradoxically of Darwinian and Zolaesque determinism.

Miss Glasgow decided that the notoriety which she achieved after the publication of her first book "could never become palatable" to her.[17] She also felt that she must reject popular success secured at the sacrifice of artistic conscience. In this resolve, she was strengthened by her first important mentor, Walter Hines Page, who was also responsible for her change of publisher from Harper and Brothers to Doubleday, Page and Company. In a letter to Page in 1897, Ellen Glasgow emphatically expressed both her willingness to meet the demands which her future career as artist might impose on her and her sense of dedication to her work: "As regards my work I shall follow your advice in full. I shall write no more short stories and I shall not divide my power or risk my future reputation. I will become a great novelist or none at all. For which determination you are in part responsible." [18] In his reply he encouraged her to concentrate upon her novels and to reject the temptation to do "minor work": "But with your seriousness of purpose and your high aim I cannot help believing that it would be a grave mistake for you to do anything except to drive forward with your greater efforts." [19] The moderate royalties from her novels and the provision made for her by her father and brother freed her from any compulsive need to make money from her writing.

Financial independence and her own sense of artistic probity enabled Ellen Glasgow, then, to write in accordance with the standards which she initially set for herself. This sense of her integrity as writer still remained with her when she consciously sought, in later years, an increased public for her work. By this time her youthful ambition of creating "a series of good books each adding to the building of the name I hope for" [20] had been achieved.

Miss Glasgow had at her disposal plenitude of materials for the writing of fiction, but she soon found that she had to rely upon her own efforts to achieve a suitable craft and technique, and a "pure and flexible" style. In an unintellectual society, she had no help in evolving her aesthetic principles and her methods as an artist except that provided by the spirit within, with its instinctive fastidiousness and with its sense of excellence and truth. She thus intuitively grasped the general nature of her standards, though their definition eluded for a time her devoted and sometimes misdirected efforts. From writers such as the genteel members of the New York Authors' Club, who exploited for their advantage the popular literary modes, Ellen Glasgow learned nothing. Like most of her other contemporaries, they did not recognize, she felt, the independent importance of literary art. In the American tradition, Hawthorne seems to have been the only novelist to secure her complete admiration; [21] and here she showed a similarity to Henry James.

As to Howells, her mind was apparently divided. In 1918 she said that "as our greatest realist" he enabled us to "see the poetry of the life he knew best" [22]; in 1938 she described his realism as "severely regimented" [23]; and in *The Woman Within* she revealed how she had consciously resisted "his charm and his influence" and "the dull gentility" of the fiction he approved. Miss Glasgow evidently sympathized with his attacks upon "romance" and with his contention that character in fiction was more important than plot. She felt, along with him, that "fidelity to experience and probability of motive are essential conditions of a great imaginative literature." [24] The finished quality of the conversational sequences in his fiction and his expert exteriorizing of psychological motive into a character's words may have been her chief indebtedness to him—or to his friend, Henry James. In 1916 she praised other American realists: Katherine Fullerton Gerould, Mary E. Wilkins, and Sara Orne Jewett. [25] Her enthusiasm for their work, I think, signifies less their direct influence upon her than her recognition in others of attitudes and principles similar to her own.

Ellen Glasgow soon sensed that the method of Howells, which depended primarily upon a scrupulous rendition of the actual, was hardly "realism" in any larger sense. For her the realist had to "illuminate ex-

perience, not merely transcribe it." If one range of reality lies in "the
absolute fidelity of the treatment" of the external world, a firmer reality
consists, she felt, in "the vision of the artist": an integral truth must
derive not only from outward appearances but from the inward world
as well.[26] In labelling herself a "verist," she seems to have borrowed
from Hamlin Garland and to have meant the same thing that he did by
"veritist"—an artist motivated by a "passion for truth and individual
expression." For him the novelist as "veritist" or "truth-stater" would
be in a poetic relationship to his subject, evincing an "impassioned
personal outlook on life." [27]

In this emphasis upon the realist's temperamental involvement with
his materials in order to reach their inner significance, Miss Glasgow's
ideas were also close to those developed by Frank Norris. He too had
stressed alternately the need in fiction for an objectively truthful representation of life and for a revelation of its meaning "to an interesting, impressionable man." [28] Miss Glasgow's own ultimate wisdom was similar
in emphasis: "For truth to art became in the end simple fidelity to one's
own inner vision."

For the most part, Miss Glasgow did not state definitely her views on
the novel until she wrote the prefaces for the collected editions of her
work in the 1930's. These prefaces have already been drawn upon in my
discussion and indicate that Miss Glasgow's deepest American affinities
were with realists like Garland and Norris who immediately preceded
her or who were her contemporaries. Even if these writers had little
direct influence upon her, they demonstrated that serious novelists from
1870 to 1914 were dominated, as Miss Glasgow was herself, by a
realism which had assimilated Darwinian concepts. Along with Garland,
Norris, and James, Miss Glasgow revealed that American realists (except for Dreiser at his most deterministic and his direct followers) have
also characteristically suffused their search for truth with a modicum of
subjectivity. The moral idealism, which underlay their conscientious
efforts to depict man and his society as they actually were, was often
present, then, in what they wrote. All these novelists exhibited, moreover, the impress of the nineteenth-century French novelists, whom Miss
Glasgow called "the great realists."

Actually it was from European literature that Miss Glasgow herself
learned most in becoming an artist. She had always been deeply interested in English writers, enjoying in particular the great novelists
and the poetry of Keats, Shelley, Browning, and Swinburne. But she did
not find in the somewhat formless abundance of the traditional English
novel the sophisticated aesthetic and the controlled command of medium
which she then believed she needed. More congenial to her development

as a novelist was the self-conscious artistry of the Anglo-American, Henry James, and of certain of his masters—the French writers, Balzac, Flaubert, and Maupassant. These were also the literary preferences of Edith Wharton (who included Stendhal) and of Willa Cather; to these three women writers and their master, James, the modern novel, of course, owes much of its sensitivity to style and form.[29]

From Henry James, whom Miss Glasgow read assiduously in her early career,[30] she learned much about the technique of the novel, particularly the temporal and spatial organization of one's materials, the uses of an objective and ironic method, and the need to control point of view to enhance psychological effectiveness. It is not surprising that the flexible, imaginative realism of James appealed to her more than the restricted theory of Howells. She felt with James that the realist should render what *is* instead of what ought to be, that the novel "is a living thing, all one and continuous, like any other organism," that the novel is "a personal, a direct impression of life," that the novelist must be adept at "catching the very note and trick, the strange irregular rhythm of life," and that art must be "essentially selection, but it is a selection whose main care is to be typical, to be inclusive." [31] Like James, she characteristically used a moral problem with all its ramifications to serve as a compositional center in the novel for holding in place its disparate characters and incidents.

Though Ellen Glasgow admired *Madame Bovary* as "the most flawless" novel ever written and *Une Vie* as "the most beautiful novel in all literature," she came to view the work of Flaubert and Maupassant as too consciously manipulated and, in its impeccable form, as too divorced from the imperfections of life. From Maupassant, her "liberator" and an inspiriting example to her of the dedicated writer, she learned the virtue of "a style that was touched with beauty and yet tinctured with irony" and the importance in her craft "of the precise word, of the swift phrase, of cool and scrupulous observation." She must have appreciated Maupassant's view, in the famous preface to *Pierre et Jean,* that the realist "will not try to present us with a commonplace photograph of life, but will endeavor to give us a picture of it more perfect, more striking, more convincing than reality itself" and that he must strive for "the skillful grouping of small but invariable facts from which the final issue of the work may be gathered." [32] From her French masters, Ellen Glasgow not only acquired a resolutely honest approach to experience but a sense that "the assembling of material, the arrangement of masses" was all-important in securing a desired total effect.[33]

Balzac, with his forceful fusion of character and environmental detail and with his self-conscious aim of writing an exhaustive social history in a series of novels, probably had the greatest impact upon Miss Glasgow.[34] Like him, she would become the "secretary" to a society which would be "the real author" of her books: "La Société française allait être l'historien, je ne devais être que le secrétaire." To Balzac (as to Ellen Glasgow) the novelist was a notable historian to the extent that his immersion in his materials allowed him to convey inevitably their truth. In the introduction to the *Comédie Humaine* his description of his method in writing social history in fiction suggests reasonably well Ellen Glasgow's own: "By drawing up an inventory of vices and virtues, by collecting the chief facts of the passions, by depicting characters, by choosing the principal incidents of social life, by composing types out of a combination of homogeneous characteristics, I might perhaps succeed in writing the history which so many historians have neglected: that of Manners." [35] In the verisimilitude and scope of Ellen Glasgow's work, there is Balzacian comprehensiveness and sympathy. Undoubtedly, Balzac's awareness of the impersonal forces which mold society and which in their turn influence human behavior impressed Miss Glasgow, who had, moreover, the added impetus provided by evolutionary science and Zola's theorizing about the novel to help her interpret the psychology of the individual in relation to his social milieu.

Miss Glasgow's theory and practice of fiction had some resemblances to the literary naturalism set forth in Zola's *Le Roman Expérimental* and exemplified in his novels and those of his followers. Her application of Darwin to the social scene was, in large part, independent of Zola's, however, and less rigid than his. Still, her fiction illustrates many naturalistic tendencies: a frequently inclusive rendition of milieu, a conviction that social laws operate like biological and physical laws, a sense that primitive and eruptive forces are part of human nature, an insistence that Darwinian premises underlie any "modern" world view, a belief that ethics are inductively derived from experience, a feeling that individualistic force is needed to break through inhibiting social conventions, and a recognition that heredity and environment are the main factors which limit mankind's effectiveness as a free agent. Like many of the other American realists contemporary with her, she accepted only a modified determinism, feeling that the individual is in part capable of directing his activity, even if heredity and environment restrict him. As she explained in 1939, the determinism of her philosophy is mitigated by a recognition that the freedom of the will, as a concept, serves a useful moral and social purpose:

The longer I observe experience, the greater emphasis I place upon determinism both in our beliefs and in our bodies. Regarding the freedom of the will, and regarding that doctrine alone, I suppose I may call myself more or less of a pragmatist. Indefensible in theory, no doubt, that exalted error—if it be an error—appears necessary to the order of civilized man, and seems to justify, on higher grounds, its long record of service as a moral utility.[36]

Miss Glasgow was not in sympathy with other aspects of Zola's theory: his insistence that the writer efface his temperament, his belief that the writer is not free to select among his materials, and his counsel that the writer dismiss the metaphysical, the poetic, and the intuitive as unverifiable.

In reconciling the realist's zeal for objectivity with the artist's sensibility, Miss Glasgow seems to have made about the same adjustment as Thomas Hardy. While Hardy proclaimed that "scientific" novelists err on the right side in their desire to present the full truth and in their hatred of the false and hypocritical, he also felt that artistic effectiveness derives less from a sensitive eye and ear than from "a sympathetic appreciativeness of life in all its manifestations." [37] He also retained, unlike some of his French contemporaries, a belief that literature ought to be devoted less to the physiological than to the spiritual, less "to the delineation of man's appetites than to the delineation of his aspirations, affections, or humors." [38] Hardy's modified naturalism is close to Ellen Glasgow's; and her novels are often reminiscent of his in tone, texture, and conception. In 1897 she thought of him as "the first of all novelists, living or dead" and of *Jude the Obscure* as the best of his books.[39] She was consistently in accord with his echoing of Novalis in *The Mayor of Casterbridge* that "character is Fate," and agreed with him that the will may be considered one of the most influential of the forces which comprise fatality.

In Chekhov and above all in Tolstoy she found presented a more comprehensive reality than she had yet encountered in English and French novelists, a reality which subjected the facts of experience to modulation by the artist's indwelling spirit. From reading Tolstoy, she was to learn that "life must use art; art must use life," and that the universal is implicit in the illuminated particular. From Dostoevsky she may have gathered hints for the tortured egotism of Christopher Blake in *The Deliverance* (1904) and some sense of the fundamental irrationality of human experience. Guided by the enlarged conceptions of the novelist's art which she acquired from extensive reading in continental literature, Miss Glasgow was now able to order her experience with competence and to capture the wider significance of the regional life which she had begun to depict in her fiction. She then came back with fuller appreciation to the British novel and found many suggestions for her own art in the work of Richardson and Fielding, of Jane Austen and George Eliot, and of Dickens, Thackeray, Meredith, and Hardy.

Hamlin Garland became aware, after a visit to Richmond in 1898, that strong forces in Ellen Glasgow were seeking expression, and he prophetically recorded in his notebook: "The order of her progress seems reversed. She is beginning with the bitterness of age. She is likely to be a marked personality in Southern literature. Her work will not be pleasant, but it will be original and powerful." [40] This prophecy was fulfilled when her revolt against the sentimentalism in Southern culture and the professed gentility of American society gathered force with each succeeding novel. To write effectively, she discovered that she had merely to exploit what lay close to hand: "the soil was deep and dark with a thick deposit of unused material," which the romancers of her day had scarcely touched.[41]

Her relationship to the historical romance, in greatest vogue between 1898 and 1908, was complex.[42] Although she succumbed to the popularity of this form and wrote *The Battle-Ground* in 1902, this novel is more realistic than those by her contemporaries in this genre. *The Deliverance* (1904) is a historical novel only in the sense that Thomas Mann's *Buddenbrooks* can be considered one. Both authors wrote with candor of a society which had existed just before they were born or in their childhood, and were only incidentally concerned with the picturesque. In *The Deliverance* Miss Glasgow was not preoccupied with descriptive detail, with a fast-paced narrative, with romantic love, nor with the recreation of historical milieu. These were the chief concerns of the Southern practitioners of historical romance such as Mary Johnston, Thomas Nelson Page, Maurice Thompson, George W. Cable (in his late phase especially), Mary N. Murfree, Francis Hopkinson Smith, Winston Churchill, and John Fox, Jr. These elements from romantic narrative are present in Miss Glasgow's book, sometimes to its detriment; but the chief emphasis in this first of Miss Glasgow's mature novels is psychological.[43] Like the earlier George Washington Cable, Ellen Glasgow was much more than a romancer; yet like him, she was sometimes inhibited by current literary convention and by the ethical and ethnic conservatism in the South after 1870.[44]

In succeeding volumes of her work, interest in colorful milieu and romantic sentiment as such decreased until in *Virginia* (1913) the novel hardly seems "historical" at all, although it is largely laid in the Virginia of the 1880's. Much creative energy went into Miss Glasgow's earlier novels and her efforts in them to prove "that things were . . .

seldom known by their right names" [45]; much creative force, she later feared, was also dissipated in these books written before the first World War.

Since realism in literature is no longer a controversial subject, her revolt is, in retrospect, less startling than it appeared at the time; but without this impulse to protest, Miss Glasgow might never have written at all and the force of her earlier work would have been less. This solitary, self-conscious nonconformity made her feel uncomfortable in both the North and the South and generated, in part, that alienation toward life in America which she was never quite able to overcome. Her perseverance in her endeavor to render with truth the experience she knew best is remarkable, considering the lucrative temptation to write for a popular audience and the isolation imposed upon the writer in an America not yet fully ready for realism in literature. In another of her early letters to Walter Hines Page she wrote: "I know, at least, that I would not write down to a sensation loving public for any amount of financial recompense, but I do want my work to be widely recognized. But for all that my methods don't belong to this generation—though I mean to stick to them." [46]

The record of the surface aspects of Miss Glasgow's literary life and associations before the Great War is unfortunately incomplete. With the destruction of manuscript materials by her sister before 1916 and with letters from the years 1908 to 1914 unavailable at this time, this important record may even be impossible to reconstruct. At least we know that among her friends were two writers with whose work she could have been only in moderate sympathy, James Lane Allen and Mary Johnston. She was Allen's close friend from about 1909 or 1910 and respected him personally as "the most gallant figure I have ever known." With the decline of his reputation after the World War some strain occurred in their relationship. In the postwar age Allen evidently found it increasingly difficult to accept the radical nature of Ellen Glasgow's realism; and she failed to display, she felt, the "adulation" which he required in speaking of his work.[47] An article on Ellen Glasgow in 1912 by Alice M. Tyler mentions "a close friendship dating back through years" with Mary Johnston; and a number of the *Letters* document this relationship. The tone of the letters is affectionate, even effusive, and Ellen Glasgow evidently appreciated her sympathy during a time of emotional upheaval. Yet the letters mention divergences between the two writers which were probably intellectual as well as temperamental.[48] The 1912 article cites Mrs. Kate Langley Bosher as a Richmond associate and May Sinclair and Beatrice Harraden as

British friends.[49] The *Letters* show that Ellen Glasgow's intimacy with Amélie Rives Troubetskoy, a Virginia writer whose modish *fin de siècle* novels were once greatly popular, began early in the century.

Ellen Glasgow was apparently more interested in knowing her British contemporaries than major American writers then and later. At one time, she and Hugh Walpole greatly admired each other: he praised her work and thought of her house on Main Street as "his American home." Later there developed some strain, after she detected an element of the pompous in the successful author and after he ignored her letters to him when she was travelling in England in 1930.[50] If they were not her intimates, Miss Glasgow thought highly of Thomas Hardy, John Galsworthy, Joseph Conrad, and Arnold Bennett, and sought them out in England. On his American visit in 1923 Conrad expressed regret that ill health prevented him from visiting her in Richmond.

At this point Ellen Glasgow seems to have been only moderately sympathetic with the revolutionary naturalism of Theodore Dreiser. For one thing, she was unwilling to sign the Authors' League of America's protest against the suppression of *The Genius* without having read the novel.[51] On this subject of Ellen Glasgow and realism in America, an interview with Joyce Kilmer in 1916, " 'Evasive Idealism' in Literature," is informative. She condemned here the reading public for avidly desiring "a sugary philosophy" in literature with little reference to actuality; she hailed the *Spoon River Anthology* as an example of a reawakened concern with robust truth in letters as opposed to a shallow optimism; and she rightly divined that the reality of the war would make a continued genteel romanticism and evasiveness impossible. Her attack upon current literary decorum was sufficiently vigorous for a cautious realist like Booth Tarkington to be led to protest. Yet when in this interview Kilmer referred to "a certain conspicuous American novelist [evidently Dreiser] whose books are very long, very dull, and distinguished only by their author's obsession with sex" as the leading realist in most people's opinion, Miss Glasgow replied that a distinction had to be made between a "realist" and a "vulgarian." Evidently she felt that Dreiser belonged in the second category and that a complete lack of humor detracted from the fidelity of his work.[52] Though Miss Glasgow as a craftsman could hardly have been in full sympathy with Dreiser's sprawling artistry, she seems to have forgotten for the moment that he was trying—as she was—to secure greater freedom for the writer and that he was being hampered by the same reticences imposed upon literature. In the 1930's her instinctive recoil from some of the violence in Faulkner's work similarly tended to disguise from her how close in spirit much of her own writing was to his.

Before the World War Miss Glasgow had become, following Ibsen and his influence in England and America, a champion of woman's rights. Along with her sister Cary, she helped form the Virginia League for Women Suffrage, but after Cary's death Ellen lost almost all interest in active campaigning for suffrage reform. By instinct and conviction she remained a feminist, however, as two articles in *The New York Times* for 1913 attest. The feminist movement was important, she thought, less for what it might accomplish specifically than for the possibilities it might open for woman's development: "For what we call the woman's movement is a revolt from a pretense of being—it is at its best and worst a struggle for the liberation of personality." [53] Several times Miss Glasgow drew upon this phase of her life for her books— in depicting the incessant agitations of Aunt Matoaca Bland for woman's rights in *The Romance of a Plain Man* (1909), for example, and in presenting with approbation the self-sufficient Gabriella Carr in *Life and Gabriella* (1916).

Transcendent emotion illuminated Ellen Glasgow's life when in 1899 she and Gerald B——, a New York financier whose exact identity she did not disclose in *The Woman Within,* fell in love. He was unhappily married and the father of two boys, for whose sake he felt he could not secure a divorce. Forced to meet in secret, the lovers increasingly experienced a sense of frustration and yearning which seems only to have increased their passion. Love brought Ellen, for the first time, full confidence in herself and freedom from her fears, especially from her morbid feelings about her growing deafness. Her sense now of spiritual power, she says, "re-created the entire inner world of my consciousness," and determined her to be well, happy, and beautiful. She also valued Gerald's intuitive understanding of her work and of her artistic ambitions. The intensity of this passion, unfulfilled though it was, enabled her to give positive direction to her life. Through her very love for Gerald, she acquired the strength needed to withstand the shock of his death and to restore herself physically and mentally. In her relationship with Gerald "the memory of longing" stayed with her, she said, to become more agonizing than "the . . . memory of fulfillment" could have been. Between her and later lovers the shadow of Gerald B——, or at least the secret laughter they had shared, was to interpose.

The agony of Gerald's loss caused Miss Glasgow to burrow deeper into the self to seek whatever reality might abide there. At first she felt an "anesthesia" of the living organism, but after shock had somewhat diminished she was absorbed again in the problem that had agitated her ever since as a child she had seen that leering face of evil in the sunset: "How can an oversensitive nature defend itself against the malice of life? How can one learn to endure the unendurable? Not the cruelty of civilization alone, but the cold implacable inhumanity of the universe." At this point and later Ellen Glasgow's sufferings were genuine, yet the shrill tone which she sometimes used in describing them implies that she considered herself aggrieved at having had to suffer at all. There were at least the mitigating circumstances of leisure and money which many writers have lacked; and Louise M. Field in 1922 remarked that Ellen Glasgow had experienced few of the privations or disappointments which ordinarily confront the literary artist.[54] For her work the tragedy in her experience was most significant in generating her protest against the injustice of the cosmos toward mankind. Anger and defiance, expressed and implied, characterize the novels and the autobiography more than does self-pity; and from the first, she reacted vehemently against an enforced submission to the inevitable: "suffering . . . makes me impatient and ready to rend the universe." [55]

Miss Glasgow described herself as instinctively a believer and intellectually a skeptic in the years which followed Gerald's death. She struggled to reconcile emotion with reason and to discover, through wide reading in philosophy, a reality which could explain to her satisfaction the facts of cruelty and suffering. Her search for a truth which might be lived was intensified, at the same time that it was made more difficult, by Frank's suicide in 1909, by Cary's agonizing death in 1911, by a brief engagement to a poet, and by "the impenetrable wall" of deafness. From her anguish she found some relief in the mysticism of Plotinus, in the disciplined aspiration of Pascal, and in the strength and fortitude implicit in the *Meditations* of Marcus Aurelius. She next studied German metaphysics, starting with Kant and ending with Schopenhauer, and then read Spinoza. She felt that Spinoza was too cold and mathematical, but responded at once to the "embittered compassion" of Schopenhauer. She may also have been impressed by his concept of the will, though, like Bernard Shaw, she interpreted the Life Force in a more positive way than did Schopenhauer. Her temperamental idealism was strengthened by these studies, by her reading of Plato and Josiah Royce, and by her admiration for the moral precepts of the Buddha, of Christ, and of St. Francis of Assisi. To her these last were also sublime figures in their avid renunciation of the senses to attain communion with a spirit transcending the self. In her "hunger" for God during this period of duress, she seems especially to have been helped by the sacred books of the East "to some kind of acceptance and reconciliation"; and toward the end of 1906, she could say that she had been happy during the past year in her "soul which is clear and radiant out of a long darkness." [56] In all this activity Miss Glasgow was as much concerned with defining ethical values as with metaphysics.[57]

Actually, Miss Glasgow's philosophical idealism was manifested more as an illumination of disparate moments of her experience than as a substratum into which all experience could be dissolved. Her idealism was, therefore, compatible with a rationalist's sense of fact, with an interest in Aristotle and Bacon, and with a Humean skepticism. In later years she spoke of her development as a journey from Plotinus to Locke and Hume, and she also developed an appreciation for Berkeley, "for destructive idealism as for destructive materialism." In her early skeptical period which preceded her idealistic phase, she would also have acknowledged, she felt, the only certainty advanced by Hume, the perception of the moment, had she then been familiar with his work.[58] Matter—or the sensations which have their basis in matter —seemed the only solid reality to Miss Glasgow in 1939; and like Hume, she felt that knowledge could be only provisional and tentative, the incremental result of our uncertain impressions as they are accumulated in the mind:

If life has a deeper meaning, it must forever elude us. Neither science nor philosophy can do more than illumine or enkindle the senses through which impressions or what we call knowledge must come. Yet it is of these vague impressions and of this uncertain knowledge that the scholar, as well as the creative artist, must assemble and build up the very substance, the feeling, sight, taste, touch, scents and sounds, of reality.[59]

The creative thinker, by energetic effort, must bring his independently derived perceptions into harmony with the inner "substance of personality," reconciling thereby the fruits of experience with the abstract. If she acknowledged that faith had its victories, Miss Glasgow also maintained that the "permanent basis of tolerance" could be found only in skepticism and that "a reasonable doubt is the safety-valve of civilization." [60] As an intellectual who was both an idealist and an empiricist,[61] Miss Glasgow had, moreover, many affinities with a philosopher she often mentioned, George Santayana. In her feeling that the light exists but that man is beleaguered by uncertainty, her views are also similar to those of a poet, contemporary with her, whom she did not mention in any published source, Edwin Arlington Robinson. But it was ironic laughter, rather than philosophy, which best permitted her, she said, to escape the insistent self within. A lightly sardonic view of her own frustrations and of the larger tragedy of the world gave her spirit release. This view remained with her to the end and brought "the steadfast . . . accord without surrender of the unreconciled heart."

The World War deeply influenced Ellen Glasgow spiritually and intellectually. Because of her love for England, she could not help being strongly sympathetic with the Allies. On the basis of the ideas expressed in her interview with Joyce Kilmer, we can conclude that she was strongly affected by the Wilsonian view of the war as a moral and political crusade. She believed that Western democracy was preferable in all respects to Prussian autocracy and she hoped that an Allied victory would mean the disappearance of barriers between nations, classes, and the sexes. Some of these ideas Blackburn directly reflects in *The Builders* (1919). With part of her being, Miss Glasgow also identified herself with the suffering engendered by the war. In the old house on West Main Street in Richmond to which she returned in 1916 after five years' residence in New York, she was not only oppressed by a heavy sense of her personal past but by a sense of calamity concerning the world at large. She was also disturbed by the fact that many people, including her fiancé, either seemed to enjoy the war or to profit from it. Looking back on the winter of 1917–18, she was to withdraw in revulsion as from "a frigid nightmare, an allegory of doom."

In this time of international crisis and of personal disturbance, Miss Glasgow fell in love again, this time with Harold S——, whose exact name Miss Glasgow also chose not to disclose.[62] Harold's strength of will, shrewdness, and intelligence enabled him to become a well-known lawyer and political leader in Richmond by the time Miss Glasgow first came to know him in 1916. At first Ellen resisted him, since she felt herself too independent for marriage and too critical of his standards. But she was so anxious to escape the burden of her past that she was readily borne away by his vitality, while he was aroused, she said, by her lack of veneration for him and by her open mockery of some of his values. During the war Harold was part of the Balkan deputation of the American Red Cross and stayed on in Romania afterwards supervising the relief program. Though they had been in love and had almost married, Miss Glasgow discovered that after the war neither she nor Harold cared enough to accept, without trying to remake, the other person.

Although they continued to see each other for twenty-one years, they were happy, Miss Glasgow declared, during only the first seventeen months. After their first quarrel in 1918 which almost ended in Miss Glasgow's death from an overdose of sleeping pills, their first fervor never revived. When at last she fell out of love, she experienced an increased freedom; but the affair had also, she perceived, partly killed her spirit. From the pain caused by illusion yielding so quickly to disillusion, she could only escape through a bemused contemplation of their uneasy relationship. The effects of this disconcerting experience are assuredly present in the late novels: in Dorinda Oakley's bitterness toward sex (*Barren Ground*), in the endeavor to tell "the whole truth about men" [63] (*The Romantic Comedians*), in Mary Victoria's moral crusading in the Balkans (*They Stooped to Folly*), and in the frustrated passion of the Birdsongs (*The Sheltered Life*).

Through these crucial years, Miss Glasgow sought diversion in travel and creative expression in her novels. She went abroad yearly until the first World War and spent the rest of her time writing at home or visiting New York. With truth she could allege that she did her best work, not when emotion dominated her but when its force had diminished to the throb of remembrance. She had written one of her strongest books, *The Deliverance* (1904), when she was in love with Gerald; but with her deepening love for him and the subsequent agony originating in her renunciation of him and in his death, she sought too conscious a release from emotion. *The Wheel of Life* (1906), *The Ancient Law* (1908), and *The Romance of a Plain Man* (1909), accordingly show her talent at its thinnest. When she was less directly involved, intense emotion did not always result in an artistic impoverishment. For instance, the suffering she experienced as a result of her brother's suicide and her sister's death may well have contributed to the grim force of two of her best books, *The Miller of Old Church* (1911) and *Virginia* (1913). With *Virginia* and *Life and Gabriella* (1916) her reputation widened, although Miss Glasgow felt that *Virginia* did not at first receive the attention it merited.

During the war years and those which followed, Miss Glasgow's creative energy again ran low. When in 1920 she was at work upon *One Man in His Time,* apathy and fatigue had apparently overcome her: "I have a very good idea, but somehow it doesn't seem as important and vital a thing to write a novel as it once seemed. That's a pity." [64] Her uncertainty about Harold and her growing awareness of the disorders caused by the war afflicted her so fundamentally that twelve years elapsed between *Virginia* and another major novel, *Barren Ground* (1925). Having worked out a code for herself which stressed the relevance of spirit only when it could face an often brutal reality, having thrust into the dim corners of her mind the emotion she felt toward Harold, and having weathered personal disillusionment and world catastrophe through an ironic mockery, she felt about 1922 that creative energy was again flooding her mind and that aspects of her being, long in abeyance, were reasserting themselves. She soon surmised that her best work was to spring from the strengthened insight into human nature which the troubled years just past had given her. The three of her best books, *Barren Ground* (1925), *They Stooped to Folly* (1929), and *The Sheltered Life* (1932), belong to the years which followed; and though *Vein of Iron* (1935) and *In This Our Life* (1941) lack uniform sureness of touch, they too reveal the effects of a reawakened artistry.

Miss Glasgow defined early her province in writing fiction, but did not exhaust it readily. Her renewal of power she rightly ascribed to a sensitivity toward contrasting ranges of experience. The strain of an existence divided between disheartening solitude and outward social gayety had made her, she felt, equally responsive to the serious and to the amusing. She was then able to transmute the two facets of life into an art with both comic and tragic manifestations. This sense of the complexities of experience became especially pronounced in her work during the 1920's and the early 1930's. When she knew herself exhausted by a preoccupation with the starkness of life in *Barren Ground* (1925), she turned to the fashioning of two comedies of manners, *The Romantic Comedians* (1926) and *They Stooped to Folly* (1929), and then to the uniting of the two strands in *The Sheltered Life* (1932). In the 1930's she further exploited the somber side of her sensibility in *Vein of Iron* (1935) and *In This Our Life* (1941).

Ironically, Miss Glasgow's creative vigor revived when her health began to fail and when the world, in the 1920's, seemed in her view about to destroy reason in the ardent quest for sensation. The war, she said, had so drained her of feeling and so inculcated "a faintly sardonic laughter" that she was led to the "experiment and revolt" [65] which found their register in *The Romantic Comedians, They Stooped to Folly,* and *The Sheltered Life.* Although she continued to identify herself with that aspect of revolt in the 1920's which protested against "parochial smugness and village *mores,*" she was outspoken in her criticism of those intellectuals who glorified the primitive, the violent, and the unconscious. Hence in these years of her own achievement, Miss Glasgow increasingly felt shut off from the main movements in American literature. Again, her intimate associations with novelists during the 1920's and the 1930's, apart from Cabell, were mostly with minor figures such as Joseph Hergesheimer, Carl Van Vechten, Marjorie K. Rawlings, and Stark Young, and indicate her own partial remove from the center of American literary activity. In the Prefaces which comprise *A Certain Measure,* in *The Woman Within,* and in her letters after 1932, her strictures upon certain phases of American writing in the 1930's were actually at variance with the best features of her own work, the powerful evocation of destructive primitive passion at the close of *The Sheltered Life* (1932), for example. At this point she condemned writers such as Hemingway and Faulkner for their recourse to the irrational, though she herself had made consistent use of it for creative renewal. The principal weakness in her criticism of these authors lies in a reliance upon the strongly asserted generality without much mention of specific books, or else in a fixation upon one book by a writer— *Sanctuary,* for example—to the exclusion of his other work.

That she did read her postwar contemporaries with interest, however, her survey, "The Novel in the South" in *Harper's Magazine* for December, 1928, attests. Only a few years after Mencken's deprecatory "The Sahara of the Bozart," she was one of the first to see in the South the beginnings of that literary renaissance which has since attained noteworthy proportions. As a pioneering realist, she was at least partly responsible for this renewed creative activity in the South during the 1920's and later. Writing before the full emergence of William Faulkner, Thomas Wolfe, and the "Fugitive" group, she mentioned the work of the following writers as evidence of a Southern literary awakening: Amélie Rives, Mary Johnston, Margaret Prescott Montague, DuBose Heyward, Julia Peterkin, Paul Green, Burton Rascoe, James Boyd, Frances Newman, Edith Summers Kelley, Julian Green, Conrad Aiken, Laurence Stallings, T. S. Stribling, Isa Glenn, Emily Clark, Eleanor Mercein Kelly, Dorothy Scarborough, Eleanor Carroll Chilton, Donald Corley, Berry Fleming, Elizabeth Madox Roberts, and James Branch Cabell.

For a time it seemed as if Miss Glasgow might achieve substantial leadership in American letters. It was at her suggestion, for example, that a Conference of Southern Writers was held at Charlottesville on October 23 and 24, 1931.[66] She suggested to James Southall Wilson that Southern writers might benefit from knowing one another better; Dr. Edwin A. Alderman, then president of the University of Virginia, proved hospitable to the proposal; and an informal committee consisting of Ellen Glasgow, James Southall Wilson, James Branch Cabell, Archibald Henderson, DuBose Heyward, Thomas Wolfe, Stark Young, and Paul Green was organized. Thirty-four writers were invited to attend the conference. The actual participants were Sherwood Anderson, Katherine Anthony, John Peale Bishop, James Boyd, Herschel Brickell, Katherine and Struthers Burt, James Branch Cabell, Mr. and Mrs. Chapman (who collaborated as Maristan Chapman), Emily Clark, Donald Davidson, William E. Dodd, William Faulkner, Ellen Glasgow, Isa Glenn, Caroline Gordon, Paul Green, Archibald Henderson, Dorothy and DuBose Heyward, Mary Johnston, Ulrich B. Phillips, Josephine Pinckney, Alice

Hegan Rice, Cale Young Rice, Amélie Rives (Princess Troubetskoy), Mrs. Laurence Stallings, Allen Tate, and Irita Van Doren. Thomas Wolfe, Stark Young, Julia Peterkin, Laurence Stallings, Burton Rascoe, and Herbert Ravenal Sass could not come. Miss Glasgow presided at many of the meetings and was evidently the guiding spirit of the conference. She emphasized, especially, the need for diversity in life and literature, and the rejection of "the standardization which is the death of creation." [67] She had previously recognized in "The Novel in the South" a growing protest in the region against "fundamentalism in ideas" and "utility in art" and had regarded such discontent as the dynamic force behind contemporary revolt in Southern letters. In an interview with Virginius Dabney in 1929 she expressed similar ideas. Though she here deplored the tendency of the New South to create a culture without including the aesthetic sense, she also found such widespread ferment in the South that she could prophetically declare, "It is entirely possible that the best writing in the United States will now be done in the South." [68] At the conference in 1931, Miss Glasgow's friendship with Allen Tate apparently began, and she had praise for two early works by Southern writers who thereafter achieved distinction, *Penhally* by Caroline Gordon and *Many Thousands Gone* by John Peale Bishop. [69] She continued to think highly of these writers and was later impressed by Hamilton Basso's books.

In a 1943 revision of the *Harper's Magazine* essay (the Preface to *The Miller of Old Church* in *A Certain Measure*) she retained only Cabell from her 1928 list of writers and revealed that she had responded to the changing literary scene by citing now, as the chief writers in the South, figures on the whole of greater stature such as Thomas Wolfe, William Faulkner, Allen Tate, Caroline Gordon, Marjorie Kinnan Rawlings, Hamilton Basso, Margaret Mitchell, Stark Young, and Clifford Dowdey. Miss Glasgow's somewhat agitated aversion to contemporary life and literature, which even in 1931 began to be evident, hardened in the years which followed and prevented her from exerting in American letters the genuine leadership which her past acomplishment and her wide learning should have made inevitable. If she failed to become a leader of others in the 1930's and 1940's, she had gained the unforced respect of older contemporaries such as Sherwood Anderson, James Branch Cabell, and Sinclair Lewis and the sincere admiration of younger writers such as Donald Davidson, John Crowe Ransom, Allen Tate, Thomas Wolfe, and Stark Young.[70]

Ellen Glasgow's antipathy toward what she deemed to be the intellectual rootlessness and mannered futility of the 1920's and the 1930's was great, since her own search had always been for an abiding reality beneath the changing surfaces of life. The "reckless" ethical experimentalism of the age, she was convinced, violated an insistent idealistic tendency within her own being, "a sense of justice and compassion that I could not betray." Her mature views on spiritual and intellectual revolt, as she voiced them in an address to the Modern Language Association, "Elder and Younger Brother" (published January 23, 1937), were ambiguous. Though she still perceived that nonconformity led to the development of new ideas, she now wished to define with care what she was protesting against. She also frankly acknowledged that her "radical" attitude in letters had been based primarily upon rebellious impulse rather than a cogently worked out set of principles.

She apparently detected an even greater lack of substance in the irreverent younger generation. In her comedies of manners written during the 1920's she viewed the excesses and pretenses of postwar youth ironically, but in *Vein of Iron* and *In This Our Life* and in her critical pronouncements in the 1930's she treated them too seriously. When war and its aftereffects—together with what she felt were the spiritual inadequacies of modern man—seemed to imply a defeat of the ideals embodied in "the new freedom," a sense of betrayal entered her thinking and fundamentally discomposed her: "That liberal hope of which we dreamed in my youth appears to have won no finer freedom than an age of little fads and the right to cry ugly words in the street." [71] Her excited opinions about the alleged excesses of the modern age reveal, in fact, an almost hysterical recoil from the complex pressures and the latent violences characterizing life in the 1930's and 1940's. Disillusioned with what she saw, she withdrew more tensely into the self than she had yet done and failed to see steadily and whole the life about her.

In her later desire to preserve the best in tradition from contamination and abuse, she ended by accepting rather uncritically some of the things she had rebelled against in her youth, the romantic aspects of her inheritance, for example: "After all, in spite of the scorn Northern reviewers heap upon the now completely discredited 'magnolia and moonlight tradition,' there have always been many magnolias in the South, and even in the fallen grandeur of the present, moonlight has never wholly deserted the Southern scene. Someday, I suppose, all this will be discovered over again." [72] Two other Jamesian realists among her contemporaries, Edith Wharton and Willa Cather, also decried the violence in life and the experimentation in letters characterizing postwar America. By virtue of her embittered self-reliance and her forcible skepticism, Ellen Glasgow was at first (until ill health and nervous irritability clouded her vision in the middle 1930's and 1940's) able to adapt better to these years than were these other two novelists. At least she did some of her best work during this period of spiritual exile from the life about her; and there was not so sharp a decline in the quality of her last books.

In the 1930's a chronic heart condition made foreign travel formidable and an active literary career almost as difficult. During this decade and into the 1940's Miss Glasgow spent her summers in New England and her winters in her imposing old house in Richmond, devoted to her friends and to the art of writing. Among her intimates, her keenness and vivacity of mind remained unimpaired to the end; and, in spite of her deafness, her conversational powers and social brilliance became legendary. Though she had resolved not to write any more novels after *Vein of Iron* (1935), the creative impulse again generated its own energies after "this long Siberian winter of the soul," [73] and the result was an interesting book, if not necessarily one of her best, *In This Our Life* (1941). If we are sensitive to the strident undertones of her autobiography, composition of which she had now begun, we may conclude that even a growing national reputation did not much sweeten these years. The solitary practice of her craft became still more insistently the organizing principle of her life, when the chaotic world outside and her own deafness increasingly forced her back upon herself. Typical of her attitude was her conviction, expressed to Stark Young in 1932, that immersion in her work would provide her with staying-power since all else seemed to have failed her: "In spite of the long tragedy of my life, I do not think I have exhausted the creative part of my mind. Now, when everything else matters so little, I may give my whole self to that. The only thing I have saved out of the wreck is the gift of work, and I shall cling to this as our ancestors clung to the Rock of Ages." [74]

With the summer of 1940 her heart became worse, after she had completed the second draft of *In This Our Life*. Through a determined effort and with the help of James Branch Cabell, she corrected in proof this draft of the novel, since she had been in the habit of making three drafts for each of her books. That the strain of writing this book and seeing it through the press was almost too much for her we may deduce from a discouraged letter to Carl Van Vechten in 1942: "I cannot work; I cannot even hate; so simple and pure despondency is my bitter brew." [75]

Toward the end of her career she enjoyed the serious recognition which had eluded her before the first World War. She was awarded honorary degrees from the University of North Carolina, the University of Richmond, Duke University, and the College of William and Mary; she was granted in 1940 the Howells medal for distinguished work in literature by the American Academy of Arts and Letters; and she was given the Pulitzer Prize in 1942 for *In This Our Life*. To the end of her life, November 21, 1945, her conviction persisted that the art of fiction had made her existence tolerable, despite the sufferings she had experienced in the past and the physical pain she was then enduring. One may question, along with Cabell, whether literary fame and the life of the mind were really compensations for the absence in later years of vital human relationships. Despite her sensitivity and isolation, Miss Glasgow saved herself from some of the extreme implications of her narrowed later attitudes by her ironical sense, by the vigor of her mind, by the breadth of her interests, and by a never completely blunted critical faculty which was most characteristically revealed as a humorous scrutiny of the incongruities of existence.

Miss Glasgow felt that, with the writing of *Barren Ground* (1925), her inner life had been reoriented and that she could afterwards "respond to a fresh, and, apparently, a different, creative impulse." [76] Her creative energy did burst forth again; at the same time, in the last twenty years of her life, the constructive break with her past life and artistry was not so sharp as she thought, and she was unable to maintain with complete poise "this heightened consciousness and this altered perspective." In emphasizing her sense of fracture between her early and her later selves, Miss Glasgow and her critics have too readily encouraged the view that her career was divided into two sharply distinct parts. Miss Glasgow's own statements have caused her integral development as artist to be disregarded and the earlier work to be too frequently dismissed as inferior to the "final achievement" and unrelated, except as apprentice work, to it. The fact, moreover, that Miss Glasgow did not generally achieve recognition as a serious writer until *Barren Ground* may have focussed attention upon the novels written after 1925. [77]

Actually, the independent vigor of mind evinced in the early novels largely compensates for what they may lack in maturity; and her forthright rebellion against social and literary conventions provided a clearer vantage point from which to write than did her later well-defined philosophy of experience. In some measure, then, the force of the earlier novels disappeared when the note of rebellion became faint. The vehemence of *The Deliverance* (1904) is equal to that of *Barren Ground* (1925), *The Miller of Old Church* (1911) is as profound a commentary upon manners as *They Stooped to Folly* (1929), and *Virginia* (1913) is as informed with pity for a noble type of woman who symbolizes a lost way of life as is *The Sheltered Life* (1932). These six books, in fact, represent Miss Glasgow at her best, and though not one of them is flawless, they form, together with many sections from her other books, a solid body of significant work, distinguished primarily for its moral insight and for its dissection of the moralism which tends to obscure a valid morality.

Though too much may have been made of it, Miss Glasgow's deliverance after 1925—emotional and intellectual—was real: the ghosts from the past were exorcised at the same time that a philosophy was precisely defined. With relief from psychic stress, Miss Glasgow more exactly formulated her eclectic view of life, which, as she outlined it in a chapter contributed to Clifton Fadiman's *I Believe* in 1939, included naturalistic, idealistic, stoic, skeptical, and humanistic concepts. Intellectual self-confidence gave rise to the four excellent books written from 1925 to 1932, even if the positiveness and more precise definition of her views sometimes resulted in an inflexibility which became still more pronounced in her last two novels. Fine as the later fiction is, it embodies with serenity and rigidity values and attitudes which had, at least, been less insistent in the earlier work. In *Barren Ground* (1925) there is an agitated denial of the life of the senses in favor of an almost inhuman fortitude, in *They Stooped to Folly* (1929) a moral passiveness possibly in excess of the ironic detachment required in a comedy of manners, in *The Sheltered Life* (1932) a too open temperamental involvement with the gentility of General Archbald, and in *Vein of Iron* (1935) and *In This Our Life* (1941) a querulous dismissal of modernity by a self-confessed modernist.

In these later novels Miss Glasgow half-intentionally, half-unconsciously neutralized the strictures she had voiced when, as spokesman for the New South, she had condemned the timidities—intellectual, social, and ethical—of the Virginia gentry. She grew more tolerant of aristocratic values when, after 1925, she became increasingly skeptical of industrial forces and of much in the liberal philosophy of progress which had dominated her at the turn of the century. She now saw that the "progressive" industrialized South she had once felt preferable to aristocratic debility had, in its turn, denied certain spiritual attributes present, if only partially developed, in the older South of tradition. Although she remained more liberal in her philosophy of experience than the Agrarians who came to prominence in the 1930's, Miss Glasgow shared their distrust of the effects of a "mad industrialism" upon civilization in the South and at one point apparently agreed with much in their program, if we may judge by one of her letters to Allen Tate: "I find myself turning definitely toward your point of view and away from the raucous voice of the modern industrial South." [78]

She now recognized in the most admirable representatives of her own class an inner strength which at times of trial turned their apparent defeat by circumstance into moral victory. As a result, spiritual endurance rather than the individual's vigorous realization of his own destiny dominates the later Glasgow fictional world. The really distinctive feature of the novels after 1925 was a comprehensiveness of view, in large part intuitive, which could see the best in both the old and the new and which tended to supplant the crisp vigor of the intellectual in active revolt against her inheritance, so notably present in *The Deliverance, The Miller of Old Church,* and *Virginia.* At the imaginative level, then, Miss Glasgow achieved an over-all tolerance in her later novels that they sometimes lack in terms of the intellectual formulations or of the prejudices found in them. Her later acceptance of her class was still provisional, however, while the liberal hope survived that the future might somehow be better than the torpid present.

Miss Glasgow's professed liberalism of thought had sometimes clashed with an inherent conservatism of the spirit, even in her early work, and continued more insistently to do so in her later career. As long as the realization of the best self was encouraged, Ellen Glasgow advocated a philosophy of change and a relaxation of moral restraints, but she became dissatisfied whenever a doctrinaire liberalism, a materialistic progress, or a crudely naturalistic art threatened the spiritual autonomy of the individual or implied that life had only a surface meaning. Against all odds the individual was to maintain his integrity, whether he were beset by deadening custom or by forces antagonistic to the living values in tradition. In her early work she reacted more against the hold of the past upon the South. In her late work she could still be forthright in criticizing the lifeless aspects of Southern culture at the same time that she increasingly distrusted the levelling tendencies she saw in contemporary democracy. A democratic liberalism and an aristocratic conservatism each fostered noble qualities, Miss Glasgow reasoned, but could each become tyrannical. Only in the solitary life of the spirit—superior both to tradition and to the distracting present—could one find equanimity. As with Santayana, this harmonizing of extremes and this high valuation of spiritual poise was, in essence, the underlying principle of Miss Glasgow's career as thinker and artist.

❖ II ❖

Disenchantment
and Aspiration:
Early Explorations

Although Ellen Glasgow excluded from her collected work her first two books, *The Descendant* (1897) and *Phases of an Inferior Planet* (1898), they anticipate the themes, situations, values, and character types elaborated in her later fiction. Despite an uncertainty in style and conception, these apprentice novels not only possess force and originality but they adumbrate significantly her later development. Miss Glasgow realized this herself when she looked back upon *The Descendant* late in her career: "the germ of my future work, as well as my philosophy of life, lay hidden in that immature effort." [1]

In *The Descendant* Ellen Glasgow expressed, through the violent Michael Akershem, her impatience with the anemic sweetness and the reticence characterizing much of the literature and culture in which she had been nurtured. When the central figure of this first novel walked into her imagination, Ellen Glasgow at eighteen decided that she "would write of an outcast, of an illegitimate 'poor white,' of a thinker, and of a radical socialist." [2] After showing the deprivations of his boyhood in Virginia, she felt impelled to place him in a scene she knew only imperfectly, the New York of the 1890's. The inference is that in a thoroughly conservative society like the Virginia of post-Reconstruction days Michael could hardly have been so aggressive in his opinions and actions. Miss Glasgow had not yet evolved, to any appreciable extent, her ironical and satirical view of her native Virginia, and evidently she did not yet feel completely at ease in writing of Southern life and manners. Nor was she yet prepared, it seems, to analyze the immediate effects of political intransigence upon Virginia caste and tradition.

In *The Woman Within* Ellen Glasgow said that she had revolted against the Southern tradition more because it was cruel than because it was false.[3] The intensity of this motivation behind her own revolt she expressed in depicting Michael's formative years.[4] Because of his illegitimacy he is relentlessly persecuted by his pharisaical guardians and neighbors, since it is easier for lower middle-class adherents of moral gentility to snub him than to try to understand him. In the animus between a bastard boy and his adoptive family Ellen Glasgow anticipated the similar tensions recorded by Faulkner between Joe Christmas and the McEacherns in *Light in August*. Discarding the comforting view that childhood is always idyllic, she conceived Michael's as squalid and tormented.

When the sensitive, vehement Michael finds life intolerable in the Virginia town of Plaguesville, he runs off to New York. After much initial distress, he becomes a noted socialist agitator and journalist, infusing into this activity the same energy and truculence which had marked him as a boy. In New York he falls in love with an ambitious and warmhearted painter, Rachel Gavin, who is at first reluctant to permit emotion to interfere with her career. Overcome by passion at last and conscious that marriage is contrary to Michael's freethinking principles, she decides to be his mistress. Ultimately he tires of her and becomes uncomfortable at her disregard of convention. He is then attracted to the conscientious Anna Allard, who has for him all those "womanly" qualities which he now finds missing in Rachel. With a sudden urge to achieve respectability and the good opinion of Anna Allard, he permits Rachel to break off their relationship and resigns from the *Iconoclast* to become editor of the more moderate *Journal of Economics*. Michael's affair with Rachel and his shift in political allegiance together form the structural center of this novel: as his enthusiastic yet self-regarding passion for Rachel diminishes, so does his generous but self-aggrandizing revolutionary ardor.

In a quarrel about his resignation Michael impulsively shoots and kills the most fanatic of his associates on the *Iconoclast* and is sentenced to eight years in prison. After his release he by chance encounters Rachel, now a well-known artist. She exults in having him with her again, but her happiness is only momentary. Blood comes to his lips in a fit of coughing, and Rachel sees that he now possesses only remnants of his former force. Aware that he is dying, she regrets, even more than her own unfulfilled life, the waste of his rare abilities. The bitterness suffusing Rachel's reunion with Michael and the vigor of his outcries against fate demonstrate the strength of Miss Glasgow's disenchantment even as a young writer: "The broken and wasted remains of a great vitality, the decay of a towering ambition, querulous complaints in place of an impassioned reserve, death in place of life—these were hers" (275). This section of the novel, depicting Michael's decline and death, balances the earlier chapters, depicting his struggles in boyhood and youth, and the whole book reveals the youthful author's already well-developed skill in handling blocks and masses of material.

Imagery drawn from Christian tradition helps define the personalities of Michael, Rachel, and Anna Allard and Michael's relationships with the two women. When Rachel first sees Michael at the *Chat Noir,* she finds in his brooding intensity the model she had been seeking for a study of John the Baptist about to leave the wilderness. Her tearing her sketch in two when Michael approaches her may foreshadow his failure to achieve his initial ambition of becoming a prophet of a new world order. Rachel is identified in part with the Magdalen she is painting in the picture which at last wins fame for her. As Rachel has envisioned her, the Magdalen displays "a great forewarning in her awful eyes" to which Rachel herself is oblivious in her own emotional life. One of her acquaintances truly declares, however, that the fallen woman in the finished painting is as "beautiful" and "brave" as Rachel. The unselfishness of Rachel's love for Michael changes her dubious relationship into something potentially noble, love being "that great transforming power which evolves an Esther from a Jael, a Madonna from a Magdalen." With her serene integrity Anna Allard seems to Michael "the sister of some holy order." Later she becomes for him a veritable Madonna when, on one of her charitable visits to the slums, she tenderly holds an unwashed baby in her arms.

It is the sinner in love's cause who stays by Michael to the end rather than love's saint. If Anna has a rustic wholesomeness about her, it is Rachel who is the vital force, "alive to her finger-tips, and warm with the flow of her rich, red blood." Miss Glasgow often thought of Rachel in images of warmth and light, seeing her bright face, for instance, across the "flame-colored nasturtiums" on her studio table. Rachel brings Michael life: when he gives her up, he loses the power to think independently, and he resents the fact that she is indissolubly connected in his mind with all the kindnesses which others have done for him in the past. With this warmth and vitality she would also protect Michael upon his release from prison, if she could.

Miss Glasgow's psychological insight into the gifted but turbulent Michael Akershem is one of the most interesting features of *The Descendant*. Uncontrolled, he shatters "meteor-like" those with whom he comes in contact. Miss Glasgow expressed this disruptive influence by the dynamic terms she often chose to describe him: "The mental energy confined within the storehouse of his brain was in a continual state of ebullition, escaping in magnetic currents through the will or the senses, as the case might be" (104). Unconfined, his energies will consume himself as well as others. This Miss Glasgow conveyed by comparing him to an ignited "brand" and by associating his personality, appearance, and utterances with fire that glows brilliantly for the moment, only to be extinguished: "his magnetic gaze illuminating her, scorching her, as though the scintillating flames were shafts of fire"; his "eyes flickered like rusty iron through which a red-hot fire is passing"; his "revolutionary spirit [was] a flame which, sooner or later, must burn itself out." [5] In short, Miss Glasgow perceived that primitive impulses surviving in civilized man exert both creative and destructive force. Whereas in Michael she demonstrated the explosiveness of primitive temperament under restraint, she also implied that his strength of will might have been productive had he met society halfway and had he been able to direct his compulsive egoism. She was never again, in fact, to be so directly concerned with ostensibly noble impulses which, through pride, become transmuted into evil.[6]

Miss Glasgow anticipated with Michael Akershem the vehement, brutal characters popular in American fiction from 1900 to 1915. In the boy Michael she subtly foreshadowed the primitive force of the man to be. At one point, his hatred for the wife of the farmer who raises him becomes suffused with a desire to kill ("to feel his fingers closing upon something and closing and closing until the blood ran down"). Later, his anger is beastlike in ferocity when he quarrels with his disciple Kyle. Throughout the novel Michael's narcissistic fervor, his fierce independence, his self-assertiveness, his love of power, and his persistent desire for a chance to be even with the whole world, ally him with the Nietzschean overmastering personality that somewhat later found definition in the novels of London and Norris. His violent egotism, his desire to inflict cruelty, his tendency toward self-dramatization, and his final surrender to his own destructive instincts are also characteristics of the undisciplined romanticist. Even if Miss Glasgow's presentation of her protagonist is flamboyant and sometimes superficial, his disordered personality recalls the much more firmly drawn characters in Dostoevsky such as Ivan or Dmitri Karamazov or Raskolnikov.

Commenting upon the murder which Michael later commits, his

patron Driscoll realizes how frenzied had been Michael's frustrations,
how undisciplined his latent passions, and how socially abnormal his
self-sufficiency:

As the result of conflicting circumstances he saw that Michael was but a
victim to disregarded but controlling laws—laws that remain ignored for
generations, and recoil upon the heads of the children of children. Now
that his anger had cooled he saw in him not the man revolting against the
system, but the abnormal development revolting against the normal. He
beheld in him an expression of the old savage type, beaten out by civilization, and yet recurring here and there in the history of the race, to wage
the old savage war against society. And he reproached himself, remembering
Michael as he had seen him last, his nature aroused in all its primitive
ferocity; the seething passion which he, John Driscoll, had laughed at because
he could not understand. It seemed to him that had he reached forth and
drawn him back, had he ventured one appeal to that better nature which
was overthrown and vanquished, this tragedy might have been averted. (246)

In this passage the fusion of nineteenth-century and anti-Victorian attitudes illustrates the transitional nature of Miss Glasgow's early work:
a conventional sort of moral dualism which presupposes an articulate
struggle in man between his lower and his higher nature is supplemented with an emphasis upon the inexorable effects of "controlling
laws" and with a consciousness of the strength of primitive drives in
personality.[7]

Miss Glasgow's first novel revealed the conflict, never quite resolved in her fiction, between her radical intellect and her basically conservative temperament. Michael's "faith in the power of truth and the
impotence of error" is impressive, she implied, to the extent that it
deflates the complacency of his contemporaries and encourages them to
revalue their prejudices and conventions. Despite his final defeat by
circumstances, she identified herself in large part with his socialist protest against existing institutions. But whenever his radical attack on
convention becomes an excuse for the gratification of immediate impulse
and of self-centered ambition, Miss Glasgow condemned it. Although
she was committed intellectually to Michael, she was often disparaging
in her detailed consideration of him. Emphasis in the novel thus becomes uncertain because of Miss Glasgow's complex, possibly confused,
conception of her central character. Yet she was able, with penetration,
to analyze the unstable, undisciplined zealot who is too easily impelled
from radicalism to conservatism.

Miss Glasgow, then, sometimes recoiled from her protagonist and
sympathized with the more conservative "liberals" in the novel. Anna
Allard, for example, modulates her idealism with a strong sense of fact

and displays a goodness which represents a "mean between spiritual unsophistication and worldly wisdom." She unconditionally deplores, therefore, the unsettling influence of Michael's theoretical tirades against society. In Driscoll Miss Glasgow projected still other facets of her mind. By regarding a valid radicalism as "unconventionally moral" rather than "conventionally immoral," Driscoll discriminates (as Miss Glasgow herself consistently did) between morality and convention. He consequently regrets Akershem's unreasoned attacks upon morality emanating from his indiscriminate hatred of convention. Michael finally approximates Driscoll's position and Miss Glasgow's own—that of the reformer rather than that of the revolutionist. As a reformer, however, Michael is less arresting than as an impassioned fanatic. Driscoll's skeptical, exploratory temper, which sees a situation in its full complexity, and his "respect for humanity" also reflect the young Miss Glasgow's empiric yet humanistic approach to experience. Driscoll's critical acumen is partially ineffective, however, since unlike the early Akershem, he has no clearly defined purpose in life: "He pursued the dangerous, sweet divinity—change."

Like her peers Ibsen, Shaw, Conrad, Henry James, Galsworthy, H. G. Wells, Robinson, Norris, Dreiser, and Crane, Miss Glasgow grew to maturity during "the late Victorian sunset." [8] Despite the unintelligent restrictions it sometimes imposed upon an artist's free expression of his vision or his ideas, this was an age which encouraged a largeness of outlook among its artists and intellectuals. Like most of the writers just named, Ellen Glasgow believed that some pattern of spiritual order ultimately determined man's destiny; and like them she also protested against the spurious idealism in this culture which, by avoiding distasteful truths, led to moral dishonesty or to a complacently materialistic society. Along with her protagonist in *The Descendant,* who echoes Carlyle and Ibsen, Miss Glasgow was convinced that "customs, like garments, wear out and lose their original usefulness, and like garments require to be discarded for a more advanced and more suitable order" (75). Like Carlyle and Ibsen, moreover, she respected the energizing influence of an idealism which was critically discriminating.

One sort of idealism which Miss Glasgow repeatedly subjected to ambivalent scrutiny in her fiction, beginning with *The Descendant,* is that associated with the earnest religious temperament. The strong religious impulse which gives to Grandmother Fincastle in *Vein of Iron* and Dorinda Oakley in *Barren Ground* their independent moral strength has affinities with the ethical seriousness of at least three characters in *The Descendant:* Driscoll whose inherited force of conscience does not

permit him to sin easily, Anna Allard whose quiet integrity organizes
her energies, and Rachel Gavin whose inner power allows her to transcend her frustrations as artist, her loss of social reputation, and her
desertion by Michael.

Several minor figures in the novel display the misdirected religious
feeling which Miss Glasgow satirized more fully in her later work. The
elderly Miss Serina Parks has developed a morbid interest in the un-
regenerate women whom she visits and prays for: "A lady who handles
the Ten Commandments with care, and collects the fragments that her
neighbors have shattered" (145). The minister, Mr. Self, forgets that
a vital religion presupposes honesty: he thus denounces the "sordid
realism" of the present day and advocates an idealism which would
"turn to the frugal existence of our Puritan ancestors, putting aside all
the vicious results of these decadent days" (168). For the labor leader,
McTibs, the letter of religion is far more potent than its spirit. When he
loses literal belief in the doctrines of original sin and predestination, he
has nothing to sustain him: "He was content to toil by the sweat of his
brow and wrestle with temptations as long as such conduct warranted
him the privilege of a heavenly seat looking hellward. But what is the use
of keeping to the narrow path if our neighbors are not damned for going
astray?" (127). And there is the Virginia minister who is relieved by
Michael's departure to New York, since he need no longer be the
champion of a young man unjustly despised for illegitimacy.

A static moral idealism was still more to be deplored, Miss Glasgow
felt, than an unimaginative, tenaciously held political or religious creed.
In the social sphere, the inspiriting precept often lost connection with
the actuality and became responsible for maintaining unchanged the
values and practices of the past in an age of transition. This obsessive
refusal to face the unwelcome truth, this "calling things by their wrong
names," [9] provided Miss Glasgow with abundant material to examine for
comic effect in *The Romantic Comedians* (1926), *They Stooped to
Folly* (1929), and in sections of *The Deliverance* (1904) and *The
Miller of Old Church* (1911). But moral sophistry could also lead to
tragedy, when innocence in woman was more highly valued than her
knowledge of good and evil, in *Virginia* (1913), in *The Sheltered Life*
(1932), and in the education of Rachel Gavin in *The Descendant:* "She
had read much in books and little in life, being wise in theories and
ignorant in facts, and possessing a good deal of that ignorance which is
mistermed innocence. Her clear glance had swept over nature, and had
found all things pure and nothing common" (70). Rachel's worldly inexperience causes her to idealize Michael and to misjudge masculine
fidelity in love; as a result she is completely unprepared for Michael's

defection. Commenting upon Rachel, her friend Madam Laroque point-edly expresses Miss Glasgow's disparagement of such innocence: "She's too innocent to come to any good. . . . In this world innocence is worse than crime" (72).

With a temperate irony deepening at times into Ibsenian force, Miss Glasgow exposed the double standard of sexual morality through her treatment of the unconventional love affair between Rachel Gavin and Akershem. Rachel is penalized by being exiled from society, whereas Michael loses nothing. Her emotional warmth estranges him, once love has been "offered up upon the altar of his own divinity," because such abandon does not seem altogether "spiritual" to him. Miss Glasgow thus revealed in Michael the paradox that the most emancipated in-dividual can at heart be the most parochial. The respectability he had previously scorned is in the end a more potent force upon him than he would willingly acknowledge.

In subjecting traditional gentility to rigid scrutiny, Miss Glasgow did not wholly support "modern" rebelliousness. Accordingly, in *The De-scendant* she described the followers of Ibsen, Tolstoy, and Zola as too eager to conclude that vice once frankly described is no longer vice but "realism." Yet she herself was more sympathetic with these moderns than with people conditioned in the fifties who had been fascinated by vice as "the old skilfully draped creature."

This ambiguity in her feeling toward modernity is projected through the characters of her novel and their relation to the age and through her descriptions of the modern age itself. Her shifting sympathy with Michael has been noted; she also seemed to vacillate in her relative evaluation of Rachel and Anna Allard. Rachel is seen as "that light, elusive essence of modernism." In her candor, her whole-souled vitality, and her rejection of pretense she represents all that is best in the new, at the same time that she is occasionally lacking in emotional balance and a sense of the true worth of tradition at its best. Anna Allard is spiritually incorruptible and personifies all that can be said in favor of an imagina-tive attachment to the proprieties.

Though Miss Glasgow apparently decided in Rachel's favor, still the modernism which Rachel represents is often associated with sickness and disease, to contrast with Anna Allard's wholeness and spiritual health. Rachel grows to maturity in the early nineties when old principles are being discarded before new ones have been evolved: she is "the out-come of an effete civilization" and has perhaps unconsciously absorbed some of the weaknesses of her time. It is difficult, therefore, to see life with complete stability and clarity if one has so completely identified herself with the present as Rachel has: "Theories floated around, like bacteria in an infected atmosphere, waiting to gain a parasitic existence upon an unsettled reason" (86). Michael is still more closely identified with this spiritual malaise. The elements of his nature meet to form "a poisonous complexity," his opinions have the effect upon others of "a subtle poison," and he himself expires from tuberculosis as if to emphasize the diseased aspect of his nature and to demonstrate the enervating effect upon him of the chaotic modernism which he has advanced and which has in turn undermined him. The obverse side to his earlier fierce idealism is "the pain and misery, and wasted strength" of his final days. A "palpitating humanity" and a "tainted atmosphere" not only characterize the overheated summer during which Michael and Rachel come to the end of their life together but reflect the disordered age which has both encouraged and eroded their relationship. That the age is new and exciting and capable of great things Michael's own fervor and Rachel's final success as painter testify; that it is also drifting spiritually and morally is implied when Michael finds in Anna's wholesomeness and honesty an anodyne for the "degeneration" and morbid tendencies of the day.

The Descendant is still unseasoned: its style is frequently trite and overblown, the situations in it are often hackneyed, and its psychological motivation is frequently unsure, as in Michael's implausible contemplation of suicide when he first arrives in New York. The intrinsic merit of the book is not great, yet it is interesting for its steadiness of vision, its sense of structure, its heralding of a sophisticated irony, and its subtle rendition of ethical conflicts within quite fully realized characters. The book must be considered in studying the evolution of Miss Glasgow's artistry and of the modern novel itself.

In her next book, *Phases of an Inferior Planet* (1898), Miss Glasgow again projected herself into her protagonist. At the beginning of the action, Anthony Algarcife is a teacher, scholar, and journalist in the New York of the 1880's, and is writing his master work: "A History of Man, with Special Application to the Science of Ontogeny." In her sympathetic presentation of his skepticism and intellectual independence—his determination to "live as I please" and to "think as I damn please"—Miss Glasgow betrayed her involvement in his inner life. With his sustained idealism and his intellectual seriousness, he embodies a different facet of her being than did the anarchistic Michael Akershem of *The Descendant*.

Algarcife's immersion in Darwin, Weismann, and Galton, and his thrilled emancipation from the theology of tradition, reflect Miss Glasgow's own youthful intellectual interests and her "radical" attitude toward religion. In 1939 she indicated how, like her hero in this book, she had founded her philosophy upon evolution: "On this foundation of probability, if not of certainty, I have found—or so it still seems to me—a permanent resting place; and in the many years that have come and gone, I have seen no reason, by and large, to reject this cornerstone of my creed." [10] Like Algarcife, Miss Glasgow, with her rationalist cast of mind and her humanistic bent, soon discovered enough that was contradictory and distasteful in Christian dogma to cause her to doubt its infallibility: "Yet I have no recollection that I ever truly believed either in the God of the Shorter Catechism or in the God of the Thirty-nine Articles. I could not trust an Everlasting Mercy, whether stern or mild, which was omnipotent, but permitted pain to exist, and the Prince of Darkness to roam the earth in search of whom he might devour." [11]

For the dogmas of Christianity, Algarcife substitutes an emergent religion in which man continually creates his God through an incremental series of spiritual intuitions. Since for Algarcife the transcendental realm as well as the observed fact has meaning, he values more the spiritual implications of a dynamically conceived philosophy of evolution than the empiric methods of laboratory investigation. Ethically and philosophically an idealist, he later evolves a Goethean morality of integrity and renunciation without admitting to himself its possible Christian basis: "it is good for a man to do right, and to leave happiness to take care of itself" (316). To some degree, then, Algarcife combines the iconoclasm of Michael Akershem and the reverence of Anna Allard as these were set forth in Miss Glasgow's first book.

"Phase First" of the novel recounts Algarcife's life as a young scientist, his defeat through the Philistinism of his age, his misalliance with Mariana Musin, and his depair at her defection. The action of this section, except for that described in the few flashbacks, is limited to approximately a year. "Phase Second" takes place some eight years later, and it is even more restricted in time. It is connected with "Phase First" through Algarcife's and Mariana's occasional recollections of the past. In this work Miss Glasgow evolved the structural method she put to good use in books like *The Miller of Old Church* (1911) and *The Romantic Comedians* (1926): an initial situation is presented in complex detail, and in a second section of the novel this same situation, reflecting the changes caused by the years, is still more exhaustively analyzed. By the time "Phase Second" begins, Anthony has become an Episcopalian priest to please his onetime mentor, Father Speares, who cares for him in his illness and mental depression after Mariana's desertion. Although Algarcife becomes renowned as leader of "a second Tractarian excitement," his mind rejects the dogmas he professes and his heart is not in his work except as he is able to help the poor.

Romantic intensity, as well as intellectual deliberation, characterizes

Algarcife and links him with the undisciplined Michael Akershem in *The Descendant*. If Akershem is the superman as defiant rebel, Algarcife is the superman as prophet, a Zarathustra who, in exaltation of the ideal, contemns the flesh for the reason possibly that its desires are so insistent:

As he stood there with the morning sunlight flashing upon his face and gilding the dark abundance of his hair, the singularly mystic beauty of his appearance was brought into bold relief. It was a beauty which contained no suggestion of physical supremacy. He seemed the survival of a lost type— of those purified prophets of old who walked with God and trampled upon the flesh which was His handiwork. (72)

To link him with humanity in the present, Algarcife exhibits the same violent drives, the same "scarlet veins of primeval nature," which lie beneath Akershem's nature. Algarcife's passions are more controlled, but their having been repressed only serves to increase their potential force. Certainly the impulse which seizes Algarcife to strike his wife when he sees her after eight years of embittered separation, "to strike her until he had appeased his thirst for blood" (247), recalls that which led the less sophisticated Akershem to murder.

Algarcife's passion for Mariana revives, however; and this genuine emotion throws into relief his hypocrisy in serving a church whose dogmas he scorns. When the contrite and chastened Mariana suddenly dies of pneumonia, Algarcife is so distraught that he contemplates suicide. At this moment a parishioner interrupts him with news that some of the poor in his congregation are on strike and need him. His subsequent anxiety for their welfare implies that he will live and devote himself to service among the underprivileged in New York.

In spite of Algarcife's—and Miss Glasgow's—essential idealism, a cynical and disillusioned atmosphere, as in *The Descendant,* pervades this novel. After Mariana leaves, Algarcife's despair verges upon nihilism. At that point he is overwhelmed by an obsessive sense of the indifference of the cosmos to his aspirations. In such moments of stress Algarcife forgets his Spencerian view of evolution with its long-range optimism, and concentrates upon the harsher aspects of the evolutionary process which are in accord with his own unbearable anguish:

A physical disgust for the naked facts of life attacked him like nausea. The struggle for existence, the propagation of the species, the interminable circle of birth, marriage, and death, appeared to him in revolting bestiality. In his bodily and mental wreckage, all action became repellent and hideous, and the slanting sun-rays bespattering the human atoms in the street produced a giddiness in his brain. (177)

His revulsion at Mariana's flight is modern in its vociferousness but Victorian in its distrust of the flesh when he concludes that happiness is to be found "not in love, which is the thirsting for a woman's spirit; not in passion, which is the burning for a woman's flesh. Did not bitterness follow upon the one, and upon the other satiety?" (182). In his conscientious loss of a theological faith and his attempt to find a "religion" in service to humanity, Algarcife is once more spiritually of the nineteenth century, in spite of his modern Nietzscheanism and his self-conscious responsiveness to the pessimistic undercurrents of this age.

This diffused mood of disenchantment, which determines much of the ultimate meaning of the book, is in part conveyed by the many references to disease in the action and imagery. Increasing discord between Algarcife and Mariana culminates in an "atmosphere of common pain" with the death of their child, Isolde. The futility of Mariana's life and her disappointed expectations are accentuated by her apathy and sickness thereafter. The somewhat fevered intellectual career of Algarcife is suggested when he falls physically ill of fever in his despair after Mariana departs. It is as if this sickness befogs his brain until renewed contact with Mariana allows him to perceive his intellectual hypocrisy for what it is. When he sees her after her temporary recovery from pneumonia, she too exhibits "the ravage of pain." It is ironical that his reunion with Mariana is prevented by her relapse after she impulsively seeks him out in inclement weather, now that he has told her of his renewed love for her. As though conscious of the inferiority of this planet and the unmerited suffering of its denizens, Algarcife as clergyman spends his time visiting the psychologically maladjusted and the physically ill. His wealthy parishioners suffer predominantly from morbid ailments of the mind, while his poorer charges are frequently victims of mortal illness. When one of them is dying of cancer, for instance, Algarcife is acutely conscious of the sordidness of her end: "the unclean odors of the disease consuming her flesh hung about the quilt and the furniture" (198). To parallel the somewhat gratuitous death of Isolde in "Phase First," there is in "Phase Second" the somewhat contrived death from croup of the son of the wealthy but discontented Mrs. Ryder.

The skull and crossbones in Algarcife's study, referred to at several strategic points in the novel, gives force to its sinister undercurrents of meaning. In some sense the skull and crossbones is an emblem of a harsh reality which Algarcife—when he first sees Mariana—wishes to keep from her knowledge: he wants her to know only "flowers and sunshine." That this reality can be overpowering, the skull hints when it seems to grin at Algarcife as he works doggedly at his articles the night that his child dies. Later when Mariana leaves him, these "remnants of dry bones" seem to typify the futility and apparent waste in his own life, now that all the purposes which once directed him seem to have vanished. In charting the apparent defeat of a noble individual, Miss Glasgow used, as the chief instrument of Fate, a woman who destroys through ignorance of her power. Worshipping art and artists with a kind of "sensuous self-abnegation" and craving the untried, Mariana rebels against her poverty-stricken family in Virginia and her boardinghouse surroundings in New York, only to be more overwhelmed by drabness in her marriage. Like Emma Bovary in her romantic malaise, Mariana has no suitable outlet for her wayward emotions, for her "swift surprises and tremulous changes." Thus compulsive artistic ambition overpowers Mariana when she attends the opera after absence from it: "She felt taller, stronger, fuller of impregnated germs of power, and, like an infusion of splendid barbaric blood, there surged through her veins a flame of color. With a triumphant crash of harmonious discord, she felt that the artistic instinct was stimulated from its supineness, and the desire to achieve was aglow within her" (118). Throughout the portrayal of Mariana Miss Glasgow grimly insisted upon the disproportion between heroic aspiration and meager talent and thereby generated realistic force for her in the novel.

At the end of the book Mariana has become aware, in Ibsenian fashion, of the malign effects of a spurious idealism ("I have lopped off an ideal every hour since I saw you"). She now realizes that a valid idealism must be leavened with a sense of the actual and agrees with her friend Ardley that "life is a continuous adjustment of the things that should be to the things that are" (236). Ironically, Mariana attains before her death that degree of spiritual poise which had been Algarcife's before she had undermined it. If Mariana's ideal of a grandiose destiny for herself as a prima donna in opera deflects her critical powers and disenchants her with the actualities of her marriage, Algarcife's own idealism is so intense and inflexible that it blinds him to the nuances inherent in the psychology of love. His expectations from women are somewhat arbitrary, his views as to her sphere are often narrow, and he sometimes fails to understand human nature as his own wife reveals it. In any event, both Algarcife and Mariana learn from rigorous experience that the intensities of romantic passion are inadequate by themselves for meeting intelligently the complexities of life. This is also the substance of Miss Glasgow's interpretation of *Lohengrin*, a performance of which Algarcife and Mariana attend separately after their eight-year estrangement. As the music proceeds, it loses its ethereal quality and becomes ominous in its implication that love's ecstasy diminishes when mundane actuality impinges upon it: "The ideal was singing the old lesson of the real found wanting—of passion tarnished by the touch of clay" (258).

While this tone of disenchantment is sustained throughout the book, the modified idealism achieved finally by the main characters not only gives direction and amplitude to their lives for an interval before Mariana's death but inhibits Algarcife from suicide. Despite the disillusion which preceded it, the fervent reconciliation between the lovers on a plane where the flesh is subordinate to exalted purpose is typically Victorian. Yet Miss Glasgow's frank analysis of Algarcife's frustrated career and buried primitive nature, her cynical concentration upon Mariana's impulsive self-aggrandizement, her sardonic emphasis upon the arbitrary element in Mariana's death, and her preoccupation with the deterministic aspects of natural law, all anticipate twentieth-century realistic fiction in America.

With a less forceful hero than *The Descendant,* this second novel has the faults of the first: an uncertain style and an inadequate motivation of characters in the main situations. Algarcife's religious struggle is too little the vital problem of a human being and too generally an illustration of the intellectual uncertainties of the advanced thinker of the 1880's to be at all credible; and Mariana's remorse and repentance are too little in accord with her former selfishness. A comparative absence of conscious irony and social satire also makes this book more ponderous than her first. Already well developed in this novel, as in *The Descendant,* is the pictorial aspect of Miss Glasgow's imagination: see, for instance, Algarcife's declaration of love to Mariana as, on the balconies of neighboring boardinghouse rooms, they overlook the city in the early evening, or Mariana's frenzied dance in a moment of Bohemian abandon at a party in this house. With some feeling for the reality, Miss Glasgow also evoked the atmosphere of artistic Bohemia in late nineteenth-century New York. Her conscious use in this novel of light and shadow for aesthetic effect anticipated her later use of this device: Algarcife's black cowl at the end of the book implies his haunted conscience, and these dark tones contrast with the sunset lights in the scene wherein Algarcife had fervently declared his love to Mariana. A minor work to be sure, *Phases of an Inferior Planet* provides further evidence of the youthful writer's structural grasp of her materials and reinforces the conclusion which she had already reached about art and life in *The Descendant,* that "truth is only truth in its complexity; our convictions are only real in their relativity" (18).

"Of Brave Men
and Angels": The First
Chronicles of Virginia

The Voice of the People (1900) and *The Battle-Ground* (1902), as chronicles, cover many years in the lives of the principal characters and in the history of a region. These books are differently organized from *The Descendant* and *Phases of an Inferior Planet* which had focussed upon a protagonist's life in a limited setting. Miss Glasgow again used this earlier structural pattern in *The Deliverance* (1904). In the two intervening chronicles, she presented numerous characters and an exhaustively rendered milieu: Williamsburg (under the pseudonym of Kingsborough) and Richmond from 1870 to 1898 in *The Voice of the People,* and the northern section of the Valley of Virginia from 1850 to 1865 in *The Battle-Ground.* The evocation of scene is, in fact, often more impressive than the vitality of the central figures.

In these narratives Miss Glasgow is the omniscient author, and the chronological line is straight and direct. With each new mass of material introduced, the characters have grown considerably older and sometimes the scene has changed. Actually, Miss Glasgow sporadically introduced too many inadequately developed characters into an extended and shifting scene to have been altogether successful in sustaining the illusion of time inevitably passing. Despite her resort to situations in ironic contrast with each other, her full renditions of family life, and her adroit use of persons and incidents in parallel sequence, structural firmness was not, in all respects, satisfactorily achieved in these chronicles. They are more diffuse than later efforts in this category, such as *Virginia* (1913), *Barren Ground* (1925), and *Vein of Iron* (1935). In these more successful chronicles the psychology of the characters is adequately developed, point of view is expertly controlled, and setting is capacious and unified. Though historical milieu generally overshadows character portrayal in *The Voice of the People* and *The Battle-Ground,* their best sections are those which incidentally etch in such eccentrics as Mrs. Dudley Webb and Aunt Griselda, or Miss Lydia and Major Lightfoot. In depicting with astuteness and tolerance the diverse types found in Virginia society, Miss Glasgow had already become a novelist of manners.

By early 1898 Ellen Glasgow had the idea for "a bigger and more ambitious work" than she had yet written: by the end of 1899 when she had finished most of *The Voice of the People,* she saw that it represented "a change of literary base" from her previous books.[1] In her first two novels she had explored an alien environment to express her dissatisfaction with the conventional aspects of the Southern scene. Now she could think of planning "a series of Virginia novels as true as I believe this one to be." [2] She perceived that her critical powers might best function through interpreting Virginia life with ironic detachment and that roots were as necessary as fervor to the novelist who would truthfully reflect his experience.

When Ellen Glasgow scrutinized the recent past of Virginia, she saw a society in transition. In *The Voice of the People,* therefore, she exploited for the first time the subject which was to absorb her in the novels written through the first World War: the transformation of the South from a hierarchical society to a social order less stable and less confident of its values, if more assertive and brash in temper. Nicholas Burr, son of a peanut farmer, struggles to achieve distinction, ultimately as governor of Virginia, and becomes emblematic of the vigorous middle class that largely came to supplant, at least in the realm of practical affairs, the once powerful planter caste and their associates who had "lived easily and . . . died hard." [3]

The germinal situation from which the rest of the book develops is presented in the first chapter, when Nicholas Burr, the "poor white" farm boy, comes to borrow a book from Judge Bassett. His very presence not only disturbs the tranquil atmosphere of the library but seems even then to embody "the intrusion of the hopelessly modern into the helplessly past." [4] The eternal calm of aristocratic life in Kingsborough and its indifference to change is thus, from the first, in strong contrast with discordant forces from the outside which eventually, as Nicholas Burr comes to represent them, cannot be completely ignored.

That aspects of the aristocratic civilization in the prewar South fitfully survived into the seventies, eighties, and nineties to resist industrial and democratic tendencies in the New South, Miss Glasgow indicated in her portraits drawn from the Battle family. The General in his generosity and impulsiveness epitomizes the essence of Southern chivalry, Miss Chris the fortitude of the South in adversity, Eugenia its romantic individualism and independence, Aunt Griselda its amenities turned sour through inner desiccation, and Bernard its enervation through a tendency to exchange moral responsibility for the pleasures of the moment. Writing about the decline in prestige of a social class she knew well, Miss Glasgow was able to give these figures symbolic value as they are related to Southern life. They seldom reach beyond the Virginia scene of the novel, however, to the general and the universal, as do the characters in Miss Glasgow's more mature novels.

The Battles and Webbs, representing Virginia's first families, stubbornly withstand the threat to their traditional authority posed by a widening democracy as the middle class is changed and augmented by the rise to influence of gifted commoners. Mrs. Webb's exaggerated pride of caste is offended by Nicholas's presence at Judge Bassett's school which her son attends; and in the college library where Nicholas studies as a young man, even the lifeless portraits seem displeased at his presence: "the portraits of painted aristocrats glowered down upon the intrusive plebeian" (86). The General best reveals the instinctive revulsion which the Battles feel toward Nicholas Burr, especially after he presumes to ally himself with Eugenia. The General refuses to discuss anything with the young man except crops, because to speak of his studies would be to condone his aspirations to rise out of his class. His shiftless, somewhat churlish father, Amos Burr, is disorderly and procrastinating; and instead of tilling his land vigorously, he sanguinely hopes that the United States government will come directly to the rescue of the farmer as it has, he thinks, already helped the manufacturer and the laborer. Amos Burr was thus caught up by the Populist movement of the 1880's and 1890's which advocated Federal relief for farmers in distress and which was, in essence, a protest against the increasing power both of capitalist financiers and of railroad magnates who exerted control from the Northeast over Southern economic life. The best facets of this agrarian unrest, as they trace back to the ideas of Jefferson, are represented by Nicholas himself in his later insurgency against the established political machine in Virginia.

Though a minor character Mrs. Dudley Webb is more directly a symbol of the aristocratic South in eclipse than are the Battles. Her deliberate withdrawal into a romantic past from her present poverty and obscurity is not only a personal predilection but a regional one. Her independence, her pride, her exclusiveness, her "unconquerable irony," her aloofness, her aversion to the unpleasant reality, and her blindness to the forces making for social change are, in Miss Glasgow's interpretation, as characteristic of the pre-Civil War South and its survival into the seventies and eighties as of Mrs. Webb herself. So great is the force of her tradition that those who go counter to her wishes feel they have violated the loyalties which ought to command their deepest reverence. Although the Judge with his reason feels her prejudice toward Nicholas Burr unjustifiable and insists upon the boy's attending the same classroom as her son, he is secretly uncomfortable at having his way: "He had gained the victory, but he would have felt pleasanter had it been defeat. It was as if he had taken some secret advantage of a woman—of a widow" (85). Characterized by quiet confidence and an "Epicurean fortitude," the Judge himself is more humane and tolerant in his conservatism; but he is still skeptical of radical programs of reform like those advocated by the Readjuster Party which repudiated the prewar and Reconstruction debt of Virginia and which then came under the control of the opportunistic General William H. Mahone.[5]

In the Webbs and the Battles Miss Glasgow recognized that in most respects the former leading class in the South was still "unreconstructed," after relinquishment of "Radical" Northern control of the South in 1877. The spiritual tenacity and the practical inefficacy of the tradition which survives inflexibly in Mrs. Webb cause Nicholas Burr to declare: "We are a people without a present" (142). He is himself responsive to the magnanimous aspects of the Southern heritage, however, as it is found in the unaffected wisdom of his Kingsborough patron Judge Bassett, in the democratic idealism of Jefferson, and in the example of Washington. As governor, Nicholas is often seen against statues of Washington in the Capitol square and in the Capitol building at Richmond; his moral character, it can be inferred, is similar in its integrity to the first president's. Through her latter-day protagonist, Miss Glasgow implied that even after military defeat the South had much that was vital in its submerged traditions and much that was indispensable to the molding of a comprehensive political philosophy for a united nation.[6]

By means of romantic passion Eugenia Battle and Nicholas Burr attempt to bridge the gulf between the classes. But social prejudice too readily allows Eugenia to believe her brother's lie that Nicholas has compromised his employer's daughter. As Nicholas perceives, she turns in revulsion from him "as she would not have turned from the brother of her blood had he been damned in Holy Writ." [7] Her denunciation of Nicholas had been anticipated when as a child she had called him "common," shortly after she had defended him from Dudley Webb's similar taunt. These roughly parallel incidents, however, do not provide sufficient motivation for Eugenia's rejection of Nicholas. Despite her strong attachment to her own class, Eugenia condemns her lover too impulsively for the situation to be entirely credible and for her moral nature, in retrospect, to seem as noble as Miss Glasgow evidently meant it to be. If Nicholas is, as Eugenia maintains, the kindest, gentlest, and most generous man she has ever known, it is difficult to see why— except for spurious pride—she allows his violent, but momentary and justified, anger to separate them irrevocably. Miss Glasgow was not yet able to fuse completely her aim as social historian in showing class division with the psychological requirements of her art.

Uncertainty of emphasis resulted from Miss Glasgow's seemingly instinctive identification with Eugenia and her exclusiveness. Actually, the situation explored in the novel called for Miss Glasgow's forthright identification with Nicholas in his partial defeat by the immobile aristocracy. She evidently accepted him more fully with her mind than with her sympathies. She was thus unable to exhaust the possibilities inherent in this relationship between lovers from different classes, because she conceived Nicholas too much from the outside. Many of the tensions existing between the lovers are left unresolved, and Eugenia too easily drifts into marriage with a friend from her own class, Dudley Webb. Despite Miss Glasgow's contrary intention, Eugenia's struggles with the farm, her anxieties over a wavering husband, and her disenchanted resignation to Fate do not incite much sympathy in view of her complacently assumed superiority to Nicholas. Furthermore, Miss Glasgow's direct praise of Eugenia becomes at times a sentimental indulgence.

Nicholas Burr, similar in many respects to Michael Akershem of *The Descendant,* evinces in this third novel Miss Glasgow's continuing fascination with the overmastering personality. Her insight into what struggle means for Nicholas as an individual is penetrating. It is a venture for him into a no man's land, a venture resulting in his complete isolation as he leaves behind his own people for an uncertain future in law and politics. His whole relationship to his age is suggested early in the novel when at dawn he is suddenly aware of "his own littleness and the immensity of the hour." If, in contrast to the greatness of nature, he may seem insignificant to himself, he is yet an extraordinary human embodiment of natural force—in his "vast fund of energy" and in his being "fearless of elemental changes"—and he transcends effectively the littleness of the hour which fails to understand him. The Old Stage Road from Kingsborough past the Burr farm against which so much of the action is placed suggests that Nicholas's destiny is forward into the unknown; and his thoughts are continually of "the vast avenue of the future" which the Judge opens for him.

When Nicholas curses Bernard Battle for his lie, Eugenia realizes how precariously balanced her lover's nature is between good and evil forces and how potentially satanic the deep-feeling individual can become: "And lighted by a glare of memory she saw his face; she saw the convulsed features, the furrow that cleft the forehead like a seam, the heavy brows bent above the half-closed eyes, the spasmodic working of the drawn mouth. She saw the man in whom, for its brief instant, evil was triumphant; in whom that self-poise, which had been to her the secret of his strength, was tumultuously overthrown" (183). After Eugenia's unjust accusation Nicholas reverts to the law of the jungle and thinks savagely that to see Bernard Battle now "would be to do murder." That a greater than normal barbarism may underlie a greater than average strength of character, Nicholas once again reveals sixteen years later when, as governor of Virginia, desire for revenge tempts him to refuse a pardon for Bernard who has escaped a prison sentence for forgery. At this point Nicholas's violent emotions all but overthrow his spiritual equilibrium. In spite of the temptation to yield to his eager demoniac impulses, Nicholas, in contrast with Christopher Blake of *The Deliverance,* still possesses enough command of self to draw back in time from gratifying them.

In the consciousness of his own power Nicholas, like Akershem, exhibits a Nietzschean self-reliance, "a regard for daring for its own heroic sake" (288). Was it not the mild Judge Bassett himself who had expressed the proto-Nietzschean doctrine which Nicholas exemplifies, the doctrine which endows the natural leader with the force to shape destiny: "It is not the times, but the man. . . . The time makes the man, the great man makes his time"? [8] Nicholas's force and integrity ultimately prevail, the largeness of his nature with its suggestion of "the breadth of the open fields" sweeps away the trivial before it, and his greatness is finally acknowledged even by Eugenia and the rest of the Battles. Nicholas is thus temperamentally secure, despite the assaults made upon him by his enemies, because his inner reserves give him power. Nicholas also learns that happiness is not to be measured in terms of gratified passion but more durably in terms "of the adjustment of individual needs to the natural laws" (259). When he once fully comprehends the indifference of the universe to the individual, he then reaches a self-contained serenity which neither his moments of amorous ecstasy nor his subsequent bitterness provided.

At the height of his prestige he is senselessly shot by one of a lynch mob at Kingsborough, when he prevents the mob from entering the prison for a Negro offender. In Nicholas's catastrophic death before he can make his principles prevail, Miss Glasgow undoubtedly reflected the failure of Populist reform elements in Southern politics in the eighties and nineties. Although he is a Democrat, he represents, like the Populists, the agricultural interests; and his tragic death in defiance of a mob demanding a Negro prisoner can be traced, like decline in Populist prestige, to the compulsive need felt in the South to maintain white supremacy under a strictly one-party system. The tradition which he has challenged in a sense triumphs over him, since it had done so little, fundamentally, to lessen racial tension. The control of politics through courthouse cliques, like that headed by the opportunistic Major Rann in the novel, was also a well-known expedient to keep the power of the traditional Democratic Party unchallenged and free from the influence of insurgent elements. At any rate, Miss Glasgow implied in Nicholas's fate that neither the decaying aristocracy nor the amorphous populace was yet ready for his independent moral strength. Eugenia is especially conscious of the waste of genius in Nicholas's death and the habitual indifference of men to the greatness which lies beyond their immediate interests. The final ironic comment upon Nicholas's career is supplied by Virginia history. The democratic principles that he personified were in large part defeated by the Constitution of 1902 which, four years after his death, disenfranchised not only the majority of Negroes but the poor whites as well.

The romanticism, underlying popular fiction in America in the 1890's and later, continued to influence Miss Glasgow, with the result that the somewhat self-conscious realism in *The Voice of the People* is sporadic.[9] In this book, for example, Miss Glasgow idealized young love to the point of unreality. Sentimentality accrues to a scene like this with its diffused air of uplift, and with its too neat envisaging of the way in which the lovers complement each other: "Eugenia's quick, untutored mind, which had run to seed like an uncultivated garden, blossomed from association with his practical, unpolished intellect. He taught her logic and a little law; she taught him poetry and passion. . . . He was the first man who had ever spurred her into thought; she was the first woman he had ever loved" (171). Similarly, Miss Glasgow's presentation of Juliet Burwell, a Kingsborough belle and later the wife of the politician Ben Galt, lacks subtlety. The effect of her goodness upon the impressionable Nicholas as a boy in her Sunday School class is too immediately salutary to be quite credible, and her slightly tyrannic domination of her husband and his friends is too directly stated.

But it is Miss Glasgow's simplification of Nicholas's upward struggles which detracts most from the verisimilitude of the novel. Instead of defining implicitly but with precision the factors involved in his rise, Miss Glasgow often resorted to summary comment:

That was his first winter and he had been nobody. Ah, it was hard work, that beginning. He had had to fight party plans and personal prejudices. He had had to fight the recognized leaders of the legislature, and he had had to fight the men who pulled the strings—the men who stood outside and hoodwinked the conscience of the powers within. He had had to fight, and he had fought well and long. (223)

Thus Nicholas's triumph at the state convention is inadequately prepared for, and the enthusiastic ovation accorded him there represents emotion in excess of the situation. Such scant analysis of character and incident was perhaps inevitable in a short novel which tried to cover too much ground.

Despite these defects *The Voice of the People* shows many evidences of Miss Glasgow's craft as novelist. Her style in the novel, for example, with its use of fresh sense impressions imparts the charm of Williamsburg in the 1880's:

Along the verdurous, grey lanes the houses seemed lonely, abandoned, filled with shade. From the court-house green came the chime of cow-bells rising and falling in slow waves of sound. A spotted calf stood bleating in the crooked footpath, which traversed diagonally the waste of buttercups like a white seam in a cloth of gold. Against the arching sky rose the bell-tower of the grim old church, where the sparrows twittered in the melancholy gables and the startled face of the stationary clock stared blankly above the ivied walls. (11)

As in her later manner, she made natural setting an integral register for the moods of her characters in the one convincing love scene, which takes place against the still autumn fields. When the love between Eugenia and Nicholas is violently disrupted, Miss Glasgow envisioned their tragedy not only against nature but against social scene. "A spectre-like suggestion of death and decay," [10] investing Kingsborough and the decline in prestige of the aristocracy (whose surroundings Eugenia views "with the tender eyes with which we mark decay in one beloved"), is linked with hints of autumnal decay along the woodland road where the lovers quarrel. Subsequently the force of their love wanes with the autumn season, still against the background of a dying social order. In after years it is not only Eugenia's radiant image but also "the effluvium of rotting flowers" which recurs to Nicholas and brings to mind his rage after Eugenia had unjustly accused him.

In this novel Miss Glasgow also revealed a flair for the vivid creation of minor characters in a sentence or two, using sharp, epigrammatic strokes to chisel a likeness, as in this rendition of the softly yielding but subtly dominating Mrs. Burwell, "who ruled her husband with the velvet-pawed despotism which was the heritage of the women of her race and day. She had never bought a bonnet without openly consulting his judgment; he had never taken a step in life without unconsciously following hers" (65). Miss Glasgow gave us in *The Voice of the People* the first of her many humorous rustics, Marthy Burr, Nicholas's stepmother, whose view of life, if unsophisticated, is yet unillusioned. In the somewhat melodramatic sequence in which Nicholas reviles Bernard for his lie, Miss Glasgow reached the intensity which she sometimes attained in later books. A still more acrid intensity underlies the scene wherein Nicholas as governor is torn between his conscience and his desire for revenge.

The Battle-Ground (1902) is surer in emphasis than Miss Glasgow's previous books, and it is her only novel with the Civil War as principal subject. It centers on two upper-class Virginia families, the Amblers and the Lightfoots, and contrasts the leisured existence of the prewar South with its mettle in battle. Shortly before the outbreak of war Dandridge Montjoy quarrels with his grandfather, Major Lightfoot, and is reunited with him only after four years of hard service in the infantry. Ironically, Dan discovers his love for Betty Ambler just before this violent quarrel separates him from the life he had always known. The break with his family and the start of war all but destroy his hopes of marrying Betty.

It was perhaps inevitable that Miss Glasgow should have written about the war, even if she had not wished to be inclusive in her social panorama. She gained her knowledge of the war from those who had participated in it and suffered from it, so that it became a living part of her imagination. The Glasgow governess, Miss Virginia Rawlings, had, for example, an inexhaustible supply of stories about the conflict. Other people whom Ellen Glasgow had known or heard about and their fortunes provided the basis for many of the characters and incidents in *The Battle-Ground*. Major Lightfoot was drawn from a kinsman of her father, Mrs. Lightfoot had for prototype a delightful relative of her mother, and the other figures in the novel were modelled in part upon people she had known directly or vicariously. Her great Aunt Cassie had saved some ancestral portraits from the burning of Mount Joy (her home and incidentally the basis for the hero's surname in the novel) as the Lightfoots had saved Aunt Emmeline's portrait from the burning of Chericoke, their plantation mansion. Like the women in the novel, Miss Glasgow's mother had suffered extreme hardship in the war (she had heard her children cry from hunger, for example) and had felt the misgivings about slavery expressed in the book by Governor Ambler.[11]

If the pre-Civil War South was "the home of brave men and . . . of angels" and if its rituals and refinements were the essence of generous living, it was, nevertheless, founded upon injustice. Miss Glasgow expressed this view through the character with whom she was intellectually most in sympathy, the morally scrupulous and conscientious Governor Ambler. He is more perceptive than his neighbors and thinks of slavery as an ancestral curse, undermining like a dry rot the ethical foundations of a gracious social order. Governor Ambler is frequently at odds with the testy Major Lightfoot who regards slavery as a divinely ordained bulwark of the aristocracy, albeit an institution for gentlemen only, as he tells the oppressor, Rainy Day Jones. When war comes the Governor turns sadly from the union he loves to the defense of home and state, bitterly conscious that the pageantry of war cannot compensate for the moral obloquy both of his forefathers and his contemporaries. Through him Miss Glasgow perceived the soul of the South as often tragically torn between instinctive knowledge of moral truth and the immediate need to temporize with that truth in the interests of self-preservation. Slavery thus becomes in this novel, as in Faulkner's work, a symbol of human guilt which must be expiated. If the impetuous Major can be identified with uncompromising secessionists such as Ruffin, Rhett, and Yancey, the hesitant Governor is to be identified with most thoughtful Virginians at this time and with the major leaders of the South such as Lee, Stephens, and Davis who respected the Union but who were in the end loyal to their native region.[12]

That the prewar South, both in its aversion to the disagreeable reality and in its impetuous aspiration, was a "romantic" culture Miss Glasgow indicated in *The Battle-Ground* by the unanimity of its gallant response to a cause which, to more realistic appraisal, might have seemed hopeless from the beginning. The "great fox-hunt" soon became a dreary war of attrition, and ruin was complete in 1865. Even then the South did not renounce the spirited yet evasive confidence which enabled it to outface disaster. There was enough truth in the widespread opinion that defeat had been the result of Northern numerical and economic superiority to confirm the South, after 1865, in its belief that the cause for which it had fought was just. In spite of sickness, poverty, and an inauspicious future, Dan and Betty at the end of the novel have not lost their self-respect and their self-pride. Miss Glasgow presented this aspect of the spiritually unreconciled South still more forcibly in the blind Mrs. Blake of her next novel, *The Deliverance* (1904). The legend of a glamorous mode of life violently brought to an end by war could survive, Miss Glasgow later contended, not only in a debilitating worship of the past but in a cultural heritage, which, with its emphasis upon beauty and heroism, ought to appeal to the imaginations of present-day writers in the South.[13]

Miss Glasgow again anticipated in *The Battle-Ground* some aspects of her later social satire, since the same Victorian standards which she subsequently criticized dominated pre-Civil War society in the South. The attitudes and behavior of Miss Lydia, Betty Ambler's aunt, for instance, exemplify the hypocrisy which the age demanded from its women. To the naive Lydia, "the sheltered life" of artificial ignorance is woman's appointed realm and an unrestricted, but unacknowledged, personal freedom is man's divine right:

She regarded heaven with something of the respectful fervour with which she regarded the world—that great world she had never seen; for "the proper place for a spinster is her father's house," she would say with her conventional primness, and send, despite herself, a mild imagination in pursuit of the follies from which she so earnestly prayed to be delivered—she, to whom New York was a modern Babylon, and a Jezebel but a woman with paint upon her cheeks. . . . In her attenuated romances she forever held the sinner above the saint, unless, indeed, the sinner chanced to be of her own sex, when, probably, the book would never have reached her hands. For the purely masculine improprieties, her charity was as boundless as her innocence. She had even dipped into Shakespeare and brought away the memory of Mercutio; she had read Scott, and enshrined in her pious heart the bold Rob Roy. "Men are very wicked, I fear," she would murmur, "but they are very—a—a—engaging, too." (41)

Through curiosity and ignorance a "pure" woman like Miss Lydia, Miss Glasgow perceived, could be charmed by what she ostensibly condemned. Miss Glasgow's later comic art, in large part, also depended upon an exposure of the disproportion between society's idealization of women and what these women actually are.

Woman indirectly imposes her desires and standards upon the society which represses her. Mrs. Lightfoot, while hovering in the background, nevertheless firmly but lightly controls her headstrong husband, who "knew all his world, indeed, except his wife." She is also more cynical than he in appraising the actuality of the war—a war which she had never expected "to be conducted like a flirtation behind a fan." Though he makes fun of her taste for sentimental novels, Major Lightfoot is fundamentally more idealistic and is basically more upset than his wife "when human nature behaves like human nature" in the war.[14] Possessing a keen sense of reality, Mrs. Lightfoot is, in her imaginative life, an extravagant romantic in a society of romantics. She can find sublimation for her strong emotions only in reading popular novels, the more Gothic or the more sentimental the better:

> The old lady, in her ruffled night cap, which she always put on when she took to bed, was sitting upright under her dimity curtains, weeping over "Thaddeus of Warsaw". . . . "None of your new-fangled writers for me, my dear," she would protest, snapping her fingers at literature. "Why, they haven't enough sentiment to give their hero a title—and an untitled hero! . . . I opened one of Mr. Dickens's stories the other day and it was actually about a chimney sweep—a common chimney sweep from a workhouse! Why, I really felt as if I had been keeping low society." (151)

In this book Miss Glasgow had not yet perfected her ironic method. Her attitude toward her materials was therefore not always sufficiently detached to create the illusion of an imaginatively compelling reality, and she was often ineffective in projecting emotion. In their lush and formal quality the love scenes in this novel show some affinity with those found in the romantic novel so popular in her early days as a writer. Then, too, the Major's rage when as a student Dan is put overnight in jail is out of all proportion to the "disgrace" thereby brought on the family name. The old man is as much infuriated by Dan's defense of a barkeeper's daughter from insult as by the fight and arrest which follow. The scene at the Richmond hospital in which Dan's reprobate father lies dying from an amputation also reveals Miss Glasgow's frequent inability at this phase of her career to discern the emotional implications of her materials—subtlety is smothered in rhetoric. When Dan reads *Les Misérables* to the soldiers about the campfire, their spellbound identification with the story is hardly representative of military life—even in an army of romantics.[15] Despite these displacements of emotion and despite a tendency to lean too heavily upon the cliché in situation, *The Battle-Ground* anticipates in many ways Miss Glasgow's later mastery.

In this novel Miss Glasgow's conscientious realism and the symbolic requirements of her art were in fuller accord than they had been previously. By presenting the objective truth about war at the same time that she grasped its far-reaching consequences, she now invested character and incident with deeper significance while still depicting them with fidelity. Especially searching is the contrast she established between the prewar South and the stern ordeal it was eager, yet ill-prepared to meet. The portrait of goddess-like Aunt Emmeline, who in times past was "the beauty and belle of two continents" and is now "the abiding presence of the place," symbolizes the gracious beauty and the apparent grandeur of this civilization which was soon to lose political power. When Chericoke is in ruins at the end of the war (evidently fired by Sheridan in his valley campaign of 1864), it is fitting that the portrait, "the one vestige of a former greatness," should survive as a reminder that a genuine greatness cannot wholly perish. The magnificence of spirit which constantly motivated Confederate civilians and soldiers prompts Mrs. Lightfoot to offer her wedding dress to furnish material for a flag. In contrast with this nobility, the partial corruption of the South is suggested in the death of Governor Ambler's slave, Mahaley, immediately before the war.[16] Even under a well-meaning master slavery is inhumane, Governor Ambler realizes, so that the gulf between master and slave cannot be bridged: "Mahaley was dying, this he saw when his glance wandered to the shrunken figure beneath the patchwork quilt; and at the same instant he realized how small a part was his in Mahaley's life or death. . . . As he stood there the burden of his responsibility weighed upon him like old age" (191). A memorable episode, too, occurs at the end of the book when the Northern soldiers feed their foes from a slaughtered ox. If human decency instead of political expediency could have administered the peace, we are to infer, an instantaneous reunion might have been possible.

Incidents involving the main characters also take on symbolic value. Borne away at Manassas by both the pageantry and the anguish of war, Betty Ambler evinces "that power of ardent sacrifice which lies beneath all shams in the Southern heart" (253) and becomes emblematic of the entire South in its great struggle. Virginia Ambler's death in pregnancy at Richmond during the Seven Days defense in 1862 implies that the Confederate cause may now be doomed and that "the war god" has demanded his choicest sacrifices and given nothing in return. Her dazed wanderings before her death, in order to find her wounded husband, mirror the agonized uncertainties of the Civil War South when its initial hope for a quick victory after Manassas had passed. Just before she dies, the magnolia tree in the garden takes on a new spurt of life and blooms lavishly; at least, the high idealism of the Confederacy, we gather, is not yet dispelled. Governor Ambler, as we have seen, manifests a moral integrity which, as long as it was heeded, was the finest quality of the Confederacy. In the death of one of the South's finest men, Miss Glasgow apparently wished to demonstrate that the prewar South failed to survive precisely because it evaded the questionings of its own conscience.

The deepest current of meaning in the novel runs through this last episode, for Betty and Dan are temporarily brought together before the war's end and reaffirm their love almost in the very presence of death. The force of life, we perceive, goes on despite the death of the great individual and the impending defeat of patriotic aspiration. Nature, including the love of man and woman, outlasts a purely man-made holocaust. At his first battle in the Virginia mountains, Dan notes, for instance, the survival intact of the delicate blue flower he had seen before going into battle. The Virginia mountains, the scene of much of the early fighting, link the prewar, wartime, and postwar sequences in the novel. At the end of the conflict, warfare has gone from these eternal hills; yet they still surround in the distance the plantation of Chericoke now in ruins, as they had done in the serene days before the war. Dan's first impression of "his own hills crowding against the sky" all but overwhelms him as he trudges home after Confederate surrender. The still unconquerable spirit of the South—of life itself—is implicit in the quiet way in which, after four bitter years of separation, Betty Ambler and Dandridge Montjoy submerge their identities in one another and in nature to face together their uncertain future. The spectral-like mountains in winter, "stripped of the mere frivolous effect of light or shade," had similarly tested the stamina of the fighting men and their capacity to endure to the end.

As if in anticipation of the later Southern novels such as Stark Young's *So Red the Rose* (1934) and Caroline Gordon's *None Shall Look Back* (1937) which honestly depict the destruction of the Confederate South, *The Battle-Ground,* an indifferent success for the most part, achieves force in the realism of its last chapters.[17] The "evocation of a lost way of living," [18] which occupies the first half of the novel, is much less authentic than Miss Glasgow's steady realization of the cost of war in terms of sheer suffering. Her realism in recreating the physical scene of war gathers weight when it is compared to the "sword and cape" fabrications of her less conscientious contemporaries.[19] Miss Glasgow's books depicts the miseries as well as the splendors of battle, though some of its crudities are beyond her. More successful than her rendition of the campaigns of Manassas, Romney, and the Wilderness is her evocation of wartime Richmond, civilian and military excitement being set against the afflictions endured by the hospitalized soldiers. It is her vision of an all but despairing South, however, which gives the last chapters of *The Battle-Ground* their somber strength. The episodes dealing with Virginia's death, with the death of General Ambler, and with the deprivations of women in the war all show a steady comprehension of its malignant power. These early examples of what Miss Glasgow termed "the revealing episode," [20] gather force through understatement, a mordant tone, and a concentration of emotion. Possibly more trenchant still are the passages which recount the total defeat of Dan's hopes as a soldier, now that his return home at the death of the Confederacy is anything but that of a victor:

For a country that was not he had given his life as surely as the men who were buried where they fought, and his future would be but one long struggle to adjust himself to conditions in which he had no part. His proper nature was compacted of the old tradition which was gone forever, of its ease, of its gayety, of its lavish pleasures. For the sake of this life, he had fought for four years in the ranks, and now that it was swept away, he found himself like a man who stumbles on over the graves of his familiar friends. (373)

⋄IV⋄

"The Old Pagan Scorn
of Everlasting Mercy":
The Deliverance

By 1902 Ellen Glasgow had begun a "big, deep, human document
. . . wrung from life itself," [1] from the life which had surrounded her
as a child and which she comprehended more fully as she matured. The
incident which formed the basis of *The Deliverance* survived in her mind
from childhood when an elderly lady had told her of a woman whose
closing years at the end of the war had been made tragic, like Mrs.
Blake's, by blindness. Ellen's family also had suffered from the conflict
and its aftereffects. Anne Glasgow had been exposed to privation during
the Reconstruction, and Francis T. Glasgow had had to begin his business career anew in middle age. It is also possible that the vehemence
underlying this novel may have reflected Miss Glasgow's frustrations in
her unfulfilled love for Gerald B——. In any event, she felt compelled to
write in order to escape profound depression: "It was this or death for
me—for I had come to the final choice that some are forced to make—
and when I left New York it did not seem to me within the remotest
range of probabilities that I should see the New Year in upon this
planet." [2]

As the novel opens, Christopher Blake is atoning in his indigent,
brutalized existence for the selfish lives of his forefathers. In Southside
Virginia he is a tobacco planter on seventy acres from the vast fields

once belonging to his ancestors, but now the property of Bill Fletcher, former overseer on the Blake plantation. Partly through exploiting his position of trust and partly through wartime speculation, Fletcher had amassed a fortune. In 1868 Fletcher arranged to have Blake Hall put up for auction, possibly through connivance with the Reconstruction authorities; there were no other bidders and he paid seven thousand dollars cash for the great estate. Ten years later, he has consolidated his holdings except for the small farm which had been deeded after the war to the maimed veteran, Tucker Corbin, brother to Mrs. Blake. Thus opportunism and rascality often triumphed during the Reconstruction and had their right to the spoils legally confirmed thereafter.

Because justice for the defeated landowners was frequently unattainable by legal means, violence like that implicit in Christopher's hatred for Fletcher was all too common in the postwar South. Christopher's animosity toward Fletcher, we soon discover, is not only personal but reaches beyond his own situation to convey the resentment of a whole region which suffered deep humiliation during "Radical" Reconstruction for the principles it had in all honor upheld by going to war.[3] Although he was not the agent of the Northern authorities, Fletcher prospered by tacit coöperation with them; at least he flourished after a war which impoverished his former employers. As a native citizen who took an almost traitorous advantage of the privations of others to enrich himself, Fletcher commands Christopher's resentment more strongly than an alien political jobber from the North could.[4] The Negroes and poor whites alike, classes which heretofore had derived little benefit from the aristocracy, instinctively continue to defer to the Blake family in obscurity as they never defer to the upstart Bill Fletcher.

If the planter caste had been sinned against during these years, Miss Glasgow realized that in the halcyon antebellum era it had been irresponsible. As Christopher Blake gazes at the portraits of his ancestors in the sitting room of Tucker's farmhouse, he perceives that they have been both genial and self-indulgent and that he has inherited their weaknesses as well as their strength: "Big, blithe, mettlesome, they passed before him in a long, comely line, flushed with the pleasant follies that helped to sap the courage in their descendants' veins" (152). From them he has derived that inflexible pugnacity, inherent in their chivalric code, which demands full vengeance for all the wrongs done him. If Blake Hall, the former seat of the dispossessed family, graciously betokens "that inner spirit which had moulded it into a symbolic expression of family pride,"[5] the secluded burial ground of the Blakes to which Christopher frequently retires to renew his hatred of Fletcher bespeaks a grimmer inheritance. If he is at first a victim of the demands of family tradition, he later throws off its stultifying influence without losing entirely the distinction it bred in him.

From a world "governed by an ideal group of abstract laws," the Blake family is thrust into a Darwinian universe governed by the law of struggle for mere survival. The extent to which the Blake fortunes had been reversed is to be measured by Christopher's having been put to the plough as a boy while the children of the former slaves trooped off to "the Yankee woman's school," a situation not uncommon in the Reconstruction South. If adjustment to a changed reality has warped the younger Blakes, such adjustment was not possible at all for the older Blakes. When at the close of the war Blake Hall passed to Bill Fletcher, the elder Christopher Blake had already become enfeebled in mind and had apparently taken to drink. The softness of his life, with its suggestion of decadence, could not inure him to the crisis of the war and the years that followed. Here obtrudes a hint of that aristocratic debility which was later to be more completely exploited in Southern literature, in the failure, for instance, of some of Faulkner's characters such as Thomas Sutpen or Jason Compson III and his son Quentin to command circumstance.

The blind and partly paralyzed Mrs. Blake is endowed with greater resilience than her husband and survives him some twenty years, though she has no knowledge of the present eclipse of her race and thinks that the former prestige of the South still remains. The members of her family connive at keeping her in ignorance of their misfortunes and support her on the lavish scale to which she has been accustomed. The blind Mrs. Blake's inability to see the present reality and her idealization of a romantic past were characteristics, in Miss Glasgow's view, of the postwar South itself: " 'The truth would be the death of her. . . . Tell her that Fletcher owns the Hall, and that for fifteen years she has lived, blind and paralyzed, in the overseer's house! Why, even if her eyes were opened, she wouldn't believe it. It is her not believing it possible that has made the long deception so easy. The sight of the change might kill her, but it could not convince her.' " [6]

To Guy Carraway, attorney for Fletcher and Miss Glasgow's "interested observer," the imperturbable Mrs. Blake in her massive Elizabethan chair is a fascinating and contradictory personality. Admiring her "wonderful keenness of perception" and her "intuitive understanding of men and manners," he finds it difficult to reconcile these traits to her living on lies and to her imperviousness to change. Like the denuded South of the 1870's and 1880's, Mrs. Blake has circumvented a distasteful reality by an indomitable strength of character—by her "wonderful will" and her "magnificent patience." Like her region, she has also suffered the last indignity; even the diamond in her ring is pawned and replaced by purple glass in order for a loan to be repaid to Fletcher. Mrs. Blake is a living figure in the novel but she does not always convince simultaneously as woman and symbol, for the reason perhaps that Miss Glasgow too forcibly directed attention to her symbolic dimensions in making her both physically blind and mentally hallucinated.

Like Chekhov's in *The Cherry Orchard,* Miss Glasgow's sympathies were with the despoiled aristocrats whose faults she could, nevertheless, anatomize with shrewdness. Tucker Corbin, clear-visioned as a result of suffering, records Miss Glasgow's own attitude when he sees how hollow the pretensions of his own class are and yet respects its sincere if misguided loyalties. Mrs. Blake, in her attachment to the luxurious life of the past, is generous and charming, but improvident and unable to see that her life of privilege has resulted from injustice to another race. Her daughter, Cynthia, is also motivated by fidelity to tradition and to values which, Miss Glasgow implied, at once foster a thorough magnanimity and an inhumane intolerance. Noble and generous to the point of self-extinction in her devotion to her family, Cynthia epitomizes the patrician generosity of the old order when, on one of her regular excursions to town to pick up sewing, she shares her meager lunch with a blind beggar. Out of a sense of hereditary loyalty she also supports Christopher when he risks death to help an old Negro retainer, Uncle Isam, bury four of his children who have died of smallpox in a woodland cabin. Brother and sister reveal that sense of moral obligation often felt by the plantation families for the welfare of the Negroes they had once owned but who deserted their service after the war. Actuated by this same uncritical acquiescence with the ancestral code, Cynthia inflexibly opposes the suit of her sister's lover, Jim Weatherby, because he is a farmer as his grandfather had been before him.

Christopher and his twin sister, Lila, are the only Blakes who come to terms with changing times: they even relish the coarse food which the other Blakes detest. It was Christopher's fate, as his father had once confessed, to be born twenty years too late to profit from his heritage; accordingly, he can only adjust to the inevitable. In contrast to Cynthia, Lila rejects the refined selfishness of her ancestors as being "worthless as the moth-eaten satin rags that filled the garret," and she is eager to marry her plebeian lover, despite the opposition of her family. In this marriage Miss Glasgow indicated that the independent small farmer with his democratic ideals has proved himself politically equal to the once dominant aristocrat, even if socially, under the old standards, he may still be unacceptable. Without possessing much surface appeal, the Weatherbys, as the yeoman middle class, possess a staunch stolidity absent in large part from both the Fletchers and the Blakes. They are survivors of a class prominent in the Southern social structure; and in them rather than in the overthrown Blakes or in the parvenu Fletchers we have the most undisturbed manifestation of continuity with the racial past.

Although her strongest predilections lay with the dispossessed aristocracy, Miss Glasgow was objective and tolerant in presenting other characters. Even in Bill Fletcher, who is in some degree the simplified villain of melodrama, she conscientiously indicated certain complexities. Insensitive to a whole range of subtle values, he compensates in some part for his indifference to tradition by a strong pragmatic sense of the present. If with his "hairy, bloated, sinister" face he is a bully and probably a thief, he has initially a vigor lacking in the more effete of his antagonists. That his energies can be applied positively, his strong devotion to his grandson, Will, indicates. That they can be reoriented in natures more sensitive than his own, the nobility of his granddaughter, Maria, testifies. Though the class origin of the two women is different, Maria, in the confidence with which she looks to the future and in her later poised integrity, suggests Anya in *The Cherry Orchard*. In a vein recalling Trofimov's sentiments toward Anya, Guy Carraway comes to regard Maria as the prototype of a stronger race rising from "the tragic wreck of old claims and old customs." [7]

The Deliverance is even more significant as a psychological than as a sociological study. For that reason, Miss Glasgow utilized the Virginia tobacco fields and a changing society in the novel less for their intrinsic interest than for a backdrop in the resolving of intricate inner conflicts. If the complexities of a whole society in flux form the matrix of this novel, the complexities of a human soul engulfed in a great passion —revenge—form its core. Christopher's savagery, induced by circumstances but also nurtured by his own narcissism and by a certain hereditary recklessness, provides the psychological impetus for this most powerful of Miss Glasgow's early books. Whenever he recalls his fierce instincts as a boy, Christopher experiences an exaltation in which he sadistically revels:

Strangely enough, it soothed him now to remember how near to murder he had been, and as he drank the summer air in deep draughts, he felt the old desire rekindle from its embers. . . . His god was a pagan god, terrible rather than tender, and there burned within his heart the old pagan scorn of everlasting mercy. There were moods even when he felt the kinship with his savage forefathers working in his blood, and at such times he liked to fit heroic tortures to heroic crimes, to imagine the lighted stake and his enemy amid the flames. (67)

There is something audacious and elemental about his jealously tended hatred, something, too, that is ultimately self-abasing, stultifying, and stagnating. According to Miss Glasgow, these contradictory qualities also characterized the animus which the South kept alive for its oppressors during the Reconstruction and afterwards.

Many of the images which describe Christopher indicate both his scorn of the Christian ethic and his commanding presence. From the mouth up his face suggests "the antique ideal," [8] though seen at a downward angle his face has a "massive power" which is "repelling." When Christopher concentrates on his revenge, Carraway sees that his face becomes "suddenly lustful like that of an evil deity"; later, Carraway refers to him as "our somewhat Homeric young neighbour." In his dealings with Fletcher, Christopher possesses a deliberation which places him at an advantage and allows him to take time "as lightly as did the Olympian deities." At other times, the stalwart rigidity of Christopher's temper and his stately appearance are established through associations with the Old Testament. When as a child he lay in wait to kill Fletcher, he felt that "the hand of the Lord was in his own—God-like vengeance nerving his little wrist." Elsewhere he is presented as undergoing in his own soul "the Scriptural wrestle between the angel of the Lord and the brute." His father likens him to Isaac, as being the son of his old age, and Cynthia regards him as possessing the beauty "of the young David."

Throughout the novel Christopher's primitive passion approaches in force, without ever quite becoming, the melodramatic. His insatiable hatred seems almost a madness, and he has a hallucinatory sense at times that his revenge has been accomplished to his entire satisfaction. His obsessive emotions generate a highly charged, almost "Gothic" atmosphere; [9] like his nearest counterparts in literature, Roger Chillingworth and Heathcliff, Christopher is also a believable character. With sure control of her material Miss Glasgow was aware of the good and evil in Christopher's nature, and she let his emotions spend themselves without herself intruding into his inner life. More than in some of her later books she was content, at least in the first two-thirds of *The Deliverance,* to present, rather than to moralize, her protagonist's struggles. In the recklessness with which he pursues his revenge, in his own and other people's consciousness of the primitive powers within him, and in his very appearance with its "effect of sheer brutality," there are also suggestions in Christopher once more of the Nietzschean superman.

A sure instinct guided Miss Glasgow in her initial indirect presentation of Christopher, as she refracted his primitive crudity and aristocratic beauty through Carraway's mind in six of her first seven chapters. Carraway's glimpse of Christopher at the beginning contains in essence the whole novel: the man's closeness to nature, his vindictiveness, and his defiance of Fletcher. The young giant at sunset in his adversary's fields tosses aside his basket of plants because he has finished a day's contracted labor, apparently satisfied that all Fletcher's tobacco is not yet planted and scornful of all suggestion that he work by moonlight to help get the crop in. Christopher's dominant rancor and submerged gentility, qualities not usually in conjunction, become effectively juxtaposed when Carraway's sensitive, yet matter-of-fact, mind reflects upon them. In his very recoil from Christopher's violent nature, the ordinarily imperturbable Carraway helps establish the reality of Christopher's extraordinary emotions.

Miss Glasgow avoided the melodramatic and made Christopher's hatred authentic by absorbing him into the natural setting of the novel, so that to Carraway "he seemed . . . as much a product of the soil as did the great white chestnut growing beside the road" (9). Even the maze of rutted roads and fields, registered in Carraway's mind as characteristic of the countryside, suggests the tangled elements in Christopher's soul. Miss Glasgow thus controlled the emotional situations in the novel by relating or subordinating them to natural phenomena. Through such objective presentation Christopher's slowly consummated revenge in primitive surroundings gains the aspect of a natural force operating inevitably according to its own laws. Christopher, however, finds that his vital contact with nature diminishes as his nefarious revenge nears completion: what had once given him pleasure no longer has the power to do so. Thereafter, in his progress toward the light, he discovers that the world about him once again assumes its former beauty and meaning. Miss Glasgow gained further credence for the unusual personality of Christopher Blake by domesticating it in a scene which depicts the details of tobacco-farming in Southside Virginia with a Balzacian "solidity of specification." [10]

A continuous hovering about her protagonist, a studied withdrawal from him and return to him, and a conscious extracting "from the situation every thread of significance, every quiver of vitality, every glimmer of understanding" [11] insure the final credibility of Christopher as a character; for if, as in melodrama, his psychology is that of the ruling passion, still all its reverberations are recorded. He is credible to the imagination because his obsession is not merely a subjective fixation but a force which drives him "beyond the normal limits of humanity." [12] He achieves, at least occasionally, dimensions which, under more favorable circumstances, would be heroic.

In a moment of fateful intuition he divines that the way to consummate his revenge upon Fletcher "for the crime hedged about by law" is to wound him where he is alone vulnerable—in his pride for his grandson, Will. In tracing Christopher's degrading of Will, Miss Glasgow demonstrated how gradually, yet inescapably, a man who tampers with another's soul becomes corrupt himself: the first three sections of the book focus exclusively upon this situation. In itself Christopher's sadistic absorption in revenge is no simple state, since he is half charmed by what he would destroy. In fact, the boy's innocence and trust in Christopher fall just short of winning out. In their troubled relationship there are even some suggestions of unacknowledged homosexual attraction, conscious as Christopher is of the boy's lips with their expression of "a singularly wistful beauty" and sensitive as Will is to the appeal which the strong man holds for the weak, "the eternal hero-worship of youth." Christopher's waverings in his dark purpose, his fascination with his object of prey, his ultimate apathy in carrying through his project but for the stimulus provided by Will's elopement, his continual conflict of motives—all indicate his divided soul. Part of the effectiveness in Miss Glasgow's presentation of Christopher derives from his final realization of the contrast between his present corruptness and the life that might have been his, had he not enslaved himself to hatred.[13]

Christopher plays upon the boy's irresponsible nature and makes a shiftless drunkard of him. Christopher's triumph is apparently complete except that he now feels increasing repugnance toward what he has done, and this incipient remorse is furthered by his awakening love for Maria, Will's sister. In a moment of rage, when the "beast" comes out in both of them, Will murders his grandfather with a hammer. Seeing that this deed has been in part his own, Christopher helps the boy escape and takes the blame for the murder. After three years in prison Christopher is reunited with Maria, and achieves through the purifying influence of love a "deliverance" at long last from the evil in his nature.

Throughout the novel Miss Glasgow stressed Christopher's degraded existence or his inherent savagery by noting his kinship with animals and the bestial quality of his design for revenge.[14] In his fallen fortunes he feels that he has become a "beast of burden" and had been broken to life as a young horse to the plough; at the end of the book, he sees himself "debased by ignorance and passion to the level of the beasts." He wishes to indulge his hatred like "a gorged beast" and to see, through his own means, Bill Fletcher and his grandson gnawing at "each other's bones." [15] Maria at one point calls him a "savage" and "a bear"; at another point, he listens with delight to the bellowing of a bull.

But it is his snarling pack of hounds which conveys most forcefully Christopher's reversion to primitive brutality; he even thinks of himself as "a whipped hound" because of the hostility of destiny towards him. He is continually seen as the master of this pack which greets him "with a single bay" and attacks all trespassers upon the Blake farm. The hounds fiercely pounce upon Will's puppies when the boy brings them to be trained by Christopher, just as Christopher himself would destroy their master. In one sequence he tosses cornbread to his yelping dogs; in another he tosses brutal oaths and coarse expressions to Will as if he were throwing them out to his animals. When Christopher has failed to detain Will from his elopement with Molly Peterkin, he has a dream of his hounds mangling a hare which turns out to be Maria Fletcher: his savage nature all but destroys the agent which alone can save it.

If Christopher is its main figure, the most tragic character in *The Deliverance* is his self-effacing sister Cynthia, whose disenchantment with life recalls that undergone by Elizabeth-Jane Farfrae in *The Mayor of Casterbridge:* "Life had been revealed to her as something to be endured rather than enjoyed" (71). The pathos of her life consists principally in the fact that her capacity for the heroic never finds expression; or if her selflessness is heroic, it is never so recognized by those she serves. With tacit cynicism, with cauterizing understatement, and with restrained sparseness of style, Miss Glasgow demonstrated how near, under such ignominious conditions, fortitude itself can approach futility. If in Christopher she embodied the rancor of the defeated South, in Cynthia she embodied the hopelessness it felt in enduring a life without hope, the hopelessness so poignantly expressed by Sidney Lanier in a well-known letter to Bayard Taylor in 1875: "Perhaps you know that with us of the younger generation in the South since the War, pretty much the whole of life has been merely not-dying!" [16]

Miss Glasgow was not nearly so fortunate in drawing Maria Fletcher and in utilizing her in the novel with dramatic effectiveness. As long as she remains peripheral to Christopher's struggle and becomes the elusive emblem of his better nature—as she does in the first three books which are mostly centered in Christopher's consciousness—she is organic to the novel. In the first two books, "The Inheritance" and "The Temptation" laid in 1878, Christopher concentrates upon his diabolical schemes for humbling Fletcher; in the third book, extending from four to six years later, "The Revenge," Christopher slowly matures his malignant plot. Maria is necessary to this part of the novel in increasing the

violence of Christopher's hatred for the Fletchers by giving it the added
force generated by an irrealizable sexual fixation. The novel largely
deteriorates in the last two books, "The Awakening" and "The Deliverance" (which take place about seven years after the first two), because a
"noble" love relationship is grafted on a drama of hatred. The divided
point of view in these last two sections, alternately that of Maria and
Christopher, also contributes to their diffuse effect and to the unreality
of the lovers' reunion upon Christopher's release from prison.

Maria throughout expresses too directly Miss Glasgow's own ideal of
renunciation. Her progress from self-illusion to self-knowledge has been
too abrupt, and this progress has not been closely enough implicated in
Christopher's own regeneration. Her realized character, in short, is insufficient to support her role in the novel of disclosing the possibilities to
which the former laboring class might now reach with the loosening of
aristocratic control in Southern society. Maria's ideas, moreover, have
too absolute a rigor for the complex situation explored in the novel, and
their portentous gravity becomes, through Miss Glasgow's direct emphasis, either sentimental or tedious. Despite Miss Glasgow's fondness
for Tucker Corbin as a "civilized" being, or perhaps because of it, his
moralizings, like Maria's, have the unreality of the appended observation,
not the reality of deeply felt truth. In the last two books of *The Deliverance* Miss Glasgow's wavering grasp of her material occasionally
resulted in prolixity or in the use of the cliché: "there came to him the
memory of their first meeting at the cross-roads and of the mystery and
rapture of his boyish love. He had found her then the lady of his dreams,
and now, after all the violence of his revolt against her, she was still to
him as he had first seen her—the woman whose soul looked at him from
her face" (282).

The excellence of *The Deliverance,* especially in variety of theme and
mood, overshadows its defects. A complexly woven book, with alter-
nating strands of the comic and tragic, it embodies, like many of Miss
Glasgow's other books, her contention of 1938 that comedy and tragedy
are "blood brothers." [17] Just as a slight change of emphasis in amusing
characters like Mary Victoria Littlepage, Louisa Goddard, or Virginius
Littlepage could have darkened *They Stooped to Folly* (1929) into
tragedy, so a slight displacement in focus might have made Christopher
Blake and Bill Fletcher of *The Deliverance* ridiculous. If the tone of
this book is predominantly grave and if Miss Glasgow painted in uniformly somber colors such characters as Christopher Blake, Cynthia
Blake, and Bill Fletcher, her skill at blending the contrarieties of experience is seen in old Mrs. Blake. Mrs. Blake's cynical humor, con-

trasting ironically with the romantic nature of her memories and deriving from her candid reflections upon life or from her own unadmitted hypocrisy, makes richly human a character overborne by adversity and somewhat arbitrarily conceived as a symbol.

In the sequences involving Mrs. Blake, Miss Glasgow's own insight into the contrast between the surfaces of polite life and the substantial realities it often evades is profound.[18] Mrs. Blake's ready wit indicates her former great powers of command in a brilliant society and her sharp if limited intelligence. There is much truth, too, in Mrs. Blake's remarks, but she would be unwilling to admit that she sees only part of the truth. Life, as she reviews it in memory, seems unexciting, though she would wish to relive it if she could. She especially singles out, as overrated entities, the male sex ("a man is not half so satisfactory a domestic pet as a cat, and far less neat in his habits") and the institution of romantic love ("your Aunt Susannah always said it [marriage] was like choosing a partner at a ball; for my part, I think it resembles more the selecting of a brand of flour").[19] In her acid view of ideal passion Mrs. Blake reflects in part Miss Glasgow's own impatience with "romance," although Tucker's assertion that "to have had one emotion that was bigger than you or your universe is to have had life" undoubtedly represented Miss Glasgow in another mood. In any event, Mrs. Blake, with almost sadistic zest, punctures the illusions surrounding youthful ardor and rejects as foolish the values normally motivating men and women in love. She refuses to see that these illusions and values may sometimes be estimable and not trivial. From her sacrosanct position as the dowager head of her family, Mrs. Blake can also muffle all objections when she speaks her mind. She thus reveals the humor inherent in a complete lack of inhibition. When Cynthia, for instance, tells her that Christopher has had no love affairs, Mrs. Blake expresses herself with an unexpected vigor and worldliness for a gently bred lady: "For a man to go twenty-six years without falling in love means that he's either a saint or an imbecile, my dear; and, for my part, I declare I don't know which character sits worse upon a gentleman." [20]

Most effective is the counterpoint established between Christopher's grim disillusion and his mother's equally radical but essentially comic cynicism. Christopher's passions thereby become more intense through being contrasted with his mother's wit. There is dramatic irony, too, in such scenes between Mrs. Blake and members of her family, an irony which again establishes the close identity of tragedy and comedy. Though Mrs. Blake's remarks are humorous, she unintentionally wounds those she loves through blindness to their indigence and through asperity of manner. For example, her admonition to Christopher to forego his

life of ease is on its surface witty; projected against his immediate sufferings and the hatred in his soul, it gathers an irony more tense than
playful: " 'A man who has taken the enemy's guns single-handed, or
figured prominently in a society scandal, is comfortably settled in his
position and may slouch pleasantly for the remainder of his life. But for
an ordinary gentleman it is quite different, and as we are not likely to
have another war, you really ought to marry. You are preparing to go
through life too peacefully, my son' " (118).

The humor in Mrs. Blake's conversation often derives from the hypocrisy inherent in the values of her society. She thus endorses without
question the equivocations found in a double standard morality: "Oh,
the family was all right, my dear. I never heard a breath against the
women" (202). As to the well-bred woman, she must conform with
exactitude to a propriety from which there is no appeal, and she must
exert herself to acquire fine manners rather than a discriminating moral
sense:

"I have never slouched in my life . . . and I do not care to fall into the
habit in my old age. When my last hour comes, I hope at least to meet my
God in the attitude becoming a lady; and in my day it would have been
considered the height of impropriety to loll in a chair or even to rock in
the presence of gentlemen. Your Great-aunt Susannah, one of the most
modest women of her time, has often told me that once, having unfortunately crossed her knees in the parlour after supper, she suffered untold
tortures from 'budges' for three mortal hours rather than be seen to do
anything so indelicate as to uncross them." (75)

In *The Deliverance* Miss Glasgow also used the rural peasantry for
comic effect. Sometimes her rustics function in the plot; at other times
they comment incisively like a chorus on the unfolding action. Like old
Mrs. Blake, they suggest through their uninhibited humor that comedy is
as vibrant a reality as tragedy. Miss Glasgow was able, moreover, to
secure an added degree of credence for Christopher's excessive hatred
by surrounding him with the ordinary folk from whom he is isolated in
spirit. These rustics are depicted with an exact realism; they are characterized solely through an expert recording of their speech. In inception and in method, Miss Glasgow's humorous use of country folk
resembles that of Thomas Hardy, although her characters are her own.[21]

Mrs. Susan Spade, the most fully depicted rustic, is typical. She is a
lower-class counterpart to Mrs. Blake; both women legalistically condemn all deviations from the conventional code. Mrs. Blake, however, is
a Puritan in matters of sexual morality only, since the antebellum
South had otherwise accustomed her to a life of luxury and sensuous
indulgence. In her long argument that Molly Peterkin's attractiveness

is synonymous with depravity ("thar's somethin' indecent about yaller hair"), the absurdity of Mrs. Spade's inflexible attitudes is adroitly implied. For a Puritan like Mrs. Spade, the only admissible pleasure is a masochistic one resulting from conscientiously doing one's duty and from suppressing the expansive natural instincts:

"It's my duty that's brought me, Mr. Fletcher. . . . You kin see very well yo'self that it's not a pleasure; for if it had been I'd have stayed at home till I died. I never saw a pleasure in my life that didn't lead astray, an' I've got the eye of suspicion on the most harmless-lookin' one that goes. As I tell Tom—though he won't believe it—the only way to be sartain you're followin' yo' duty in this world is to find out the thing you hate most to do an' then do it with all yo' might. That rule has taken me through life, suh; it married me to Tom Spade, an' it's brought me here to-day." (213)

Mrs. Spade's absolute distrust of the senses leads her to think that a person's misfortunes are a sure sign he had yielded to pleasurable impulses. Imbued with this standard, humorous in its humorlessness, Susan Spade with complacent relish ascribes the unhappiness of Maria Fletcher to the wrath of God who will see that, in the long run, poetic justice prevails and that sinners, such as Mrs. Spade imagines Maria to be, are punished: "The best rule to follow, accordin' to my way of thinkin', is to make up yo' mind right firm that no matter what evil falls upon a person it ain't nearly so bad as the good Lord ought to have made it" (273). In Mrs. Spade's unflattering view of men and in her easily outraged sense of propriety, there is a decided echo in homespun of Mrs. Blake's radical cynicism.

Such comic verve was as typical of Miss Glasgow in *The Deliverance* as her psychological insight, and both provided an assured measure, for the first time in her career, of the range and flexibility of her talent. A matured sense of form and of the structural requirements of the novel is also in evidence to contrast with the diffuseness of *The Voice of the People* and *The Battle-Ground*. Miss Glasgow's informed presentation of the social scene in Reconstruction Virginia and later, her expert analysis of varying character types during a period of transition, and her exhaustive probing of the emotions of her central characters under personal stress, all contribute to the merit of this novel.

·V·

Versions of the Ideal
and of Social Reality

With the death of her lover Gerald B—— in 1905 Ellen Glasgow entered her "mystical" phase; and in two books, *The Wheel of Life* and *The Ancient Law,* she reflected her endeavor to find solace deep within herself for her grief. She rightly felt that these books, written soon after her emotional crisis, lacked the detachment to be memorable and she excluded them from her collected work. We are not apt to question this judgment, even though some parts of these books are residually interesting.

In *The Wheel of Life* particularly, Miss Glasgow was seeking "an antidote to experience, a way out of myself." [1] It is natural that she should have been interested at this point in expressing through her characters the moral and philosophical idealism which, during a period of personal anguish, gave her some sense of stability. For the purposes of art, however, the philosophizing in this book is too direct and intrusive, even if the ideas expressed are basic to an understanding of Miss Glasgow's mind.

Judged by this novel Miss Glasgow had absorbed the values found in much nineteenth-century literature and philosophy. She was responsive at once to natural evolution and to idealistic protests against the constricting materialism sometimes fostered by the new science. She divulged her own version of the truth in the ideas of Roger Adams, the earnest editor in New York of the *International Review,* and of Laura Wilde, a young poet of Virginian ancestry. Through hero and heroine Miss Glasgow affirmed the partial relevance to modern life of the spiritual absolutes inherent in the Western tradition or assimilated into it—goodness, beauty, truth, love, honor, and so on—as they had been defined in Christianity, in Platonism, in the thought of the Enlightenment with its stress upon man's possible perfectibility, in the intuitive perceptions of Romanticism, in the religion and literature of the Orient, and in the transcendental philosophers of all ages. Laura Wilde, for example, finds inspiration in Shelley, Spinoza, and *The Imitation of Christ,* and writes luminous, somewhat ethereal poetry. She is convinced that she is "set apart for a predestined good, an exalted purpose," and has managed to convince Adams of this also: "It was a face that had followed after the ideal beauty. . . . And it was this inspired divination, this luminous idealism, which had caused Adams to exclaim when he put down her first small gray volume: 'Is it possible that we can still see visions?' " (52).

Roger Adams, in his turn, adapts the modern theory of evolution to his idealistic, aspiring view of life by accepting Spencer's cosmic meliorism and spiritualizing it. Adams's views also have affinities with the dynamic adaptations of Darwin made by Whitman, Meredith, and Butler. Into the eclectic philosophy behind the novel went Arnold's concept of God as an impersonal ethical force, Browning's gospel of effort, Tennyson's idea of the lower and higher nature in man engaged in ceaseless struggle, Carlyle's and George Eliot's emphasis upon renunciation as leading to the highest beatitude of spirit, Meredith's gospel of the needed proportion between the senses and the soul, and Emerson's doctrines of self-reliance and the absorption of the individual by the Oversoul. Though she was earlier and later a professed Darwinian, Miss Glasgow at this stage was somewhat removed from the empiric modes of scientific thought in contending, through Roger Adams, that the objects of existence are "less the forms of a material substance than the result of some shadowy projection of mind" (344).

Because Adams has carefully specified for himself the nature of reality, he has the power to renounce the world to the extent that it is the source of false illusion. In *The Wheel of Life* Miss Glasgow nevertheless too completely insisted that "all life is forfeiture in one way or another" (239). In demonstrating the futility in the lives of her happiness-seekers, she argued persuasively that some more vital ideal in life is needed than "the oscillation between fugitive desire and outward possession—between the craving of emptiness and the satiety of fulfilment" (244). The expression of her ascetic philosophy through the central characters of the novel, however, is forced. Roger Adams is too forthright a spokesman for the view "that renunciation may become the richest experience in the consciousness of man," and his achievement of saintliness, of "simple goodness in a manifest form," is too simplified. Despite his sympathy and tolerance, Adams is a shadowy figure and too insubstantial to exert the moral force he is assigned in the novel.

Toward the end of the book Adams, as the mentor of Laura Wilde, is impossibly noble and pretentious, while Laura, in her role as spiritual outcast, is impossibly humorless and self-conscious. She finally withdraws in horror from the selfish hedonism of the man to whom she is engaged, the magnetic Arnold Kemper. Adams's love for his erring wife, Connie, had originally been a sensuous indulgence; in its last phase it becomes "a love so sexless, so dispassionate that its joys were like the joys of religion." Notwithstanding Miss Glasgow's sincere valuation of it, this transfigured sexuality is so emphatically presented that doubts arise as to whether she found it an entirely valid rationale for living. Adams's view of the highest love as beatific unfulfillment may have derived from the adjustments which Miss Glasgow had perforce to make to the inevitable in her relationship with Gerald B——, both before and after his death. At their most credible, the satisfactions deriving from renunciation are affirmed by Laura's elderly and undemanding admirer, Mr. Wilberforce: his age and his experience imply that he can inevitably embody "the 'enchantment of the disenchanted.' "

Though Maxwell Geismar's praise of *The Wheel of Life* as the best of Miss Glasgow's early novels is excessive,[2] he rightfully holds that the portraits of the sophisticates—Perry Bridewell, Gerty Bridewell, and Arnold Kemper—provide its chief distinction. These characters who incessantly sacrifice self to "the inevitable and agonising pursuit of pleasure" are not so sharply drawn, however, as the postwar sophisticates in Miss Glasgow's later comedies of manners. In this novel she typically used satire and irony to attack the hypocrisies, ordinarily hidden, in social intercourse. In presenting Kemper's views on love and marriage, she thus laconically exposed masculine complacency and conceit: " 'Men were not born monogamous'—it was a favourite cynicism of his, for he was inclined to throw upon nature the full burden of her responsibility" (218).

If a shallow flippancy characterizes that "graduate of the world" Gerty Bridewell, she also has her depths: she resents her passion for her "florid and impressive" husband, she respects the moral sincerity of Laura Wilde and Roger Adams, and she shrewdly and candidly appraises her own traits and those of her associates. Roger Trent, a young playwright, pierces through her worldliness to discover "a deep disgust, a heavy disenchantment" beneath, and she herself is restive though resigned to her fate as "a mere bond-slave to my body." At least she honestly recognizes that, like too many other women in the fashionable world, she has sacrificed her integrity to retain the attention of men. At an even more cynical moment she maintains that all she or anyone else needs from life is forgetfulness, whether that comes from "religion, dissipation, morphia." No wonder then that Laura Wilde, as a sensitive observer, views this predatory society "as a hideous battle in which the passions preyed upon the ideals, the body upon the soul" (109).

Although Gerty's husband Perry is supremely selfish, he has certain mitigating qualities: a lack of pretense, a blustering good nature, and an unaffected kindness. An amusing scene occurs when Perry informs Adams that Connie has been unfaithful. Perry declares "it's the men who are such confounded brutes," only himself to leer sensually at the pretty women who pass by. A certain callow wisdom is one result, too, of his frank pursuit of amatory pleasure. He knows, for example, the spiteful jealousies which dominate fashionable women in their judgments of other women: "Unless she's as flat as an ironing board, somebody is sure to say she's vulgar. For my part I like shape" (276).

Arnold Kemper, the most deftly conceived figure in the novel, is an unprincipled adventurer in human emotions. Except for his latent cruelty he is a rough sketch for the Jonathan Gay of *The Miller of Old Church*. Both gratify at all costs their natural impulses while demanding absolute purity—or ignorance—in the women they love. Thus Kemper is annoyed with Laura for possessing enough knowledge of the world to suspect his rendezvous with his former mistress, as though Laura's purity rather than his fidelity were at stake: "he was honestly of the opinion that their whole future happiness was wrecked by the fact that she believed him capable of the thing which he had done" (383).

In her insight into the tangled motivation of the man of the world, Miss Glasgow displayed a mastery of psychology and an ironic objectivity which eluded her in her portraits of Roger Adams and Laura Wilde. If Kemper is largely a "surface," Adams recognizes "depths of pleasantness" below that surface, and sums up the good and bad in Kemper by seeing him as "half libertine" and "half hero." Kemper is at once a generous man and a confirmed egoist. His refined sadism in a hedonistic temperament, reminiscent of George Eliot's Grandcourt and Henry James's Gilbert Osmond, is balanced by a quality they lack, a sincere tenderness when his emotions are engaged. Though he speculates, for example, over the pleasure of trying his wife's constancy and is curious to see how Laura would play the part of the neglected wife, he is really devoted to her—to the point of compromising with his disgust for marriage. If his ironic skepticism prevents his commitment to purposes other than his search for new sensations, his irony is at least genial; and he prefers "a cultured abstinence" in the pursuit of pleasure to the animal indulgences of Perry Bridewell. While Kemper and his fellow sophisticates are not quite central to the novel, they do furnish its chief interest for the modern reader.

The protagonist of *The Ancient Law* (1908), Daniel Ordway, "had sinned and paid the penalty of sin" and had "asked of humanity the right and the freedom to begin anew." But Ordway never really gets his second chance. This apparent defeat, as in Roger Adams's case, is transmuted through force of character into hard-won spiritual victory. Like Hardy's Michael Henchard, Ordway finds that he cannot escape the consequences of his past acts: "the price that a man pays for being a fool, he pays but once and that is his whole life long" (251). Though character is destiny, a crime and a prison sentence are almost too much for an individual to live down. Another Jean Valjean, Ordway makes his way in Tappahannock after an imprisonment for embezzlement as Wall Street financier.[3] When he is assured of his victory in the campaign for mayor of the town, a fellow convict Wherry turns up as his nemesis, his sinister nature suggesting an evil character in Dickens. Since he feels bound to prevent a misalliance between Wherry and a local girl, Ordway exposes him as a blackguard and would-be bigamist. For Ordway such confession means ruin.

Achieving wisdom through suffering yet becoming something of a martyr, Ordway is a Christlike figure in this novel. As such, he evokes for his aim in life an almost mystical "vision of service" and he exemplifies, except when his patience is inordinately tried (as Christ's was by the money changers in the temple), a philosophy of nonresistance, also reminiscent of the later Tolstoy. Like Daniel Ordway, one must lose one's life in order to find it, Miss Glasgow implied, and like his aunt one must come to realize that "happiness is like everything else, it is only when one gives it back to God that one really possesses it" (326). The strenuous ethical idealism in the novel recalls the philosophy of Browning, when, for instance, Ordway sees himself, "not as Banks pictured him, living quietly in Tappahannock, but still struggling, still fighting, still falling to rise and go on again" (484). Miss Glasgow stressed in this book not only the need to renounce a self-centered happiness and to live with stoic fortitude but the spiritual isolation which such moral independence inevitably brings.

Ordway's isolation is most pronounced when he goes back to live in Botetourt at the death of his father and finds that his crime alienates him from everyone except his daughter and two kindly aunts. His trespass, he discovers, had been not only a personal misdemeanor but a sin against his class. His daughter Alice, despite her kindness to him, is an irresponsible, morally weak pleasure seeker, not greatly different from the Stanley Timberlake of *In This Our Life*. When Alice forges a check in his name, Ordway accepts the blame for her crime and again leaves Botetourt in disgrace, this time with the reluctant admiration of his wife and brother who know the guilt is Alice's. He thus symbolically turns his back on his class, which he now sees as decadent. When he returns to Tappahannock and finds the workers at the Trend cotton mills on strike, he buys the establishment and is persuaded by his friends to remain there where his services are most needed. At the end of the novel he thus exemplifies the benevolent paternalism which often characterized men from the best families when they assumed industrial leadership in the early days of the New South. The previous owner, Jasper Trend, had, on the contrary, felt that his prosperity depended upon the maximum exploiting of his laborers.

To some degree interesting in relation to Miss Glasgow's other work, *The Ancient Law* from an aesthetic standpoint is inferior. Its moralizing is dull and overt, the ideas being too directly presented through Ordway and Emily Brooke to generate imaginative assent for them. Miss Glasgow not only assigned too much psychic weight to the characters who express her ideas, but she also sentimentalized situation: witness Ordway's amateur preaching to the natives of Tappahannock, and his mediating in the strike there to the accompaniment of cheers from a previously sullen mob. Failure in motivation, particularly in the later sequences of the book, is also apparent. Ordway too easily gives in to his daughter's impetuosity, and her capricious, outrageous actions are not sufficiently warranted by the psychological substratum which Miss Glasgow established for her character. At times the style is strained (Geoffrey Heath, Alice's husband, is described as a "large red and black male animal"), at times commonplace ("it seemed to him that his feet were inert and lifeless weights which were dragged forward by the invincible torrent of his will"), at times rambling and diffuse.

Like *The Wheel of Life*, *The Ancient Law* is of interest less for its philosophizing than for its psychological perceptiveness and its social commentary. Surprisingly modern in tone is Miss Glasgow's candid presentation of the "pure" Lydia Ordway whose frigidity gains for her the respect which such an intractible neurosis often elicited from the Victorian public. Since, according to the code of her class, it is "unwomanly" for a lady to know about crime, she can, with public approval, be indifferent to her husband when he needs her most. In that his crime has been an outrage to her "virtue," she is also conveniently provided with a pretext for severing unwelcome sexual relations with him after his return to Botetourt. Ordway accepts her decision and is, ironically, as reluctant as the rest of his family to admit the true nature of her frigidity:

Yet it was with difficulty even now that he could free himself from the conviction that her emotional apathy was but one aspect of innocence. Would he admit to-day that what he had once worshipped as purity of soul was but the frost of an unnatural coldness of nature? . . . Was there death, after all, not life hidden for him in her plaintive beauty? The next instant, as he watched her, he told himself that such questions belonged to the evil promptings of his own nature. (339)

Her family is convinced that Lydia is a saint, although one of her perceptive aunts has the feeling that this belief may have been induced mostly by the way Lydia wears her hair. Actually, in her legalistic virtue and in her uncritical, self-centered acceptance of convention, she becomes the destructive force—"like some heathen deity above the sacrificial altar"—which defeats Ordway at Botetourt. His mistake, he later sees, had been to worship Lydia as "divinity" instead of seeing her for the mortal being she really is. When he fights Geoffrey Heath who, according to Alice, has mistreated her, he gains an unforced respect from Lydia which years of gentle devotion to her had failed to produce. Miss Glasgow's neurotic women almost always prefer an overmastering man to the considerate gentleman.

In *The Ancient Law* Miss Glasgow's attitude toward the post-Civil War aristocracy was ambivalent. In the ineffectual Beverley Brooke who has ruined his family with an "irreproachable demeanor," this class is seen in decadence. His sister Emily, however, has been formed by the finer qualities in tradition: "Her confidence belonged less to personal experience . . . than to some inherited ideal of manner—of social values" (116). At the Brooke homestead the cedars that Emily refuses to sell are the symbol of an integrity which she cannot violate and which derives from an idealism held over from the past. As for the Ordways, their dishonesty and inhumanity have been induced by rigid adherence to values formulated in the past; yet it is in a flexible responsiveness to these same values that Daniel Ordway is himself able to transcend unfavorable circumstances. At the close of the novel, Ordway's rejection of his family and its subservience to "tradition, inheritance, instinct" is almost complete, when he decides that his future home is to be in Tappahannock in association with the laboring class. Like an American Tolstoy he finds in the lower class a vigor and honesty too often lacking in his own, a freedom from inherited prejudice, and an outgoing kindness. His continuing reverence for Emily Brooke implies, nevertheless, that his rejection of his class is not total, for its fine qualities have made them both what they are.

The Romance of a Plain Man (1909), a chronicle of Southern economic and social life from 1875 to 1908, traces the emergence of an optimistic and bustling New South from "the terrible lethargy which had immediately succeeded the war" (21). As Miss Glasgow judged the New South in her thirties, she saw it as a dispensation in which "the air . . . was already full of the promise of the industrial awakening, the constructive impulse, the recovered energy that was yet to be" (71). The book demonstrates that "the road to reunion was a forked road" [4] and that the Redeemers of the South, represented in the novel by General Bolingbroke and his protégé Ben Starr, chose the way of Eastern capitalism as opposed to the way of Western agrarian protest. Actually, redemption in Virginia came from the businessmen of Richmond and resulted in "the city man's rule of a country-man's state." [5] Richmond itself, fifteen years after Appomattox, had made a rapid recovery and was beginning to know its greatest prosperity.[6] Some sense of this excitement and material achievement is conveyed in Miss Glasgow's account of the multifarious activities of the General and Ben Starr. In a region waiting to be exploited, leadership came from two sources primarily, from the old families or Bourbons and from the increasingly powerful middle class.

General Bolingbroke, son of a great planter, had fought for the South's honor in the war and at one point had tried desperately to save Johnston's army. But with the new age after the war, he thinks that there may be more honor in developing a country's wealth than in winning battles. As a "Redeemer" of his section from political dependence on the Northeast, the General wishes this epitaph: "He brought help to the sick land and made the cotton flower to bloom anew" (24). He outwitted the carpetbaggers financially, he bought up railroad property in the depression after the war, and he helped open the South again to commerce and industry. He is now the head of an empire comprising factories, banks, and, above all, the Great South Midland and Atlantic Railroad. Unlike the other aristocrats in the novel, the General has adapted himself to social change and has prospered with the times. In fact, his greatness, as Ben sees it, springs from "an erratic departure from traditions," but it could also be argued that his social prestige gives him added authority in business. He has the moral limitations of a business leader devoted solely to materialistic ends; and in adopting him as his model, Ben Starr is sometimes false to his own honorable instincts. From the first, therefore, Miss Glasgow's attitude toward the New South and its leaders was critical as well as enthusiastic. This note of criticism was to become stronger in *Virginia* (1913) and in the fiction written after the Great War.

As time passed, trade, manufacturing, and finance became less and less the province of the best families. Like George Bolingbroke and Theophilus Pry in the novel,[7] the aristocrats were often unfitted for and uninterested in such pursuits, or else they could not exert influence over a democracy expanding too rapidly to be controlled by their decreasing numbers. It was fairly common, then, for an average man of capacity like Ben Starr from the lower middle class to rise to power through superior ambition and talent. Miss Glasgow concentrated upon his single-mindedness and implied that after the war the upward path was clear at least for men with his strong energy and marked ability. In this novel more than in her preceding work, she dealt directly with the developing alliance between the increasingly powerful middle class and economic leadership in the New South.

Although he respects General Bolingbroke for his attainments and appreciates his help, Ben Starr recognizes that his own success will involve the partial supplanting of the social attitudes upheld by the General and his generation. Ben also perceives that in the less fluid society before the war there would have been little opportunity for a man of his low birth. His quick rise is symptomatic of the rapid emergence of a bourgeoisie in the South after the war. What took two generations in England was achieved in much shorter time in the postwar South: the passing of social control from a landed aristocracy to industrialists of middle-class origin.[8]

The novel is a "success story" tracing the rise of Ben Starr from the lower middle class to financial power in Richmond. Such a tale is sentimental when, as here, business success and failure are only vaguely related to economic milieu, and when the drive for financial power is an insistently mentioned fact rather than an imaginatively recreated reality. Thus Miss Glasgow was at fault in presenting Ben's ambition too rhetorically and abstractly, without embodying it fully in the commercial life outside him or in the meaningful symbol: "To dominate that living organism [the Great South Midland and Atlantic Railroad], to control in my turn that splendid liberator of a people's resources, this was still the inaccessible hope upon which I had fixed my heart" (113).

Although Ben is another of the "strong men" of Miss Glasgow's early fiction, a romantic egoist and an individualist, he is less forcefully drawn than Michael Akershem, Nicholas Burr, and Christopher Blake. For example, his altercation with a crowd during a panic outside the bank of which he is president is theatrical.[9] He vouches for the probity of his bank but becomes fiercely impatient when the people he addresses demand a cash settlement at once. In this scene the violence of the buried forces in Ben's nature too greatly exceeds the strength which Miss Glasgow had previously been able to secure for them. Actually, his habitual gentleness and psychic uncertainty are too greatly at variance with the brutality of business enterprise in an age of intense competition. As a result this novel lacks the impact of Norris's and Dreiser's work.

Miss Glasgow was true to the facts of history, however, in depicting industrial development in the New South as largely the result of railroad expansion. From the start, railroad enterprise was especially favored by the Reconstruction governments and by Northern investors. In Virginia after 1871 the former state-owned roads enjoyed under private ownership the same privileges they had had as publicly owned ventures.[10] Virginia businessmen, like General Bolingbroke and Ben Starr, would naturally respond to the public interest shown in the roads and to the encouragement given to rail entrepreneurs by the state governments. Southern leadership most often built and managed the roads while Northern capital most often financed them.[11] Ben's frequent trips to New York and Washington indicate that Northern investors almost certainly played a part in his projects.

The years 1870–1900 saw the building of new roads and the consolidation of existing ones. Ben Starr's ambition of absorbing "the small adjunct lines" into "the main system" of the Great South Midland and Atlantic, parallels the actual amalgamation during the 1880's of the smaller lines by the Richmond and Danville Railroad and then by the Richmond and West Point Terminal Company.[12] General Bolingbroke also takes advantage of his competitors to enlarge his holdings. He buys up at his own price the Cumberland and Tidewater after it has fallen into receivership during a business depression; and his road, the South Midland, swallows it "like a regular boa constrictor." Ben's purchase of the small West Virginia and Wyanoke road in order to tap the coal fields, charts another of the directions taken by rail enterprise in postbellum Virginia: the extension of the roads westward over the mountains. Ben's vision of the Great South Midland and Atlantic's destiny truthfully sums up, then, the ambitions which the South's "Redeemers" had for their region: "I saw it to-day, sweeping in a bright track over the entire South, lengthening, branching, winding away toward the distant horizon, girdling the cotton-fields, the rice-fields, and the coal-fields like a protecting arm" (113). Miss Glasgow's failure, however, to discuss the disturbingly close alliance between the railroad interests and the Democratic political machine in Virginia in the early twentieth century detracts from the verisimilitude and significance of the novel.

In *The Romance of a Plain Man,* Miss Glasgow's intermittent realism actually found firmer expression in her commentary upon manners than in her presentation of masculine psychology and the economic scene in the Gilded Age. The work is most cogent in so far as it defines Ben's diffidence toward, and impatience with, the Richmond aristocracy. The chronicling of the "industrial awakening" becomes less central to the book, then, than the analysis of the social disruptions caused by such change. In the business world, Ben Starr's talents cause him to be readily accepted even by his associates from the first families. In the social sphere, he finds that these families instinctively regard him as an inferior. Thus the conflict "between democratic ideals and old-world institutions" did not end with the Civil War.

The tradition of gentility, embraced by the first families, is confident of its rightness and controls the social and intellectual South in the novel. In relinquishing political and economic power to the vigorous new democracy, the aristocracy, as Miss Glasgow saw, reluctantly yielded to main force without budging in spirit or tolerating the slightest compromise in habits or beliefs. Even when the class itself succumbed to decay, the values it stood for were more than ever respected. Defeat in war left essentially unchanged the Southerner's attitudes, including an instinctive reverence for his social superiors. Ben challenges this complacency and condescension by marrying Sally Mickleborough over the protest of her tradition-bound aunts, Mitty and Matoaca.

To Ben this reverence for the past, the eagerness of Miss Mitty "to think as my grandmother and my great-grandmother have thought before me," is stifling. Secure in its "stained-glass seclusion" and suspicious of all suggestions of change, the aristocracy extinguishes useful ambition, not only in the lower classes, but in its own members as well. Ben would agree, therefore, with Michael Akershem's scornful view, expressed in *The Descendant,* of the aristocrat as "a man who sits down to think about what his grandfather has done while other men are doing something themselves" (43). In this conflict between the individual and the Virginia heritage Ben Starr feels frequently at a disadvantage. He is ill at ease with his wife's relatives and friends, he resents their condescension toward him, and he is self-consciously aware of his lack of the "external graces."

More disturbing to him is his inability to respond to age-old values, his feeling that he lacks the intuitive understanding of Sally and her life which his rival, George Bolingbroke (Sally's cousin), constantly displays. This alienation of Ben from Sally's class is symbolized in the sprig of sweet alyssum which, to Ben's chagrin, George leaves for her each time that he has been to see the estranged Aunt Mitty. Ben is irritated by this elusive barrier between him and his wife's caste, and he is determined to make tradition yield to his possession of financial power, even if in the process the amenities prized by Sally must be sacrificed. In that Ben does succeed financially and does marry an aristocrat, Miss Glasgow disclosed that the Southern economic and social scene had been shaken by the war and the Reconstruction. The first families were unable to exclude entirely from their ranks those who possessed economic power; yet these families could exclude the new arrivals from the inner circle where ancestry, gentility, and the backward view counted most.

Implicit in the evasive and static life of these aristocrats are inequalities and hypocrisies which Miss Glasgow ironically exposed by permitting the complacent upholders of tradition to speak for themselves. The most humorous touches in the novel are those provided by General Bolingbroke, who breaks with his family by entering commerce and becoming a railroad king but who is all the more conventional in his distaste for intelligence and candor in woman. He is continually impatient with his onetime sweetheart, Miss Matoaca, who had not been content to let buried hypocrisies stay buried and who had actually been "unwomanly" enough to prefer her principles to his own jovial society as youthful libertine. Only an indelicate woman, the General feels, could be guilty of Miss Matoaca's indelicate view that men ought to observe the same rules of morality as women:

"Now, what do you suppose Miss Matoaca said to me on Sunday? We were talking of Tom Frost's running for Governor, and she said she hoped he wouldn't be elected because he led an impure life. An impure life! Will you tell me what business it is of an unmarried lady's whether a man leads an impure life or not? It isn't ladylike—I'll be damned if it is! I could see that Miss Mitty blushed for her. What's the world coming to, I ask, when a maiden lady isn't ashamed to know that a man leads an impure life?" (104)

Although Ben Starr looks to the future, he is himself imperfectly emancipated from the tradition which he condemns. Like the General, he accepts the premise that love and domesticity should limit a woman's activity and that she should be kept sheltered from the outside world. Ben is responsible for the alienation which develops between him and Sally because he is insufficiently critical precisely of the customs which oppress him. Assuming that woman is by nature too fragile to withstand contact with the world, he is reluctant at the time of the panic to tell Sally anything specifically of his trouble, "restrained by some masculine instinct that prompted me to shut the business world outside the doors of home" (229). He agrees with the General that a woman should do no more than "merge the ideal into everyday life." He is therefore opposed to woman suffrage, since a voting woman would have to know more about a man's world than tradition could countenance. When Sally objects to her "doll house" existence and passionately defends her Aunt Matoaca's feminism, Ben still minimizes her need for self-realization.

If the first families induced inertia and impeded social progress, Miss Glasgow again concluded in this novel that they possessed many admirable qualities. Thus it is Ben who feels the most embarrassment when his blustering brother, President, interrupts a formal dinner; Sally, whose aristocratic inheritance helps her in a trying situation such as this, regains her composure immediately. Some sense of the finer virtues of the Old South are apparent, even to Ben, when he becomes conscious that the New South has emerged in terms of the old: "In the ground the seeds of the new South, which was in truth but the resurrected spirit of the old, still germinated in darkness" (71). At the time of the financial panic he is already aware when he holds Sally in his arms of a force streaming through him "welding . . . the finer qualities in both our natures." He realizes, if but nebulously, that the hope of a resurgent South lies in this joining of the tenacity of the old with the vigor of the new.

Sally is emblematic of Ben's better nature and is his good angel, whereas General Bolingbroke with his cynicism, his dominating ambition, and his materialistic values represents a malign influence which Ben counteracts only after much difficulty. As a result Ben almost destroys Sally's spirit, and in the tainted atmosphere of his home his son cannot survive. When Ben burns the cablegram offering him the presidency of the Great South Midland Railroad, he conclusively renounces the world to gain his soul. This book, like *The Deliverance* and *The Wheel of Life,* has for implied theme, then, the conflict between an individual's lower and higher nature, a theme presented here with morality-play directness when contrasted with its more subtle development in *The Deliverance.*

If there are symbolic overtones in this contest between love and ambition, the characters and situations lack suggestive power and psychological force. The method utilized in this book—reminiscence by its central figure—accounts for its diffuseness. A first-person narrative, episodic at best, runs thinner still when twenty-five years are spanned in short compass and when, to indicate passing time, resort is made principally to summary statement. One result of this is that the caricatures in the book—Ben's mother, his brother, Mrs. Cudlip, and Mrs. Chitling—are its most lifelike figures, since extensive analysis is not necessary to establish their reality. What there is of the symbolic—the dominant flower imagery, for example, underlying the love sequences, which apparently relates to the unforced beauty of Sally's nature—is out of place in a novel supposedly depicting the crass vigor of the new industrialism. The psychology of Ben Starr is also elementary, in that Miss Glasgow's genius required greater amplitude for the development of a central character than that provided by the first-person technique. For one thing, Ben has too little opportunity to dwell upon his mental states since he must continually be describing his actions. For another, the leisurely space required for Miss Glasgow's characteristic technique of incremental repetition—whereby variations are developed upon a central theme and achieve for the theme a cumulative force that commands assent—is absent from a directly unfolding first-person narrative. The method of autobiographic reminiscence, unless better controlled than in this book, also directs too much attention to the narrator himself. As a result Ben Starr seems objectionably complacent when he describes his good qualities and singularly obtuse when he muses upon his shortcomings. If he realizes his shortcomings, we might ask, why need he continue to indulge them? As an example of the unintentionally pompous, here is Ben's completely satisfied self-analysis at the time of the panic:

A certain readiness for decision, a power of dealing with an emergency, of handling a crisis, a response of pulse and brain to the call for action, stood me in good stead now, as in every difficult instant of my career. They were picked business men and shrewd financiers before me, yet I was aware that I dominated them, all and each, by some quality of force, of aggressiveness, of inflated self-confidence. The secret of my success, I had once said to the General, was that I began to get cool when I saw other people getting scared. (238)

Some of Ben's more overt actions, too, lack fullness of motivation. Except as it might derive from a perverse irrationality induced by his illness, Ben's lighthearted squandering of his wife's legacy from her aunt is hardly plausible. If it is supposedly the result of an uncontrollable instinct to play for high stakes while gambling on the future, the act does not fully grow out of elements organic to the book—in the same inevitable manner that Christopher Blake's tampering with Will Fletcher's soul does in *The Deliverance*. *The Romance of a Plain Man* is too much a romance, too little a psychological analysis of Ben Starr and his problems as man and leader of the New South. The moribund aristocracy of Virginia and the advance of a "plain man" were to be more expertly rendered in *The Miller of Old Church* (1911); the South's ideals of womanhood and the impact of the industrial New South upon established modes of thought and conduct were to be more firmly defined in *Virginia* (1913).

◆VI◆

Convention and Fatality in The Miller of Old Church

The Miller of Old Church was written when Miss Glasgow was disturbed about her brother's suicide and her sister's incurable illness. Despite humorous elements in the book, it is predominantly grave in tone, possibly as a result of the sobering quality of Miss Glasgow's own experience at the time. Like *The Voice of the People* and *The Deliverance, The Miller of Old Church* combines her feeling for the soil and her interest in manners. It represents in fact the most successful fusion of these two major preoccupations in her fiction, though she was to develop each of them separately with more distinction in her later work. Except for use of a too variable point of view and a consequent dissipation of creative force, *The Miller of Old Church* (1911) would be unmistakably a work of first importance. All things considered, this novel does deserve the good opinion of several of Miss Glasgow's critics.[1]

The Miller of Old Church is set in rural Southside Virginia from 1898 until 1902, and depicts the daily existence and the passions of those who live with nature. In its bucolic atmosphere, in its chorus of humorous peasants, in its stress upon the irrational in human behavior, and in its dependence upon chance, the novel strongly suggests the influence of Thomas Hardy. Describing the yeoman-type predominating at the political convention in *The Voice of the People,* Miss Glasgow had spoken of "that enduring aspect which comes from contact with natural forces" and had exemplified it in Nicholas Burr, who soon leaves behind him his poor white origins. Abel Revercomb in *The Miller of Old Church* is a figure comparable to Nicholas Burr. He also rises superior to his poor white background, and he also responds with his whole being to the steadying influence exerted by the land. Both his sturdy integrity and his uninhibited emotion spring, Miss Glasgow insisted, from the soil under his feet: his is a largeness of spirit, "a dignity . . . which had in it something of the quiet and the breadth of the Southern landscape" (316). This unsophisticated accord with the forces outside him has given Abel his depth of perception, it has refined his being, and it has provided a firm basis for his moral earnestness. Just as external nature regards all human pretensions as too insignificant for notice, so Abel Revercomb's austerity of mind, simplicity of soul, and singleness of purpose permit no trifling with the serious business of life. Through him rather than the aristocrats, continuity between the present and the future generations will be assured: his dream of a future with Molly Merryweather and their children is as much racial as individual and emanates from "the integral structure of life." [2]

Molly Merryweather is at first wild and untamed, a less worldly Eustacia Vye. Sexual emotion in her has the strength of a natural force, and the virginity overlying it is "fierce and passionate, not shy and fleeting." In depth of feeling like the miller, she has something of his high-mindedness so long as she lives close to the earth. When she first becomes a member of the Gay household, she easily discerns the inadequacy of the elder Gay's expiation—in leaving his money to her—for the wrong done her mother. Later, she adopts some of the pretentious amenities of the upper class and ends in misjudging Abel for his surface crudeness. As in Thomas Hardy's fiction, a sophisticated environment beclouds moral vision, whereas rural simplicity possesses an elemental wisdom.

Miss Glasgow also skillfully related the course of the lovers' troubled passion to external nature. During the sadness of the closing year Abel's love for Molly reaches apparent fulfillment. Yet the lovers quarrel the next spring and draw apart when reawakened nature is bringing its other creatures together; with Molly gone, the spring season to Abel "became as desolate as winter." A year later Abel marries Judy Hatch without love in the wan autumn when the fallen leaves seemingly find "some frenzied joy in this dance of death." The Indian summer splendor of his wedding day, moreover, is made a torment to him by its hint of a lost beauty in his own life. The lovers are at length reunited with as much sadness as joy after Judy's death the succeeding fall "when the earth wears its richest and its most ephemeral beauty."

In contrapuntal contrast with this genuine, if ill-fated, relationship between Abel and Molly, which varies its mood to harmonize or contrast with nature's, there is the less sincere love affair between the younger Jonathan Gay, the worldly intruder into rural Virginia, and Blossom Revercomb. Because Gay's values derive from the artifices of a now decadent upper class, he is only partly responsive to the spiritual influence of unspoiled nature. Yet even Gay comes to feel that, in so far as his passion for Blossom is real, it is part of the larger drama of the world immediately surrounding him. In his mercurial mind his love has followed the course of the seasons to attain autumnal fruition and an attendant hint of decay: "His passion had run its inevitable course of desire, fulfilment, and exhaustion. So closely had it followed the changing seasons, that it seemed, in a larger and more impersonal aspect, as much a product of the soil as the flame-coloured lilies that bloomed in the Haunt's Walk" (289).

If Miss Glasgow's sense of the inevitable quality of natural forces contributed an astringent flavor to *The Miller of Old Church,* so did her satiric picture of the Southern aristocracy. A perceptive study of Southern life and manners at the beginning of the century, this novel reveals Victorian values as still supreme but nearing dissolution. An unsteady equilibrium characterizes this social order as tensions mount between it and those who challenge it: the older and the younger Jonathan Gay (though they do not break loose from it), Molly, the miller, and Aunt Kesiah Blount. More than in any other of Miss Glasgow's books, the old order is corrupt and possesses none of the redeeming qualities which she found for it in *The Voice of the People* (1900), *The Romance of a Plain Man* (1909), *Virginia* (1913), and *The Sheltered Life* (1932). In different ways the older Jonathan Gay, his nephew, and his sister-in-law Mrs. Gay represent their class in its decadence: in turn they exhibit its ineffectual good intentions, its self-indulgent weakness, and its petty tyranny. Mrs. Gay and her son Jonathan, moreover, have little interest in life at Old Church and illustrate the increasingly common tendency among the descendants of the prewar aristocracy to become absentee holders of their lands.[3]

By the most insidious of ironies "the fragile little lady" Mrs. Gay, with her resplendent "virtue" and her "soft, unfathomable eyes," becomes the destroying woman in two generations. In presenting Mrs. Gay, Miss Glasgow abjured the nineteenth-century myth that *la femme fatale* was destructive in proportion to her forthright evil and demonstrated with greater verisimilitude how effectively, without the guidance of a free intelligence, a real or alleged goodness can "smother." In Mrs. Gay, woman as "inspiration" is transformed into woman as "devourer," and she destroys without ever having had to exert herself. She had dominated the elder Jonathan Gay through her extreme pride and ill-health, and had prevented him from marrying the lower-class woman he had seduced, Janet Merryweather. The ultimate result of the forced separation of the lovers was Janet's death from insanity. Mrs. Gay's son, Jonathan, likewise cannot tell his mother that he is married to a rustic, Blossom Revercomb, for that would certainly induce in her a violent "heart attack." The secrecy surrounding this marriage is misinterpreted by Blossom's father Abner, brother to Abel and Janet Merryweather's former rustic lover. He is generally believed to have shot the elder Gay for trifling with Janet, and at the end of the novel he does shoot the younger Jonathan when it appears that the young man has, in his turn, trifled with Blossom. Because she is kept from knowledge of the tragedies she is actually responsible for, Mrs. Gay is confirmed in the rightness of her principles. Something of a romantic about her own "beautiful" nature, she yearns for "a richer century" wherein she might have caused "the moral regeneration of distinguished historic sinners of the opposite sex, like Lord Byron or Alfred de Musset" (252).

If Mrs. Gay prefers fastidious unreality, she is, nevertheless, a realist to the point that it pays her to be one. She has "surrendered all rights in order to grasp at all privileges" (55). Taking full advantage of her own devious nature and physical frailty, she triumphs through indirection. She uses men to her own ends through their more open natures and exploits to the full her "remorseless tyranny of weakness" (332). She even resents her brother-in-law's partial expiation of his sin, because his provision for his natural daughter Molly focuses attention upon an unpleasant situation which would have been better forgotten and which besmirches Mrs. Gay's pure memory of him, now a basic part of her "religion." After Mrs. Gay's rabid "innocence" demands her son's life rather than knowledge of the truth of his marriage, Miss Glasgow, with a consummate irony, depicted Mrs. Gay as consoling herself with the thought that she had never spared herself for her son's happiness.

Mrs. Gay is at once real in the psychological framework of the book and larger than reality in view of her role as the eternal feminine. The idealized femininity incarnate in Mrs. Gay is aborted and decadent, however, since she has assimilated the moral dishonesty of her social class in its decline. Men see her as more than mere woman by worshipping her as "saint" and "angel," whereas she is far from angelic in her disregard of Christian charity. As Miss Glasgow remarked in the preface to *They Stooped to Folly,* the ineffably feminine as an object of universal veneration had reached its apogee in the Amelia of

Thackeray and the Agnes Wickfield of Dickens.[4] Mrs. Gay is but a more unscrupulous and intelligent woman of the same sort, more neurotically vigorous than her virginal compeers; and she represents what they might have been, after induced neurosis had become inflexible. In her delicacy and sweet radiance men are only too ready to find their "ideal," generated by centuries of their inbred fixation upon it. Mr. Mullen, the local Episcopalian clergyman, who is himself strongly addicted to Mrs. Gay's "beautiful" spirit, says of her: "it is not possible, I believe, for any woman to approach more closely the perfect example of her sex" (149). She is, in essence, the "womanly woman" of his sermons, the woman who wants only to be "an Incentive, an Ideal, an Inspiration." The feminine domination of Southern society, noted by one authority during the Reconstruction, evidently persisted into the years 1898–1902 to become one of the enduring traditions of the region: "Women were the most uncompromising part of Southern creation and their power was great. The war had put them in a considerable majority in many communities, and by setting the tone of society they came near establishing a matriarchy." [5]

If "evasive idealism" makes a hothouse plant of Mrs. Gay, it makes sentimentalists of the men who encourage her and who mistake for virtue and character her weakness and obstinacy. Miss Glasgow's analysis of masculine deficiencies is, therefore, as amusing and sharp as that of feminine pretense. The younger Jonathan Gay, for example, calls it "philosophical" to regard none but the pleasant facts. Mr. Chamberlayne, Mrs. Gay's lawyer and spokesman for a hypocritical society, is confirmed by the magnificence of her great virtue in his conviction that divine goodness really exists. His belief in God's beneficence is momentarily shaken at the end of the book by the spectacle of Mrs. Gay's grief for her son: an angelic woman ought by rights to have been shielded from tragedy by God as well as by man. Miss Glasgow thus disclosed how natural it was, under the aegis of such failure to see straight, for an accomplished rake like Jonathan Gay, in keeping with the indulgences he allows himself, to demand a proportionate "innocence" from the women in his circle. Molly's active resentment of the wrongs which she and her mother have borne from the Gays argues, in his mind, too great a knowledge of the evils of the world, too great a failure to bear her cross with humility. She is, indeed, far removed from his ideal, the sweet and passive "woman of the early Victorian period."

Woman's sphere in late nineteenth-century America was characteristically that prescribed by unimaginative tradition: woman was to be permitted a mere existence but not the pursuit of purposeful activity. Since under such a convention intelligence becomes a masculine virtue and a feminine liability, Mrs. Gay's sister, Kesiah Blount, discovers that rebellion against the established order is futile. Miss Glasgow's analysis of Kesiah's aspirations and frustrations results in another impressive feminine portrait. Kesiah is endowed with sensibility and discernment but lacks grace, beauty, and the spirit to resist. She is, accordingly, forced to give up her ambition to be a painter, since "it was out of the question that a Virginia lady should go off by herself and paint perfectly nude people in a foreign city" (57). Ironically, the same feminine charm which would have made protest needless is also required to make it effectual: "Women in novels had revolted against life as passionately as she; but, one and all, they had revolted in graceful attitudes and with abundant braids or curls. A false front not only extinguished sentiment, it put an end to rebellion" (61). The unconscious cruelty of a civilization which reverences the purely feminine attributes is most directly illustrated in its intolerance of those who, through no fault of their own, lack them. Custom weakens Kesiah to the extent that when she does become financially independent, she no longer has the energy to rebel. Kesiah, having had sufficient strength to renounce what she desires, is subjected to humiliations in proportion to what she has sacrificed, whereas a "weak" and unscrupulous woman such as Mrs. Gay has had all things added unto her.

In other characters also Miss Glasgow explored the tensions existing between heredity and environment, the effect of environment being even stronger than usual in her fiction. To balance Kesiah's defeat by life in the upper class, there is Reuben Merryweather's in the lower. A victim of the monopoly of resources and political power by the Old South aristocracy, he was unable, in the widening democracy after the war, to develop his formerly repressed initiative.[6] He had never really flourished, even as overseer at Jordan's Journey, when his former commander, the elder Jonathan Gay, had bought the estate after the war. He is endowed with "a simple wisdom of the heart," but he lacks the sterner qualities which would have enabled him to adjust better to a changing society. He in some ways personifies the inhumanity of the aristocracy, for the elder Gay repaid Reuben's soldierly devotion by seducing his daughter. As his drab existence drags on toward death, Reuben realizes that none of his hopes has been fulfilled because the forces against him have been too powerful. In her presentation of Judy Hatch, who has been made distraught through an unreturned infatuation for Mr. Mullen, Miss Glasgow's determinism was still more pronounced. Because of Judy's great passion, her will becomes power-

less and her destiny beyond her control. In part a result of the work-
ings of natural Darwinian laws, Judy's death is also invested in Miss
Glasgow's eyes with some of the impersonal grandeur of the martyr's,
with "a sense of the pathetic futility of individual suffering in the midst
of a universe that creates and destroys in swarms" (312).

The affair between Jonathan Gay and the goddess-like Blossom
Revercomb provides a delicate register for the intricate interplay of these
antagonistic forces of heredity and environment. Gay himself, more
insouciant than aggressively evil, works his own doom because he is, at
bottom, not serious enough for life in the religiously serious community
to which he returns. Blossom Revercomb, on the other hand, has inherited the moral seriousness of her Calvinist forebears. Though passion
may be strong in Blossom, it is controlled by stronger principles. Accordingly, she exacts from the amorphous Gay the legal bond of marriage
before she yields to him. Such is Blossom's temperamental, if nominal,
victory over Gay's cavalier instincts. If character is destiny in Miss
Glasgow's view, this basic principle is less effective than usual in shaping
the eventuality: in Gay's case a tribal hedonism results in the loss of
the power to control events, and in Blossom's case an inelastic tribal
strength meets defeat when it confronts forces too devious for it.

With the possible exception of Molly Merryweather, Abel Revercomb is the only character who transcends hereditary limitations and
environmental obstacles. External impediments to success yield to the
determined enterprise of a man like Abel, now that the aristocracy's
hold over the land has been loosened by the impact of the Civil War.
Under "the beneficent charity" of the Jordans, Reuben Merryweather
was ground down and a man like Abel could not have risen: "In that
pleasant idyllic period the one act which went unhonoured and unre-
warded was the act of toil" (37). That character is destiny in this
lower class, however, Abel reveals when he, alone of his family, resists
the traditional shiftlessness of the poor white. He secures an education,
farms diligently according to improved methods, and goes beyond his
class to become financially prosperous and politically influential. The
genuinely sincere Abel with his simple establishment at the mill sup-
plants in power the genial but temporizing Jonathan Gay with his two
thousand acres.

Abel Revercomb is a more believable character than Nicholas Burr
or Ben Starr, since his force derives more directly from his natural
environment and since he is more independent of aristocratic sanctions.
His rise to political power is also probable in terms of his moral
seriousness, though Miss Glasgow failed to convey all that must have
been involved in the process. For once, Miss Glasgow's sympathies

were completely with her lower-class hero, possibly since in this novel there is so little to be said for the "dilapidated aristocrats," as Mr. Chamberlayne himself terms them. Since Abel is a complex individual whose nuances of personality Miss Glasgow fully caught, the love scenes in which he figures are more forceful than usual in her fiction.

If the will and critical intellect are indispensable in determining an individual's destiny, they are often of little weight in regulating the vagaries of love. Both Abel and Judy Hatch are powerless to resist the strength of their passions for Molly and Mr. Mullen respectively, both Blossom Revercomb and Jonathan Gay yield after some resistance to the currents of instinct, and Molly Revercomb enjoys the authority which her instinctive coquetry confers. Love is possessive (Abel's jealousy is unreasoned), love responds more readily to indifference than to tenderness (Abel's considerateness to Molly when she leaves Jordan's Journey injures his cause), love without mutual understanding soon evaporates to bitterness (Blossom's disappointment that "the reality of love was different from her virgin dreams" is intense), love as physical passion wanes with its consummation. Love, in short, becomes an irrational agitation of flesh and spirit which may deny peace even to those who are happily mated. Anticipating D. H. Lawrence in these reflections of Molly, Miss Glasgow depicted the probable struggle for supremacy in marriage between even a devoted man and woman:

She wanted to run into his arms, but her knowledge of herself told her that once there she would not want to stay. The sense of bondage would follow; on his part, the man's effort to dominate; on hers, the woman's struggle for the integrity of personality. As long as he did not possess her she knew that emotion would remain paramount over judgment, that the longing to win her would triumph over the desire to improve what he had won. But once surrendered, the very strength and singleness of his love would bring her to cage. (199)

Molly's aversion to men early in the novel ("I'm all hard and bitter inside") recalls in tone and intensity that expressed by Estella in *Great Expectations* and derives from a similar source, the effects upon a susceptible child of an older woman's revulsion from love after being betrayed.[7]

Miss Glasgow expertly analyzed in Jonathan Gay another sort of restlessness in love, that characteristic of the venturesome but soon satiated rake. Her investigation of his motives is discerning because she recognized their complexity and because her insight into masculine weakness was acute. Though Gay is a reprobate, he is also, like Hardy's Wildeve and George Eliot's Arthur Donnithorne, a human being. In spite of his own weakness of will he can admire strength in others; he is the only one of the aristocrats, for example, who appreciates the miller's virtues. Gay even undergoes a rudimentary struggle between good and evil, and would do the right thing if it involved less effort. As it is, he is not quite serious enough about his good intentions: "So all his life he had done the things that he condemned, condemning himself because he did them" (298). A tendency to drift, a passion for novelty and change, and a surrender to the flux inside his own soul are Gay's most salient psychological traits. His emotions, intense but short-lived, produce a nature "cursed with swift fancies and swifter disillusionments"; a Don Juan in temperament, he is more stimulated by amatory pursuit than by fulfillment. Though his love for Blossom quickly fades, his desire for her while she is yet unattained is sharp agony. He is as illogically ashamed of his marriage to her as he is swiftly borne into it by the force of his passion.

If Jonathan Gay represents the Cavalier, Sarah Revercomb, with as great authority, represents the Puritan. She is the third of the great feminine portraits of the novel, and like Mrs. Gay she exudes the malign influence of an over-anxious virtue. Sarah is as firm in her cheerless religion as Mrs. Gay is in the absolutes of the social code. Like Mrs. Gay she is never self-conscious nor often visited by doubt: "Entrenched behind an impregnable self-esteem, she had never conceded a point, never admitted a failure, never accepted a compromise" (89). If she occasionally questions God's beneficence, she has her confidence restored by dogma: "there wasn't any explanation of . . . seeming injustice except original sin" (188). The same simplicity which permits Sarah to accept at its most literal the Biblical word of God permits her to interfere complacently in other people's lives. Since she disapproves of Molly Merryweather's coquetry and is anxious for her son's eternal rather than his temporal welfare, she has no hesitation in applying to Reuben Merryweather to break off the engagement between his granddaughter and Abel. Because she discounts happiness as fleeting and welcomes affliction as the Lord's will, she deems it sinful to indulge in violent transports of ecstasy as Abel had done in loving Molly or in headlong fits of depression as he had done in losing her. Mental maladies do not exist for her, since behavior apart from the set patterns of the Calvinist ethic is not to be countenanced: "She was on her knees busily sorting a pile of sweet potatoes that she suspected of having been frost-bitten; and by sheer force of character, she managed to convince the despairing lover that a frost-bitten potato was a more substantial fact than a broken heart" (127).

An abundance of humor pervades *The Miller of Old Church,* a subtle sort hovering about the hypocrisies of the rich and a broader, more explicit sort finding expression in a chorus of rustics. The scenes in which Mrs. Gay triumphs are not only tragic in implication but, seen in true perspective, they are also ridiculous. When the disagreeable reality is mentioned, she continually flashes with quavering eyes a warning to everyone that her sensibilities are delicate. If this sign goes unheeded, she has recourse to a fainting fit; and sometimes she finds a "heart attack" necessary before unpleasant facts are withdrawn from her notice. If it has grievous results in Jonathan's violent death, the social conspiracy is also absurd which keeps from Mrs. Gay the knowledge of his misalliance to Blossom. It is laughable—though such confusion among values is also fateful—that to Mrs. Gay's immediate circle her reaction to her son's death is of more concern than his death itself: " 'She bears it beautifully, just as we might have expected,' he [Mr. Chamberlayne] said. 'I have seldom witnessed such fortitude, such saintly resignation to what she feels to be the will of God' " (332). A controlled irony also marks the somewhat extravagant scenes in which Mrs. Gay figures, when, for example, she compliments her son, by this time Blossom's secret husband, for leading a purer life than his uncle: " 'Oh, my boy, my darling boy,' Mrs. Gay sobbed, with her head on his shoulder, 'I have but one comfort and that is the thought that you are so different' " (151).

To round out the comic range of the novel Miss Glasgow used once again, as she had in *The Deliverance,* the unsophisticated country folk, "slow of movement, keen of wit, racy of speech." [8] The frequenters of Bottom's Ordinary are indispensable in the novel both for introducing the central characters in the first chapter and for deepening our later apprehension of them. The rustics comment upon these people and their actions, while, as parallel figures from a different class, they also provide colorful variations upon the situations and themes developed in the novel. Betsey Bottom in her own realm, like Mrs. Gay in hers, is the "helpless" woman who rules through calculated weakness the allegedly dominant male. In her own colorful way Betsey also realizes the irrationality of love and summarizes, without knowing its existence, the nature of Blossom's fascination with the dashing Gay: " 'Some women try to make out they ain't got an eye for the shape as long as the sense is all square and solid; but I ain't never been one of 'em. Sense is all right in its place, no doubt, but thar're times when a fine figger is mo' convincin' than any argyment' " (123). When old Adam Doolittle (whose altercations with his son repeat the conflict between generations in the Revercomb and Gay households) discourses on religion, he challenges the validity of Mr. Mullen's sentimentalized faith and becomes, without realizing it, an unsophisticated proponent of the Darwinian view of nature:

"When twenty seeds rot in the ground an' one happens up, thar're some folks as would praise the Lord for the one an' say nothin' about the twenty. These same folks are for ever drawin' picturs of wild things hoppin' and skippin' in the woods, as if they ever had time to hop an' skip when they're obleeged to keep one eye on the fox an' the hawk an' t'other on the gun of the hunter. Yet to hear Mr. Mullen talk in the pulpit, you'd think that natur was all hoppin' and skippin'." (174)

In comic and ironic sequence, the peasants in their sphere make use of the same moral sophistries and the same prejudices as their superiors do. Mrs. Gay's and Mr. Chamberlayne's "evasive idealism," for example, has its grotesque reverberation in the peasant class when Old Adam heartily admits his desire to escape the unpleasant: "When you ax me to pin my faith on any p'int, be it for this world or the next, my first question consarnin' it is whether that particular p'int happens to be pleasant" (7). Old Adam also shares the restrictive sexual morality which exalts Mrs. Gay and ruins Kesiah's life, and which assigns an abject role to woman. The inhumanity of this code Miss Glasgow ridiculed when Solomon Hatch would have Molly Merryweather treated as an outcast, simply because she is illegitimate. At this point he is addressing Jonathan Gay who turns away from him in disgust; yet ironically it is Gay who most ruthlessly exploits a double-standard morality to satisfy his own desires. Solomon is also wretched at Judy's passion for the rector after she has married Abel Revercomb, since unconventionality in the women related to him makes Hatch as wretched as it would Jonathan Gay.

Even though their political authority declines, the aristocratic Gays are still responsible for the tragic outcome of the various love affairs in the novel. Jonathan is embroiled disastrously, as it turns out, with Blossom, because his mother's delicacy causes him to keep his marriage secret. Mrs. Gay refused to allow the terms of the elder Jonathan's will to be set aside so that Molly would be free to go to Abel if she should care to: the compulsive need to keep scandal hidden becomes a more important consideration than the securing of justice.[9] Miss Glasgow expressed this social power of an aristocratic class now in decay by directing attention in Book One to the influence of Jonathan and his mother. Three of the seven opening chapters are centered in Jonathan Gay's consciousness and an omniscient point of view is used in two others. Mrs. Gay effectively permeates Book One—and the whole novel—although she is almost entirely seen from the outside. This long first section Miss Glasgow entitled "Jordan's Journey" after the estate which Jonathan's uncle had bought from the Jordans after the war.

In this first section, the scene remains constant and unity of time is also well observed, the action being limited to six months. Only in the broadest sense is unity of action observed, since the linking of many characters in an intricate plot is sometimes tenuous and point of view is variable. There are at least three main strands in the action— the first involving Mrs. Gay, the second involving Jonathan and Blossom, and the third involving Abel and Molly. These threads of the story are expertly interwoven, but none of them clearly predominates. As we have noted, the action is sometimes seen from an omniscient spectator's vantage point. At other times, it is seen through the eyes of Jonathan Gay, Abel Revercomb, Molly Merryweather, Blossom Revercomb, Sarah Revercomb, Reuben Merryweather, Kesiah Blount, and Judy Hatch. Thus point of view may shift too often to permit the fullest probing into character and situation. What the novel lacks in depth it may gain in breadth, however. By entering the minds of many characters, Miss Glasgow was best able to convey perhaps the widespread effect of the social transition upon the inner lives of people from different classes, even in the country where change penetrated slowly.

If in the first part of the novel the aristocracy dominates, in the second the yeomanry has begun to exert increased power. Abel triumphs at last over the devious influence of Mrs. Gay by winning Molly; and Abner Revercomb avenges the wrong done to the honor of his family by shooting the aristocratic seducer, Jonathan Gay. The lower classes —whose best representative, Abel Revercomb, challenges the supremacy of Jordan's Journey—have for local haunt Bottom's Ordinary which is located where three roads meet at a former turnpike gate. Symbolically, Abel, Molly, Jonathan, and Blossom are all confronted with moral decisions which mark turning points in their destinies; appropriately then, Book Two is entitled "The Cross Roads." This section, which begins with Abel's miserable marriage to Judy Hatch a year after the conclusion of Book One, provides an extensive commentary upon the preceding action and is a kind of epilogue to it. The novel goes forward for about a year more and encompasses Judy's death, Jonathan's violent end, and the lovers' reunion. The unified setting and the restricted time sequence do much to tighten a short novel with many characters and a complex plot; as a result, most of its incidents seem inevitably the outcome of ordered natural and social forces.

As with so many of Miss Glasgow's books an early scene contains the whole novel in embryonic form. In the first chapter as the central characters—Jonathan, Abel, and Molly—come by Bottom's Ordinary, their entrances are preceded by comments from the peasants assembled at the tavern. Molly is seen to be headstrong and independent in having failed to replace a road barrier, and Abel's disposition is regarded as testy. The conflict between the classes is established when Abel is offended with Jonathan Gay for casually remarking that Molly is "a pretty bit of vanity"; the conflict between the lovers is indicated when Abel is angered by the encouraging glance which Molly throws to Jonathan. An undercurrent of fatality emanates from old Adam Doolittle's ready recognition of Jonathan as a Gay. Doolittle associates Jonathan with the elder Gay, and then he recalls that he was the one who had closed the uncle's eyes in death. Solomon Hatch and Betsey Bottom maintain that the elder Gay's death was murder rather than suicide, and they add to Jonathan's uneasiness. The innovations of the Reverend Orlando Mullen at Old Church, the rise of Abel Revercomb to prosperity from a shiftless family, and the unfortunate history of Molly Merryweather are aspects of this novel, introduced in the rustics' comments, which are extensively developed thereafter.

The Miller of Old Church again reveals Miss Glasgow's unevenness as a writer. She lacked in this novel that complete control over disparate materials which her ironic intelligence and perceptive humor promised. As foil to the precision and conciseness of her style at its best, there are wordy, lifeless sentences such as this: "Then his figure standing under a stunted cedar on a small raised platform, which was used for school celebrations or out-of-door concerts, appeared to gather to itself all that was magnetic and alive in the atmosphere" (300). Despite her sure grasp of the complexities of character and her knowledge of human nature, sentimentalizing occurs in the novel. This is seen, for example, in Abel's political conversion by a "good clergyman," or in Reuben Merryweather's disquisition upon God: "but I've yet to see the spot of natur, either human or clay, whar we couldn't find the Lord at work if we was to dig deep enough" (168). A failure to motivate Abel's marriage to Judy Hatch except in terms of sheer pity is the most salient defect of the novel. Her fortuitous death—the result of a miscarriage when she learns that Mr. Mullen's horses have bolted with him—increases the unreality of the later scenes. Her sudden end too easily permits the estranged lovers to come together. If Molly and Abel in the end had remained apart, Judy's death with its overtones of the ludicrous would have been more organic to the novel by contrast with another tragic situation, more dignified in its tone and implications. As it is, the symbolic intonations and the ritual significance with which Miss Glasgow wished to invest the reunion of hero and heroine do not register decisively. If their reunion had been due less to chance, or if Jonathan Gay had been more of a temptation to Molly, her salvation as a Gay through marriage to a man of integrity from a lower class would have been more compelling.

Like *The Deliverance* and Miss Glasgow's other best novels, *The Miller of Old Church* as a whole rises superior to its incidental defects. As one evidence of its artistry, a deepening atmosphere of fatality accompanies its unwinding skein of incident. Ominous overtones, in particular, gather about the younger Jonathan Gay whose weakness of will from the first points to a tragic destiny. That the elder Gay's ghost supposedly appears to the superstitious from time to time in the Haunt's Walk at Jordan's Journey, suggests the continuing debilitating influence of ancestral irresponsibility upon the last weak-willed survivor of the race. In spite of his rational dismissal of this legend after his return home, the younger Gay is upset. On another occasion he is disturbed when a piece of paper with the word "tomorrow" inscribed in his uncle's handwriting drops from a book he picks up. Abner Revercomb's alleged murder of the elder Gay, in the "middle distance" of the narrative, continually hovers about its unfolding action and hints at Abner's precipitate revenge upon a Gay of a different generation. Blossom's primitive abandonment to emotion when she confesses to Molly her marriage to Gay also foreshadows the violence of her lover's death. As a result of this sustained tension, Gay's death is as convincing in the novel as Judy Hatch's is contrived. In this sensitivity to the violence which often attends social decay, Miss Glasgow once again seems to have anticipated a preoccupation of later Southern writers. Expert also is Miss Glasgow's handling of a modified stream of consciousness technique when Gay, in his few minutes of reprieve after the shooting, becomes fascinated with approaching death and, reviewing his past, recognizes the triviality of his life.

Although incidents in the novel thus accrue symbolic weight and produce the cumulative effect which Miss Glasgow desired, individually they sometimes seem factitious, as though they had been consciously added to the novel after its original inception. For example, when the Negro Uncle Toby sees a ghost in "the Haunt's Walk," Sarah Revercomb remarks that the Gay ghosts walk only when someone in the family dies or marries. This is too patly fitted in with Gay's secret marriage to Blossom to be entirely effective. More impressive as a symbol is the grove of pines—where Abel planned to build a home for himself and Molly—representing that inviolable strength in his nature which is beyond injury at Molly's defection.

The symbolism more organic to the novel, that expressed through the containing landscape and through the individual members of the conflicting social classes, is the most forceful. In particular, the scenes from aristocratic life are, sociologically and morally, richly allusive. Gay, for example, is the helpless victim of a mother-image carefully implanted in his mind by Mrs. Gay and her acquiescent friends: such is the purport of the scene upon his arrival home in which his mother quietly muffles her son's struggling instincts toward an upright life based upon a recognition of the truth. Conceived as it is with imaginative vigor, this novel represents a confident, sophisticated artistry that was to be yet more surely displayed in Miss Glasgow's next novel, *Virginia*.

◆VII◆

"The Feminine Ideal
of the Ages":
Virginia

Miss Glasgow did her most distinguished work when, as in *Virginia* (1913), her vision was sharpened by a radical irony. Through the clarity of mind provided by such irony, she crystallized into a destined form her panorama of a society at "a dissolving moment in time." [1] Although it gave her critical strength, Ellen Glasgow's irony was nevertheless flexible and sensitive to the essence of a character's mood or situation. In *Virginia* her world, with its diverting surfaces and ominous depths in near juxtaposition, is more complex and commodious than that in her other books, with the exception of *The Sheltered Life* (1932). The atmosphere of *The Sheltered Life,* however, is elegiac rather than incisive, and the acrid mood of satire yields sooner to the brooding pity which does not dominate *Virginia* until its close. The bitterness which permeates *Virginia* may be partly attributed to the fact that the idea for the novel came to Ellen Glasgow while she "sat, waiting in agony, for an end without hope" [2] at her sister Cary's bedside. *Virginia* and *The Sheltered Life,* moreover, gain scope and authenticity because Miss Glasgow in these books refracted a dying passion against a dying culture and thereby invested the emotions of individual characters with general as well as sociological significance. The pressure exerted by these novels is, accordingly, greater than that exerted by more diffusely con-

ceived works like *The Miller of Old Church* (1911) and *They Stooped
to Folly* (1929), and their texture is richer than that of works like
The Deliverance (1904) and *Barren Ground* (1925) in which the mores
of a whole society are less fully set forth.

Virginia, which is laid in Dinwiddie (a pseudonym for Petersburg),
records exhaustively the defeat of its heroine, Virginia Pendleton, by
the years. After an ecstatic marriage, Virginia's energies are absorbed by
her young children to the point that she neglects her husband, Oliver
Treadwell, or else fails to comprehend his ambitions as a playwright
absorbed in his work. In part, the novel explores the conflict between
the sexual drive and the maternal and reveals how they are, to some degree, mutually exclusive. According to the Victorian standards observed
in Virginia during the 1880's and 1890's, the responsibilities of mother-
hood precluded any further need for a woman to seek self-realization,
even in sex itself. Thus Virginia's sexuality is consumed by the demands
of her family upon her affections, whereas Oliver retains unimpaired
his youthful vigor. Failing to appreciate fully Virginia's innate goodness and tiring of her limited intellect, Oliver ultimately finds a more
understanding companionship in a New York actress, Margaret Oldcastle, and asks an astounded Virginia for his freedom. Since her
children are now grown and Oliver is her husband in name only, the
middle-aged Virginia has, in her father's words, "outlived her usefulness." In her unselfish sweetness and her unmerited suffering, she is
reminiscent to a degree of the heroines of Maupassant's *Une Vie* and of
Fielding's *Amelia,* books which Miss Glasgow esteemed highly. Though
Virginia Pendleton is memorable in her own right, she also resembles
the virginal Eugénie Grandet of Balzac, who, through no misdeed of
her own, is bitterly defeated by life.

More adroitly than in Mrs. Webb of *The Voice of the People,* Miss
Glasgow suggested in the minor figures of *Virginia* the qualities, questionable and fine, of the old order in the South as it survived into the
Virginia of the 1880's. Miss Priscilla Batte and Mrs. Tom Peachey,
who are characterized by personal integrity and intellectual timidity,
are both representative of this phase of Miss Glasgow's craft. Thus in
her vignette of Mrs. Peachey, Miss Glasgow regarded this impoverished
gentlewoman, with her high ideals and temperamental inflexibility, as
a symbol of the postwar South itself:

When, after a few hurried mouthfuls, he [Oliver] asked permission to return to his work, she received his excuses with the same cheerful acquiescence
with which she accepted the decrees of Providence. It is doubtful, indeed,
if her serenity, which was rooted in a heroic hopelessness, could have been
shaken either by the apologies of a boarder or by the appearance of an

earthquake. . . . Courage, humour, an adherence to conviction which is wedded to the inability to respect any opinion except one's own; loyalty which had sprung from a principle into a passion; a fortifying trust, less in the Power that rules the universe than in the peculiar virtues of the Episcopal prayer-book bound in black; a capacity for self-sacrifice which had made the South a nation of political martyrs; complacency, exaltation, narrowness of vision, and uncompromising devotion to an ideal:—these were the qualities which had passed from the race into the individual and through the individual again back into the very blood and fibre of the race. (101)

If their attitudes are usually obsolete, the majority of people in Dinwiddie and, in particular, aristocrats such as Miss Batte and Mrs. Peachey, possess an enviable equanimity which made the South in defeat still unconquerable in spirit. Even Miss Batte's house seems to have stamped upon it her chief attribute, "the look of cheerful fortitude with which her generation had survived the agony of defeat and the humiliation of reconstruction" (8).

In spite of its high-minded enthusiasm and magnanimity, the post-Reconstruction South had become sterile because of its resistance to contemporary thought. Most of the advanced ideas in the late nineteenth century ran counter to a feminized culture and were bitterly opposed by the average Southerner who regarded them fearfully as Yankee or foreign influences. C. Vann Woodward in his *Origins of the New South* notes this obdurate resistance to the intellectually new and untried: "The South of the eighties was a bleak place for the younger scholar. 'The studious man is pronounced impractical and is suspected as a visionary,' wrote young Woodrow Wilson from Atlanta in 1883." [3]

On Virginia's bookshelves are those "sweet" works—Mrs. Hemans, Adelaide Anne Proctor, an expurgated Shakespeare, Miss Strickland's "Lives of the Queens of England," *Thaddeus of Warsaw,* Miss Yonge's novels, and other innocuous tales—which exemplify the anemic conceptions of Miss Priscilla Batte, who, as head of the Dinwiddie Academy for Young Ladies, is cultural arbiter for Dinwiddie. Such timorousness Miss Glasgow often exposed by an expert use of the irony of direct statement. Thus Miss Batte qualifies for her role because her father, a gallant Confederate general, had died at Gettysburg; like the rest of Dinwiddie, "she was capable of dying for an idea, but not of conceiving one" (10). What knowledge a young woman acquires is unimportant, just so long as she assimilates the right attitudes, "such fundamental verities as the superiority of man and the aristocratic supremacy of the Episcopal Church." [4]

In education, forces which unsettle the mind and encourage originality were suppressed or disregarded. Thus Dinwiddie in 1884 is still unaware

of *The Origin of Species;* and the freethinking Oliver discovers that if
his ideas were generally known, they would make him as much an
outcast as if he were to declare himself a Republican.[5] Even poetry is
suspect to Miss Batte, for was it not "the ruination of Poe?" In a
culture of this sort, all women who deviate even slightly from inherited
norms of behavior are immediately suspect: Susan Treadwell with her
active mind, Mrs. Payson with her quick intelligence ("Mrs. Payson is
a college woman and it seems to me that she is always trying to appear
as clever as a man"), Abby Goode with her vigorous amiability, and
Virginia's own children with their frank sophistication.[6]

The "evasive idealism" characteristic of the Victorian age in England
and America reached its possible apogee in the South, Miss Glasgow
felt, where the legend of a glorious past reinforced an instinctive aversion
to unpalatable truths. As a result her fiction richly illustrates the similar
contention of at least one other commentator on the South: "Nowhere,
indeed, did this Victorianism, with its false feeling, its excessive nicety,
its will to the denial of the ugly, find more sympathetic acceptance than
in the South." [7] By such concentration upon the romantic and the
pleasant, the characters in *Virginia,* especially those of aristocratic
descent, easily slip several steps from actuality. Thus Gabriel Pendleton
and his wife see only what they wish to see. Unconscious hypocrites
both, they instinctively cling "to the belief that a pretty sham has a more
intimate relation to morality than has an ugly truth" (28). An un-
realistic optimism also characterizes this view of life, so that in Panglos-
sian fashion Mrs. Pendleton can rationalize, after initial shock, almost
any fateful or violent occurrence:

If Mrs. Pendleton had ever reflected on the tragic fate of pullets, she would
probably have concluded that it was "best" for them to be fried and eaten
or Providence, whose merciful wisdom she never questioned, would not
have permitted it. So, in the old days, she had known where the slave market
stood, without realizing in the least that men and women were sold there.
"Poor things, it does seem dreadful, but I suppose it is better for them to
have a change sometimes," she would have reasoned, no doubt, had the horror
of the custom ever occurred to her; for her heart was so sensitive to pain
that she could exist at all only by inventing a world of exquisite fiction
around her. (52)

In the normal exigencies of life Virginia and her mother have a nervous
attitude toward evil, a "conviction that to acknowledge an evil is in a
manner to countenance its existence" (28).

When it seems that Virginia may lose Oliver to Abby Goode, Mrs.

Pendleton's counsel conceals a genteel hypocrisy and an essential
moral cowardice:

"Oh, Virginia, a scandal, even where one is innocent, is so terrible. A
woman—a true woman—would endure death rather than be talked about.
I remember your cousin Jane Pendleton made an unhappy marriage, and her
husband used to get drunk and beat her and even carry on dreadfully with
the coloured servants; but she said that was better than the disgrace of a
separation." [8]

There were, indeed, some close similarities between provincial Virginia
of the eighties and sophisticated New York City of the seventies, as
Mrs. Wharton depicted it in *The Age of Innocence* (1920). At the time
Newland Archer and his wife are giving a send-off dinner to the
Countess Olenska—the guests wrongly believe that she is his mistress—
he thinks how these are people "who dreaded scandal more than disease,
who placed decency above courage, and who considered that nothing was
more ill-bred than 'scenes,' except the behaviour of those who gave rise
to them." [9]

As her parents had done before her, Virginia persistently tries to
outface a complex reality by looking elsewhere. In one of her moments
of insight—when she is struggling with Omnipotence for the life of her
boy ill with diphtheria—Virginia understands that a law of compensation determines the nature of human experience: "Never pleasure without pain, never growth without decay, never life without death" (271).
Ordinarily, however, she resists the implications of such truths by
failing to acknowledge them. She also learns that love never exists without an increase or a decrease in its intensity and that change is the
only constant aspect of life, despite her own inability to adjust easily to
new conditions. "The inherited mould of fixed beliefs" has formed her, so
that in a dynamic age she is left behind by husband, children, and
friends, and seems to act "in the aimless way of a person who is not
moving toward a definite object" (348). Only in her youth, in the
quest of love, had she been positive; from the moment that Oliver
possessed her, she later perceives, he had been moving away from her
and her fixed principles and prejudices.

Miss Glasgow insisted that this same evasiveness operated, with unhappy results, in other social classes and in spheres other than that of
personal relations. To the Pendletons the problem of the South, the
Negro question, does not exist; to Cyrus Treadwell, realistic with respect
to his profits, this same problem can be potentially disturbing only if
it is acknowledged as one. By his pretense that an alien race has no

rights or feelings, Cyrus had been able to use casually as mistress the Negress Mandy, at that time his servant. His reputation for respectability and his determined adherence to the letter of Christian principles compensate for his sensual lapses, he feels, and justify him in rationalizing out of existence his former mistress and their child. Having refused to help Mandy and his own illegitimate son, Cyrus in the best known scene of the novel turns with complacency to thoughts of his nephew, Oliver: "Even if the boy's a fool, I'm not one to let those of my own blood come to want" (133). Throughout the novel Miss Glasgow insisted that the effects of social dishonesty become compounded and demand eventually an expiation commensurate with them. Hence the conscientious and high-minded, if evasive, Gabriel Pendleton becomes the victim of the evil which his own pious forebears had encouraged, when he intervenes disastrously to save the grandson of his former slave from being bullied by several white men.

Disregard of reality becomes a fine art when ritualized in the "code of beautiful behavior" for woman. Moral passivity, emotional reticence, the uncomplaining endurance of disappointment, a cheerful recognition of masculine superiority, a joyful acceptance of one's enslavement to the comfort of the family, an unreal existence among the conventions, a distrust of originality, a reliance upon the emotions rather than the intellect, a pragmatic adoption of the "short view" rather than the unsettling "long view"—all these sanctified qualities of the "ideal" woman of the race mark Virginia and her mother. With a whimsical irony Miss Glasgow emphasized how, until too late, Oliver fails to realize that being married to "the feminine ideal of the ages" has been, of all fates, the worst for his intellectually active temperament.[10] That Oliver, as Virginia's young lover, writes a play about the "new woman" when he is sighing for the old-fashioned one he has just met is in itself ironic; he would, moreover, introduce on the stage the reality he avoids in his own life. At this point in his career he guilelessly imagines "how easy it would be to work if she [Virginia] were somewhere within call," little realizing what a burden his wife's uncomprehending presence will be to him later. That Miss Glasgow, in general a proponent of the "new woman," could view caustically what she endorsed is implied in the terse comment upon one of Oliver's early plays: "The play dealt with woman, with the new woman who had grown so old in the last twenty years, with the woman whose past is a cross upon which she crucifies both herself and the public" (98).

Though Oliver instinctively admires intelligence in women, he paradoxically at first recoils from any display of it. As a young man, confirmed in "the historical dogma of the supplementary being of woman," he prefers the softer sexuality of Virginia to Susan Treadwell's independence of mind. Only when change in society at large modifies his provinciality does he search in woman for what he had never in his courtship days desired in Virginia.[11] If this enthusiastic veneration of woman as ornament and divinity has its tragic consequences in Virginia's misalliance, it has its comic phase in Gabriel Pendleton's gullibility: to him all women are pure because they are women.

In describing the teeming Negro quarter as a place where "the more primitive forms of life swarmed like distorted images under the transparent civilization of the town" (36), Miss Glasgow implied that the highly conventional life of Dinwiddie inadequately conceals the currents of emotional violence running beneath its surface. Realities are often sharply at variance with appearances in a society which deliberately cultivates artifice. The apparently staid Cyrus Treadwell had responded to primitive impulse in making love to Mandy, the handsome Negress; his subsequent antipathy to her is to be measured in terms of a primitive instinct of race antagonism. Mandy herself is seen as a hunted animal whose emotions still border on savagery.[12] Even the self-effacing and genuinely charitable Gabriel Pendleton recalls, from his own life as a soldier, that in war "the savage seems to sleep in the most peaceable of men" (59). When the gentle and refined Virginia is inflamed by jealousy, she responds to a normally repressed pleasure in cruelty which has made the hunt so popular with men and can feel her enmity toward Abby Goode translated into "the rapturous baying of the hounds." She had, moreover, yielded previously to primordial instinct by falling unabashedly in love with Oliver, as though she were "the first woman seeking the first man through the vastness and the mystery of an uninhabited earth" (40). Oliver likewise struggles for a time against his passion for Virginia, but desire "like a hot wind blowing over him" is too strong to be denied.

As in *The Voice of the People, The Deliverance, The Romance of a Plain Man,* and *The Miller of Old Church,* all in varying degree novels with social transition as one chief theme, *Virginia* also traces the inroads made by the new bourgeoisie upon the dissolving aristocracy. An ambiguity of conception, similar to that utilized for Bill Fletcher's character in *The Deliverance,* marks Miss Glasgow's portrait of Cyrus Treadwell, whose tobacco factory awesomely dominates the sky line of Dinwiddie. This small-spirited Titan is both "the destroyer and the builder; the inexorable foe of the old feudal order and the beneficent source of the new industrialism" (57).

The reaction Cyrus provokes among the aristocrats in Dinwiddie is complex. They hate the gratuitous meanness which keeps his wife in abject poverty and which he has expressed for over thirty years by spitting upon a bed of sunflowers outside his window. Yet they cannot help admiring him, because his strong will has induced, by means of industrial power, a greater abjectness in them than had defeat in war, a subservience which, masochistically, they almost seem to enjoy. The apathy resulting from the extinction of high ideals in war rendered the typical Southerner liable to materialistic exploitation by the unscrupulous. Miss Glasgow was thus conscious of the spiritual price which the New South paid for "progress," despite her conviction that there was no choice but to adopt industrialism as a means for economic salvation.[13] Cyrus also represents a different aspect of the new industrialism in the postwar South from that found in *The Ancient Law:* the paternalistically motivated aristocrat like Daniel Ordway yields as leader to the opportunistic financier who need not have blue blood in his veins. Instead of feeling any responsibility for his workmen, Cyrus can only scornfully conclude that "there are too many of them." From the fact that Cyrus spends two days of each week in Wall Street, it is obvious that industrial expansion in the New South was as much the result of Northern capitalism as of a newly awakened aggressiveness in the region itself.

The descendants of the aristocracy resent the materialism which Cyrus stands for, but lack the vigor to keep this resentment active. Gabriel Pendleton thus tolerates in Cyrus what he intrinsically loathes, and the genteel Miss Batte lauds the *fait accompli* of power seized and exploited. Deficient in qualities such as self-denial, sensitivity, and spiritual endurance which characterize the old order, the industrialist, avid for power, is too often narrowly pragmatic when his immediate interests are at stake and inflexible when they are not. The force which Cyrus exerts as a person, coupled with his repulsiveness and meticulous parsimony, suggests his possible Balzacian origins. Despite his faults he does reject the deadening influence of the past. Some even of the newest generation of aristocrats, John Henry Pendleton, for instance, have grown tired of "the endless lip-homage to a single moment in history." He comes to feel, perhaps too uncritically, that there is at least vitality in the Treadwell point of view and willingly exchanges a moribund culture for commerce. In the Southern industrialist, the obverse to John Henry's attitude was sometimes seen: the entrepreneur often exhibited a lingering fondness for the Old South, so long as its chivalric ideals did not affect the conduct of life. Thus Cyrus acknowledges to himself that Gabriel Pendleton, who personifies the older civilization, has been the "single romance" of his life: both men had fought in the ranks and Gabriel had displayed a great courage which secured

Cyrus's admiration. Yet Cyrus immediately distrusts the idealism of the rector when the latter would extend it to include a vexing problem of the present, the Negro. In Cyrus's view the law of Christ "wouldn't do" for the subservient race.

Since there is not much choice to be made between the old and the new, between Miss Priscilla Batte and Cyrus Treadwell, between quixotic ancestor worship and irresponsible materialism, Miss Glasgow's irony—emanating from her scorn of both factions in the late nineteenth-century South—was broader in scope in *Virginia* than in any of her other books and produced the superior vigor of this novel. Her own feelings of impatience with the restrictions imposed by the old order and with the inhumanity of the new were infused into her portraits of Susan Treadwell and the youthful Oliver. An example of the "new woman" at her best (more human than Gabriella Carr in *Life and Gabriella*) and of an enlightened future (like the Maria Fletcher of *The Deliverance*), Susan Treadwell is caught between the intellectual apathy of the old order and the one-sided practicality of the new, yet achieves by force of character a vigorous, tolerant, and serene mind. As a young artist, Oliver Treadwell is still more outspoken in his criticism both of the enfeebling past and of the soulless present. The commercial spirit is as inhospitable to metaphysical speculation—to "the thought that did not construct a heroic attitude or a concrete image" —as the romantic spirit of tradition had been. Radical as it was in some respects, business enterprise, Miss Glasgow saw, was primarily interested in preserving the moral and intellectual status quo. With much sympathy, therefore, she presented Oliver as an intellectual out-cast in a commercial society; at the same time, Oliver finds it impossible to turn for understanding to representatives of a dying culture like the Pendletons and the Peacheys.[14] It is significant, too, that Miss Glasgow's sympathies were more equally divided in 1913 between the unspoiled Oliver and the defeated Virginia than they were in the late 1920's and 1930's when, revising the novel for the collected editions of her work, she appears to have become more impatient with masculine than with feminine weakness. The only significant deletions are several paragraphs at two points in the novel which adjudge, in sympathetic terms, Oliver's dilemma.[15]

Though she admired its honesty, Miss Glasgow's sympathy toward modernism was qualified. To her ironic vision, the concern of modernism with aggrandizement of the self no more represented an integral purpose in life than did the escapism of the Virginia gentry. If Virginia's children are more honest than she, they are far less kind, gentle, and human. In Oliver modernism works still more dubiously. After his youthful revolt, a consistent moral integrity eludes him; "the slow, insidious devil of compromise" undermines his nature. He lacks an outside scale of values—divorced from a corroding egoism—which might have permitted him to use the increased resources of the modern age for constructive ends:

Like his age, he was adrift among disestablished beliefs, among floating · wrecks of what had once been rules of conduct by which men had lived. And the widening responsibilities, the deepening consciousness of a force for good greater than creed or rules, all the awakening moral strength which would lend balance and power to his age, these things had been weakened in his character by the indomitable egoism that had ordered his life. There was nothing for him to fall back upon, nothing that he could place above the restless surge of his will. (355)

Miss Glasgow's steady comprehension of the energetic intellectual from the provinces who gradually grows beyond his unsophisticated origins, suggests once more a resemblance to Balzac whose provincials, Lucien de Rubempré and Eugène de Rastignac, are similarly intelligent, personable, ambitious, and somewhat unscrupulous.

Just as *The Deliverance,* despite its fully elaborated social milieu, is ultimately more important for its psychological insight, so is *Virginia.* As in *The Deliverance,* regional atmosphere is subordinate to Ellen Glasgow's pensive humanity and gives it tangible habitation. Thus Miss Glasgow's fully elaborated milieu in the novel—the town of Dinwiddie —mostly provides the requisite background against which human beings and incidents possessing universal import can be placed:

Human nature in this town of twenty-one thousand inhabitants differed from human nature in London or in the Desert of Sahara mainly in the things it ate and the manner in which it carried its clothes. The same passions stirred its heart, the same instincts moved its body, the same contentment with things as they are, and the same terror of things as they might be, warped its mind. (12)

Virginia bears the imprint of Henry James in its psychological involutions, and much of its power derives from an exhaustive exploration of the mixed motives of its central figures. Contrasting sorts of blindness in Virginia and Oliver culminate in a situation beyond their power to alter. Virginia's nature is a complex of inherited ignorance and goodness; Oliver's, of incisive intellectuality and of moral complacency. They both contribute to the defeat of Oliver's high ideals, she by unintelligence, he by enervating selfishness. If Virginia lacks the power of criticizing those she loves, Oliver lacks the power of criticizing him-

self. If, like her mother, Virginia is juvenile in her philosophy, she has
great capacity to endure; if Oliver's mind is keen, he lacks moral stamina.
Mutual anguish thus results when two individuals, who have been yoked
together through emotion only, drift apart.

Love, Miss Glasgow asserted, can "survive the shocks of tragedy"
more readily than "a gradual decline of interest." Oliver, accordingly,
reaches a time with Virginia "when to shed his blood would have cost
less than to make conversation" (355). When Virginia struggles for
the life of her boy, she is visited with a momentary cynicism unusual for
one of her sanguine temperament, and asks: "If every woman told
the truth to herself, would she say there is something in her that love
has never reached?" (277). Virginia evades the purport of this insight until it is too late: if love has not been quite enough for her with
her circumscribed interests, it must have been less adequate still for her
restless and sophisticated husband.

Miss Glasgow constantly predicated in this novel her apparent belief
that sexual love may in itself be eventually nugatory. The chief situation
in the novel—the final disappointment of Virginia's dreams in proportion to their initial intensity—is squarely based on the device of ironic
contrast and in fact determines the structure of the novel. The first book,
"The Dream," culminates in the bliss of Virginia's wedding; in the
succeeding books, "The Reality" and "The Adjustment," she passes
imperceptibly from beatitude to the misery of entire loneliness and
abandonment by those whom she had loved. Miss Batte's conviction
that Virginia is destined for supreme happiness and Virginia's own feeling that her existence will be certainly more glorious than the prosaic
lives of her fellow townsmen is painfully far removed from the reality
which overtakes her in middle age. After the ruin of her life in New
York she undergoes a baffled withdrawal from present pain. She finds
solace only in her symbolic wanderings at night, because only then does
she recapture the ecstasy of a youth suffused with love. Her present
anguish is made almost unbearable by such compulsive recalling of
happier days. The first part of the novel, which conveys the passion of
the youthful lovers, is often lush in tone and contrasts with the sustained sobriety of the rest of the book which conveys the lovers' disillusion.

When, as in *Virginia,* Miss Glasgow was exploiting to the fullest her
realistic and satiric vision, her affirmations were tentative and did not
interfere with the objective artistry of the novel. They were effectively
muted because in large part they were voiced by the Pendletons whom
she also satirized, or by the youthful Oliver whose later callousness
she presented unsympathetically. Miss Glasgow's basic premise seems

to have been the one which actuated Gabriel before his sudden death: "the greatest belief on earth, the belief in Life, in its universality in spite of its littleness, in its justification in spite of its cruelties" (288). As to Mrs. Pendleton, Miss Glasgow could condone to some degree her intellectual dishonesty, for Mrs. Pendleton has directed her energies to the forging of character and has thus "translated into action the end of all reasoning, the profoundest meaning in all philosophy" (305). She also exemplifies the familiar Glasgow precept of the need to lose one's soul to find it: "In spite of her trials she was probably the happiest woman in Dinwiddie, for she had found her happiness in the only way it is ever won, by turning her back on it" (112). Through Oliver's reflections upon the tragic life of his Aunt Belinda (Cyrus Treadwell's wife), Miss Glasgow indicated that "to make allowances" is the only acceptable "philosophy of human relations"; yet Oliver himself later fails in imaginative kindness to Virginia. In the end, though Virginia is defeated by life and by her unintelligence, her intrinsic goodness has greater substance than Oliver's distinction without moral foundation.

With fine control and firm insight Miss Glasgow established the completeness of Virginia's catastrophe by underplaying it emotionally. In the moving scenes at the close of the novel, emotion is forceful because it is held in abeyance: the effect produced is similar to the restrained power in the death-house scenes of *An American Tragedy*. In Virginia's encounter with Miss Oldcastle nothing really happens on the surface; underneath, however, Virginia's emotions and those of the actress are in turmoil. In terms of Miss Glasgow's artistry, the impact is the stronger for emotional tensions being thus unstably held in equilibrium:

Then, because it was impossible to say the things she had come to say, because even in the supreme crises of life she could not lay down the manner of a lady, she smiled the grave smile with which her mother had walked through a ruined country, and taking up her muff, which she had laid on the table, passed out into the hall. She had let the chance go by, she had failed in her errand, yet she knew that, even though it cost her her life, even though it cost her a thing far dearer than life, her happiness, she could not have done otherwise. In the crucial moment it was principle and not passion that she obeyed; but this principle, filtering down through generations, had become so inseparable from the sources of character, that it had passed at last through the intellect into the blood. She could no more have bared her soul to that other woman than she could have stripped her body naked in the market-place. (376)

In Virginia's meeting with Miss Oldcastle Miss Glasgow stressed the ambivalent nature of the actress's "freedom" and "nobility." The largesse of spirit deriving from these qualities commands admiration, but it has been secured through disregard of weaker, less selfish individuals. A predatory Darwinism of the emotions thus assures to Oliver and his mistress their victory over one whose strength is that of fortitude, not of pugnacity. The pathos in Virginia's situation is intensified by the very fact that she is inarticulate and cannot objectify her strong emotions into effective words or actions.[16]

In the subsequent scene when Oliver asks for his freedom, Virginia's pain is the greater for not being voiced. With aseptic vision Miss Glasgow depicted a harassed Virginia whose anguish in itself enfeebles her in the struggle to keep her husband. The result is that, Desdemona-like, she can only yearn after her unjust executioner: " 'Do—do you want her so much?' and she, who had learned from life not to want, looked at him with the pity he might have seen in her eyes had he stabbed her" (379). Even to the humorless Virginia her shopping expedition, while her heart breaks, appears comic in the wan light with which she now sees the incongruity between her outward activity and her inner turmoil. A sheen of sinuous absurdity often accompanies the tragic, in Miss Glasgow's view, since at times of crisis these disproportions between appearances and the truth can be so pronounced.

Other aspects of Miss Glasgow's artistry are prominent in *Virginia*. Her characters, for instance, are symbolic in terms both of social milieu and of moral value. The strength and the inadequacy of Southern tradition and morality in the eighties is distilled into the romanticism of the Pendletons; the spiritual hardness of the industrialism which is supplanting the older culture is implied in the materialism of the Treadwells; and the uncertainties that both this culture and the modernism which rejects it face when looking to the future are inherent in Virginia's —and Oliver's—bleak prospects at the end of the book. Virginia's role as a symbol for the South is, in many respects, well realized: the finest product of tradition, Virginia in her beauty and bright future at the beginning of the book suggests the South as it was before the war; in her fine qualities—"service, pity, loyalty, and sacrifice"—she suggests those which actuated the South in its unequal struggle with the North; and in her defeat by life, except for retaining "the inviolable sanctities of the spirit," she suggests both the declining prestige and the surviving pride of the postwar South. Virginia is unable to adapt to a new situation in her life because of her inherited inhibitions; nor can Oliver—in some sense a symbol of the "modern" recoil against Southern tradition—adapt to a new situation in his life because of his spiritual insensitivity. The chief defect of the novel is that, in spite of her real difficulties and her admirable qualities, Virginia is often dull and uninteresting. By implication, then, in her utter lack of resourcefulness, she is sometimes an inadequate symbol for the Old South even at its least progressive. Since she only incidentally commands full sympathy, the book is too loosely kept together psychologically. When a heroine is in part created ironically, we may intellectually become too insistently aware of her defects even when emotionally we may be engaged by her pathetic fate.

Flower and light imagery are also implicated in Virginia's tragedy. Light and flowers (roses, honeysuckle, the paulownia blooms in the rectory garden) connote Virginia's ecstatic emotion, her abandonment to love, and her expectations in the early part of the novel. The visualizing of Virginia in terms of brilliant light or the soft pallor of dusk and stars; the frequent mention of the beauty and the enthralling scents of honeysuckle, roses, and other springtime flowers; and the use of flame and fire images to convey the intensity of the lovers' passion, all signify that universal nature, animate and inanimate, has worked to the inevitable end of bringing Oliver and Virginia together.

When a drab middle age comes to Virginia, flowers only recall to her a lost youth, and light has edged off into shadow. It is fitting, therefore, that Virginia return from her defeat in New York in a dark, disagreeable slush storm. Absence of light and a bleak winter season mean that she is no longer an energetic embodiment of the Life Force with which, as a young girl, she was so perfectly in harmony. Loss of love and decline in beauty keep pace with the rotting of the paulownia trees which have been previously associated in her mind with her once overpowering happiness. When she comes back heartbroken from New York, she hears with anguish that the wife of the present rector is anxious to have them cut down.

Through repetition of motif the novel also gains force and authority as Virginia's unhappiness culminates. Virginia's slow decline in beauty achieves added pathos, therefore, from such incremental emphasis as the following:

She was still lovely, but it was a loveliness, Susan felt with a pang, that would break early. (188)

. . . around her gentle blue eyes appeared a group of little lines, brought out by the nervous contraction of her forehead. Was it the wan, smoky light of the dusk?—Susan wondered, or was Virginia beginning to break so soon? (245)

Though she was not yet thirty the delicate, flower-like bloom of her beauty was already beginning to fade. (259)

Though variously symbolic of social forces and of moral qualities, Miss Glasgow's characters in this book are imaginatively incisive as individuals because of her paramount interest in their conflicting motives.

All are brilliantly presented from such "flat" characters as Belinda Treadwell, Miss Priscilla Batte, and Miss Willy Whitlow, to more fully dimensioned figures like the Gabriel Pendletons, Cyrus Treadwell, Oliver Treadwell, and Virginia herself. More than in any book except *The Sheltered Life,* all the characters in *Virginia* are to an equal degree inevitable expressions of its structural strands; they all equally convince. Neither does social and ethical commentary impede the free movement of the characters though they have often, openly and latently, assimilated Miss Glasgow's own attitudes. Immersed so thoroughly in their Virginian milieu, these figures have the verisimilitude of natural objects in a landscape: they could not have been different, as Miss Glasgow herself said.[17] In *Virginia* the setting is so well realized and so capacious as not only to absorb the individual characters but the successive generations as well. The major characters, Virginia and Oliver, are embedded in an extended matrix organically including both themselves and the minor figures. These latter then become, in part, Jamesian "ficelles" to bear the burden of momentarily extraneous emphases.

In particular, this is the function of Miss Priscilla Batte. Like Guy Carraway in *The Deliverance,* Miss Priscilla Batte is the Jamesian "interested observer" at the start of the novel, through whom there filters our first knowledge of Virginia, Susan Treadwell, and Oliver Treadwell. The approach is indirect in Book One: of its ten chapters only two are related from Virginia's point of view, while the other eight are presented partly from the author's point of view as omniscient story teller, partly from that of Miss Batte, and partly from that of Oliver. But in the last two books of the novel Virginia's fate becomes its compositional center, and its action is then registered almost entirely in her consciousness. With the end of achieving economy through indirect characterization, Virginia Pendleton is, to a great extent, made parallel to her mother in personality and social attitudes.

In her later novels Miss Glasgow utilized a modified stream of consciousness, where, at a connected rational level, the flow of thought in an individual's mind is recorded. This technique had been adumbrated in Ben Starr's sick-bed musings in *The Romance of a Plain Man* and in Jonathan Gay's reminiscences as death approaches in *The Miller of Old Church:* it is also found in *Virginia* in the reflections upon life made by Cyrus, Oliver, and Virginia. In this rendition of Virginia's agony, for example, Miss Glasgow gets beyond summary statement to interfuse into her analysis of Virginia's mind some sense of the actual flow through it of thought and emotion:

As she sat there in silence, with her eyes on the brilliant street, where the signs of his play stared back at her under the flaring lights, she began to

think with automatic precision, as if her brain were moved by some mechanical power over which she had no control. . . . "It is not new. It has
been coming on for years," she thought. "He said that, and it is true. It is
so old that it has been here for ever, and I seem to have been suffering it
all my life—since the day I was born, and before the day I was born. It
seems older than I am. Oliver is going from me. He has always been going
from me—always since the beginning," she repeated slowly, as if she were
trying to learn a lesson by heart. But so remote and shadowy did the words
appear that she found herself thinking the next instant, "I must have forgotten my smelling-salts. The bottle was lying on the bureau, and I can't
remember putting it into my bag." The image of this little glass bottle, with
the gold top, which she had left behind was distinct in her memory; but
when she tried to think of the parting from Oliver and of all that she was
suffering, everything became shadowy and unreal again. (381)

Stylistically, *Virginia* is one of Miss Glasgow's best novels, especially
in the briskly satiric passages. In spite of its greater vigor and the larger
creative vision it embodies, *Virginia* still lacks the uniform, poised
restraint of *They Stooped to Folly* (1929) and *The Sheltered Life*
(1932). The main criticism one may make of *Virginia,* technically, is
Miss Glasgow's failure to maintain uniformly its excellence in style.
Overwriting is the chief deficiency, with a consequent addiction to the
cliché or to the consciously declamatory. The strength of Miss Glasgow's ironic vision of life in the novel, however, compensates for these
occasional lapses. The lasting impression produced by this novel is that
of a vibrant panorama in which consciousness of a brilliant past, kept
alive by the Pendletons, struggles ceaselessly and somewhat blindly with
the energetic modernity embraced by the Treadwells.

⋄VIII⋄

Fiction of the War Years and After

Life and Gabriella (1916) was written during Ellen Glasgow's voluntary exile in New York City from 1911 to 1916 following the death of Cary McCormack. It is an ambitious book but not one of Miss Glasgow's best: it betrays a too immediate involvement with Gabriella's surface problems and too little concern with more substantial issues. Miss Glasgow acknowledged in a 1914 letter to Mary Johnston the spiritual exhaustion which had its aesthetic counterpart in the deficient energy found in this work: "I am somewhat over half through a book, but the flesh and particularly the hands grow weary." [1] Even after her return to Richmond in 1916, her inspiration ran low. Accordingly she felt, rightly, that her next two books, *The Builders* (1919) and *One Man in His Time* (1922), were perfunctory; and she was evidently dissatisfied with them.

In *Life and Gabriella* Miss Glasgow once again assessed the impact upon Virginia social tradition of modernism with its rejection of inherited moral authority. Her sympathies, for the most part, lay with the "modern" Gabriella Carr as she battles "the enveloping twin powers of decay and inertia" in the Richmond of the 1890's. The distinction of the novel resides, however, in the deft, humorous projection of inflexible traditionalism in the minor characters. Sustained by a sportive tolerance and a faint mockery, the first third of the novel and its last chapter provide a lively exposé of decadent gentility. Unfortunately, the astute discrimination and the ironic objectivity which are notable in Miss Glasgow's satire of the old disappeared when she presented the new.

127

Book One of the novel, "The Age of Faith," is centered upon Gabriella's revolt against Richmond tradition in the early nineties and her subsequent marriage to George Fowler in which, despite her common sense, she succumbs to romantic illusion. Book Two, "The Age of Knowledge," recounts over a twenty-year period Gabriella's emotional recovery from her disastrous marriage and her succeeding to ownership of Dinard's, a fashionable woman's shop in New York. In her New York sojourn Gabriella illustrates the well-known tendency of those who most actively rebelled against Southern tradition after the Civil War to seek a future for themselves elsewhere, particularly in the North.[2]

In *Life and Gabriella* Miss Glasgow traced the rise of a new spirit in the South in terms of the emergence, against strong opposition, of a new independence and new opportunities for women. Although the South was fundamentally conservative on this whole question, the hardships experienced by women in the region during the Civil War and the Reconstruction paradoxically led to their enlarged freedom and to their direct agitation for increased rights.[3] The Carrs have been impoverished by the war, but Gabriella decides that she will no longer willingly endure her family's indigence. She therefore decides upon an active life, at variance with the traditional view of her sex's role in society. In Chapter 1 of Book One, her relatives suggest to her various "respectable" ways of earning money: sewing, making lampshades, crocheting, cooking, and teaching. To the consternation of her mother and her timorous relatives, Gabriella wants to work in a store and learn "business methods." She admits the attractiveness of "the sheltered life" but feels she can't "afford" it; her mother feels that Gabriella is going out of her class because she "won't stay at home and work buttonholes." Mrs. Carr's view is thus Reverend Orlando Mullen's in *The Miller of Old Church* who categorically proclaimed in one of his sermons: "No womanly woman cared to make a career" (100).

Among the many people whose dominance Gabriella resists in Richmond, her mother most fully typifies the inefficiency and hypocrisy which originate in subservience to custom. With a finely disciplined irony Miss Glasgow exhibited Mrs. Carr, "a weak person of excellent ancestry," failing always in a crisis—such as that continually provided by her daughter Jane's unhappy marriage—because her nature is to "twine," not to assert. The strength of Mrs. Carr's stubborn mind is obvious early in the novel, however, in the determined silence with which she—as a person "brought up not to do anything"—opposes the "disgrace" of Gabriella's working for a living in a shop.

Miss Glasgow emphasized Mrs. Carr's prejudices more than her ineffectual nature. Mrs. Carr guilelessly assumes, for example, that God has endowed men, but not women, with passion. Reticent and evasive, she feels that "true" women ought to be glad to lead more sheltered lives than men, and she assumes rather too confidently that the spirituality of women removes them from worldly temptation. Mrs. Carr's conventionality is amusingly revealed when she comments by letter upon Florrie Spencer's divorce from her second husband. According to Mrs. Carr, a divorcee ought to lead a semi-retired life to show that she realizes her fallen position, and under no circumstances, if she is a "pure" woman, ought she think of remarriage while her former husband is alive. She is likewise determined in her opposition to any manifestation of the modern spirit, such as suffrage for women: "I shall never knowingly bow to one [a suffragette] even if she is related to me" (406). Since the actuality continually violates Mrs. Carr's inelastic standards, she is often disillusioned by experience and drifts into a resigned pessimism. That life is too much for her languid, faintly masochistic temperament is, in fact, Mrs. Carr's one consolation. Even Gabriella's misalliance gives her the melancholy satisfaction which a martyr to life derives from the unhappiness of another.

Ellen Glasgow achieved spirited comedy in exploring with zest the domestic situation of the Graceys. Possessing all her mother's softness, moral conservatism, and humorless view of life, Gabriella's sister Jane is externally so sweet that her "virtue" becomes insufferable. Charley, her scapegrace husband, is on the other hand a personable fellow, despite his indifference to moral philosophy. Instead of reclaiming him from his "lower" nature, Jane's nagging only confirms Charley in his tendencies to waywardness; marriage changes him "from a gay bird of the barnyard into a veritable hawk of the air" (5). Jane's confident assertions of her own virtue, Miss Glasgow implied, are hypocritical since the spirit of goodness is not in them and since she does not doubt her own moral superiority. Without the "heart attack" which each time follows news of her husband's infidelity and without the elaborate ceremony of "forgiveness" which her wifely duty later imposes, Jane would, Gabriella sees, have no real motive for being. Miss Glasgow demonstrated with satiric malice that Jane's chief hypocrisy lies in an unwillingness to modify her situation by leaving Charley. Jane really loves him for his vices and, without being able to admit it, she even resents her eventual success in reforming him. His transformation into a temperance worker and a brisk Rotarian spokesman for the New South leaves her with nothing to think about and with an increased sense of self-pity at having been cheated by life. She becomes, as Charley himself had predicted, "a martyr without any martyrdom." One fundamental aspect of the woman question was, then, to persuade women themselves that they

must renounce "the crown of the martyr and the manner of the Phar-
isee," [4] in spite of the short-range advantages that they might lose
thereby.

Other minor characters in the first half of the novel, who are mostly
survivals from the South of tradition into the late nineteenth century,
Miss Glasgow also conceived with lucidity and adroitness. There is the
hard businessman with a sentimental streak concerning women, Jimmy
Wrenn, whose practical sagacity is in contrast with his mental naiveté,
"the incorruptible innocence of a man who had never imagined anything" (16). There is Uncle Meriweather, "feebly violent" in the support
of convention, whose old-fashioned complacency the capable Gabriella
continually disturbs. There are the Peterborough sisters on the second
floor of the Carr House in Hill Street whose lives are a beautiful and
futile pretense: Amelia looks back upon youthful love with a jaundiced
memory and Jemima looks back upon a loveless youth with a jaundiced
regret. There is the vivacious woman of fashion, Mrs. Spencer, whose
gossip everyone fears but who outfaces criticism by convincing people
that "she never meant any harm." There is Colonel Buffington, whom
Gabriella meets in New York, an exile from Virginia who nonetheless
characterizes the charm of manner and the barren intellect of "the old
school." As another Virginian transplanted to New York, there is Mrs.
Fowler who compensates for her evasion of moral fact by her compulsion
to maintain social appearances, and who, like Gerty Bridewell in *The
Wheel of Life,* has sacrificed peace of spirit to "the tin gods" of the
world. There are the other New York hedonists: Judge Crowborough
with his monumental vitality and ugliness, and Florrie Spencer with
whom "dash" successfully supersedes "intelligence . . . feeling . . .
imagination, virtue, breeding, or good taste" (180). There is also the
aging woman of the world in New York, the much married Madame
Dinard who ends by fighting physical decay more ruthlessly than she ever
had her business competitors.

In Arthur Peyton, Gabriella's first fiancé, Miss Glasgow more exhaustively presented an ineffectual, feminized man to symbolize the old-
fashioned, presently decadent South. To suggest how completely ingrown Arthur's nature had become, Miss Glasgow made him the victim
of a doting mother who herself is a perfect emblem of the tradition
which has formed—and enervated—her son. With firm grasp of Arthur's
psychology Miss Glasgow could comprehend the unreasoning aspect of
his opposition to Gabriella's working. Propriety is more urgent than
disconcerting facts like "poverty and starvation" to a man "whose thinking had all been done for him before he was born," and pride seems
preferable to economic security. It is ironical, then, that a conventional

man should fall irrevocably in love with an independent woman and that he should attempt to rationalize her progressive modernism out of existence. His incapacity for change also has ironical repercussions for his destiny, since he cannot give up a woman obviously not suited to him. His nobility and his generosity of response to Gabriella's "unladylike" declaration of interest in another man is as typical of the Old South which he represents, Miss Glasgow pointed out, as his irrational conservatism.

As a realist who has her hidden vein of romanticism, Gabriella responds to this admirable side of Arthur's nature when she is away from it, and she falsely idealizes him after her unhappy marriage to George Fowler. This enslavement of the realist to illusion—to the point that she gives up an admired suitor in New York, Dr. French—is one further ironic involution of Miss Glasgow's artistry; Gabriella is, in this one matter at least, as sentimental as the people she had rebelled against. When she goes back to Richmond to see Arthur after seventeen years in New York, his charm is still powerful over her, but she realizes anew how immobile and hesitant his tradition has made him. She then turns with relief from the bloodless Arthur to the energetic Ben O'Hara and is finally freed from her constricting heritage.

There are indications that Miss Glasgow less completely severed herself from admiration for Southern tradition in this book than she had in *The Miller of Old Church*. True, Miss Lancaster, at Brandywine and Plummer's store in Richmond, is seen to be engulfed by the past to the point of losing her identity separate from "a world where things happened to-day just as they happened yesterday, where no miracles had occurred since the miracles of Scripture, where people hated change, not because they were satisfied, but because they were incapable of imagination" (59). Yet she and the other impoverished gentlewomen who work at the store, Miss Glasgow insisted, possess the "courageous and yet essentially light-hearted Southern spirit" which is impressive. Although Mrs. Peyton almost annihilates her son's identity with the force of the values to which she adheres, her faith in life and her self-sufficiency are heartening to Arthur and to others: "she demanded nobility of being, and it existed; she exacted generosity of nature, and it was there" (74). Even Gabriella who rebels so loudly against tradition is a "lady" at heart and brings into the business world of New York "the finer attributes which Nature had bred in her race" (277). The satiric surface of the book is at variance in some respects, then, with Miss Glasgow's own deeply felt loyalties to her race and culture. That in an essentially "liberal" book Miss Glasgow could evince questionable reactionary tendencies is revealed by Gabriella's thoughts about the "foreign" population of New York. As if to illustrate the myth of Anglo-Saxon supremacy especially prevalent at the turn of the century, Miss Glasgow had Gabriella complain of "those lethargic foreign faces which crowded out the finer American type" and become apprehensive "before the impending destruction of higher forms by masses of inert and conscienceless matter" (390).

Despite such deviations Miss Glasgow's "liberalism" was fairly consistent in the novel. For example, she saw fit in a feministic novel to prefer through Gabriella the masculine attributes to the feminine, in that men have greater breadth of view and are less the creatures "of the elemental impulses" than women. Gabriella, accordingly, values more highly the active virtues than the passive ones: as a morally strenuous individual, she finds the meaning of life in "endeavour, enterprise, and courage." With the years she discards successive illusions and substitutes an independently derived morality for the "tradition," the "accepted opinions," "the dogmas and the ideals of the ages" which had been her inheritance.

The deterioration of Gabriella's marriage and the characterization of the irresponsible George Fowler are well-realized aspects of this novel. Miss Glasgow reversed the marital situation she had presented in *Virginia:* the disintegration of the Fowler marriage is traceable to an unintelligent man rather than to an unintellectual woman. Miss Glasgow adroitly analyzed this marriage between unequals as it declines into a struggle of opposing wills, then into mutual toleration, then into repugnance, and finally, on George's side, into hatred. George Fowler, the modern man of the world, has ironically the same inflexible attitude regarding woman's sphere and behavior as did the aristocratic, unworldly Arthur Peyton. Before they are married, George recoils somewhat from the strength of Gabriella's ardor; afterwards, he insists that she has charm for him in proportion to how little she knows about stocks or realities of any other sort.

With a strength and a sharpness her own dislike of him provided, Miss Glasgow firmly established the outlines of George Fowler's personality. Like Jonathan Gay, Jason Greylock, and George Birdsong, he is at first the good-natured man without principle who manages, through physical appeal, to win a superior woman. Like these men George Fowler is attracted by a noble nature so long as it does not interfere with his own inclinations. With firmness of touch Miss Glasgow created in him a character of some complexity who is at first a charming egoist, and finally a sadistic one. George is also a victim of the destructive potentialities of a love unregulated by the intelligence: his moral nature has unwittingly been destroyed by his mother's indulgence. Arthur Peyton and George Fowler, the two men who figure most prominently in Gabriella's sexual life, are thus, in being Oedipal sons, no match for her independence. In depicting the shabby violence of George's death from delirium tremens in Gabriella's apartment, Miss Glasgow used "naturalistic" convention in fiction to good effect. This episode augurs the quieter death from alcoholism of Jason Greylock in *Barren Ground,* a man who also dies in the home of the woman who had formerly loved him.

Despite its bright and powerful sequences, the book fails mostly because Gabriella is not an engaging individual. In a book organized so closely about its heroine, the disparity insistently present between Gabriella's alleged superiority and her actual complacency results in a personality unintentionally fractured. She is always too precisely conscious of her own attributes—of "her primal qualities of force, restraint, and capability"—for these attributes to be registered conclusively through the incidents presented in the novel. Her lack of humility, of hesitation, and of perplexity detracts from the veracity of her psychology and from the representative quality of her life. When in New York she gets to Dinard's, the world becomes her oyster. Her confidence has more bravado in it than exact knowledge of the forces arrayed against her, and it is too overweening to have been inevitably the result of hard-won experience: "Of her competence to earn a living, of her ability to excel in any work that she undertook, of the sufficiency and soundness of her resources, she was as absolutely assured as she had been when she entered the millinery department of Brandywine and Plummer" (207). Miss Glasgow, moreover, became sentimental in describing the instantaneous effectiveness of Gabriella's optimism: "The children grew and strengthened in its bracing air; Miss Polly quickly responded to it; the women in the workroom breathed it in as if it were the secret of health, and even Madame showed occasional signs that she was not entirely impervious to its vital and joyous influence" (265).

The sequences which close the book, those between Gabriella and Ben O'Hara, are likewise unconvincing. A mellowed superman, O'Hara possesses the strength without the latent brutality—and reality—of figures like Nicholas Burr, Christopher Blake, and Abel Revercomb. Nothing about O'Hara is real, neither his past history nor his psychology, neither Gabriella's priggish obsession with his cultural crudity nor her later realization that he has gotten beyond wealth and worldliness to the "broad fields of vision." Nor does his talk sound like that of a self-made man who had once been immersed in degrading circumstances. A completely idealized figure, he possesses in actuality none of the "exuberant vitality" which Miss Glasgow said was his, nor is he believably a symbol of the insurgent democratic spirit in the America of Theodore Roosevelt. A reliance upon the intellectual commonplace, when for example Gabriella convinces a fellow lodger never to underrate "the importance of food as a prop for philosophy," further diminishes the strength of a book which starts well but whose intrinsic merit vanishes when its most serious scenes begin.

Miss Glasgow's next novel, *The Builders* (1919), is interesting for its expression of Miss Glasgow's initial idealistic attitude toward the first World War. The heroine, Caroline Meade, is similar in resiliency and moral strength to Gabriella Carr but is more feminine. As a trained nurse in her early thirties she supports her three sisters and her widowed mother. She is hired by the Blackburns for their child, Letty, and at first believes the rumors about her employer's sternness and his cruelty toward his beautiful and "innocent" wife, Angelica. In Caroline's artless intruding into a tangled domestic situation and in her intensifying love for a somewhat mysterious, wealthy, but unhappily married employer, there are hints of the situations found in *Jane Eyre*. Fully aware in his turn of Caroline's integrity and self-sufficiency, David Blackburn judges her to be, at the time he entrusts Letty to her care, "a woman who had met life and conquered it, who could be trusted, he felt, to fight to the death to keep her spirit inviolate" (274).

Despite the somewhat attenuated nature of her main characters, Miss Glasgow kept firm her sense of reality in charting their love affair, as she had failed to do in the concluding scenes of *Life and Gabriella*. At the end of *The Builders* the unloved wife, Angelica, comes back a permanent invalid in mind and body; and notwithstanding her previous persecutions of him, Blackburn feels he must go back to her. If he were to seek romantic fulfillment with Caroline, he would, he feels, not only be deserting the wife he once loved when she needs him most, but he would also be violating the selfless idealism which had motivated him in the war. Caroline herself had been jilted several years before and had learned that she could still live with a broken heart. As a nurse, sometimes in touch with degrading reality, she has had to modify her youthful view that love is always ennobling; yet she manages to keep alive her early illusion to the point of believing that the best part of life is "the love that some people keep to the end." Her Southern heritage—her strong responsiveness to emotion—encourages her to love with full devotion; but her mature wisdom teaches her that love, if at times transcendent, "is not the only good." Her sense of proportion, won by experience, thus enables her to be transfigured by the passion for Blackburn which she must renounce. Though love is basically a madness and an irrationality—as in Blackburn's involvement initially with a woman unsuited to him—Miss Glasgow also maintained through Blackburn's and Caroline's attachment that, in its most permanent form, love is as deeply rooted "in thought as in desire."

Except that she is in a more modern environment and is more aggressive, Angelica Blackburn is similar to the malign, evasive Mrs. Gay of *The Miller of Old Church,* and her ostensible goodness is just as destructive. Like Mrs. Gay's, Angelica's "virtue" is poisonous because it is too abstract and lacks humanity. The principal disparity in Angelica's character consists, therefore, in public pretension to a virtue which, except for what basis it may have in the conventions, she is incapable of understanding. She assumes as a result of being trained as a "lady" that she can gratify instincts ordinarily deemed reprehensible, so long as she observes the proprieties. When it seems that her sister-in-law may marry advantageously, Angelica out of malice hastens to disrupt the engagement by securing the affections of the lover. Amusing, albeit distressing for those who see her true nature, is the ease with which she persuades everyone that duty rather than desire causes her to fulfill, at all cost, the promptings of instinct. Equally ludicrous is the widespread delusion that her special excellence lies in "bringing out the best in people."

Angelica becomes symbolic of the repressive aspects of tradition in that she is actively antagonistic to her enlightened husband and often expresses openly a timorous political conservatism. It can't be right, she feels, for a man, especially one she does not love, to doubt, or even to examine critically the principles which Virginians—and Democrats— have held for fifty years. She supports the popular view, expressed by her friend Lucy Colfax, that there is something "black" in a man who votes Republican and aligns himself with the party associated in the South with the Negro.[5] She also derides his political conviction that the World War is a moral struggle in which America must eventually become involved. When it seems her husband may really distinguish himself and become the nucleus of an independent movement in politics, she deliberately circulates untruthful rumors about his sadistic treatment of her, rumors which destroy his career. Since Miss Glasgow could utilize for presenting Angelica an irony and a malice which derives from an objective viewing of her personality, Angelica towers over everyone else in the novel and dominates its imaginative world.

In her relations with husband and wife, Caroline learns to distinguish between a genuine and a false idealism. In "Book First" ("Appearances"), she is impressed with Angelica's beauty, sweetness, and "goodness" and accepts her at her own valuation. In "Book Second" ("Realities"), Caroline comes to grasp Angelica's sinister nature and to realize,

as Blackburn had, that her virtue is only "thinness of temperament."
Concurrently, Caroline revises her earlier estimate of Blackburn and
now finds him to be a man of principle and strong vision. The chief
defect of the novel is Miss Glasgow's clumsy handling of Caroline's enlightenment. Caroline is too credulous when she first hears of the situation in the Blackburn establishment to be elsewhere the perceptive individual that Miss Glasgow depicted.

Caroline's idealism of temperament is partly elicited, and thoroughly
reinforced, through her contact with Blackburn. Actuated in large part
by nineteenth-century utopianism, Blackburn in Wellsian fashion dreams
of a more perfect human nature and of a more perfect society eventuating
from the war. He is, like other "Progressives" in his region, protesting
against the political apathy of the New South where *"laissez faire* became almost a test of Southern patriotism." [6] In his own political activity he thinks always of America's role in the future, when she will
have become a nation of real "builders" who embody their vision of a
renovated humanity in a renovated society. He feels that political
progress will ultimately depend upon the individual's instinct for rectitude and the potential perfectibility of human nature; accordingly, he
distrusts the "officialism" of tightly organized programs for social better-
ment like socialism. Despite the suffering and cruelty it has engendered,
the war has also served a spiritual purpose, Blackburn thinks, in making
men conscious of larger forces outside the self and in causing them to
see thereby that "the reality is not matter, but spirit." The intellectual
Blackburn is a mystic as well, piercing through the mask of the actual
to come at the bare substance beneath. In writing the novel Miss Glasgow also wished to set forth the relationship existing between Blackburn's vision of America's political destiny as an international power and
the reality of world war: with a German victory, America would be
unable, at home or in Europe, to realize her role as spiritual leader.

Caroline comes to see that a regenerate politics in America must look
to the future and cease to depend upon the past. Her father had wished
to set the South apart politically from the rest of the nation; but Blackburn hopes that the individualism prevalent in the South, together with
the sense of social solidarity found in the North, may provide a basis for
a renewed national consciousness and for a third political party to express
it. Such enlightened patriotism will be prepared, when the necessity occurs, to make any sacrifice required to preserve liberty when it is threatened from without.

America has at last entered the war, Blackburn contends, because
she has at last realized "that civilization is better than barbarism, that
humanity is better than savagery, that democracy has something finer

and nobler to give mankind than has autocracy" (375). Regarding the war as a means for eliminating outmoded institutions, Miss Glasgow, through Blackburn, contended that a more dynamic political economy in America would have to supplant the present government, "sentimental, evasive of realities, idealistic in speech, and materialistic in purpose and action" (22). Thus her protest against "evasive idealism" in manners and morals was, at the time of the World War, enlarged to include her sense of the political inadequacies of the age. In the closing scenes of the novel the individual's sacrifice of fulfillment in love, in the interest of preserving his spiritual integrity, is linked to the nation's foregoing of imperialistic prestige in war, in the interest of preserving political integrity.

Miss Glasgow's sense of America's international responsibilities which she expressed insistently, sometimes stridently, through Blackburn, manifested her political perceptiveness when principles were involved; but she seems to have been too far removed from the conflicting pressures operating during these years for her delineation of life in wartime America to possess much real substance. The ideology of the novel is also questionable when Blackburn elaborates his Nietzschean and Carlylean views of the political leader: "The man whom God has appointed sees his road straight before him, and he does not glance back or aside" (224). A pronounced ethnic snobbery, moreover, is found in Blackburn's exaggerated consciousness "that we Virginians are Anglo-Saxons, and that we share the sporting spirit which is ready to fight for a principle." [7]

The Builders records several interesting facets of social history: the decline in Southern political prestige after the Civil War, the partial recovery of national influence by the South with Democratic presidential victories in 1912 and 1916, the reawakening of Southern patriotism with the entry of the United States into the Great War, the permanence and inflexibility of the political machine in twentieth-century Virginia, and the assumption of the new leaders in the South (like Blackburn) that progressivism was meant for the white man alone. This last assumption at once makes the novel a typical statement and impairs its effectiveness. One cannot question Blackburn's sincerity, his contention for example that the securing of increased social and economic justice must be our main concern for the next fifty years. Nor can one doubt the validity of his bitterness against the Solid South, the one-party system, and an established machine in Virginia so reactionary that it failed, under the control of Senator Thomas Martin, to support the candidacy of a progressive native Virginian for president in 1912. Blackburn, however, reveals nowhere any concern for the disinherited among the Negroes:

racial problems are hardly ever in his mind. His attitude is essentially one of relief that the Constitutional Convention of 1901 had curtailed the Negro vote and so eliminated racial tension, for the present, as a political problem. Whether Blackburn is justified in thinking of social reform in terms of its benefits to the white man alone is, of course, a matter that Miss Glasgow need not have debated in the novel. What does detract from the novel is Blackburn's failure to perceive that the Negro exists as an unassimilated entity, and therefore as a disturbing element in the South. In the novel Miss Glasgow criticized America for an "evasive idealism" in foreign policy without noticing that she herself was being similarly evasive in her presentation of the Virginia political scene. Paradoxically this novel is less politically effective—despite its explicit concern with the present—than *Virginia* had been; in the earlier novel, Miss Glasgow at least recognized that race relations constituted "the problem of the South."

In *The Builders* Miss Glasgow failed to incorporate fully her abstract ideas into the book's organism. The analysis of these ideas—in Blackburn's talks with Caroline or with his political friends and in his letter to Caroline from France—form essays detachable from the novel instead of motivating vitally its characters. Just as Caroline's and Blackburn's passion for sacrifice and service seems too abstract and forced, so does the militant idealism evinced by Mrs. Dandridge's boarders. The vehement desire, moreover, of the elderly spinster, Cousin Matty Timberlake, to kill a few Germans herself is not carefully enough drawn forth from the strands of her personality. At the philosophical level Miss Glasgow took the war too seriously when she wrote about it in this novel. The result was that she lost sight of some of the subtleties—not to mention some of the crudities—involved in the war's effects upon the American people, even at the height of Wilsonian idealism.

Caroline's moral strength is peremptorily assumed rather than forcefully conveyed through individual incidents in the novel. Since an extraneous approval for Caroline is all too evident throughout the novel, her consciousness lacks identity in its own right, and the situations involving her, as a result, lack incisiveness. For example, her struggle with the Eternal when Letty is fighting diphtheria loses vigor because of Caroline's vaguely defined personality. In her final renunciation of Blackburn's love, moreover, she is almost fatuously preoccupied, at an articulate level, with self-sacrifice. She fails in effectiveness largely because she takes herself too seriously—this despite Miss Glasgow's contrary insistence upon Caroline's sense of humor.

Blackburn's strength of character and his idealism are also overdrawn. The sequence in which he recalls his mother and how she had inspired him to a selfless career is trite in the extreme. A like cliché of situation occurs when Caroline clasps Blackburn's hand over Letty's head and swears at his behest a lasting fidelity to the child. After Caroline's high seriousness and Blackburn's grim conscientiousness, the gossip and garrulousness of Daisy Colfax provide reassuring evidence that Miss Glasgow's spirited comic art was only in abeyance. It is an irony unintended by Miss Glasgow that a book in which she tried hardest to be portentous turned out so entirely contrived and so little impassioned.

One Man in His Time (1922) is a better book than *The Builders* though Miss Glasgow had no high opinion of it.[8] In this novel a young Richmond aristocrat, Stephen Culpeper, has been unsettled by his experiences in the World War and finds himself caught between the social traditions embodied in his family and the new energies which have made these traditions obsolete. The first twelve chapters set the conflicting forces in operation; the last twelve, in the spring season six months later, resolve them, with Stephen's decision to reject the gentility of Margaret Blair. In the book Miss Glasgow examined not only the changing social scene after the war but the expression in politics of the influences which have brought such change—the effect, in short, of energetic democratic forces, surviving from the prewar progressivism in the South, upon a cultured but devitalized aristocracy. Gideon Vetch, the present governor, represents these forces at their best, while some of his fanatic followers represent them at their worst. Vetch in fact seems to be the "one man in his time" who has had the vigor to disregard custom in the pursuit of his humanitarian ideals. Miss Glasgow's reformer in this novel, of poor white origin and once a circus rider, thus sharply contrasts with the aristocratic Blackburn of *The Builders*.

Through the Culpepers, Margaret Blair (the woman Stephen's mother has selected for him to marry), and John Benham (a gentleman and politician of the old school), Miss Glasgow scrutinized the inadequacies of a social order which "never doubted anything that was old and never discovered anything that was new" (59). With its air of "security, permanence, possession" the Culpeper house is a symbol of the once powerful but now ineffectual authority of the aristocratic tradition; and the Culpepers themselves are oblivious to all that goes on outside this citadel though the threat of an unstable future sometimes disturbs them. This family, Corinna Page feels, is too highly bred and has lost the vigor of its colonial ancestors except at times of unforeseen emergency. Its intellectual deterioration, she says, is similar to the blindness which overtakes a cave-dwelling fish when it no longer wishes to see. Completely passive and devoid of force, the genteel Mr. Culpeper is ruled by

precedent. Proper pride, "the expression of a man who hopes that he is
a Christian and knows that his blood is blue" (67), has also prevented
him from any energetic expression of the self in active life. Like her
husband, Mrs. Culpeper is impervious to the realities which exist outside her home and is so immersed in the "enchanted fairy-ring where
no fact ever entered" [9] that she cannot see, for example, the tenements
in the Culpeper estate for what they are. Political events have meaning
to her only in their personal effects—when the Great War temporarily
takes her children away or when the Governor's daughter threatens to
entangle her son. The Culpepers illustrate the tendency of their class in
the twentieth century to reject a paternalistic concern for the welfare
of others while yet holding tenaciously to the notion of paternalistic
privilege. As to Margaret Blair, she is in theory Stephen's ideal woman—
gentle, passive, unselfish, and colorless. Now that his inherited standards
have been relaxed by the war, he finds that he does not want her though
he continues to admire her.

The desiccation of the old order has had still more unfortunate effects upon Benham, Vetch's political opponent, for he has the potentialities of greatness. In contrast to the Culpepers he stands for a
potentially enlightened conservatism, with its reliance upon stability,
good sense, and moderation. But tradition forestalls the development in
him of vigor and originality. Although he criticizes Vetch for being un-
couth and for repudiating the cult of manners, Benham, with his "mental
thinness" and "emotional dryness," lacks the fine qualities of his opponent: humanity and complete dedication to a cause. Stephen concludes
that a median position between Benham's ordered, reasoned approach
to politics and Vetch's vital iconoclasm is essential. The true leader, he
feels, "must vitalize tradition and discipline progress." Of the two,
Vetch, in being more natural, more nearly attains the spirit "that comprehends, that reconciles, and recreates" (321). In refusing to go to
extremes with any faction, Vetch realizes the need in polity for the
harmonizing of conflicting interests. For attempting to prevent a disastrous general strike and for standing between the unprogressive con-
servatives and the unprincipled agitators, Vetch is destroyed by the
radicals who put him into office and who distrust his course of moderation as thoroughly as do the privileged aristocrats. Under the one-party
system in the South, strikers would often feel impelled to violence to
make themselves heard at all, while reactionary elements in the Democratic party would use such outbursts to marshal public opinion against
the workers.[10]

Vetch also illustrates Miss Glasgow's conflicting views about "modernism." Corinna Page reflects Miss Glasgow's own conception of

Vetch's complex character and his mixed influence, regarding him as a "great demagogue," who, with his "power to inspire equally devotion and hatred," is "saviour" and "destroyer" both. Vetch has freshness, sincerity, veracity, integrity, vitality, and most important of all, vision. Because his political thought is ethical rather than institutional in nature, Vetch's practical program, a kind of minimal socialism, is ultimately of less importance, his devoted follower Darrow feels, than his conviction that man must be regenerated before his environment can be modified constructively.

Vetch's positive qualities which amount to genius—his magnetism, his capacity for leadership, his ability to instill confidence in others—are counterbalanced by others more questionable. In moral stamina he transcends the directionless forces of the transitional period which has produced him, yet as the quintessence of the modern spirit, he is crude as well as vital. In its prizing of material values, in its worship of size, and in its drive for power, modern democracy, which has produced Vetch, has been as much a degrading force, Stephen feels, as an emancipating one. If it has somewhat chaotically led to increased social justice, "the progressive principle" also "makes a wilderness of beauty" and disregards the more intangible phases of Southern tradition, especially manners and a reverence for the heroic.

Perhaps Vetch satisfies his drive for power too readily by assuming that what he does must redound to the benefit of others. This assumption allows him to accept the support of unscrupulous politicians like Gershom who do not understand his principles. It could perhaps be argued, though, that Gershom's methods are not greatly different from those used by the Democratic machine. Even if, as Vetch says, he must use the tools available, the fact remains that he compromises his principles in the eyes of the public by too expedient resort to questionable methods to gain his ends. He has some of the qualities associated with the Southern "demagogue" in the twentieth century, and his aristocratic opponents in the novel do not hesitate to apply that term to him. He is allied with radical labor leaders and "new factions" in the state; he controls "the undisciplined, the half-educated, the mentally untrained" by the force of his will and eloquence. Still he is a type rare among such popular leaders, a patriot and a statesman as well as a politician. He is therefore saved from the authoritarian excesses of Robert Penn Warren's Willie Stark by his devotion to Jeffersonian principles and by his realization that he must mediate between opposing factions. As in *The Builders,* an absence of all reference to the Negro contributes to the unreality of a book which analyzes the newer type of progressive leader in the South who often secured his power not only through a vocal interest in the welfare of the common man but through appeals made to his sense of racial superiority.

Miss Glasgow was apparently less provisional in her judgment of Vetch's adopted daughter, Patty. To Stephen she represents the modern spirit, with its boldness and venturesomeness, with its violent energy and its lack of formulated purpose. Although she is too independent and too coarsened by her experience to adapt to their standards, both Stephen and Corinna find in her an indefinable and compelling attraction. In her courageous vitality she sums up Corinna's contemplated audacities in the past and Stephen's suppressed urges in the present. She may substitute, perhaps too readily, a "sporting instinct" for Victorian morality, but she wins Stephen not only by her charm but by her innate, if sometimes ill-defined, force of character.

The book is chiefly notable for the way in which Stephen Culpeper and Corinna Page, aristocrats by heritage, come to terms with the new age. They are also the principal individuals through whose minds the other characters and the incidents of the novel are presented.[11] At the outset of the novel the war has destroyed Stephen's faith in the past without giving him anything in its place, except the vision, briefly but almost universally held during the war, of a world rebuilt upon the foundations of social justice. With the fading of this vision apathy sets in. He therefore lacks the energy to break with tradition though he is more than ever irritated by its stolid inertia: the "ancestral custom of good breeding closed over him like the lid of a coffin" (200). Nevertheless, his moral sensitivity and his war-engendered disillusion with the complacency of his family overcome in time his paralysis of will—and his social exclusiveness. The act finally catches up with the liberalized idea when he chooses the vital Patty in preference to the lifeless Margaret Blair, thereby rejecting Oedipal domination by his mother. In turning from Margaret he decides to go along with the new age in thinking that his first duty is to himself.

The most revealing figure in this novel, Corinna Page, exhibits more directly than Stephen the graciousness of the older culture as it is tempered by the sincerity of democratic modernism at its best. As Miss Glasgow pointed out, the enduring part of Corinna's inheritance is her fighting spirit, akin to that evinced so often in the past by the South, and her capacity to endure with gallantry a disenchanted existence. The modern spirit, indeed, often disregards the arduous example set for it by the past, the need for discipline and for patriotism in addition to the exalting of liberty and equality. Corinna has also learned from her ancestors to reject mediocrity, "the increasing cult of the second best" (104). What they stood for—"dignity," "manners," "social culture"—

is in danger, she feels, of succumbing to a worship of the dull average. Some sense of the way things ought to be and her own steady view of things as they are, permit her, then, to assimilate the best in both the progressive and the conservative principles. An inherited decorousness, however, finally inhibits genuineness of response when, after learning the facts of Patty's birth, Corinna has momentary doubts as to Stephen's wisdom in deciding to go on with her.

One Man in His Time has some marks of a major novel, but an intellectual softness in conception and execution interferes with its full effectiveness. Corinna, who with her "royal soul" is meant to be inspiriting, becomes tiresome, for she strains too much in her nobility and is too appreciative of it herself. In curing the ills of Alice Rokeby and of Stephen, Corinna displays a nettlesome officiousness, and she influences the lives of others with an effortless ease that fails to convince: "With a little song on her lips, and her gallant head in the red hat raised to the sunlight, she went out of the house and down the steps into her car. 'Fools are very exhausting,' she thought, as she bowed to a passing acquaintance, 'but I think that she will be cured' " (315). She is patronizing not only toward those who seek her help, but toward the plebeian governor himself, who is, unfortunately, not a gentleman by birth. Corinna's interest in Patty Vetch is, moreover, condescending and proprietary, and Miss Glasgow exaggerates its importance in the novel. In the cheerful acquiescence with which Corinna gives up Benham to a worthless woman, her impossible nobility is actually immoral in implication. Corinna is so determined to do the right thing by Benham and Alice Rokeby that she fails to consider his preferences. For an intelligent woman she too peremptorily rejects an interest in public affairs. She thinks of political strife, for instance, as affording an opportunity to cure Stephen of instability, not as important in itself.

Miss Glasgow also failed to set forth perceptively the motives and the values of other characters in the novel. Stephen's self-pity, for instance, often irritates rather than incites to sympathy, for who can sustain interest in an individual who so self-consciously proclaims that he is a "prig" and that he is in "a chronic blue funk about living"? His reactions to finding slum tenements on the Culpeper estate are too naive to be significant, and his timorousness is often less typical of vociferous postwar disillusion than Miss Glasgow evidently wished it to be. Sometimes, though, his disillusionment with the war is out of proportion to the scant analysis of his mind which Miss Glasgow gave, even if her presentation of his psychic trauma is discerning. Patty's joy at securing the friendship of Corinna is likewise extreme; and her conversation with Corinna on Stephen's love for herself is too extended

for its intrinsic importance. Even Vetch's expression of his values
sometimes seems arbitrary, when, for example, in talking to Corinna
he says that he has been guided through life by the circus "fat lady's"
proverb: "When the skies fall we shall catch larks." He also pompously
declares to Corinna: "Life is all right . . . as long as there's a fighting
chance left to you. That is the only thing that makes it worth while,
fighting to win" (118). In short, a tendency to overwrite and a tendency
to overdraw the traits and sentiments of the characters detract from
the authority of this novel.

Miss Glasgow seems to have needed the leisured form of the novel
to develop her characters and situations, so that, as a short story writer,
she is not particularly adept.[12] With two exceptions her stories, collected
in *The Shadowy Third and Other Stories* (1923), are negligible because in this form she turned primarily to an investigation of the supernatural, an inquiry which did not consort well with her predominantly
realistic bent of mind. Most of the stories deal with the occult, but too
baldly and literally. The subtlety which frequently distinguished Miss
Glasgow's studies of moral conflict and of the manners of the aristocracy
is absent from most of these thinly imagined tales.

In "The Shadowy Third" a child appears as an apparition to his
mother and to the nurse-narrator of the story, although he remains
invisible to the father, Dr. Maradick. When his wife insists that she
still sees the spirit of her infant son, her husband thinks she is suffering
from delusion and has her put in an asylum. After his wife's death, Dr.
Maradick plans to marry a shallow woman who had rejected him before his first marriage and who will benefit from the first Mrs. Maradick's
money. The child again appears to the nurse, prior to the time the
doctor's wedding is to take place. At this point the doctor is killed
when he falls downstairs, the result of "an invisible judgment," the
nurse is convinced. Why the boy should be visible to the mother and
not to the father is never satisfactorily developed, nor are the relations
clear between the doctor and the women with whom he is involved.
In "Dare's Gift," otherwise a mediocre tale, Miss Glasgow stated the
belief which she had also expressed in *One Man in His Time* through
Corinna Page, that in Virginia "the personal loyalties have always been
esteemed beyond the impersonal." [13] Miss Glasgow made clear her
views on the psychological nature of time in this story: it is, she has
her narrator conclude, "the high moments that make a life, and the
flat ones that fill the years" (104). In "A Point in Morals" she had
concluded in 1899, as she did later in "Dare's Gift," that the highest

civilization is the one which places the highest value upon the individual life.[14]

The two best stories in the collection are "The Difference" and "Jordan's End," stories of real life rather than the supernatural. In "The Difference" Miss Glasgow enlarged upon her familiar theme that women love with their imaginations and whole souls, whereas most men love only with their senses. George Fleming makes light of an affair with Rose Morrison to his wife, Margaret, thus revealing to her his essential triviality. Margaret now sees that she has been too easily satisfied with the second best. She comes, therefore, to despise her husband more than his mistress and actually to feel for her an unconventional bond of affection, originating in "woman's immemorial disillusionment" with man.

In "Jordan's End" Miss Glasgow effectively presented a physically decadent aristocratic family, the Jordans. This family has deteriorated because of hereditary insanity deriving, in part, from too much inbreeding. When Miss Judith marries into the family, she is happy with Alan Jordan, her husband, for three years until the hereditary taint shows up in him. At this point, she sees her life stretch out bleakly before her and is overcome by the thought of her physically strong husband miserable for years in an asylum. Three days later the doctor discovers that Alan is dead and that all the opiate he had left behind is gone. In spite of his suspicions, the doctor will never know how the husband died. He cannot question Judith because she is too impersonally removed from her own misfortune: "she was beyond all consolation and all companionship. She was nearer to the bleak sky and the deserted fields than she was to her kind" (291). For once Miss Glasgow wrote with power and discernment about the completely degenerate aspects of the South, and in this short narrative anticipated major works like *The Sound and the Fury.*

⬥ IX ⬥

"The Perpetual Broomsedge": Barren Ground

Miss Glasgow thought *Barren Ground* her best book; with its single-ness and sobriety of vision, it is one of her strongest. During the hiatus in her creative energies which set in after the publication of *Virginia*, she evidently bore the idea for *Barren Ground* within her mind, but was unable to start writing on the book before 1921 or 1922.[1] In a letter to Hugh Walpole she confessed that she was conscious of a falling off in achievement after *Life and Gabriella* and that she had "slipped somehow . . . away from what I had won"; in the writing of *Barren Ground* she became conscious that she was gaining back all that she had lost and more.[2] The experience which drained her of vitality and creative power was the affair with Harold S——, as she told us in *The Woman Within*. It was only when emotion waned that she repossessed her spirit and wrote *Barren Ground* as, among other things, a gesture of liberation. In a reminiscent letter to Signe Toksvig in 1944 she recalled that the novel "was torn out of myself," and written "in one of those blessed pauses that fall between the 'dark wood' of the soul and the light on the horizon." [3] Not only did the book set her free from her past and indicate the direction that her future might take, but it seemed to her to sum up all that was significant in her experience.[4]

A spaciousness unique in Miss Glasgow's fiction derives from her

146

symbolic use of the land: the wastes of broomsedge at Pedlar's Mill—
in the Piedmont region of Virginia—dominate characters and action in
the novel, much in the way that bleak Egdon Heath pervades Hardy's
The Return of the Native. In both novels, too, the degree to which the
principal characters can adjust to primitive existence close to nature
determines their fortunes. The relationships fully probed in *Barren
Ground* between characters and their native region demonstrate that
Miss Glasgow was responsive to Southern agrarian sentiment and
that she also anticipated the preoccupation of later twentieth-century
Southern writers with the inescapable influence of soil upon soul.[5]

The omnipresent broomsedge becomes a symbol of fatality in the
novel—a potentially hostile force to those who must live with it.
From the first, Dorinda Oakley has a sense of the land's intent to
close in upon the farmers of Pedlar's Mill who struggle endlessly to
conquer it. One chief aspect of the book comprises Dorinda's efforts to
frustrate its sinister influence. When the broomsedge intrudes upon the
Oakley Farm, she is oppressively aware that it does not relinquish what
it catches, that the more determinedly it is grubbed out one year the
more vigorously it thrives the next. The one-man tragic chorus in the
novel, old Matthew Fairlamb, a creaking figure of doom as ancient
as the landscape, contends that "you've got to conquer the land in the
beginning, or it'll conquer you before you're through with it" (14).

At the close of the novel the broomsedge is potentially triumphant
once again at Pedlar's Mill. After the first World War, when the high
cost of labor brings ruin to many farmers, the broomsedge is ready to
absorb the cultivated fields and to bring the roads into disrepair. This
circular aspect and continuity of the processes of nature is implicit in
the undulatory images used to describe the motion of the broomsedge
wastes (and of other phenomena like the wheat fields and the patches
of life-everlasting in the autumn) or the progress of light and shadow
across them:

Wave by wave, that symbol of desolation [the broomsedge] encroached in a
glimmering tide on the darkened boundaries of Old Farm. (107)

A slow procession of shadows was moving across the broomsedge, where
little waves of light quivered and disappeared and quivered again like ripples
in running water. (252)

These flowing and ebbing rhythms also characterize the pattern of the
year so that in retrospect the same season from different years seems
but one season to Dorinda. As she looks forward at the end of the
novel to experiencing repeatedly this cycle of the year, she finds herself immersed again in the ceaseless energies of nature: "The spirit of

the land was flowing into her, and her own spirit, strengthened and refreshed, was flowing out again toward life" (449).

To Dorinda's animistic sensibility the land and the things it affects become living forces and objects. For her the land wears "the expression
of an animal that man has forced into sullen submission," but one
which is only waiting for the most propitious time to turn against him.
Even the house in which she lives, when seen at a distance, seems to
her "a frightened thing," huddling close to the earth as if to escape
disaster, while the surrounding landscape comes alive like a beast
waiting to devour it. Miss Glasgow did not hesitate to utilize kinetic
imagery of this sort—in essence, the pathetic fallacy—to give the land
a forceful, vigorous life of its own. Thus in the late summer of Jason's
courtship of Dorinda, the broomsedge "sprang up in a running fire
over the waste places"; on the journey to Aunt Mehitable, Dorinda is
conscious of "the perturbed murmur and movement of the broomsedge";
when she returns from New York, the landscape at dawn seems to be
"flying upward to meet" the day; and at the time of her marriage to
Nathan Pedlar, "the landscape looked as if it were running away from
the wind." [6] The distinctive sounds of this country alternate with its
strange silences to establish its elusive aspect, while the continually
shifting colors and lights of the broomsedge mirror subtly the ever-
changing moods of nature.

From the time of her mother's mental disturbance as a young woman,
Dorinda has felt that the land exerts a terrifying power, working for
good and evil. She realizes that she and her parents derive inevitably
from the same spare soil as do "the scant crops and the exuberant
broomsedge," that the land has entwined itself into the basic fibers of
their beings. This relationship between soil and its inhabitants Miss
Glasgow made explicit in describing how the farmers of Queen Elizabeth
County have devoted centuries to uprooting broomsedge—the wild
and the free in nature—and to uprooting the free, spontaneous, sometimes sinful impulses in human nature itself. In either direction these
efforts have only been partly successful, since the broomsedge lurks always at the edges of the cultivated land to repossess it and since the
primitive instincts in man's nature lurk always beneath a superstructure
of the civilized to reassert their power. Despite her Calvinist upbringing,.
Dorinda responds to primitive impulses in her attempt to kill Jason
after he betrays her. In the almost hysterically religious Mrs. Oakley
herself, there is a wild streak which she has been able to sublimate only in
intense visions of missionary endeavor amid splendors of tropical lands.

The Oakleys have given all their energies to the farm, only to get
nothing in return. Mrs. Oakley's face, "with its look of blended physical

pain and spiritual ecstasy," suggests to Dorinda the harsh but in-spiriting countryside in which her mother has always lived. Old Farm may have swallowed up Mrs. Oakley's life, but Dorinda knows at the same time that leaving the farm would be death for her mother. Even more pitiably, Dorinda's father, Joshua, a product of the soil even to the stale briny odor which exudes from him, struggles against the impersonal power of the land to no productive end. He thus reveals the same steady but frustrated effort to conquer his surroundings evinced by John Bergson in Willa Cather's *O Pioneers!* Resignation to his fate, "the earth's passive acceptance of sun or rain," not an active rebellion against it, characterizes Joshua. Miss Glasgow confirmed the submerged grandeur in his nature by continually associating his counte-nance with that of the youthful John the Baptist pictured in the Oakley Bible. To Dorinda her father is both archetypal and inarticulate. As she sees him in the dawn looking out over his acres, he seems prehistoric, at the same time that he has in his eyes the expression "of a dog that is uncertain whether he is about to receive a pat or a blow" (47).

If he lacks the chief defect of the poor whites in general, the tendency to "slight," he is still inherently inefficient and a failure because he lacks the knowledge and the energy that would enable him to farm differently from his forefathers. Many independent farmers in the South were thus no more prosperous after the Civil War than before.[7] The old one-crop system (tobacco in Virginia and North Carolina, cotton elsewhere) flourished while it impoverished the soil; capital was often impossible to secure or else the interest rates were exorbitant; and declining farm prices after the Civil War meant agricultural depression. At Pedlar's Mill, Joshua and his class distrust all departures from agricultural tradition, such an innovation, for example, as rotation of crops: "a corn-field at Pedlar's Mill was as permanent as a grave-yard" (16). The new manner of farming also emphasized the need for raising livestock and legumes to supplement the staple crops and to provide fertilizer for a worked-out soil. The pathos of her father's death resides in the contrast between his valiant efforts and their inefficacy in the cosmic scheme. His death, Miss Glasgow wryly observed, means no more than a tree's falling and disintegrating into the earth which had sustained it. In a talk with Jason, Dorinda had quoted her father on the disastrous effects of the tenant system, in widespread use after the war: "No man will work himself to death over somebody else's land" (27). Though Joshua Oakley owns his land and is superior thereby to the tenants who surround him, he is unable to borrow money easily; he would possibly be too apathetic to do so, even if he could. Dorinda triumphs where her father had failed, not only because her energies

are more forcefully directed but because her New York friends lend her
the money with which to farm "progressively."

The land, in Miss Glasgow's conception, often simultaneously causes
an individual to suffer and endows him with an invulnerable tranquillity. If Joshua senses that the farm has crushed him, he has, nevertheless, Dorinda feels, exchanged for a merely human perspective a
serenity which is superhuman. To Dorinda in later years, the farm is
associated with the brooding aspect of her father's face. In his spiritual
responsiveness to the elements Joshua is typical of the other farmers
in the district who frequent Nathan Pedlar's store and whom Miss
Glasgow described in a style memorable for its pithy, close-grained
quality:

The few farmers who had lounged about the track were now waiting in the
store, while Nathan weighed and measured or counted small change into
callous palms. Here and there a negro in blue jeans overalls stood patiently,
with an expression of wistful resignation which was characteristic less of an
individual than of a race. There was little talk among the white farmers,
and that little was confined to the crops or the weather. Rugged, gnarled,
earth-stained, these men were as impersonal as trees or as transcendental
philosophers. In their rustic pride they accepted silence as they accepted
poverty or bad weather, without embarrassment and without humility. If
they had nothing to say, they were capable of sitting for hours, dumb and
unabashed, over their pipes or their "plugs" of tobacco. They could tell a
tale, provided there was one worth the telling, with caustic wit and robust
realism; but the broad jest or the vulgar implication of the small town was
an alien product among them. Not a man of them would have dared recite
an anecdote in Pedlar's store that Dorinda should not have heard. The
transcendental point of view, the habit of thought bred by communion with
earth and sky, had refined the grain while it had roughened the husk. (63)

This same dignity "inherent in all simple, profound, and elemental
forces" also characterizes Negroes like Aunt Mehitable Green who
have attuned themselves to the nuances of nature's moods. With its
dominant aspect of weariness passing over into a suggestion "of un-
resisting fortitude," the landscape itself becomes a symbol, among
other things, of the strong qualities in Dorinda's nature. Her struggle
with adversity and her refuge in fortitude are authentic in the novel since
the landscape, in its granite endurance, emphasizes independently
Dorinda's own moral force.

The cruelty of the land to those who do not adjust to its stern power
is seen in the fate of the Greylocks: the elder Greylock, the son Jason,
and Geneva, Jason's wife. As for the elder Greylock the monotony
of life at Pedlar's Mill has led him to drink and to sexual dissipation.

The completeness of his degeneration—and later, that of his son—is suggested by the inexorable way the sumac, sassafras, life-everlasting, and broomsedge devour the fields at Five Oaks, once the Greylocks lose the will to farm them and to keep them subdued. Between Jason and the landscape there has been alienation from the time he returned from school. Since his character is not equal to his intelligence, he is unable to concentrate upon his constructive impulses, his ambition, for instance, to bring back the exhausted land to health. Ironically, Miss Glasgow had his vision of a restored earth realized by the woman he has betrayed, when she has come to hate him and when he is sinking deep into alcoholism. With finesse Miss Glasgow demonstrated how father and son, oppressed by nature, are in turn cruel and remiss toward others, precisely because they are out of harmony with their surroundings. Old Greylock has only sadistic contempt for his son; and Jason causes Dorinda and Geneva, his wife, much suffering because of the weaknesses he himself admits to possessing. In her pitiful insanity and accidental death from drowning, Geneva Greylock is a pathetic Ophelia-like figure. From her fate we can gather the indifference of the land toward those who, because of temperamental fastidiousness, cannot adjust to its ruggedness.

This excellent novel has as its central insight the paradox that Dorinda is both victor and victim in her struggle with the soil. The land exerts a powerful spell upon her which she must listen to in the end. She therefore returns from New York City to a countryside far less inviting in the actuality than it had seemed in her imagination when she was away from it. Yet the grimness of her existence on the land is offset by her sense of a kinship with its strength "filtering through her blood into her brain," a feeling compounded of "pity, memory, and passion." Though Dorinda squanders her youth in restoring the "dead land to life," she has her reward, after her night of spiritual travail at the end of the novel, in her knowledge that "the land would stay by her" until the end. When she is reclaiming the Greylock farm and fires the scrub pine and sassafras and broomsedge, she has the sense that all her past illusions of romance are being consumed; such is the exaction imposed by nature for control of the land. Only ascetics like Dorinda or the Alexandra Bergson of Miss Cather, who no longer dissipate their energies in gratifying the impulses of the flesh, can summon the force to bring the land to heel. Mastery of the impersonal powers of nature is assured only when mastery of the self is complete. Dorinda occasionally feels that she may have paid too high a price for her success, but such misgivings are, for the most part, momentary.

With greater concentration than she had marshalled in *The Miller of Old Church,* Miss Glasgow again utilized the countryside to harmonize with the emotions of her characters or else to contrast ironically with them. The countryside is therefore presented at different seasons to complement fully the ranges of feeling expressed in the novel. To accord with Dorinda's inner mood while she dreams of romance, the awakening spring is seen in conjunction with awakening passion: the landscape is suffused with light to suggest the brightness of her thoughts. To accord with her secret misgivings when she listens to Jason's complaints about life at Pedlar's Mill, the broomsedge becomes impenetrable in the dusk. She has her first hint, moreover, of some division from him during summer heat and drought, while the tobacco plants turn yellow, the corn wilts, and the tomatoes blister to a pulp in the sun. When she goes to see Aunt Mehitable Green and learns that she is pregnant by Jason, it is a threatening October day; and as she faints away there, she feels that "the broomsedge plunged forward, like a raging sea, and engulfed her" (118).

After she has learned of Jason's perfidy, her soul becomes barren ground, withered and blackened like the fields after the broomsedge has been burnt out, and brightness passes from the scene. But when in contrast to the bleakness of her soul she cannot deny the beauty of the landscape, she is in torment, since part of her suffering springs from her present sense of divorcement from nature. In effect, the placid beauty of the October countryside forces her to come to the decision to turn from it and her suffering and to go to New York. She then leaves at dawn in a drizzling rain, the surrounding fields answering to the blankness of her mood and suggesting in their stillness her own solitude of spirit. "The dull glow of the broomsedge" is her last impression of this countryside as she leaves behind a ruined youth. When she is in New York the broomsedge lives at the edges of her memory and causes her to experience again at intervals the sufferings of the past; in another mood, its powerful spell becomes inescapable and draws her back to Virginia. Most of the crucial scenes in the book—Dorinda's betrayal, her departure for New York, her brother's involvement in Peter Kittery's murder, her mother's perjury and death, her marriage to Nathan Pedlar, and Jason's death—take place against the broomsedge in the autumn and establish an autumnal melancholy as the dominating mood of the novel.

Dorinda realizes once again the depth of her affinity with the earth when, in a revulsion against sex after Jason Greylock's betrayal of her, she refuses the hand of Dr. Burch and denies the personal relationships which Miss Glasgow in other books valued so highly. The farm, she feels, represents more than soil to be tilled. In it resides an inscrutable force which forever promises renewal after disillusionment—the land becomes "the birthplace and burial ground of hopes, desires, and disappointments" (233). If Dorinda too readily assimilates the knowledge needed to set up a successful farm, this unreality is offset in Miss Glasgow's having conveyed Dorinda's sense of inadequacy before her task of reclaiming the abandoned fields, toward whose poetry and chill indifference she is consistently sensitive. That nature is the one inescapable reality Dorinda acknowledges, even with some feeling of relief, when, the night before the inquest concerning the murder of Peter Kittery, the cows have to be milked, in spite of Mrs. Oakley's anxiety for her culprit son, Rufus. Both the material and immaterial aspects of nature thus possess for Dorinda more durable existence than do human beings and their emotions.

Purely man-centered struggles like the Great War seem also unreal, if not trivial, when they are referred to earth and air and to the broomsedge covered with snow: nature lifts Dorinda beyond humanity into consciousness of a transcendent Power. At such times she is glad that her destiny has made her the bride of the soil rather than that of any man. At other times, the beauty of the spring or the hint of desolation in the autumn landscape troubles Dorinda with a suggestion of emotional unfulfillment in her own life, and she feels a vague restlessness stirring deep within her being for the experiences she has never had and for the truth she has not yet reached. Her independent force and sexual coldness find their register in her implied sense of kinship with the elements on the winter night when Nathan meets his death, when land and air have been refined by the snow "into some frigid zone of the spirit." This ingenious interweaving of Dorinda's emotions and the stark incidents of the narrative with vital nature produces that unity of impression and effect which is one measure of the artistry of this novel.

Barren Ground is organized about Dorinda's sexual experiences, unimportant as she sometimes declares them to be in contrast to the abiding earth with which she is so fully in harmony. The first movement of the novel (Part One) is relatively static until violence overcomes Dorinda at Jason's betrayal; it covers one year, 1894–95, when Dorinda is twenty, and is appropriately entitled "Broomsedge," since broomsedge, the adjunct of barren ground and of wild nature, physically and symbolically dominates this section. The second movement of the novel (Part Two: "Pine") covers the years from twenty-one to thirty-eight in Dorinda's career. The chief episode is Dorinda's marriage, never consummated, to a man she does not love, Nathan Pedlar, just as the main incident in "Broomsedge" had been her abandonment by the man she had loved. The central image of the harp-shaped pine, with its living roots in the family graveyard, denotes both the great endurance by which Dorinda overcomes her personal frustrations to become a success as a farmer and the continuity of life itself amid the presence of death. In the concluding movement (Part Three: "Life-Everlasting"), Dorinda's career from forty-two until fifty (the years 1916–24) is traced. Most salient in this section is the contrast between Dorinda's deserved but somewhat sterile triumph over the land and her nursing the man she had once loved until he dies, a victim of his own inertia and of alcoholism. Despite Dorinda's loveless existence and Jason's wasted energies, eternal renewal is still possible through the agency of earth, the donor of "life-everlasting." The silvery radiance and the pollen of this flower suffuse this part of the book, connoting at once the elusive beauty and the vital abundance of nature. This flower, which flourishes in the autumn, again accentuates the somber atmosphere characteristic of the novel.

Miss Glasgow analyzed with fidelity the inner lives of the human beings set against the land. In the early sections of the novel she described typical descendants of the Presbyterian pioneers in frontier Virginia. In spite of their outwardly prosaic lives, these settlers were so thoroughly immersed in the subjective intensities of their religion that they became romantics in spirit. Mrs. Oakley, their descendant, exposes this romanticism of her grandfather, John Calvin Abernathy, when she mentions that he had only come to religion with rapt intent after he had thirsted for blood.[8] In contrast to Joshua Oakley, the "poor white" who eventually inherits the ancestral acres, Abernathy throve on the land, which responded to his qualities of "integrity, firmness, and frugality." Both the worldly energy and the otherworldly enthusiasm of her grandfather survive in Mrs. Oakley.

In a still different manner John Abernathy's Presbyterianism is a formative influence upon his great-granddaughter, Dorinda. In her the evangelistic impulse to redeem the world is transmuted into a passion to restore the attenuated life in abandoned fields. She is aided in this endeavor by the virtues which had enabled the Virginia pioneers, like John Abernathy, to endure and prosper in a hostile wilderness: "Firmness of purpose, independence of character, courage of living, these attributes, if they were not hers by inheritance, she had gleaned from those heavy furrows of her great-grandfather's sowing. 'Once a Presbyterian, always a Presbyterian,' her mother had said when she was dying." [9]

No less a theme in the novel than the moral pervasiveness of religious inheritance is Miss Glasgow's insistence that the memory of love's sweetness continues to haunt at a physical plane, when, at a conscious plane, love has turned to hate. Much of the pain associated with a love broken off by violence, by infidelity, or by indifference, Miss Glasgow asserted, is caused by the survival in the senses of an emotion which the mind and the spirit despise. Aching memories of Jason's sexual magnetism remain in Dorinda's nerves, despite her conscious efforts to eradicate his presence from her being. Dorinda is, in some sense, a modern Medea, as James Branch Cabell pointed out,[10] and like her prototype she becomes the psychological prisoner of the man who has betrayed her. In the concluding sequences Dorinda—who has more cause to feel outrage at Jason than anyone else at Pedlar's Mill and who would be glad to abrogate his claim over her if she could—is the only one who will take him in. Physical intimacy thus establishes psychological bonds which can only be nominally broken. If love is most often ephemeral, there is paradoxically no substitute for its intensities. By brooding over her lost ecstasy in spite of her determination to forget love, Dorinda tacitly concedes its pervasive power; and by her very aversion to sexual emotion, she tacitly acknowledges its force.

If Dorinda gains a final optimism as a result of her sheer ability to endure, it is, as Miss Glasgow pointed out, only "a cheerful cynicism," and a philosophy which does not have much basis in "any convincing lesson of experience." The strongest sections of the novel are those which express Dorinda's sense of futility, despite her intermittent sense of renewal from contact with the land: ultimately she looks forward to "the ample leisure of the time when she should expect nothing" (401). "The gnawing worm at the heart of experience" is her sense of disenchantment that nothing lasts, that love and hatred, too, pass before they can be completely known. Her later success with the farm brings depression rather than elation because she continually contrasts her present prosperity with the deprivation of her parents' lives in the past. When in his last days Jason comes to stay with her, she finds her sense of futility aggravated by thoughts of the contrast between Jason as youth and dying drunkard: "How futile, how unnecessary, it had all been,—her love, her suffering, her bitterness." [11]

In her indeterminism—her view that the active will governs a person's success or failure in life—Miss Glasgow was at times so insistent as, paradoxically, to seem deterministic. In order to affirm the superiority of Dorinda, Miss Glasgow too emphatically built up her heroine and too expeditiously brought about the defeat of Jason by moral weakness and by circumstance. He is a forcefully drawn character but an unequal antagonist for Dorinda. His "bad blood" is too undiluted, his lack of hereditary fiber too pronounced, for the result to be other than it is. A more completely presented struggle in Jason with fatality would have made Dorinda's own exertions more compelling; as it is, the contrast between Dorinda's success and her lover's failure is too stark. Dorinda has so sure an idea of her goal that not much freedom is given her, after all, to choose among perplexing alternatives, to exercise in the tangled exigencies of ordinary life that mastery presupposed in the heroic dimensions which Miss Glasgow used to limn her moral nature.[12]

Less interest accrues to Dorinda's life as farmer than to the symbolic encounters with the land, previously analyzed. Miss Glasgow recounted Dorinda's struggles with the soil in a concentrated manner which assures power for the book. Yet certain complexities involved in the situation become blurred: the tentative effort, the false start, and the abortive enterprise ought to figure more than they do in Dorinda's career. Her heroine's singleness of vision is so positively described that the emotional register of the book becomes thin. A greater dryness and spareness than was necessary characterizes the texture of the novel and prevents it from becoming, at all times, a full transcription of human psychology with its inconsistencies as well as its consciously defined ambitions. There is, in short, too great a disjunction between the depth of Dorinda's emotional life—wherein she does respond to the irrational—and the oversimplified nature of her daily existence. Miss Glasgow also too easily approved of Dorinda's most questionable quality, her arrogance. Miss Glasgow evidently did not see that Dorinda's sense of superiority could be irritating as well as admirable. By romanticizing her heroine's chief deficiency, Miss Glasgow was unable to sustain complete interest in her and in her fortunes. A more candid appraisal of her protagonist's qualities might have led Miss Glasgow more often to the deepest levels of Dorinda's personality.

A few of the scenes also betray a strain for effect rather than an effect inevitably attained. This strained quality is pronounced in the New York sequences. Dorinda's miscarriage is too contrived in allowing Miss Glasgow to get rid of an intrusive minor character, Dorinda's illegitimate child. Furthermore, her winning the confidence of the Faraday family is too direct, her dismissal of Dr. Burch is too peremptory, and her reactions to symphonic music are possibly too strident. Only when the land is in the background does the narrative sweep on with full momentum and attain the full intensity which Miss Glasgow desired. In these "broomsedge" sections Miss Glasgow maintained a consistency of tone and a veracity of outlook which are impressive. The one exception is the part of the novel which relates the death and heroism of

Nathan Pedlar. The scenes here are the most unreal in the whole chronicle, not because they lack—like those in New York—emotional force, but because they carry unwarranted emphasis. Miss Glasgow was so highly laudatory of Nathan's virtues that they do not seem quite genuine; too many people after his death unrelievedly sing his praises. One chief defect in the novel is Dorinda's offhand and unintelligent dismissal of Nathan's good qualities prior to his death and her casual expediency in marrying him. As a result his heroism is inadequately prepared for and his elevation to a kind of "popular sainthood" has little relevance to the informing center of the book, Dorinda's consciousness.

Despite all such reservations, the book has many merits which give it power. Chief among these is Ellen Glasgow's ironic vision which, while remaining in the background, shapes the unfolding panorama of the novel. This vision depends chiefly for effect upon the reversals brought about by the years in a character's situation and fortunes. When she questions early in the novel how Rose Emily could have married Nathan Pedlar, Dorinda then has no way of foreseeing that she herself will marry him. When, in the determined spirit of her Calvinist forebears, Dorinda proclaims that she will not allow any man to spoil her life, she does not know that such resolutions can be nullified by powerful emotion. Her whole situation is the painful one of the strong woman, in all innocence, putting herself into the power of a weak man; her struggles to free herself of Jason's ascendancy over her, as we have seen, are only partly successful. At the beginning of Jason's final illness, the contrast between her standing by the poorhouse wall and the ecstasy of the meetings on the summer nights thirty years before is full of pain for her. Quite unintentionally, Jason prefigures his own fate when he says that if he stays in the country for life, he is sure to take to drink or worse. In the case of Nathan Pedlar, Dorinda misses him for the first time the night of his fatal accident, when, significantly, it is too late. His whole fate is meant to be ironical, since dead he gets all the esteem and affection he had never had when he was alive.

Not only the concentration of Ellen Glasgow's irony, but other aspects of her artistry confer distinction upon this book. Miss Glasgow endeavored to subordinate, when she could, the expression of her own ideas to the over-all contours of the novel. She thus skillfully used old Matthew Fairlamb to reflect some of her own views. The old man, close to the soil for so long, possesses an oracular, cynical wisdom which accords with the strength of Miss Glasgow's own disillusioned view of life. Other minor figures like Aunt Mehitable Green or the members of

Dorinda's own family are sharply etched in, and take their place as necessary persons in Dorinda's world even when they are encountered briefly. The tableaus of farm life, in their realism and pictorial immediacy, inevitably recreate the country scene: the Oakleys' gathering around the fireside in silence after the day's work, Joshua Oakley's struggles with tobacco to make it grow, Mrs. Oakley's drying of apples, and so on. Miss Glasgow's marked ability as a writer to create sequences of parallel significance and to use them to intensify each other is abundantly present in this novel. As Dorinda's love for Jason dies its violent end, for example, so does Rose Emily, Nathan Pedlar's wife, die of tuberculosis. Dorinda's success at reclaiming the land gains added force when constantly counterpointed with Jason's moral decline. Subsequently her prosaic marriage with Nathan is intensified by being contrasted with the ardor of her early romantic feeling for Jason.

The impact of the novel, in large part, depends upon Miss Glasgow's skillful handling of the passage of time, so that the years go by naturally and inevitably. Time passes unobtrusively because the generations are linked with each other. Thus Dorinda repeats enough of her parents' experiences to evolve in her own life a pattern similar to that found in the generations of her forebears. She concludes that the bleakness of her existence will end in the same round of ceaseless activity as had characterized her mother's life, to disguise a similar sense of unfulfillment. Time thus reduces the individual quality of experience to a less exciting racial norm. The unchanging aspect of time has for counterpart the unchanging aspect of the basic features in the landscape; thus time, like the landscape which it has conditioned, seems to wear the aspect of eternity. In this novel time and space unite to dwarf the significance of the human actors and their problems; in Miss Glasgow's own words, "the land and the sky, time and space, are the great harmonies" [13] to which the artist ought to be sensitive.

Both the uncertainties and merits of the novel are reflected in its style. If commonplace sentiments in the novel are recorded in a commonplace style, at times of great emotional stress in the action Miss Glasgow wrote with enviable energy and directness. In this long novel there are flat and verbose passages, the occasional presence, in particular, of the trite or the inept comparison—"bring order out of chaos," "caught like a mouse in the trap of life," "unfathomable as the sea," and so on. In the main, however, the style of the novel admirably evinces the strength inherent in the situations which Miss Glasgow presented.

In the first chapters, Miss Glasgow established a superior artistry through a varied style. She made use, for example, of the sonorous periodic sentence with its stately rhythms to convey the grandeur and the austerity of the landscape. To communicate concurrently some of its harsh and rugged atmosphere, Miss Glasgow combined with these rhythms a terse, epigrammatic mode of expression. With this dignified, yet vigorous style Miss Glasgow recounted the many attempts made by adventurous farmers to conquer the "old fields":

Now and then a new start would be made. Some thrifty settler, a German Catholic, perhaps, who was trying his fortunes in a staunch Protestant community, would buy a mortgaged farm for a dollar an acre, and begin to experiment with suspicious, strange-smelling fertilizers. For a season or two his patch of ground would respond to the unusual treatment and grow green with promise. Then the forlorn roads, deep in mud, and the surrounding air of failure, which was as inescapable as a drought, combined with the cutworm, the locust, and the tobacco-fly, against the human invader; and where the brief harvest had been, the perpetual broomsedge would wave. (4)

When Miss Glasgow described the pioneer stock of the region as divided into "good people" and "good families," she used a wit subdued to an assured knowledge of her subject. Through such a style she secured not only a full control of her medium but also an ability to comment implicitly, as well as explicitly, upon her materials:

Though Queen Elizabeth County had never been one of the aristocratic regions of Virginia, it was settled by sturdy English yeomen, with a thin but lively sprinkling of the persecuted Protestants of other nations. Several of these superior pioneers brought blue blood in their veins, as well as the vigorous fear of God in their hearts; but the greater number arrived, as they remained, "good people," a comprehensive term, which implies, to Virginians, the exact opposite of the phrase, "a good family." The good families of the state have preserved, among other things, custom, history, tradition, romantic fiction, and the Episcopal Church. The good people, according to the records of clergymen, which are the only surviving records, have preserved nothing except themselves. (4)

With a similar pungency Miss Glasgow commented upon Virginia politics, when urban influences began to predominate over the rural and the depressed farmer migrated to the city to make his fortune and to become corrupted by organized politics: "The old men stayed by the farms, and their daughters withered dutifully beside them; but the sons of the good people drifted away to the city, where they assumed control of democracy as well as of the political machine which has made democracy safe for politics" (5).

A parallel concision in some of the characterizations and descriptions in the book give it pace, a quality sometimes lacking in the lengthy novel of rural life. Examples of Miss Glasgow's crystalline, caustic vein are the description of Almira Pryde (Dorinda's cousin) as uniting "the physical burden of too much flesh to the spiritual repose of too little mind," the description of Dan (Mr. Oakley's horse) as having "the doleful face of a Presbyterian gone wrong," and the description of Dorinda's thoughts concerning her relations with men: "She felt that the hidden flaw in her relations with men was her inability to treat a delusion of superiority as if it were a moral principle." [14]

Also generating force in the novel is Miss Glasgow's—or Dorinda's —use of understatement and of stylistic compression in the summary comments made upon situations in the narrative. There is the authority of finality, for example, in Dorinda's reaction, as she comes out of her swoon, to definite knowledge of Jason's defection: "And while life fought its way into her, something else went out of her for ever—youth, hope, love—and the going was agony" (135). This same concentrated force characterizes Dorinda's judgment of Jason after she does not see him for several years: "He was not yet forty, but life had already used him up and flung him aside" (314). At the aesthetic level, this fairly consistent compression of style is the equivalent, at the philosophical level, of the measured cynicism which is Dorinda's fairly consistent approach to life. The sustained combination of a unified stylistic texture and a unified philosophical tone is the quality which most definitely constitutes the merit of *Barren Ground.*

"The Brilliant Air
of the Mind":
The Comedy of Manners

Ellen Glasgow's comedies of manners, *The Romantic Comedians* and *They Stooped to Folly*, were the result of recoil from her long pre-occupation with "the sense of tragic life" while she was writing *Barren Ground*.[1] Her realization of the disorders of the time remained acute; but in the later 1920's she viewed them at an ironic distance from which she could perceive the humorous as well as the serious disproportions existing between the surface brilliance of aristocratic society in Virginia ("the Castile and Aragon of American Bourbonism"[2]) and the realities outside it or imperfectly concealed beneath it. After the war an attitude of satiety was prevalent almost everywhere, Miss Glasgow sensed, and she wished to crystallize that attitude in literature. By a sophisticated use of dispassionate irony or aggressive satire, the comic vision could most appropriately refract, she felt, the cynicism and futility of a dis-ordered, purposeless age. The tragic vision, she also perceived, is generally concerned with the defeat of higher aspirations than those exhibited by the restless hedonists and the strident egotists, old and young, who were vocal in the 1920's. Wit, humor, irony, and satire predominate in *The Romantic Comedians* and *They Stooped to Folly*, although Miss Glasgow's sardonic view of the postwar age and of the psychology of her characters contributed a somber atmosphere to these books.

Through the agency of her comic spirit which in these years was beginning to struggle "against the bars of its cage," [3] Miss Glasgow tried to capture the essence of a world thrown into violent flux as a result of pressures like the war, Freudian psychology, and the widespread rejection of moral responsibility for vigorous self-realization. In Queenborough ("the distilled essence of all Virginia cities," [4]) "everything was becoming—or so it seemed at the moment—nothing was finished, except the Great War and the great tradition." [5] In *The Romantic Comedians,* for example, Judge Honeywell's tortured dreams of nymphs who spin round him "whirling, drifting, flying" and his observation of the same ceaseless motions in the dancing of the girls at Amanda's party are in part manifestations, psychological and social, of a time-spirit which is dynamic but without direction. Reacting to these agitations within and without, the Judge experiences a "shifting sensation," an "indefinite feeling that he was losing control of his faculties" (87); and after his marriage to Annabel he senses that she belongs in spirit to the new age by her apparent "aimless wandering through a labyrinth of blind impulses" (121).

As principal themes in *The Romantic Comedians,* Miss Glasgow enlarged upon love's tyranny over the constructive impulses of the mind and upon the folly of the male, especially, in seeking an evanescent sexual satisfaction. The novel is mainly centered in the consciousness of Judge Gamaliel Honeywell, a distinguished lawyer of aristocratic descent, who begins to experience at the age of sixty-five, with the death of his wife Cordelia, inexplicable but unmistakable longings in his autumnal years for a fulfillment which had been denied him in his prime. At Cordelia's grave he sighs to himself that he is "a bird with a broken wing," only to find disconcertingly that "his broken wing was helplessly trying to flutter" (3). In the 1880's he had impulsively married Cordelia after a passionate involvement, and a passionate quarrel, with the impressively beautiful Amanda Lightfoot. At Amanda's party for Annabel Upchurch's birthday early in the novel, the Judge's fluttering wing carries him away from Amanda, despite her thirty-seven years of fidelity to him and her still stately appearance, to the young, volatile Annabel, the woman above all others least suited to him. Distraught at the loss of her lover to a French woman, Annabel lures the Judge with the vitality which her violent grief accentuates and which he has never intimately known in a woman. The elderly man's pursuit of the youthful woman is neither an original situation nor a promising one for extensive treatment; and the unhappy denouement of an artificial union between old and young is hardly unexpected. What Miss Glasgow brought to the situation is, however, significant: witty intelligence, in-

sight into masculine delusion, perceptiveness as to the relationship between individual disillusionment and the postwar scene, and knowledge
of the various facets of the feminine mind.

To Mrs. Upchurch (Annabel's mother)—and presumably to Ellen
Glasgow—the Judge, Amanda Lightfoot, Annabel, and Annabel's new
lover, Dabney Birdsong, are "a troupe of romantic comedians" because
they think only of personal gratification in a world which could not have
been designed for everyone's gratification. With a sustained, faintly
mocking note, Miss Glasgow indicated how their compulsion to achieve
a selfish satisfaction is so strong that they fail to see the obstacles in
their way for what they are. Only Edmonia Bredalbane (the Judge's
scandalous twin sister) and Mrs. Upchurch herself possess the realism
and the cynicism to pursue pleasure with entire confidence; they are
undistracted by personal scruples and the unforeseen contingency, since
they have so perfectly estimated themselves and their situations.

In this band of happiness-seekers, Miss Glasgow had the Judge,
in Edmonia's view "a great lawyer but a perfect fool," suffer most from
illusion. Despite his eminence in the community, he is primarily a survival from a world "unaware of its own innocence." Intended as a
latter-day Sir Willoughby Patterne, Judge Honeywell is as foolish as
Meredith's "hero" in analyzing his own nature, the people in his orbit,
and his effects upon them. The Judge may conclude that "the power of
loving and the need of love" remain unequal, but he is unable to apply
this truth to himself. He comically embroiders, moreover, the actualities
of Annabel's nature by continually relaxing the truth in her behalf:
she is so pretty, he decides with passion instead of logic, that she cannot help being "good." He does not see how free she is—free from moral
responsibility as from moral duplicity—and how unsuited she is for the
role of matron: this despite the fact that he thinks always of her charm
in terms of wild nature, of "fields and streams," of "tall wind-blown
grasses," of the swallow's flight, of the "April mist" in her gray-green
eyes, and identifies her with the rose and ivory-colored nymphs that
trouble his imagination. The Judge is made uncomfortable in his marriage chiefly because Annabel does not exhibit that sense of domestic
responsibility which would have diminished—or killed—his interest in
her during courtship.

As she turns in revulsion from him, he is slow to realize the significance of the images which he now uses in thinking of her effect upon
him. These are images primarily of light without heat, which connote a
vitality without the warmth for which he hungers: her head is like
"November leaves in the sunlight"; her happiness with her new lover
"illumined her as if it were the fire at the heart of an opal"; her inner

life seems to glow at this point with a "secret incandescence"; shortly afterwards she seems like a "Byzantine saint" and her face is "as fresh as a flower after rain"; and when she has run off with Dabney she becomes alive "not as a flower, but as a jewel." At first he complacently interprets this contrast between her outward energy and her coldness toward him as a sign of normality, at least of maidenly reserve. He even fatuously feels he can mold her nature nearer to his ideal by being her perfect teacher. That she is not the placid woman venerated in Southern tradition and that she finds him physically repugnant, he fails for a long time to perceive. Masculine blindness and the evasive idealism of the culture which had formed him conspire to keep him ignorant, for too long a time, of the truth.

Savoring "the waywardness which rules our destiny," Miss Glasgow, with an impassive irony, could suavely expose the disparity between the Judge's actual conduct and the motives to which he ascribes it. Though he is fascinated by "the unwholesome, the prohibited, and the immoral" and longs for youthful renewal instead of peace of mind, he seeks always to justify himself in terms of convention. Unwilling to admit his awakening passion for Annabel, he at first rationalizes his instinctive withdrawal from Amanda as a need to remain faithful to Cordelia's memory. Later, he complacently persuades himself that Annabel needs him more than he needs her. Not only does she require his money and his kindness to recover from her disappointment in love, but, being a delicate woman, she may come to prefer, he hopes, his considerate caresses to the ardor of a youthful man. The Judge, in reality as egocentric as Annabel, disguises his egoism from himself and others by calling it unselfishness.

To the Judge, Annabel embodies not only sexual ecstasy, but, more abstractly, "all the assembled beauty of the world" (130), some seductive essence lacking from his conventional existence in the past. His aspiration for spiritual as well as sexual fulfillment in alliance with youth largely determines the structure of the novel. Part One is organized about the Judge's high hopes for physical and psychic restoration in his marriage to Annabel. From the first, when "the spirit of youth rushed through him like a tinted flood, like a river at sunrise" (43), his passion for Annabel is profoundly disturbing and finally a torment to his nerves. Part Two, of course, charts the defeat of the Judge's hopes and leads away from his marriage with Annabel to its dissolution. In the April one year after the awakening of his youthful impulses at Amanda's party and the subsequent failure of his marriage, it seems that the Judge may turn again from Amanda, this time to his young nurse whose cool flesh stirs in the convalescent the embers of yet unappeased desire. In the emotional life, we are to gather that wisdom is hard to come by and that reason cannot regulate to any clearly defined end the pressures of instinct: the human being all too often begins anew the same futile activity which had previously brought disaster. Miss Glasgow thus indicated that life follows cyclic as well as forward propulsions. The significance of the "apocalyptic light" which floods the last scene of the novel is artfully ambivalent. Under its spell, the Judge will probably pursue once again the same round of fugitive enchantment and final disillusion; it is possible, however, that he may find this time the fulfillment which has in the past escaped him.

Sometimes, in thinking of Annabel or in her presence, the Judge experiences the existence of a divine harmony, an ineffable radiance, a transcendent force, which includes him but which flows out beyond him. In so far as he loves unselfishly, he has these glimpses of the Eternal; in that he is incapable of bringing happiness to his beloved—since both he and Annabel are fundamentally self-centered—he cannot hold fast to his vision. He knows that her vitality warms him, but he cannot see that this same vitality takes her away from him; her very kiss is elusive like "the wings of a butterfly," as she slips out of his grasp in the bedroom and beyond his influence. Thus she is a symbol not only of the fulfillment the Judge has never had but also a symbol of the fact that such absolute fulfillment is, in most instances, an impossibility. His marriage to her is, as he suspects in a moment of honesty with himself, "a fruitless regeneration." [6] The humorous and the more serious disproportions in the novel emanate, then, from Annabel's thinking of the Judge only as a convenient means of escape from genteel poverty, while he thinks of her as a source of life-renewing energy.

Because he elsewhere fails to see her as she really is, the Judge, in his more realistic moments in Part Two, experiences an overpowering futility, which deepens to desolation when Annabel abandons him for Dabney Birdsong. Deserted by youth before his hunger for life can be satisfied, he feels "the ultimate negation of being, the encompassing solitude of the end" (221), a sense of spiritual obstruction and isolation which both benumbs and terrifies. In the Judge's agonized prostration of himself before Annabel, there is indignity and morbidity, something vaguely unwholesome in his fascination with her dressing and undressing, something hysterical, too, in Annabel's strong aversion to him.

In that the Judge has aspirations for spiritual completion common to all men, Miss Glasgow apparently intended not only to expose him to ridicule but to arouse a sympathetic interest in him. But Mrs. Upchurch's view of the Judge is, unfortunately for Miss Glasgow's purpose, the one which dominates in the novel: "Could anything, she asked herself, be more unmanly than an elderly man in the clutch of an emotional crisis?" (192). Miss Glasgow's conception of the Judge's character was too greatly divided for her to attain the philosophic dimensions she sought to establish in him. He becomes both a man whose quirks of character she satirized for their departure from the norms of a vital morality and a man whose failings she tolerated for their supposed relevance to the failings of all humanity. For trenchant satire, the Judge ought to have been presented more objectively as the laughable old man which he all too certainly is. For the most effective comedy, he ought to have been presented more exhaustively. Miss Glasgow most signally failed to convey the "greatness" which she imputed to the Judge's intellect. The realized character of the Judge is too slight, his moral nature too trivial, for his folly to be representative in any valid sense; and it is sometimes difficult, therefore, to find in the failure of his second marriage the generic significance, imputed to it by Robert Spiller, of a whole society's inability to find inner restoration.[7] The Judge is supposedly to find completion and renewal in sex; his failure to do so is understandable in terms of his complacency and egoism; what detracts in part from the authority of the novel is Miss Glasgow's denigration, through Mrs. Upchurch and Mrs. Bredalbane, of the Judge's source of fulfillment, the worth and value of love itself. Annabel is also a simply achieved character, and, even more than with the Judge, her problems have little philosophic import. She is "an intense little thing," granted, but apart from a firm honesty and an impulsive sympathy she has no depths of nature which sex or money cannot reach.

While the book does not fully achieve the over-all meaning which Miss Glasgow desired for it, it can be enjoyed as a vignette of an observable masculine type and as a *jeu d'esprit* depicting the humorous interactions of various temperaments upon each other. It is fastidiously and beautifully written with only that hint of artifice in the style which befits the brittle texture of a comedy of manners. When, as in this work, Miss Glasgow's sensibility was controlled by her ironic vision and by her ironic sense of the disparity existing between convention and reality, her style and thought lack the looseness and triteness they sometimes show. The novel is suffused with light and shadow and with vivid impressions of the senses—with perfumes, with brilliant visual images, with faint echoes from the world which rumbles on outside the charmed circle inhabited by the faintly ignoble "romantic comedians." As a witty and sometimes wise book, as a book which depends for much of its effect upon Miss Glasgow's own cleverness, as a book which "seemed to bubble out with an effortless joy," [8] *The Romantic Comedians,* if not a great novel, is always bright and diverting, and remarkable for its consistency of tone and mood.

The conservative and provincial aspects of the traditional South as it lasted into the postwar age are perceptively satirized in the novel. The Judge and Mrs. Upchurch represent those people formed by nineteenth-century tradition who have had to come to terms with the modern, but whose adjustment to new modes of thought—mostly imported from Europe—has not been easy. They are continually upset by shocks to their sense of propriety, inflicted by a generation which casually denies the claims of all it considers to be outmoded. In the face of such irreverence Mrs. Upchurch is fearful of being brought too close to facts which do not bear public discussion: in her opinion postwar youth is too fond of "vital statistics." To the Judge, liberal thought is permissible so long as it does not lead to liberal views. He can countenance evolution until it threatens the absolute reality of a personal God; he can even tolerate honest doubt so long as it remains in "a smothered condition"; sex "as a topic for speculation" he can't tolerate at all. There remains in him some of the suspicion inherent in the Victorian age toward a vital, candid art; he accordingly deplores the chief tendencies in modern literature, agreeing with Mrs. Upchurch that such writing may stimulate the mind but that it can hardly be expected to improve the morals. Annabel is only too modern, he feels, in having assimilated more "depravity" through books than he has even known about, in reading "from curiosity the things that could be said only in print" (116).

Miss Glasgow deftly explored for its humor the gulf existing between the intellectual boldness which the Judge ought to display and his actual timorousness. In her comedies of manners she thus mirrored her view of the society which surrounded her as being characterized both by an "immaturity that was old and tired and prudent," and by a gracious "code of manners." [9] Woman is still the controlling force in Southern social life, but the brash young girl is now supplanting in influence the queenly woman of passive sweetness. After some months of marriage to Annabel, Judge Honeywell has enough insight to suspect that his failure to distinguish fleeting pleasure from a more substantial happiness may have been in part the result of his having lived in a society which lacks intellectual depths and which has, therefore, blunted his critical faculties. The Judge, moreover, perceives some of the superficialities in his environment. He sees the intellectual flatulence of the first families in these terms: "Where else on earth . . . could people know so little and yet know it so fluently?" (9). He is critical, too, of middle-class values as they have determined the development of the New South. He calls the present "The Age of Pretense, The Age of Hypocrisy, The Age of Asphalt," and regards the dominance of the bourgeois point of view as "the tyranny of the inferior" (9). The modern confusion of material prosperity with genuine social well-being is the principal pretense and hypocrisy which the Judge protests against. In the moral sphere, the Judge and his associates exhibit pretenses and hypocrisies toward which their adversaries in the younger generation are contemptuous.

Having been exposed to the harsh honesty of the younger generation, the Judge, with his rational mind at least, does learn to be more tolerant, even if he does not become more sensible in his own behavior. After his misalliance with Annabel, he is dubious of all attempts to interpret life by abstract principles, though some of his inherited prejudices still survive in him. This acquired skepticism toward the absolutes which he had too easily assimilated as the core of his moral code becomes, in fact, the most likeable aspect of his personality. He is enabled thereby to be more generous to Annabel after she runs off than she perhaps deserves.

Mrs. Upchurch is one of the most clearly imagined figures in the novel, and like the Judge she belongs in most respects to the party of convention. To achieve variety in this novel Miss Glasgow used Mrs. Upchurch as an additional intelligence to interpret character and incident. Mrs. Upchurch is most often used in this way toward the end of the novel when Miss Glasgow desired a mind outside the Judge's to deliberate upon his folly and misadventures.

In spite of her homage to convention, Mrs. Upchurch conceals a corroding skepticism when in her thoughts she pragmatically reduces morality to sheer expediency. Motivated by a thorough cynicism which goes counter to her surface cheerfulness, she is, as Miss Glasgow asserted, "a century older in worldly wisdom" than Judge Honeywell. A fundamentally innocent man who thinks of himself as sophisticated is easy prey, then, for a worldly woman; and the Judge naturally feels warm regard for a woman who is "too wise ever to be original and too tactful ever to argue" (155). Actually, Mrs. Upchurch's docility, conveyed through such epithets as her "dove's eyes" and her laugh "soft as a pigeon's note," is the outward form of a disenchantment so deep that others beside the Judge mistake it for "softness of temper." In particular, her disillusion with sex is profound. Young and old talk too much about love simply because they have not reached her own state of superior wisdom, "the tranquil immunity of a mind that had finished with love" (211), the conviction that time wasted in love could more properly have been devoted to other more rewarding pursuits.

In Amanda Lightfoot Miss Glasgow skillfully portrayed a woman completely formed by tradition. Somewhat laughably, yet pathetically, Amanda in the postwar age becomes a martyr to concepts of virtue and moral responsibility which now have lost the universal respect of her contemporaries. Though Miss Glasgow appreciated Amanda's strength of character and considerateness, she also saw her ridiculous side, particularly her divorce from reality. The actualities in the life of the poor, for example, are outside her comprehension, and despite the number of her ardent admirers in the past, she has no real knowledge of men. If she is superior to Annabel in graciousness, kindness, and sweetness, she is Annabel's inferior in intelligence and honesty. Annabel at least sees that her own mother and Amanda, because they are so ladylike and delicate in sentiment, have encouraged men to be "morally flabby." After she tries directly to discover Amanda's true feelings about the Judge, Annabel concludes that "beautiful behavior" in a lady is more often "impenetrable" than morally defensible. The final irony of Amanda's situation is this: her fidelity and her sacrifice grow less significant to herself and to others by her heroic efforts to hide her broken heart.[10] The Judge himself is no longer interested in the woman he has worshipped as his ideal for nearly forty years. Instead, he takes advantage of her maidenly reserve, which prevents her from criticizing him in any articulate way, to court a young woman; and he confidently assumes, because he wants to, that she now must be too old for romance.

Miss Glasgow displayed her consummate skill in characterization by pervading the novel with the personality of the dead Cordelia. Cordelia's surviving influence upon the Judge's values and habits is so strong that she actually has the vitality of living flesh and blood. Like other women in the novel, she is, in part, the Judge's nemesis. Amanda is a reminder of the fidelity which the Judge wants to disregard; Edmonia, of the physical old age which he would as soon forget; Annabel, of a missed ecstasy which he now finds unattainable; and Cordelia, of the conventions and creature comforts which he rejects too lightly in pursuing sensual fulfillment. His honest reaction to Cordelia's death is relief, but convention prevents him from admitting this even to himself. She triumphed over the Judge by almost obliterating pleasure from his life, with the result that he came to realize, instinctively, that the worst of all possible worlds would be one invented by such a "good" woman. He is thus more genuine when his instincts rather than his prejudices give rise to his judgments. As a result of Cordelia's repressive influence he even feels guilty in enjoying Annabel's scent; the Puritan distrust of sensation, bred in him by tradition and by Cordelia's gentle asceticism, is not easily dispelled in a man who is only half-emancipated. After her death, the Judge lightly lays aside her inhibiting influence and prefers, perversely perhaps, to remember her as the mildly interesting young woman he married, not as the admirable matron she became.

Though no multi-dimensioned character, Edmonia Bredalbane is the most vivid creation in the novel and one of Miss Glasgow's most successful humorous figures. In characterizing Edmonia, Miss Glasgow made use of a laconic irony, of a penchant for the epigram, and of the somewhat ludicrous disproportions existing between the candid Edmonia and the people she shocks:

. . . there was his twin sister, Edmonia Bredalbane, an intrepid woman of liberal views and loose behaviour. After one early scandal, she had indulged herself through life in that branch of conduct which was familiar to ancient moralists as nature in man and depravity in woman. Moreover, she had lost her character, not quietly, as was the custom in such matters, but with a loud explosion which had startled Queenborough and involved her innocent family. Deaf alike to the whispers of conscience and the thunder of tradition, she had declined to remain a picturesque ruin in company with other damaged virgins of quality. While the rumble of her fall was still in the air, she had detached her loosened foundations and sailed by the next boat for Paris: a city that was regarded in Queenborough as little better than an asylum for determined profligates of both sexes. . . . Yet even after a world war, which had shaken everything but the unalterable laws of biology, he [the Judge] could find no milder word than reprehensible for Edmonia's flourishing career. (7)

With Edmonia the reversal of ponderous Victorian morality has been effected. The virtuous no longer flourish, they aren't even popular, whereas the sinner is not only tolerated but celebrated by the young for that same "wickedness" which had banished her from proper circles in Queenborough of the 1880's:

While elderly ladies of vacant memories and unblemished reputations nodded by lonely firesides, Edmonia was eagerly sought after by the inquisitive youth of the period. They clustered about her . . . in candid pursuit of some esoteric wisdom of sex; . . . at Amanda's dance . . . they treated her scarlet letter less as the badge of shame than as some foreign decoration for distinguished service. (60)

The Judge thinks Edmonia's uninhibited candor most unwomanly, and her effect upon that feminine exemplar of propriety, Mrs. Upchurch, is similarly disconcerting. The latter is unenthusiastic, then, when Edmonia suggests herself as travelling companion for Annabel, in order to allow the young woman a respite from the Judge. Edmonia defends herself by saying that there are other standards for behavior than those implied in a parochial gentility:

As provincial as you are in America, it is hopeless to try to make you understand that behaviour as much as beauty is a question of geography, and that my respectability increases with every mile of the distance I travel from Queenborough. In France, my reputation is above reproach; by the time I reach Vienna, I have become a bit of a prude; and contrasted with the Balkan temperament, I am little more than a tombstone to female virtue. (215)

In her rejection of traditional morality and the obligations it imposes, Edmonia unforgivably, to the Judge's staid mind, cuts through its hypocrisy. He may not be any more enthusiastic about this code than she is, but he is content for women to be bound by it and for men to profess admiration for it. Accounting in part for the humor in the byplay between Edmonia and the Judge is the reversal of a generally accepted relationship of men to women: in this novel the woman is emancipated and the man is tied by convention.

In thinking of Annabel's inability to feel guilt at deserting her husband, Mrs. Upchurch comes to see that the "high tragedy" of one generation may become the "low comedy" of the next. Goldsmith's advice to indecisive woman had been "a convenient household remedy" in her grandmother's day for curbing the excesses of emotion; if his advice failed to deter a woman from sin, she was at least unable to escape the shame which she had brought upon herself. With grace and intrepidity, Miss Glasgow developed this theme in *They Stooped to Folly,* depicting the "fallen" women of three generations. In Queenborough of the 1870's the woman who yielded too easily to an ardent admirer, Aunt Agatha Littlepage, had her mind and personality warped by the secluded life which Victorian convention forced upon her. In the more relaxed 1890's Mrs. Dalrymple had possessed, like Edmonia Bredalbane, the strength to defy convention and to mend her damaged reputation in exile; but as "a romantic ruin" she could not be received in respectable society. In the 1920's Milly Burden, a more intense Annabel Upchurch, feels no compunction for having loved a man outside of marriage. The newer generation approves her indifference to inherited standards and finds quaintly ridiculous the enforced retirement formerly visited upon the "lady" who fell from virtue.

In Miss Glasgow's scheme for this novel, characters at various stages of "emancipation" in 1924 react toward these three unchaste women from different generations. For humorous effect Miss Glasgow continuously set forth their divergent attitudes toward these women. Even in the same person different views prevail at different times. Thus Virginius and Victoria Littlepage, who provide the two main reflective intelligences in the novel, are harsh in judgment when their prejudices, originating in inflexible convention, dominate them, but charitable when they obey the dictates of the heart. The superiority of *They Stooped to Folly* over *The Romantic Comedians* can be partly measured through Miss Glasgow's consistent counterpointing of this positive theme with her satire upon worn-out institutions and the inconsistencies, in general, which mark human behavior and human value judgments. The movement which Northrop Frye prescribes for comedy—"from a society controlled by habit, ritual bondage, arbitrary law and the older characters to a society controlled by youth and pragmatic freedom" [11]—is certainly present in the freer morality which Virginius and Victoria attain, often as it were in spite of themselves.

Miss Glasgow centered Part One ("Mr. Littlepage") in the consciousness of Virginius Littlepage, a wealthy lawyer of aristocratic descent; and she evidently intended the novel to belong to him as a man who is intuitively drawn to the modern revolution in attitudes and morals while he remains intellectually unsympathetic toward it. He has married a "moral influence," whose name is, perhaps symbolically, Victoria. Because his comfortably settled life is uninteresting to him, he is drawn after the war to the buxom Mrs. Dalrymple. In using a humane though somewhat timorous individual to reflect upon his own past, his family and friends, and the unsettling effects in general of the war, Miss Glasgow was able to secure her desired effect of the prevalence of widespread conflict between the old and new modes of thought. In Chapter 1 all the characters who figure in the somewhat extensive canvas of the novel are introduced through Virginius's thoughts, with the exception of Milly Burden who appears in person and of Louise Goddard who does not appear until Chapter 3.

With Chapter 5 of the novel all the chief themes and conflicts have been set forth, at least embryonically. In the first two chapters Virginius muses over the three women who have stooped to amorous folly; and in Chapter 2 some hints of the developing triangular situation between Virginius, Victoria, and Mrs. Dalrymple emerge in the process of nostalgic remembrance of a brief encounter with Mrs. Dalrymple before the war. In Chapter 5 Louisa Goddard, a quasi-intellectual clubwoman and spinster friend of the family, enlightens Virginius as to the marriage of his daughter Mary Victoria to Martin Welding, who had been Milly Burden's lover. Mary Victoria, an even greater and more self-conscious "influence" over men than her mother had been, lacks her tact and discretion. Despite her knowledge that Martin Welding had been previously involved with Milly Burden, Mary Victoria came to feel, when her father commissioned her to find Martin in Europe, that it was her duty to save him from relapsing into Milly's arms. Thus the second sexual triangle in the novel is formed. In inevitable and ingenious fashion the book then proliferates from these initial situations, characters, and themes. The only unexpected, but not improbable, developments are Victoria's mystical withdrawal from life and her sudden death, and the revelation of Louisa's lifelong love for Virginius.

Other sharply defined characters, more or less peripheral in the novel, contribute to its crowded scene. There are the Littlepage sons, Curle, the "booster" and Rotarian voice of the New South,[12] and Duncan, the misanthropic cynic. There is Virginius's outspoken brother, Marmaduke, who has defied the conventions in Queenborough by being both modernist painter and bachelor. There is, finally, the self-righteous religious fanatic, Mrs. Burden, who cannot reconcile herself to her daughter's "disgrace." With the various people thus far described as part of its universe, Miss Glasgow was able to project in the characters of the novel varying crosscurrents in the social and moral life of postwar America. In wit, irony, polished style, and aristocratic décor, *They Stooped to Folly* inevitably recalls the studied artifice of that side of British tradition in comedy represented by Congreve, Sheridan, Meredith, and Wilde.

As Miss Glasgow remarked in her Preface to the novel, Virginius did not stay consistently at its center.[13] As she progressed with Part Two ("Mrs. Littlepage") in which the action is seen through Victoria's sensibility, Victoria became much more important than had been contemplated originally. Miss Glasgow herself was surprised how Victoria, whose passive moralism ought to have been tiresome, developed into a dynamic person when her instincts led her away from institutional to heartfelt responses—to the point where for the moment she can be more sympathetic with Milly Burden than with her own strenuous daughter. The nice balance established between Victoria's inadequacies and her radical goodness led to an unexpected piquancy in her personality; her very inconsistencies made her fallibly human and tended, too, to counterbalance her ordinary dullness. In this section of the novel, part of Chapter 2 is centered in Aunt Agatha's mind, and Chapter 8 comprises Mrs. Burden's review of her past history and present sufferings.

In Part Three ("False Spring") the various conflicts are resolved: Virginius, as a result of fortuitous outside interruption, fails to surrender to Mrs. Dalrymple, Victoria dies, Martin Welding escapes from woman, Mary Victoria feels deeply humiliated at the loss of her husband, and Milly Burden attains spiritual independence. In the first chapters, where the situations become more complex before they can be seen firmly by the characters, the point of view is less rigorously confined to one character than had been the case in the two preceding parts of the novel; it is alternately that of Virginius and Victoria. Some later chapters in Part Three are split between Virginius and other characters, when it becomes necessary to see him through eyes other than his own or Victoria's: Chapter 5, before he knows of Victoria's death, is divided between him and Mrs. Dalrymple, and Chapter 7, after he learns of Victoria's death, between him and Louisa Goddard. Throughout the novel, characters such as Victoria Littlepage, Louisa Goddard, Mrs. Burden, and Marmaduke Littlepage, who have been released from the sexual struggle, comment upon the follies of those still pursuing emotional aggrandizement, and form loosely a comic chorus.

Miss Glasgow lightly satirized in the novel the constricting influence and the hypocrisies inherent in the conventional social morality of the American nineteenth century as it endured into the next century. In criticizing this tradition, Louisa Goddard paints its inadequacies as Miss Glasgow herself might have done: "Nothing was worth all the deceit, all the anguish, all the futile hope and ineffectual endeavour, all the pretense and parade, all the artificial glamour and empty posturing, of the great Victorian tradition" (287). As in *The Miller of Old Church* and *Virginia,* Miss Glasgow gave prominence in *They Stooped to Folly* to the unreal exaltation of woman in the nineteenth century—an age when "a graceful feminine style softened the manners, if not the natures, of men," and when "womanhood was exalted from a biological fact into a miraculous power" (12). Thus Virginius recalls, without much sense of the incongruities involved, how much easier it was in a prudish society for his father "to commit adultery than to pronounce the word in the presence of a lady." [14]

Miss Glasgow's originality in *They Stooped to Folly* was to reveal feminized gentility as more completely on the defensive than it had been in Southern society before the first World War. When, sometimes, the man resists her influence, the earnest woman like Victoria Littlepage, Miss Glasgow perceived, will tend to think that all standards are dissolving, since she had been educated to think of America as a society "in which the superiority of wives is as firmly established as the divine right of averages" (170). Although Virginius had been ready for an affair with Amy Dalrymple, he is bound securely by Victoria's death to the pallid moralism and the discreet aspiration which she had exemplified in life. With her death the wife as mother, rather than the living woman as a sexual force, exerts an inescapable influence over the gently bred Virginius.[15] To Louisa Goddard his strained feeling seems exaggerated if genuine. Though she had appreciated the living Victoria far more than

Virginius had, she realizes that Victoria was dull and unintelligent. In Louisa's case, cynical candor toward the deceased is compatible with the deep affection she had once felt for her. When Mr. Littlepage invests Victoria with the quality of "stainless legend," Louisa knows that he will never again be capable of seeing his wife as she actually was.

In Mary Victoria Miss Glasgow skillfully modulated the lineaments of the mother's character to create a more hypocritical, less appealing personality. Whereas Mary Victoria pretends to be open-minded in the modern manner, she is, in reality, less flexible in her sympathies than her old-fashioned mother. Actually, as N. Elizabeth Monroe has observed, her marriage to Martin is, in essence, a victory of the older morality over the new freedom advocated by Milly Burden who has loved Martin passionately but indiscreetly.[16] Virginius reluctantly admits that Mary Victoria has profoundly disillusioned him—when he had so confidently counted upon her to do the right thing—by lightly marrying another woman's man. He had too sanguinely hoped that she might have been one of an advance guard of individuals to formulate a more genuine morality than his own generation had known.

With Mary Victoria Miss Glasgow demonstrated how readily a confident rectitude becomes an aggressive self-righteousness and a convenient disguise for the satisfaction of selfish desires and ambitions. Like her mother, Mary Victoria especially desires to reform the male—as her brother Curle remarks, to Virginius's annoyance, about her marriage to Martin Welding, "Perhaps she wanted to make an honest man of him" (48). Martin himself is ready to admit not only that Mary Victoria has been his "good angel," but also that, after saving him, she may have married him because she did not know what else to do with him. After several months of marriage, her ideal as to what a man ought to be leaves him feeling forlorn and inadequate. With discernment, Marmaduke observes that Mary Victoria ought to have loved her husband less and liked him more. Her humorless seriousness—her complete lack of a sense of proportion—becomes then one of the most humorous aspects of the book. Miss Glasgow also utilized, with good effect, the delayed entrance to present Mary Victoria and Martin Welding initially. Through the mentality of Virginius and the conversations he has with other characters, these two figures are fully depicted before they actually appear to confirm impressions about them already formed in the mind.

Through being sensitive to Mary Victoria's latent insecurities beneath her surface confidence, Miss Glasgow deftly foreshadowed the girl's collapse at the end of the novel when Martin flouts her egotism by running away. Her prostration is only temporary, for confidence rushes back to her when Virginius reminds her that she may exert an "uplifting" in-

fluence upon her still unborn child. She does not attain the humility which
her suffering ought to bring, however, and she is far from realizing the
truth expressed by Marmaduke to her father—that she cannot be saved
until she is first destroyed. Nor does she arrive at true charity or generosity.[17] Throughout, Miss Glasgow probed into the distortion resulting
from Mary Victoria's desire to shape the lives of others when she is in
greater need of spiritual rebirth than anyone else.

Even more vehemently, the neurotically religious Mrs. Burden attempts to dominate the people about her. One of Miss Glasgow's most
caustic portraits, she is in the same group as Mrs. Revercomb in *The
Miller of Old Church* and Mrs. McBride in *Vein of Iron*. Dreariness of
conscience is so exaggerated in the evangelically inclined Mrs. Burden
that the other characters in the novel find it grotesque when it is not
disturbing. Even the gentle, genial, conventional-minded Victoria comes
heretically to feel that worldly people are much less "depressing" than
religious women like Mrs. Burden, who seems to her to have "had the
pleasure of living wrung drop by drop out of her body and soul" (200).
Mrs. Burden's father had been a circuit rider in the days when sin was
death, not life, in contrast to the decadent present. Mrs. Burden and her
father illustrate, in part, the widespread return in the South to religious
fundamentalism in the years succeeding the Civil War and the opposition
then to sophisticated modes of thought.[18] Mrs. Burden is especially
grateful to Providence for having escaped the fate of an Agatha Littlepage, which her parents and her preacher ascribed chiefly to the worldly,
frivolous, and godless life of the upper class:

> It seemed only yesterday that she had tingled with horror and indignation
> and gratitude for her own escape from the snare of the fowler. "This came,"
> scoffed her father (a plain man, and proud of it), "as a punishment for
> round dances and wine-bibbing and bare necks in the evening, and neglecting
> to hold religious revivals in the spring of the year." "This came," moaned
> her mother (a simple woman, and proud of it), "from forgetting your
> modesty and failing to spurn the brazen instincts of men." "This came,"
> thundered her pastor (the voice of God, though a worm, and proud of it),
> "from braving divine wrath and embracing the frivolous dogmas and the
> Popish ceremonies of the Episcopal Church." (189)

With humorous intent, Miss Glasgow contrasted the fundamentalist
ideas of Mrs. Burden with the secularism of those, particularly women,
who reject them. It is a severe trial to Mrs. Burden's faith to find that
sinners sometimes do prosper, to discover that Mrs. Dalrymple, for example, has "safely wriggled past the wages of sin" (190), and that she
has been brazen enough to return "to flaunt her gilded shame in the
presence of the stout matrons and lean virgins of Queenborough" (193).

According to Mrs. Burden, a female sinner should be kept on her knees scrubbing to remind her of her fallen condition. Mrs. Burden even resents the sympathy which Virginius has shown to Milly by employing her in his office. The intensity of this resentment is humorous by the contrast it suggests between what Mrs. Burden feels and the sympathy for an erring daughter which a mother might normally be expected to feel.

Mrs. Burden is united with the other conventionally "good" women in the novel, Victoria and her daughter, by an obsession with "duty" as the only acceptable motive for human behavior. With sardonic humor, Miss Glasgow set the earnestness of these women against the apathy of those whom their strenuous virtue envelops. Virginius prefers to let his wife think of duty and not to think about it himself at all, except when it helps to keep woman in her place. Martin Welding is crushed by trying to live up to the high ideals of Mary Victoria, who is too sure of herself to wonder about her effect upon a husband. Mr. Burden ran away when his wife insisted that it was his duty to love her; and Milly becomes increasingly restive the more her mother appeals to her conscience. In Mrs. Burden the distrust which these other women show toward the pleasures of the senses is aggravated by a life of personal privation. She therefore feels that her daughter should not have happiness since she herself has never had it. Thus one facet of Mrs. Burden's depressed evangelicism is an addiction to self-pity. Having always been respectable and having always done her duty, she cannot understand her failure to influence her husband and her daughter to an upright life.

Virginius's recurrent disenchantment reflects the widespread sense of spiritual dislocation prevalent after the first World War. More deeply based than that of Judge Honeywell, his discontent becomes so pervasive that he can only conclude that we have all "lost our way in the universe." New modes of thinking set in motion by the war are also in vigorous opposition to the conventional point of view, represented so differently by Victoria Littlepage and Mrs. Burden, to some extent by Virginius himself and Mary Victoria. Speaking for the dismay felt by these people, Virginius asserts that the war had become a "Witches' Sabbath of released desires." He has, in particular, been disillusioned by the hypocrisy of noncombatants, especially women, who found in the war satisfaction for their hidden instincts. With comic exaggeration, Miss Glasgow revealed how Mary Victoria, despite her professed hatred of militarism, is only too happy to give expression to her intent energies by becoming an "inspiration" for war-torn Europe. With barbed understatement, Miss Glasgow has Marmaduke declare that Mary Victoria "patronized the war as if it were her favourite charity" (110). In her characterizations in this novel Miss Glasgow habitually made use of such alternations of exaggeration and understatement. These contrasting devices take the form sometimes of comment by an omniscient author, sometimes of reflection by the point-of-view characters, sometimes of statement by the objectively presented characters.

For humorous effect Miss Glasgow reversed the normal expectations of the conventionally virtuous when she reviewed the rehabilitation by the war of the two older wayward women in the novel. Prewar society was scarcely prepared for wartime indifference to its precepts and for witnessing the casual acceptance of those formerly ostracized. Aunt Agatha experienced a late flowering when she made pajamas for the Red Cross and when afterwards she found some consolation for her withered life in the romance and excitement of the movies. To Mrs. Dalrymple the war provided a more exciting release for her energies than had sex. As a result she distinguished herself both for bravery under enemy fire and for an impoverishing generosity in the years which followed.

Because of the war the substance of many of Virginius's beliefs has departed, and only their form remains. As to morals, many of Virginius's prejudices have no useful implications for his actual life, and as to religion, all the conviction of his youth has disappeared though God still remains as "the oldest and the most venerated of his traditions" (104). The persistence in him of these lifeless attitudes means that he is true less to personally determined standards than to what other people expect of him. When he can react spontaneously, he is aware of complexities and concealed violences in experience which an inherited moralism generally screens from him: "Life! There it was again, with its cruelties, its frustrations, its beauty, its splendour, and its unconquerable isolation" (269). At the end of the novel when he feels how unwomanly Mary Victoria and her whole generation are (she is running after her husband), Virginius again judges himself to have been an alien in the prewar age and to be one still in the modern era.

Dissatisfied with his placid marriage and "the sober pleasures" of his past which now seem "worthless as cinders," Virginius yearns for fuller expression of the self with Mrs. Dalrymple. He thinks of his earlier encounter with her as having lifted him to a "starry altitude of the spirit"; and somewhat later in a despondent mood he sees from his bedroom the light in her window as "a single fiery star" in the gloom of his present universe. At the close of Part One, a "clement" star in the twilight sky again signifies to him "the lost sweetness of life" and Mrs. Dalrymple as its incarnation. Her sexuality is thus as mysterious and vital as the light given off by the far-distant stars, and, for a man of his civilized temperament, as unattainable. In view of her coöperativeness, his hesitations in the abortive seduction scene are comical at the same time that they are natural in a fastidious male.

If Virginius through Mrs. Dalrymple achieves the bitter wisdom that desire is as transitory as it is vivid, he might have been made more bitter still at discovering how nearly Victoria's disillusion with sex and marriage approximated his own. He does not suspect that the "pure" Victoria has been more attuned to postwar disillusion than she has appeared to be or has been prepared to admit. Virginius would have been shocked to know that Victoria had found something missing in marriage and that she regretted his lack of ardor when they were first married. Victoria, in her turn, is thankful that her husband does not have "that other side to his nature," at the time his slumbering primitive energies are going out toward Mrs. Dalrymple. Victoria is complacently convinced that she has made him happy, while he becomes increasingly aware that the proprieties, embodied in her, have denied him the ecstasy he seeks. These long-standing misconceptions between husband and wife add to the quiet humor of the novel and manifest Miss Glasgow's own full grasp of the ironic divergence between an individual's illusions and the realities which habit and convention obscure from him.

Other characters are also aware that time-honored standards are dissolving and respond to the acid temper of the age. Because Milly Burden feels "there's murder in the air," she is able to justify her preoccupation with self. At first she determines, at all cost, either to have happiness or its barren substitute, pleasure; but finally discovering how futile her passion for Martin has been, she attains a more substantial inner freedom and peace. Her reaching this modicum of spiritual light is the sole bright aspect of the book's concluding sequences. They take place in Mrs. Burden's somber house at Juniper Hill, in the dreary November garden behind the house, or in the dark street outside; and they pulsate with the subterranean violence of an age which even a few years back, Virginius recalls, had been willing "to think murder and call it idealism." The omnipresent darkness which shrouds these final pages—engendered by the chill air, the sharp wind, and the scudding sunset clouds—is symptomatic of how profoundly the disenchantment of the postwar age has everywhere penetrated beneath the outward veneer of manners.

Similarly the bleak and ominous surroundings at Juniper Hill had depressed Victoria after an earlier visit to Mrs. Burden and an encounter on the shadowed street with Martin, apparently rushing to see Milly. The oppressiveness latent in these final pages is also closely linked with the melancholy that dominates Virginius in the opening chapter as he responds to the mood created by "a depressing afternoon in November" which he gazes out upon from his office window. Granted that *They*

Stooped to Folly is a comedy of manners, it is a comedy of manners with consistently sinister undertones.[19] At the novel's end even the redoubtable Mary Victoria succumbs to disillusion: "Doesn't everything come back . . . if you wait until you have stopped wanting it?" (303). A more genial iconoclasm is seen in the elderly Marmaduke Littlepage, who with his sixty years and brilliant war record has more of a right to be cynical. Though Victoria and Virginius try to be tolerant of this philosopher with his "one leg and even less reputation," they hardly condone his Bohemian candor and "the hilarity that recollections of a well-spent life so seldom afford" (214).

In presenting the clash between the older culture—which fears an extensive or an experimental probing of experience—and the brusque modern age, Miss Glasgow projected in Marmaduke Littlepage all that the conservative inhabitants of Queenborough distrust. Their dread of the unusual is crystallized in the frustration which the Littlepages feel when they view Marmaduke's *avant-garde* paintings. Virginius can't understand his brother's painting in primary colors the inside rather than the outside of things, his penchant for reddish nudes, and his terminology in describing his work:

. . . surrounded by Marmaduke's improbable nudes, Virginius was assailed afresh by the suspicion that every woman was purple under her clothes. Directly in front of him, an undraped female figure was standing beneath a florid sky, with her feet buried in splashes of orange beach and vermilion sea. On her right, another naked woman with indelicate limbs was (of all unlikely occupations!) sewing a white seam in the midst of an apple-green hill, under the pink boughs of a flowering almond-tree. "What on earth!" Virginius thought, turning away. "Is the world going mad? Or is Marmaduke already demented?"

"I've done something new in this one," Marmaduke was saying in the jesting tone in which he talked of art to Virginius. "It isn't only the loosening of technique, though I've tried to see how far I could go that way. But you'll notice a new fluency both in the design and the brushwork. There's a kind of symphonic rhythm—." (104)

By confronting convention with something it fails to comprehend, Miss Glasgow achieved the same humorous effect as she had in *The Romantic Comedians,* wherein she had confronted Judge Honeywell with the worldliness of Edmonia Bredalbane. Victoria is in her turn suspicious both of an art which does "violence either to her womanly instincts or her religious convictions" (180) and of an artist who is as indecorously vital as her brother-in-law. In the Littlepage suspicion of Martin Welding for being a writer anxious to reflect the truth of experience, Miss Glasgow further satirized the intellectual provincialism of the Virginia aristocracy. In that Marmaduke and Martin are artists alienated from a complacent society and mildly persecuted by it, they can be regarded as the scapegoats of those who do not wish to understand them.[20]

In Virginius's ambivalent attitude towards his brother, Miss Glasgow analyzed the complexities and inconsistencies of human nature. Judging by all the conventional standards which persist in him, Virginius can only disapprove of Marmaduke as a man "obviously designed to be an enemy to society" (237); yet he is drawn to him because of his moral courage and his lack of pretense. Marmaduke, then, appeals to that side of Virginius which propriety calls upon him to suppress, a rebellious longing to identify himself with "faithless husbands and other undesirable acquaintances" (24).

Though decorous people regard Marmaduke as a reprobate, he is more truly generous and charitable than anyone else in the novel and voices, as a result, many of Miss Glasgow's own valuations of experience. In so far as he rebels against the hypocrisies found in a formalized morality, he undoubtedly reflects her desire to make more human, comprehending standards prevail. In maintaining that pity is a sounder moral instinct than that of possessive sexual love, Marmaduke substantiates his claim, he feels, of being the only idealist, except for Victoria, left in Queenborough. She believes sincerely in the proprieties but administers her judgments with charity, and he tries to be humane and forbearing towards others despite his own violation of these proprieties. Marmaduke's generosity is proved when he champions Milly as a courageous woman, when he insists that the persecution of Aunt Agatha by moral sanctimony had been cruel, and when he becomes impatient in recalling the hypocrisy of his profligate grandfather, who had nearly died over Aunt Agatha's disgrace. An omniscient wisdom is partly responsible for his imperturbable tolerance. Though he would awaken people from their complacency, his frequent failures to do so do not disturb him. In that he regards history as an alternation between periods of barbarism and civilization, he sees that moral progress is uncertain, and, at best, slow. The development of the individual provides our best hope, Marmaduke thinks; he himself has been dedicated to his craft as artist in a culture which encourages conformity to standardized ideas.

Through the distending of stock characters, Miss Glasgow achieved many of her comic effects in this novel. Mrs. Dalrymple, for example, is the goodhearted woman whose private life will not bear scrutiny by the "virtuous." Miss Glasgow's originality was to make her courtesan a world-weary and disillusioned woman who had "approached the ascetic point of view by the downward path" (89) and who is tired of sex though she still must play at it for a living. In literature it is generally reserved for the male roué to voice candidly a radical satiety like Mrs. Dalrymple's and to pretend in love a personal interest he does not feel in order to secure his own ends. Other characters in the novel also represent adept variations upon familiar social types. Victoria is predominantly the prim matron, but her instincts, seldom made articulate, are subversive of the morality she incarnates. Marmaduke is predominantly the artist-icono-clast, but his humanity enlarges his soul and modulates his external cynicism. Martin Welding is predominantly the pampered aesthete but his bitter critical sense saves him from triviality. Milly Burden is pre-dominantly the young woman made rebellious by a too severe upbring-ing, but her honesty and sense of fair play give her dignity. Mrs. Burden, finally, is predominantly the grimly religious Presbyterian, but her some-what grotesque self-pity is as strenuous as her piety.

As in *The Romantic Comedians,* part of the distinction of *They Stooped to Folly* lies in Miss Glasgow's expert delineation of feminine types. Victoria is one of the most vividly presented of Miss Glasgow's naturally frigid women who are secretly satisfied that convention re-quires them to be passive. Her lingering death, while to others she seems in apparent health, is one of the most skillfully realized aspects of this novel. Continually emphasized is the contrast between the tedium in-volved in her normal selfless existence for others and the intermittent glimpses she has of a supernal reality which makes her apathetic before the demands of her family. The indefinable presence which at intervals pervades her consciousness is associated with images of light: she finds that "a luminous veil had dropped between her and life"; in her inmost being "spirals of golden dust quivered and vanished and quivered again"; and she experiences an incursion "of sparkling energy . . . spreading in rivulets of light, scattering a rainbow spray through her mind and soul." [21]

Another of Miss Glasgow's fine sketches, marked by an acrid ac-curacy, is that of the capable, self-sufficient Louisa Goddard. To Vir-ginius she seems to lack vitality, and he can't understand why "a brick . . . deficient in charm" should have received—and refused—so many proposals of marriage. In his masculine blindness, he does not see Louisa's passion for himself until his brother enlightens him. Through-out the novel, her primness of manner is comically incommensurate both with the violence of "contemporary mannerless youth" and with the depravity of the "antique manners" which she lectures upon. Vir-ginius's distrust of Louisa's intellectual pretensions reflects his heritage; one authority thus quotes from a Southern spokesman in 1870: "We want no 'strong-minded women,' no female lecturers, no female voters, no office holders. We have no wish to see our wives and daughters unsex themselves." [22] Miss Glasgow developed yet another whimsical contrast between Virginius and Louisa. Despite her virginal demeanor, Louisa is ages older in worldly wisdom than Virginius and has far fewer illusions than the man who patronizes her. Through abstinence rather than satiety, she has come to the same disenchanted view of life as Mrs. Dalrymple. Both women honestly admit that the comforts of life are more valuable than the discomforts of love, especially when it is illicit. Just as honestly, they also concede that, despite the excesses of a rebellious generation, the world has changed for the better in rejecting a false morality.

In this novel Miss Glasgow did well with the comedy of manners: the limitations of the book inhere more in the genre itself than in Miss Glasgow's talent. The absence of a truly significant conflict or of a commanding theme somewhat detracts from its excellence. Yet the book is remarkable for what it does achieve. In it Miss Glasgow consummately conveyed the multifarious facets of a society which she was later to characterize in terms of her own actual evocation of it in *The Romantic Comedians* and *They Stooped to Folly:* "For the essence of social life in the South, old or new, is in this feeling of abundant vitality and animation, in the closely multiplied effects, in the perpetually shifting surface over an illusion of permanence." [23] As often happens in the comedy of manners, wherein surfaces are so important, the characters, even those fully elaborated like Virginius and Victoria Littlepage, do not possess great depth; they are involved in real conflicts but do not seem vitally implicated in them. As it is, the novel lacks the power and the symbolic fullness of *Virginia* and *The Sheltered Life,* books in which psychological tensions are more urgently concentrated.

For the comedy of manners it is enough, perhaps, if characters live and move in "the brilliant air of the mind" (Miss Glasgow's remark on Santayana's characters in *The Last Puritan*).[24] The figures in *They Stooped to Folly* possess a credible attachment to their immediate milieu even if ultimately they are unable to command our fullest sympathies. Some loss of creative force may have resulted from Ellen Glasgow's inconsistent attitude towards her central characters, Virginius and Victoria Littlepage, who indecisively become, like Judge Honeywell in *The Romantic Comedians,* subjects for both sympathy and satire. Yet with all reservations made, there is nothing in our literature, in wit and satiric gayety, quite like *The Romantic Comedians* and *They Stooped to Folly.* They constitute a brilliant evocation of contemporary civilization in

Virginia which has been elsewhere described as "aristocratic in manner, orthodox in religion, courteous in daily intercourse and conservative in politics." [25]

Despite Miss Glasgow's realistic purpose in writing these novels and their truthful reflection of the postwar milieu, the characters often seem to be acting at that remove from reality which constitutes fantasy.[26] In *They Stooped to Folly,* however, the realistic substance of the novel remained firm enough for Ellen Glasgow to imbue her satire with sobriety. Accordingly, the discordances engendered by the war and by disenchanted sexual emotion determine its somber tone. The sense of fracture between surface pleasantry and barely acknowledged submerged forces operating in society and human nature, if not always fully developed, is the most original aspect of this novel. Its delightful humor and wit, sometimes possibly too obtrusive, were to be muted in *The Sheltered Life.* In that novel, which depicts a prewar society still unruffled by aggressive spiritual revolt, the deep-lying, uncontrolled forces in human nature, customarily concealed under a code of manners, erupt violently instead of being held in equilibrium.

⋄ XI ⋄

"The Immeasurable Joy and Anguish of Being": The Sheltered Life

During the composition of *They Stooped to Folly,* the chief figures in *The Sheltered Life* (1932), the Archbalds and the Birdsongs, had, Miss Glasgow said, developed a submerged life of their own in her imagination.[1] Not until the autumn of 1929 did these characters, drawn in part from girlhood remembrances, become insistently alive and demand Ellen Glasgow's full concentration upon them.[2] The result was the finest work traceable to the artistic rejuvenation which she had begun to experience in the writing of *Barren Ground* (1925). One of the themes of *They Stooped to Folly*—Virginius Littlepage's conclusion that love is "the creator and the devourer of life"—is even more forcefully present in this novel.[3] When General Archbald observes the futility evinced in the Birdsongs' fitful passion, he sadly concludes that "possessive love makes most of the complications and nearly all the unhappiness in the world" (186). Though she has given up everything for his sake, Eva Birdsong has always a reluctant suspicion that her husband is not worth her devotion and that the world for her has not been well lost.

The disturbed relationship between Eva and George Birdsong is central in the novel, although it is refracted through the sensibilities of two other characters only tangentially involved in it, the old man, General Archbald, and his granddaughter, Jenny Blair Archbald. The General

185

worships Eva as a person and an ideal, whereas Jenny Blair Archbald is an amoral young girl in whom the "sheltered life" has encouraged an idle hedonism and a compulsive desire to satisfy her instincts. The superior artistry of this novel is to be measured in part by Miss Glasgow's skilled contrapuntal presentation of her "point-of-view" characters, the General's tragic unfulfillment being contrasted with Jenny Blair's fulfillment which brings tragedy. For when Eva Birdsong, in her distraught illness at the end of the novel, finds Jenny Blair in her husband's embrace, she allows a primitive jealousy to possess her. With an energy born of desperation and of disordered nerves she brings an end to her long life of pretense by shooting him.

George Birdsong that day had had fine hunting and had brought home handsome ducks to distribute to his friends. When Eva, discovering him with Jenny Blair, had summoned him into the library and the girl had followed a few minutes later in panic, the first thing Jenny Blair saw—a pair of ducks on the floor, instead of on the furniture, with blood on their beaks and breasts—signified what she was to find in the room: her lover dead and his wife in a state of dazed shock. The ducks as natural objects of beauty destroyed by human ruthlessness refer by extension to Eva herself whose beauty and vitality have been undermined by the persistence of her husband's moral weakness. These birds, which George each year hunts according to established custom, are also meant to be, as Frederick Hoffman has pointed out, "ritual victims" of a tradition just as the Birdsongs themselves are the "neurotic victims" of long-established mores.[4] At this crisis the Archbalds and the Birdsongs will stand by each other to outface criticism and scandal, just as in the recent past they united to resist the influence of industrialism and just as their compatriots, the Goddards, the General remembers, once disarmed the law and popular suspicion when a nephew had shot Breverton Goddard in a quarrel over the latter's young wife. Like the Archbalds and the Birdsongs at the end of the novel, the Goddards had simply pretended that the murder was accident: "By force of superior importance, they had ignored facts, defended family honour, shielded a murderer for the sake of saving a name, turned public execration into sympathy, and politely but firmly looked the law out of countenance" (128).

The Archbalds thus prove that in an emergency they can also recover some of the moral strength which they had formerly displayed as leaders during the South's most desperate days—a moral strength which at present ordinarily dissipates itself in a continued effort to maintain appearances. The early twentieth-century aristocrats in this novel thus illustrate the slow decline that typically overtook a finely bred race which lacked vigor, a phenomenon described by W. J. Cash in *The*

Mind of the South (1941) who wrote as if he had had the Archbalds and Birdsongs in mind: "Decay, as it came to them, came rather obliquely than directly; came, for long at least, and ironically, not so much through any even partial surrender to the demands made upon them as through the inevitable consequences of their failure and their refusal thus to surrender. . . . And if the majority survived, they commonly survived to a steadily declining estate." [5]

The symbolic meaning of this novel is most fully revealed through Eva Birdsong, though she is presented completely from the outside, like Amy in Katherine Anne Porter's somewhat similar novel, *Old Mortality*. Through being so fully in the thoughts of Jenny Blair Archbald and the General, Eva becomes the pervasive, yet elusive spiritual center of the novel. With her enigmatic smile, she represents for the General all that his era had idealized in woman: beauty, spirit, mystery, legendary glamor, courage, gallantry, a personality impervious to the inroads of time. As a queenly woman of rare beauty and charm, she had become the crown of a hierarchical society. In that her love represents a lost cause and her gallant nature is defeated more through circumstances than through spiritual weakness, she may symbolize the Old South, caught in its unequal struggle during the Civil War.[6] To the General, she also conveys some hint of the indomitable quality of the South which allowed it to survive defeat unscathed within, "a strong soul, still undefeated by life" (100). Though the General admits the cruelty of the old order and had as a boy suffered from the brutality of his own grandfather, he yet discerns that this older civilization was rich "in an established feeling for life," a feeling which survives in Eva Birdsong's personality.[7] To him she becomes an incarnation not only of the eternally feminine but of the highest spiritual possibilities in life, of a "lost sense of glory."

At the time of her sickness, she also seems to the General an emblem of humanity itself, "loving, suffering, hating, hoping, going into hospitals, coming out of hospitals, laughing, weeping, trying fruitlessly to make life what it is not" (144). In her pride, which comes to mean more to her than love and life, there is some trace of the stoical force which allows the Birdsongs and the Archbalds to resist the intruding tyranny of industrialism in Washington Street and to stand fast against the evil smell blown up from the industrial bottomland of Queenborough.

At the end of the novel the General is forced to admit that what Eva has stood for is overwhelmed. What has happened to Eva Birdsong is substantially what Mr. Compson in Faulkner's *Absalom, Absalom!* (1936) describes as the fate of the Southern gentlewoman in Eva's era: "Years ago we in the South made our women into ladies. Then the War came and made the ladies into ghosts." [8] As Eva yields "gallantly to the slow deposit of time," so does a whole civilization vanish. Because she possesses both a delicate sensibility and a fine intelligence, her tragedy as a sacrificial victim to the inflexible ideals of her race is more poignant than the immolation of the less perceptive Virginia Pendleton; or, as Alfred Kazin put it: "Intelligent enough to grasp the disastrous implications of her code, she was blindly committed to it." [9] Eva Birdsong's fate becomes a convincing illustration, moreover, of Northrop Frye's definition of "sophisticated pathos," as "the story of how someone recognizably like ourselves is broken by a conflict between the inner and outer world, between imaginative reality and the sort of reality which is established by a social consensus." [10]

Eva's antagonist, Jenny Blair Archbald, also worships the woman whom she would not willingly betray. When, toward the end of the novel, she wanders over to the Birdsongs to keep a tryst with George, she finds that Eva has come home three days earlier than had been expected. For the moment her heart is once more on fire with her old love for Mrs. Birdsong, and all thoughts of George vanish from her mind. Jenny Blair then honestly admits to all that Eva had meant to her: "order, beauty, perfection, an unattainable ideal of living" (266).

A dominant facet in Eva Birdsong's personality is a consciously contrived artifice, made necessary, Miss Glasgow revealed, by the life of pretense she has led for so long. Eva's preference for hothouse orchids and gardenias over garden flowers is one indication of the exotic conventionality which tradition has bred in her. Her cousin, John Welch, a young doctor who lives with the Birdsongs, asserts at the time of Eva's illness that part of her trouble may be a wounded spirit, since she has never known a natural moment in her marriage. "The code of perfect behaviour," which has "supported her as firmly as if it had been a cross" (143), prevents Eva from breaking down and from admitting to anyone her knowledge of her husband's disloyalty. Her patient smile, even when her lips are quivering with pain at the hospital, is thus a symbol of her heroic pretenses, and it only wavers and dies when, in her illness, she summons the energy to defend George to the General. To George himself her smile is a haunting reminder of conscience, of his temporizing with the noblest qualities in his own nature.

Miss Glasgow described Eva's privations with both sympathy and ironic aloofness. The only thing she could not have borne, Eva tells the General, would have been for her husband not to love her. Ironically enough she makes this avowal while George is having his first significant encounter with the maturing Jenny Blair. After a quarrel some years before, Eva had told George, with Desdemona-like faith, that even if he killed her she would love him. Though he then unwittingly proceeded to kill her in spirit, she still loves him all too possessively, as her jealousy attests. Yet if she demands so much, an additional irony is that the moral tradition formed by men like George is mainly responsible for her idealization of marriage. Vibrant as her influence and personality are, there is also a hint of sterility in Eva: she had never, for example, wanted a child, as if to imply that the obligations of maternity and the intensities of sexual passion are incompatible.

With a fine sensitivity Miss Glasgow continually alluded to the tensions and the dissimulations in the Birdsong marriage. After the operation Eva's tarnished beauty and depressed spirit engender an ominous note in the novel. As with Thomas Mann's characters, sickness in Eva is an outer sign of traumatic dislocation within. Increasingly, she experiences a frantic sense of terror at losing something already irrecoverably lost. In a moment of rare honesty with each other, Mrs. Archbald and the General agree that Eva did not wish to survive her illness to begin anew her life of pretense. With this deepening sense conveyed in the novel that the truth must be faced no matter what the cost, Eva tires of "being somebody's ideal" and is impatient to face reality at last. After she kills her husband, she gazes through and beyond him with a look of benumbed apathy, itself symbolic of an implacable Fate which has exacted retribution in proportion to the depth—or thoughtlessness—of the betrayal.

Miss Glasgow's artistry is forcefully apparent in making George Birdsong more likeable than a man of his limitations would ordinarily be. Through stressing George's liberality, his uncalculating impulsiveness, and his magnetism, Miss Glasgow rendered credible Eva Birdsong's initial infatuation with him and her continued loyalty to him, despite his inability to remain faithful to her. She tells the General at the hospital that as a boy George evinced a heroism which won her heart: he rushed into a burning house to save a Negro child, Memoria, who was years later to become his mistress. If Eva loves George for his unreflecting courage, the General likes him for his unreflecting generosity. He remembers that when he needed money, George alone of his friends had come to his assistance with all of a small inheritance. The General thinks, too, that George has a full and rich humanity which only infirmity of purpose prevents him from fully realizing. To George's credit, he tries to extricate himself from the entanglements he falls into. In the case of Jenny Blair, for instance, she is the one who will not let things rest when George decides that he can go no further with her. As Maxwell Geismar has observed, George is more the victim of Jenny Blair's "infatuation and his own vanity" than of waning love for his wife.[11]

One other form which George's behavior assumes under pressure is a compulsion to escape intense reality. Thus he diverts himself by teasing Jenny Blair outside the hospital while they are both waiting for the General to finish talking to Eva, and he half welcomes the unexpected amorous skirmish which develops between them. After Eva's operation the General hopes that George can "keep his nerve" and his capacity to feel for his wife, but he is not reassured by what he knows of George's mercurial nature. Though the General is disheartened, he is not too shocked, therefore, at seeing George, before Eva has left the hospital, come home at dawn "florid, refreshed, invigorated by his escape," now able to "return with replenished sympathy, no doubt, to Eva's bedside" (202). The spectacle of George's weakness suggests to the General a hint of lurking evil in the universe which chills his own morning fresh-ness of spirit. A powerful irony in the book is George's rapid recovery from his flamboyant grief, while his wife, though no longer in immediate danger, loses all will to live. In that he prospers while she loses hold on life, he seems to flourish physically at her expense, at the same time that his moral deterioration parallels her physical decline. Miss Glasgow revealed with restrained cynicism how convention, in its aversion to un-pleasant reality, protects the weak like George and the shallow like Jenny Blair as long as they are discreet, but demands a continuing sacrifice to false gods by the noble Eva and the large-minded General.

Jenny Blair Archbald is another of Miss Glasgow's subtle portraits: the girl is a victim not only of the uncontrolled forces in her own nature but of an evasive morality. More passionate, predacious, and uncon-ventional than May Welland in *The Age of Innocence* (1920), Jenny Blair Archbald can be regarded, like Mrs. Wharton's young woman, as a "terrifying product of the social system . . . the young girl who knew nothing and expected everything." [12] The mores that shield the woman from a genuine contact with life bring results which had not been antici-pated and which, paradoxically, the upholders of tradition in the novel still will not acknowledge. The General and his daughter Mrs. Archbald, in their attempt to keep all knowledge of suffering from Jenny Blair, fail to see that prolonged inexperience may result in the inability to form any moral perceptions. A sheltered life may cause the innocent woman to expose herself to evil with no realization of what she is doing; it also prevents her from being exposed as an agent of evil, since all people around her unite to pretend that the unmentionable does not exist. The ending of *The Sheltered Life* is, therefore, ambiguous: things have been driven out into the open and concealed deeper than ever before. This is the purport of that final embrace between the General and Jenny Blair which Mr. Geismar has aptly described as one "of mutual falsehood and deception." [13]

Miss Glasgow's detached vision in this novel allowed her to present the General with objectivity as well as sympathy. Consequently, the self-pity informing the characters who more directly reflect her own alienation is, in most instances, missing from him. Because of his worldly experience, his great age, and his depth of perception, his wisdom is more authentic than that of John Fincastle and Asa Timberlake. When Miss Glasgow has the General remark that "fortitude may be the last thing to go," the utterance is the more authoritative for being tentative. In General Archbald, Miss Glasgow presented resignation as the inevitable result of a full experience, rather than as the result of a narrowly intense one.

He was one of those aristocrats or "Confederate brigadiers" who adapted to new circumstances after the Civil War, but who refused to identify himself with materialistic values when these went counter to his native sense of integrity. Regret for a lost ecstasy embitters him deeply —he was able to make a living, he once told Jenny Blair, only "by putting an end" to his real self—but does not induce in him a lasting neurotic recoil from life. As a result of his negative conviction that, in the long view, his own individual destiny is insignificant, he attains the positive conviction that old age may, in fact, contain his best years, "that final peace without victory which turns a conflict of desires into an impersonal spectacle" (196). One of the finest aspects of the General's character, his tolerance of people like the Crockers for what they are rather than scorning them for their origins, derives directly from this acceptance of experience. Though he knows that love decays, he also shares the belief of his era that the echoes from an intense passion survive somewhere in the outer cosmos. He is true, then, to the faith which he has, with his rational mind, abandoned; and Eva Birdsong is also connected in his mind with this lingering idealism.

The General and Eva are vestiges from an era which, in spite of its hypocrisies, had a noble simplicity and an implicit grandeur, symbolized in part by the great old elm trees on Washington Street which he and George Birdsong have struggled hard to preserve. These elms represent all that is fine in the Old South: the fact that they are now "disfigured" may indicate that the older way of life is now on the defensive. There is, in fact, considerable direct criticism of the industrial New South in the novel. The General condemns present American—and Southern—indifference to beautiful surroundings: "Did ugliness . . . conform to some automatic aesthetic spring in the dynamo?" (106). He deplores, for instance, the replacing of colorful red brick pavements by "neutral asphalt." In the General's eyes, Jenny Blair's beauty lacks the dignity and grace of Eva Birdsong's; yet he perceives that it is sufficient to satisfy "the less elevated standards of our democracy" (135). The General recognizes that increased suffrage has meant the prevalence of an increased sense of social justice in America; but he also finds a standardizing tendency which is inhospitable to the producing of "great beauties . . . great men or great heroes." [14] The General, however, perceives that the old order, despite its precious qualities, lacks vitality to survive its inanition and that salvation can only come to it from without: "Perhaps new blood, new passions, and new social taboos were the only salvation of a dying order" (76).

Like John Fincastle in *Vein of Iron,* Archbald seems to have been an idealist born out of his time. In his long monologue, "The Deep Past," the General adheres to the philosophical values of the romantic movement, and is disturbed by the tendencies of scientists later in the century to discredit the transcendental point of view. Eva's cousin, John Welch, is, the General thinks, typical of the advanced thinker of the latter age in regarding the subjective as nonsensical. In the least convincing section of his monologue the General avers that a green bench is more than the green bench he touches. As with John Fincastle, Miss Glasgow seems to have underplayed the subtlety which ought to have marked the mind of a man as intelligent as Miss Glasgow wanted the General to be. As an abstract thinker he is not impressive since, in his revolt from a materialistic world-view, he embraces with little qualification the philosophical idealism of the earlier nineteenth century.

Despite his real chivalry and high-mindedness, the General is a victim because he lacks the power to express his inmost self. The General, led on by "the pity that becomes a torment to the nerves," had in youth at least protested the injustice of the prevailing morality by helping a runaway slave to escape capture. But in the conflict between his prejudices which place him on the side of the established order and his instincts which make him sympathetic toward the revolt of the individual, his prejudices win out. Genuinely persuasive as the General is, he does not fully attain the stature which Miss Glasgow sought for him as a man representing "the tragedy, wherever it appears, of the civilized man in a world that is not civilized." [15] In particular, he lacks decisiveness and the absolute integrity which a more forthright struggle against convention might have conferred. He has, in fact, many similarities to the Newland Archer of Mrs. Wharton: both men are unable to escape the demands of convention because of their inbred gentility and their conscientious consideration for others, and they both miss as a result the best part of life.

The other characters in the novel were conceived with a uniform steadiness of vision. John Welch, with his self-reliant intellect, has a genuine but hardly tolerant insight into human nature. Evidently approving his humanitarian idealism, Miss Glasgow was closer to him with her mind than with her emotions. He is seen always as having sound sense and generosity, but he is less sympathetically portrayed than the irresponsible George Birdsong whom he so justly criticizes for his neglect of Eva. In place of George's magnetism, John has a vehemence out of proportion to what he criticizes and he is too humorless.

Etta, the General's soured and defeated daughter, suffers from a genteel nymphomania which, because she is homely, she has no chance to satisfy; and like Katherine Anne Porter's Cousin Eva in *Old Mortality*, she resents the fact that the Old South made outcasts of those women who lacked charm. As her father considers her plight, he comes to regard it as symbolic of "those harsh and thorny realities" which have blocked his own expression of self. In a more general way, Etta represents aristocratic debility and decay, when, for example, her sister-in-law Mrs. Archbald describes her as "ingrown." She finds at best a twisted expression of self when, for no rational cause, she bites the arm of a woman friend who has been more fortunate in securing masculine attention.

The General's other daughter, Isabella, is Etta's antithesis, though both women live only in the emotions. If in her elopement with a carpenter, Joseph Crocker, Isabella had the decisiveness to be unconventional, Miss Glasgow also indicated with scrupulous irony how timid she is later in most of her views: "a little too wide for the sheath skirt which was just going out, and not quite broad enough for the modern ideas which were just coming in" (167). Isabella, and to some degree Jenny Blair, embody those rebellious instincts in General Archbald's nature which, for propriety's sake, he has kept repressed.

The General's daughter-in-law, Mrs. Archbald, is another of those women in Miss Glasgow's fiction whose vision is bounded by tradition and who is capable of enduring "any discomfort of body so long as one was not obliged to be independent in act" (18). She is more aggressive than Mrs. Pendleton in *Virginia:* she is generous and kind but lacks Mrs. Pendleton's ready sympathy. Miss Glasgow also modulated through the use of a tolerant irony the somewhat harsh outlines of Mrs. Archbald's character, describing her in one place, for example, as having "been left a penniless widow at an age when widowhood had ceased to be profitable" (18). Her endeavor to find a suitable family tree for the Crockers after her sister-in-law's elopement with Joseph, illustrates not only Mrs. Archbald's pragmatic wish to make the best of things but also the widespread general tendency in the South to justify the inadequate present by recourse to authority conferred by the past.[16]

Part of the force of this novel results from Miss Glasgow's skillful anticipation in Part One of later tragic incidents: as a result many situations gather full meaning only when they are viewed in retrospect. "The Age of Make-Believe," a prelude in 1906 to the main action eight years later, is principally centered in Jenny Blair's mind when she is nine. This section of the book is one of two slight masses of material which form a pair of overtures to the main drama; the second of these, "The Deep Past," presents in 1914 the General's reflections concerning his personal history as that is refracted against the history of the South. The much longer Part Three, "The Illusion," oscillates between these two characters. In Part Three Jenny Blair and the General are more closely bound together than they had been in the previous two sections, and the narrative threads are expertly brought closer together and entwined as the tragic pattern of the events becomes increasingly inevitable.

First asserted in the novel is Jenny Blair's rebelliousness when she protests against reading *Little Women* and wishes to receive her reward for finishing it before she has done so. Her vital energy which later causes so much damage is prominent throughout Part One; she proclaims at the beginning of this section and also at its close: "I'm alive, alive, alive, and I'm Jenny Blair Archbald!" An experimentalist in sensation and the emotions from the beginning, she later exemplifies how ruthless the undirected and unacknowledged Life Force can become.

That as a child she was drawn to the unknown and the prohibited, her venture into Penitentiary Bottom reveals. There she has a roller-skating accident outside the house where George is visiting Memoria, his colored mistress. Jenny Blair's hedonistic enjoyment of the brandied peach which Memoria gives her is indicative of her relish of this forbidden adventure; she finds herself accepting naturally George's presence at Memoria's place rather than asking why he is there, just as later she accepts her feeling for George without thinking of it. George enjoins her to secrecy about their encounter; and their conspiracy of silence, of course, anticipates the later deception of Eva. Miss Glasgow thus foreshadowed in this part of the novel Jenny Blair's subsequent conflict: shall she be loyal to George as the man she wants or to Eva as the woman she greatly admires?

The novel's effectiveness lies largely in the powerful yet subtle way Miss Glasgow suggested both the cruelty and wildness which lie hidden beneath the layers of social usage. The despair which the General finds in the eyes of the hunted and persecuted among animals and human beings renders him skeptical of any benevolent interpretation of human nature or of Divine Providence. He remembers the cruelty of his grandfather toward him at the hunt and the cruelty of William's former master when the dog did not show himself apt for the chase. That strong instincts often triumph over the civilized amenities is true throughout the novel. Thus Memoria, George's colored mistress, with her deep voice recalling to Jenny Blair "the scent of earth," is stronger at the given moment as an influence over George than the more delicate, ethereal Eva Birdsong, just as later the youthful freshness of Jenny Blair is more potent with him than fidelity to his long-suffering wife.

The General recalls, moreover, that the Archbalds have always been subject to disturbing visitations of instinct. His sister, Margaret, had eloped with an Italian musician who was, unknown to her, already married, and she died obscurely in Vienna. His great-aunt Sabina had publicly defied God and had been saved from suspicion of witchcraft only because of her high connections. His brother, Rodney, had lost heart with life and had shot himself, leaving behind a cryptic note: "Shadows are not enough." [17] The General is somewhat uneasy, therefore, at finding not only that his daughter Isabella has some suggestion of Rodney's profile but that his granddaughter seems to combine the vigorous skepticism of Sabina with the eyebrows of his brother. He senses that she is unsettled within, discerning an anarchic streak in her even as a child. Later Jenny Blair mentions her grandfather's great-aunt with approbation, sympathizing with her willful singularity. The dream Jenny Blair has after her first contact as a woman with George, of being unable to elude a constant pursuer, signifies further the degree to which she is the victim of the undirected impulses of her own nature. Incidentally, this sequence ingeniously anticipates the panic she experiences after Eva, nemesis-like, discovers the guilty lovers.

Hints of spiritual corruption and of moral decay, which also attend the decline of the old order itself, accompany the fruition of the illicit affair between Jenny Blair Archbald and George Birdsong. As Jenny Blair freely follows her instincts, her innocence becomes overlaid for the moment with "the hardened look of a woman who is disenchanted with life" (229). As a child she had noticed how flushed and heavy George's features became when, after an afternoon's dissipation, he had come home to his discontented wife and quarreled with her. Jenny Blair sees some of this same ugly coloring suffuse his face when he gives in to his feelings for her before she goes to the mountains, yet his bloated face does not diminish her desire. When Jenny Blair comes back from her vacation in the mountains, she sees a blown curtain at an upper window of the Birdsong home sucked back into the room: thus she is drawn back into the vortex of her pernicious passion for George which she had almost escaped. The unkempt Birdsong garden at the end of the novel connotes not only the decline of Eva and the aristocracy she represents, but also the wild, lawless nature of Jenny Blair. The April wind blowing with unrestraint over the clover and grass as George and Jenny Blair are first attracted toward each other is one more sign of the unrestrained, primitive feeling which draws them together.

Moral decline in the individual and the decline in prestige of a social class, both implicit in the affair between Jenny Blair Archbald and George Birdsong, are also symbolized in the bad odor which wafts up to Washington Street from the chemical factory in Penitentiary Bottom. After Eva interrupts the lovers' embrace at the close of the novel, the evil odor is so pronounced as to become associated with the corruption in the depths of human nature itself. In addition to its principal suggestion of abstract evil, the odor signifies the unfriendly aspects of the new industrialism which are antagonistic to the real graces of the aristocracy and to its spiritual capacity to endure. The stench has already dispersed the upper-class families except for the Archbalds and the Birdsongs, and the General regrets that it is one of the misfortunes of civilization that some underprivileged people must live in the Bottom itself. The General himself can hardly detect the smell when it oppresses the others. This may imply that he is too chivalrous to suspect the existence of evil in his immediate surroundings and too innocent, despite his wisdom, to see adequately all aspects of reality. To Jenny Blair as a child, the smell exerted the fascination of the forbidden; and against the orders of her mother, Jenny Blair explored the Penitentiary Bottom —to partake, as it were, of the fruit of the tree of knowledge. When, as a young woman, Jenny Blair lets her thoughts wander to the charms of older men, the evil odor is again borne in upon the breeze. Then when George comes to the Archbalds for dinner after several weeks' absence, he pays no attention to her, but talks of indifferent things like the weather, woman suffrage, foreign politics and finally of the evil odor (they "wonder if it would end by driving them out of the neighbourhood").

References to this sickly, all-pervasive odor are thus woven into the very texture of the book and do much to establish its tone. With penetration and complete knowledge of the local social reality and the larger political scene, Miss Glasgow illustrated how the local decadence in these essentially admirable families had its parallel in the hidden decadence of the contemporary world itself, where, underneath a ripe culture and a flourishing prosperity, the forces of corruption were about to erupt in world war. Jenny Blair's destroying passion for George awakens in the spring of 1914, when she is seventeen and he is in his forties; it reaches a fateful climax in the autumn of that year when, with the outbreak of a total war, the world itself seems on the point of a fateful, almost self-willed destruction. Jenny Blair's drifting into an illicit love affair parallels the drifting of her social class to decay and the drifting of the larger world outside into cataclysm. The apparently innocuous, but actually subversive, temperament of Jenny Blair has its inevitable correlation with the hypocrisies at large of an effete civilization.

To exhaust the possibilities of her situations, to elucidate more plainly their symbolic implications, or to accentuate a mood, Miss Glasgow frequently had recourse to light and shadow. As to her earlier practice, Miss Glasgow admitted in the preface to *The Deliverance* that she deliberately contrasted light and dark tones in that novel. In this aspect of her technique Miss Glasgow evolved a more subtle, less mechanical approach: in the prefaces to *Vein of Iron* and *The Sheltered Life* she argued that light and shadow should be incorporated into the texture of the prose itself. Tonal gradations in her later work are not, therefore, so stark and melodramatic as they had been in *The Deliverance* and in her other early books. Instead of using light and darkness for external effect, she came to feel that they should be refracted inward and become interweaving strands in the stream of the narrative and in the souls of her characters.

Among her later books, *The Sheltered Life* pre-eminently absorbs light and shadow into its inner substance. In 1906 the Archbalds and the Birdsongs, in harmony with a social order which has only partially lost its vigor, still radiate confidence. Therefore, brightness is everywhere, flooding the Archbald library, hovering over the Birdsong garden in soft waves, and etching in the figure of Eva Birdsong. In 1914 as Eva Birdsong yields to the dissolution wrought by suffering and the years, her brightness fades, although in her decline her form is illumined from time to time with its former glow. The guilty passion between George and Jenny Blair, which will destroy Eva, significantly gathers force during the sultriness of the summer. Then under the lengthening shadows of autumn Eva's sense of impending disaster intensifies and her beauty slowly wanes. In contrast to the sunny Archbald library at the beginning of the book, twilight darkness creeps over the Birdsong library when Eva learns of her final betrayal. The vapors with their evil smell roll up from the Bottom as the sun sinks with a "tarnished light" and as night envelops the Birdsong garden and the house where George lies dead. In this book nuances of mood and symbol, of feeling explored and suggested, are caught up in a luminous prose: light and shadow become varying manifestations of a vibrant reality at the very core of existence. As if in illustration of this truth, the light images in *The Sheltered Life* are dynamic in character rather than passively descriptive.

In this novel, Miss Glasgow adroitly contrasted muffled noises with sharp clear sounds to communicate both the presence of concealed evil and the resulting violence when that evil is exposed. The restive quiet and the muted sounds pervading the prose thus anticipate the crashing within and without which overwhelms Jenny Blair in the Birdsong garden at the end of the novel, when for the moment at least, truth rises superior to the hypocrisies which customarily obscure it. This final rupture of moral pretenses Miss Glasgow had also prefigured throughout by a continued use of kinetic images of cutting, tearing, piercing, fracturing, and jerking:

. . . and immediately the darkness was slashed by a pearly glimmer. (62)

Joy as sharp as light pierced her nerves. (67)

Suddenly, while he meditated, it seemed to him that the shape of the external world . . . broke apart and dissolved from blown dust into thought. (108)

Her death had left a jagged rent in the universe. (115)

Her hidden features shuddered with grief; a spasm jerked its way through her thin body. (268)

The water imagery, extensively present in the novel, serves a complex function. Among other things, it implies the flowing and progress of time, the onward motion of life itself, and the irregular but constant surging of mental experience. Often in combination with references to light, these water images are used to evoke the most meaningful moments of emotional revelation. Thus when Jenny Blair as a child was going to the Peyton party, delighted impressions raced through her mind as "the current of life rippled and broke into waves and scattered a sparkling spray through her thoughts" (75); and the General, in contemplating Eva's pain at the hospital, still could yield to despair while he felt that "the sinking back on belief . . . rippled in flashes of energy through his mind" (138).

The Sheltered Life is typical of Miss Glasgow's later books in showing her absorbed with the representation of the flow of time. In these books, she linked this flow to the consciousness of her characters: upon their mental vision, the onward-flowing stream of time opens; they see themselves as part of this stream, while it obliterates in its forward pulse all but the most vivid moments of the past. These, however, are ineffaceable and are heightened by the glow given them by memory (Preface to *In This Our Life*). As Victoria Littlepage in *They Stooped to Folly* approached death, she was acutely sensitive to the enigma of time, so that her struggles with the proprieties lost their point as she saw time stream on around and beyond her. The only things that seemed important then were residual memories from childhood (her affection for her dog and her love for her mother) and her own desire to escape from time into the Timeless. The constant ebb and flow of time in its forward propulsions fascinates General Archbald who is also nearing death. At eighty-three in "The Deep Past" he looks back over his life. At this transparent moment the stream of time momentarily seems to stand still: "And what was time itself but the bloom, the sheath enfolding experience? Within time, and within time alone, there was life—the gleam, the quiver, the heart-beat, the immeasurable joy and anguish of being" (109). Certain golden moments precipitate from time; these, he concludes, must have become part of a perdurable cosmic memory; otherwise he would have forgotten them. After this moment of mystical insight, the General feels time flow out and away from him once more, an onward movement which will continue, he realizes, when he is no longer actively part of it, but passively absorbed into it at his death. Somewhat less obsessively, then, both Victoria Littlepage and General Archbald evince the same desire as Quentin Compson in *The Sound and the Fury* to pass beyond the temporal into the fixity of the Eternal.

To capture this illusion of time's permanence and change, Miss Glasgow endowed the General with a tremulous sensibility, not unlike that possessed by the central figures in Virginia Woolf's fiction. In Mrs. Woolf's novels, Miss Glasgow noted how the external edges of character seem to dissolve into the immediate flow of mental life so that the individual tends to become passive before the stream of energy passing through him. In the following description of Mrs. Woolf's fiction, Miss Glasgow admirably suggested her own modified use of the stream of consciousness, not only in General Archbald's review of his past life but also in sections of *Barren Ground, They Stooped to Folly, Vein of Iron* and *In This Our Life*:

In her novels the point of view has dissolved into mist and the vision is as diffused, as transparent, as luminous as a shower in sunlight. Not the characters in "Mrs. Dalloway," but life itself, is the spectator. Life, fugitive, variegated, erratic, has become both the observed and the observer. Among

English and American novelists only Mrs. Woolf has succeeded with this method, if it may be labeled a method, of the magnified vision.[18]

Mrs. Woolf, said Miss Glasgow, managed with such energy to combine the world of intuition and the world of intellect that the abstract mind became illuminated with visionary intensity. Thereby Virginia Woolf approximated in the written word the energy and evanescence of mental activity itself. In summing up the style of *To the Lighthouse* Miss Glasgow also suggested the kind of prose and the range of effects she tried to attain in *The Sheltered Life,* particularly in "The Deep Past" section:

. . . long lovely sentences, wreathing clause within clause, are poured upward by a fountain of energy and scattered like a luminous spray in the mind. In "To the Lighthouse" the world and time itself appear as frail, fugitive and exquisite as a breaking wave, and there are no fixed stars in a firmament composed of pure spirit.[19]

Miss Glasgow found in the Russian novelists a similar absorption with the dissolving, yet all-important, vistas of mental life. Discussing these writers, she defined—in terms that might have been more applicable still to the work of Proust—her conception of the unconscious as a clear illuminating power from within the depths of personality, which inevitably colors, harmonizes, and universalizes the experience of the conscious mind:

When the Russian stream of consciousness overflows it is out of the actual into the universal experience. . . . With Tolstoy or Dostoievsky the spring of the unconscious mind is not a sluggish outlet, as colorless as sand, but a fountain of images transfigured by a luminous spray of emotion. No novelist, living or dead, with the possible exception of Dostoievsky, has equalled Tolstoy in his use of those tremulous and palely phosphorescent states between thought and sensation.[20]

In Miss Glasgow's own work the direct transcription of mental life thus tended to become "a fountain of images" transfigured by "a luminous spray of emotion," as these sentences from General Archbald's soliloquy in part disclose:

A multitude of women people the earth: fair women, dark women; tall women, short women; kind women, cruel women; warm women, cold women; tender women, sullen women—a multitude of women, and only one among them all had been able to appease the deep unrest in his nature. Only one unit of being, one cluster of living cells, one vital ray from the sun's warmth, only one ripple in the endless cycle of time or eternity, could restore the splintered roots of his life, could bring back to him the sense of fulfilment, completeness, perfection. A single personality out of the immense profusion, the infinite numbers! (120)

Here and elsewhere in the novel, Miss Glasgow accomplished what she set out to achieve, a style "delicate yet unbreakable," [21] a rich texture of dense impressions caught up into the patterns of experience she was to incorporate into the novel itself.

The emotional depths found in the best passages of *The Sheltered Life* create a rich texture for the whole novel, vibrant enough to include, without strain, expressions which in another context might seem trite. When George is described as "instinct with vitality," the cliché does not obtrude because it fits him so well. Similarly, when the General thinks of Eva Birdsong's bosom as being "pure as alabaster," the commonplace quality of the comparison is effaced in a recognition that this is the idiom a courtly gentleman of the old school would use in referring to a queenly woman. In general, the writing in the novel keeps above this level. Miss Glasgow's style at its best, with its delicacy of nuance and its toughness of fiber, is found in a passage like this which pictures Etta Archbald as a disappointed spinster of thirty-three:

Aunt Etta sat up on the couch and smoothed the hair from her forehead. She held a novel with a yellow back in her long thin hands, and her eyes, the colour of frosted plums, were fixed on the feathery blossoms of a mimosa tree. When she came home every day from the doctor's office, her nostrils were packed with an ointment which was supposed to relieve her pain, but had never done so except for a few minutes. She was interested now, Jenny Blair knew, in the strange young physician who treated her every morning, and then forgot all about her until he saw her again. Poor Aunt Etta's infatuations began always with this kind of false dawn and ended in a sultry twilight of disappointment. It did not seem fair that she should have exactly the same mistake happen over and over again; but, then, did anything ever seem fair? Mamma said she had fallen into the habit of being disappointed in love, and that it was one of the very hardest habits to break. (227)

In this passage Etta's faintly repulsive appearance leads by degrees to hints of her neuroticism, and these elusive touches are then caught up into the final brittle, ironic sentence which points to the completeness of her alienation and to the imperfect sympathy which her plight arouses in others. With delicacy of perception and lucidity of style Miss Glasgow throughout *The Sheltered Life* exhaustively yet compassionately analyzed the devious interplay between inner decay and outward appearances to establish this novel as her best.

⋄XII⋄

"Confirmed in Fortitude":
Vein of Iron

In the 1930's Miss Glasgow wrote two long books which treat incidentally of the Southern past and focus, for the most part, upon the
contemporary scene. *Vein of Iron* (1935) and *In This Our Life* (1941)
are substantial books, but reveal, in general, attenuated artistry. They
show that Miss Glasgow did not comprehend fully the intricacies of
the age, despite the frequent pertinence of her insights into it. A relative
failure to grasp the ramifications of her materials resulted in vagueness
of social commentary and psychological analysis; and a too positive
certainty as to the immediate relevance of her own values caused her to
proclaim them too directly through the principal figures in these novels.
Put on the defensive by the conditions of modern life, she also became as insecure as some of her own ostensibly independent characters,
who somewhat too aggressively proclaim their positive standards. Except for the ineffectual John Fincastle of *Vein of Iron,* the characters
who have their creator's approbation significantly lack the serenity
which an intrinsic confidence in their beliefs would confer.

Miss Glasgow left behind, in large degree, the disinterestedness of her
previous ironic approach to experience and became immediately involved
in what she wrote. Her poor health and her increased sense of personal
isolation and frustration, revealed in the *Letters* and *The Woman Within,*
undoubtedly led to the irritated tone of parts of these novels. What
these books lack in balance as convincing interpretations of modern life,
they gain, in a measure, as eloquent presentations of Miss Glasgow's

own values. Her sense of the distinctive marks of personality stayed with her, moreover, so that the characters in these novels are alive and solidly real, even if at times we may judge them differently than Miss Glasgow apparently did.

The two books are of considerable technical interest. Not only is point of view virtually restricted to that of two individuals—John Fincastle and his daughter Ada in *Vein of Iron,* and Asa Timberlake and his daughter Roy in *In This Our Life*—but there are also contrapuntal passages, where successive chapters, related from varying points of view, impart the reactions of several individuals to a single situation. Though these chapters in the novel are arranged spatially in a consecutive pattern, they deal with one incident and are temporally simultaneous. These chapters, radiating from a single event as a focal point, give the part of the novel in which they occur a fanlike structure, similar to that found in certain sections of Virginia Woolf's *Mrs. Dalloway* or in "The Wandering Rocks" episode of *Ulysses,* where time stands still while the reader enters the minds of successive characters. Early in *Vein of Iron* (Part One, Chapters 4, 5, 6, 7, and 8) Grandmother Fincastle, John Fincastle, Mary Evelyn Fincastle, Aunt Meggie Fincastle, and Ada Fincastle (as a child) reflect in front of the fire at the Ironside manse; later in Part Two, Chapter 12, John, Ada, and Grandmother gather about Mary Evelyn's coffin and ponder simultaneously upon her death. In *In This Our Life* (Part One, Chapters 5, 6, 7, and 8) a polyphonic technique again provides varying reactions to one subject: the oppressive atmosphere in the Timberlake household as it is felt in turn by Asa Timberlake, Lavinia Timberlake, Roy Timberlake, and Minerva, the Negress. In her later years Miss Glasgow experimented continually with the structure of the novel without abandoning her basic methods and without adopting fully any of the devices she evolved.

Notwithstanding its significance to the student of Miss Glasgow's work and its solid provincial scenes, *Vein of Iron* is the least vital of the novels written after 1925. It is a chronicle depicting three generations among the descendants of the Scotch-Irish settlers in the southern part of the Great Valley of Virginia. This is the part of the state from which Francis T. Glasgow's people came; from long visits with her relatives, Ellen Glasgow knew this section almost as well as her native Tidewater and the Southside. It is part of Ellen Glasgow's accomplishment to have written with complete knowledge of the normal, solid, substantial folk of Appalachian Virginia instead of the degenerate and oppressed upland natives who have more frequently figured in twentieth-century fiction.[1]

Prior to the opening of the novel, John Fincastle had been ordained a Presbyterian minister; but to his mother's lasting chagrin he had, as a result of conscientious scruples, resigned his ministry in a large church at Queenborough, and retired to Ironside to become the contemplative philosopher. At this point the novel begins, with Part One, "Toward Life" (1901), centered in Ada's childhood. Part Two, "The Single Heart" (1911–17), is primarily concerned with Ada's loss of her lover, Ralph McBride, to the shallow, irresponsible Janet Rowan and with John Fincastle's strong feeling for his racial past. The short Part Three, "Life's Interlude" (1917), is an idyll of love between Ada and Ralph on Eagle Ridge when after six years he separates from his wife. Chronologically at the halfway mark, this brief section acts as a pivot upon which the first two parts in this long chronicle are connected with the last two. In Part Four, "God's Mountain" (1917–18), the principal events are Ralph's going to France in the war, the birth of his illegitimate son to Ada, and Grandmother Fincastle's death. Part Five, "The Dying Age" (1918–33), recounts the married life of Ada and Ralph in Queenborough in the 1920's and early 1930's, their misfortunes during the depression, and their determination in 1933 to return to the Great Valley after John Fincastle journeys there alone to die.

John Fincastle sets the somber mood of the novel by thinking of Schopenhauer's favorite Hindu prayer, with its recoil from the agony of life: "May all that have life be delivered from suffering" (96). From the first scene in which the Ironside children, out of wanton perversity, chase the idiot Toby Waters, until the closing sequences in which the McBrides and their neighbors struggle to keep going during the great depression, Miss Glasgow viewed man as ordinarily struggling against indifferent, arbitrary fatality, and suffering inexorably as a result of the failure of his efforts. The juxtaposition of Ada's reluctant renunciation of Ralph with Mary Evelyn's death further accentuates Miss Glasgow's sober view of human existence. To Mary Evelyn, who loved life more tenaciously than anyone else had in her family, life awarded privation, sickness, and death; her mother's camphor and mustard meant to Ada "the odour of pain—of the dying flesh, of the spirit struggling to release itself from the clay, of loss, grief, helpless pity and heartbreak" (142). When Ada does get to marry Ralph, reality again disappoints. After his return from war, Ada feels that her relationship with Ralph has changed, that impassioned ecstasy has gone from it. The loss, she feels, may be part of the structure of being, though Ralph's hypersensitivity has been aggravated by the war. She trusts, but somewhat tentatively, that another kind of love with potentially deeper springs in fidelity may take its place.

That the inequities of the world are to be endured, even welcomed, as a sign that God is not indifferent to man and that He causes suffering out of ultimately benevolent motives, were ideas implicit in the Calvinism of the aboriginal settlers in the Great Valley of Virginia. Grandmother Fincastle, their present representative in the first parts of the novel, maintains that, even if people are half-wits, they must produce all the children possible to suffer God's curse. The morality of these descendants of the frontier Presbyterians is one of prescription and derives from the Old Testament. When a Power terrible for good or evil has been offended, it must then be placated by sacrifice, though this may mean the ruin of several people's lives. When Janet Rowan accuses the innocent Ralph McBride of rape, there is nothing Ralph can do to withstand the social pressures placed upon him. He must marry her since the code of these descendants of the settlers is a literal one which considers only the convention—this time that a woman's word is not to be doubted in sexual matters—and not the individual incident. The penalty imposed upon Ralph for his supposed infraction of an unwritten law is so high that even Grandmother Fincastle momentarily has her doubts as to its justice; but faith in the Lord and His decrees triumphs over such momentary questioning of His will.

If life is mostly anguish to be endured, Miss Glasgow insisted that the pioneers and their descendants had the "vein of iron" to meet its sometimes unexpected and inexplicable demands. The Calvinist settlers in the Great Valley of Virginia led hard and dangerous lives; and their descendants possess, sometimes latently, the sustaining qualities of their ancestors: moral integrity, self-reliance, devotion to a cause of their own or of God's formulation, endurance, and fortitude. Frontier heroism in action has yielded to a heroism in the suffering of privation, but an animating idea—predestination with the pioneers and stoic uncomplaint with their descendants—inspires all generations of this race. To Grandmother Fincastle, the real exploits of her ancestors have the fascination of legend; and through her their moral fervor is impressed upon her family, so much so that Ada in later years thinks of the past in terms of her grandmother's strength and not in terms of her mother's grace.

John and Ada Fincastle, through whose minds the novel unfolds, are more directly responsive to the values transmitted to them from their ancestors than is Dorinda Oakley in *Barren Ground*; and it is clear, by the sympathy with which they are drawn, that Miss Glasgow in later years became increasingly dominated by her father's moral seriousness in spite of her intellectual rejection of Presbyterian dogma. Like the John Fincastle of old who was drawn on by a visionary frontier when at eighty he went off into the wilderness to become a missionary, the

John Fincastle of the novel, working late in his study at the Ironside manse, feels the links between himself and the community dissolve and his spirit fly off into "the unconquerable solitude," there to be refreshed and restored. The strength of vision he inherits becomes a stabilizing influence in his struggle with poverty and obscurity, and a compensation for the frustrations of his solitary inner life. By having him live chiefly in the mind in an environment which discourages intellectual activity, Miss Glasgow established the autobiographical aspects of John Fincastle's character; for Miss Glasgow, as she expressed herself in *The Woman Within,* also suffered from this same kind of isolation.

In physical contact with the land that had been wrested from the wilderness, Ada feels the hardiness of the pioneers infused into her own spirit. The "vein of iron" which runs from her ancestors over the years to her, she is sure, connects the generations and proves that the resisting spirit is immortal. When Ralph is forced to marry Janet, John Fincastle's countenance, "confirmed in fortitude," enables Ada to bear her misery; when she is giving birth to her illegitimate child, she feels that the steadying strength of the pioneers has passed into her spirit; and when she despairs at her grandmother's silent condemnation of her "disgrace," the fortitude, which lies beyond courage and which derives ironically from her grandmother, revives and sustains her.

As Stark Young has perceptively said of this novel, the elements of predestination and courage in the Calvinist creed go beyond dogma "into a passion for finality and life." [2] With John a pattern for life is provided through sheer animal faith; with his mother, through the will of God; with Ada—despite separation from Ralph and her mother's death—through the positive energies of the life-urge itself. To John and Ada and Aunt Meggie, to Ralph in lesser degree, life in Queenborough after the war lacks substance, so that Ada hopes they may sometime go back to Ironside. The fact of death, though unavoidable, also seems less final to the surviving characters at the end of the novel when the ideals of Grandmother Fincastle, Mary Evelyn, and John still live. Meggie, her brother feels, has a beautiful poise, a natural dignity that is her legacy from her forebears: "the frontier, for all its savage impulses and brutal habits, had created, if only now and then, characters that rose superior to destiny" (363).

Possessing the same poise he praises in his sister, John Fincastle retains, like Asa Timberlake of *In This Our Life,* an enduring faith in some purpose he can only dimly see. This is the symbolic importance of his final journey to Ironside, when irresistible impulse takes him to die where he has most productively lived, and to renew his spirit even in death. He has his victory in spite of the fact that on the surface he is, like so many Glasgow characters, "a splendid failure." At least, he can, without conscious sentimentality, take the long view; out of the ruins of our civilization and the abstract systems spun out to meet its problems, he is sure that something better will still arise.

The most memorable character in the book is the objectively depicted Grandmother Fincastle; and the book's most memorable sequences, the Ironside chapters, involve her. As long as the novel is spiritually organized about her commanding presence as a living exemplar of the pioneer virtues, it holds together. From the time we first see her, through Ada's eyes, etched against the landscape gathering sticks about the Ironside manse, she dominates the book. Self-sufficient and commanding, her features "carved into granite fortitude," she is, Ada thinks, the strongest and the happiest member of their household, that is, until Ada herself knows the ecstasy of awakening love.

Miss Glasgow acknowledged that a rigid stoicism may be an incomplete philosophy for living when she opposed the delicacy and fragile beauty of Mary Evelyn to the bleakness of existence at Ironside and to the iron regime of Grandmother Fincastle. Grandmother, unlike her daughter-in-law, has no sympathy for the softer, more refined and sensuous pleasures. Mary Evelyn needs beautiful trifles about her whose use and enjoyment can be ritualized: her red geraniums, her candlesticks, her crocheted mats, and her blue bowl filled with flowers or berries.

The various forms which Grandmother's striking energies assume reveal Miss Glasgow's thorough understanding of this strong, somewhat forbidding woman. With equal assurance, Grandmother can deplore the decline in moral responsibility which marks the wild behavior of the young in 1911; she can decree that Ralph must marry Janet although she suspects that Janet is lying; and she can preside over the local Red Cross meeting in her fervor for a righteous war, although she is too infirm to stand. Since Grandmother's condemnation of Ada for her sexual trespass had been harsh, her succor of Ada in labor is the more forceful. At this point, emotion and the morality inspired by the heart triumph over the abstract principle:

"Hold tight to me, Ada," she said. "Hold tight as you can. I won't let you go."
"Grandmother! Oh, Grandmother!" The steadfast life of the house, the strong fibres, the closely knit generations, had gathered above, around, underneath. She might sink back now, cradled in this blessed sense of security. "Now pain may have its way, and I may give up. Grandmother will know what to do." [3]

Generally, Grandmother Fincastle's character is strongly drawn, although her religious musings, especially her certainty at Mary Evelyn's death that the latter is beholding the Lord, are occasionally seen too much from the outside. Ellen Glasgow sometimes tended to make picturesque what ought to have been dignified, and, in effect, patronized her strongest figure by imagining her to possess a greater complacency than the fervent Calvinist could. When, for example, Ada is miserable at being separated from Ralph, Grandmother's reliance upon the Lord is too unruffled for a person who so strongly felt her religion: "For she had spoken only the truth. The Lord had never failed her. She was in the hands of the Lord" (131). At other times, Miss Glasgow implied that Grandmother must be rather naive, after all, to believe so piously in God.

The first four parts of the novel are superior to the long fifth part, not only in the incisive portrait of Grandmother Fincastle, but in atmosphere and in their incidental characters and moving incidents. The Great Valley is given with complete knowledge, so that the village of Ironside and its inhabitants and the neighboring mountains are in themselves graphically imposing. God's Mountain and Thunder Mountain and Eagle Ridge and Shut-in Valley, the manse and its pasture, the houses and streets of the village, the hovel of Toby Waters and his mother out by the Murderer's Grave—these are all so fully imbued with the feeling of place as to become more vital in the novel, in some instances, than the principal characters themselves. The rural types are also caught with sharp accuracy: Doctor Updike, the country doctor somewhat soured after an unhappy marriage; Mr. Black, the minister oppressed by the world's misery; Mrs. Rowan, the efficient housewife and proud parent, anxious at the same time for a capricious daughter; Mrs. Waters, the subnormal village prostitute and her idiot son Toby; and, most vivid of all, Mrs. McBride, Ralph's pious and self-righteous mother. Like the Mrs. Clennam of Dickens in her effect upon her son Arthur, the formidable Mrs. McBride has undermined her boy's confidence in himself and has tormented him in childhood from the highest motives. If Miss Glasgow emphasized in Ada Fincastle the positive virtues deriving from Presbyterian forebears, in Ralph McBride she recognized the detrimental aspects of this inheritance and the destructive possibilities, in general, of family feeling.[4]

The Ironside scenes of the novel generate a reality which the Queenborough sequences lack. The most forceful section of the book—that in which the Ironside elders come between Ada and Ralph and force him to marry Janet Rowan—convinces at a surface level even if Miss

Glasgow did not make it clear that for this situation no other solution was possible. The lovers' smoldering conflict with convention, following the pressures put on Ralph by the Rowans, his mother, and the Fincastles, is so strongly felt that Ralph's agony and Ada's despair are both plausible. Ada's grief at her ruined life reaches its most impressive expression at the Murderer's Grave when Toby Waters, like an apparition, appears to her. She is repulsed by his appearance; yet she now feels kinship with him, as with his harlot-mother, with the murderer, and with all other outcasts: "he was a creature like herself, she thought, more repulsive than any animal, but born, as she and an animal were born, to crave joy, to suffer loss, and to know nothing beyond" (138). Only the world's pain, she knows, can relieve her own; and Toby's sufferings, in her anguish, become transferred to her. Equally notable in the novel is the pictorial immediacy of the scene on Thunder Mountain, where the lovers elope before Ralph goes to war. The physical recreation of milieu in a measure compensates for Miss Glasgow's relative failure to capture at this point the fullness of sexual ecstasy. The effects of war upon Ironside are subtly realized, the birth of Ranny is recounted with power, and the death of Grandmother, akin in the impression it conveys to the levelling of a stout forest tree, fastens securely upon the imagination.

The novel fails chiefly because of Miss Glasgow's inadequate portrayal of her idealist philosopher, John Fincastle, through whom she meant to express her own respect for "the life of the solitary spirit." [5] He too easily assumes that the modern world is hostile to intellectual inquiry; his belief, then, that no man with a family to support should seek the truth has the sentimental emphasis of self-pity. In the main, his speculations lack a firm basis and a precise definition. To account for the origins of his career, Miss Glasgow resorted to flat statements that in youth he had revolted against the world of facts, that he had hoped ultimately to know enough to justify God, and that, in a moment of vision, he had tentatively seen how "will" could be reconciled with "idea." If he were to discuss credibly this latter difficult question, he ought surely to have done more than ask if "pure philosophy" had ever advanced beyond Plotinus' affirmation that Destiny is a flight from the alone to the Alone, before positing the pious hope that "the forgotten paths of blessedness and mystic vision" might once again be remembered and "the inventive mind" be forsaken.

John Fincastle's notion of philosophy as a consolation, "the only infallible antidote to life," is too sentimental for a professional thinker to hold so unreservedly. In a complacent exchange of the God of Christianity for that of Spinoza, there is—despite John's moments of mystic insight—the rationalist's frequent incomprehension of the complexities of religious experience. In that his tranquillity is too readily achieved, spiritual urgency is mostly absent from his metaphysical activity, as this colorless summary of his career attests: "If he were remembered by others, it would be either as a dangerous skeptic, or as a man of simple faith, who believed that God is essence, not energy, and that blessedness, or the life of the spirit, is the only reality" (248).

In view of Miss Glasgow's insubstantial analysis of Fincastle's mind, it is hard to believe that a philosopher at the University of Edinburgh considers Fincastle's work, *God as Idea*, the greatest of the last twenty years. The publication of his work by a Hebrew mystic and the enumeration of Fincastle's half-dozen European admirers is also contrived. That Miss Glasgow's understanding of modern philosophy was imperfect is made clear by her account of Dr. Hardenberg's visit of homage to John Fincastle. Hardenberg, "the last great German Idealist," asks, "After James and Bergson, what now?" John replies, his oversimplified "vitalism" asserting itself with a spurious profundity:

"God, maybe. It is true that under a microscope God may be only a cluster of cells. But, then, who has ever put God under a microscope? The intellect has survived Bergson. Ultimate truth will outwear James by an eternity. It is possible that God is more than motion. It is even possible that modern man is more than glandular maladjustment. You and I can afford to wait." (364)

Miss Glasgow portrayed Fincastle more persuasively as a man than as a philosopher, especially when she examined the tensions developing in his relationships with his delicate wife, Mary Evelyn. Commanding love for her alternates in him with a reluctant admission that love may be insufficient; as a result, Mary Evelyn's single-minded devotion to him becomes both inspiration and trial.

Another weakness in the rendition of Fincastle—and in Miss Glasgow's own creative vision—was an incomplete realization of the external realities confronting the philosopher in a world dominated by the effects of science. This weakness obtrudes especially in Fincastle's judgments of the 1920's and the 1930's. In the modern age he finds it impossible to escape "the purring of ceaseless dynamos" and thinks of the new generation as being without standards, "without a pattern, without a code, without even a centre." As descriptions of the spiritual sickness of the times, these remarks are not excessive; but excited excess of emotion tinges his further observations that all personality is in danger of being extinguished by the mass consciousness, that American culture is neither bourgeois nor proletarian but potentially infantile, and that the moron, not the meek, may inherit American democracy. As speculations even, these views are too sweeping, their negations too unqualified. The social conditions in America which might have justified Fincastle's hysterical pessimism are never fully recreated. True, the bank failures in the thirties are described with intensity, but even here there is insufficient appreciation of the terror produced by the unleashing of uncontrollable forces.

The chapters in the novel given from the point of view of Ada Fincastle even more conclusively reveal the superiority of the sections laid in Ironside. At the barn dance, for example, the conflict is accurately perceived in Ada between the inherited pride which prevents her from being with Ralph when he is drunk and the great physical attraction he has for her. Miss Glasgow also gained sympathy for Ada by contrasting Ada's integrity with Janet Rowan's unscrupulous exploitation of sexual allure. Ada is also appealing in her rebellion, ineffectual at first, against the fatality and the Puritan morality which sever her from Ralph; and she eventually rejects, with full justification, "the last refuge of fortitude" for "a living happiness," even though this decision leads to illicit love. When she goes to Eagle Ridge with Ralph, Miss Glasgow's grasp of Ada's psychology is firm. Desiring to surrender herself to the full ecstasy of the moment, Ada is, with her intellect, distrustful of the senses and finds that she can't surrender herself fully. With her, as with her father, the inherited self within the self is impervious to the intensities of emotion alone. In these sections of the novel Ada is so fully immersed in her surroundings that she possesses some of the same inevitability as her grandmother, as the valley and surrounding mountains themselves.

When she gets to Queenborough, this full accord between character and milieu is lost in Ada's excessive irritability with urban life. In many of her reactions she is unintentionally made a prig, fussily concerned, for example, over trifles like Minna Bergen's "wide insatiable mouth, painted as red as a wound" and the fact that men now shout words like "lousy" which little boys had once hesitated to write on fences. Even though Ada has endured much from the depression and from her husband, her calm consciousness of her own powers is too casually expressed: " 'I like getting the better of life,' she tossed back gaily, 'and I'm not ashamed that I do' " (325). In telling her husband when he begins to get well after his automobile accident that he has not lost his knack of selling, Ada ruminates rhapsodically on an essentially mundane matter: "Merely to say this was not enough; she must believe it. All her strength was poured into an act of faith, into a glowing affirmation of life" (311). In her criticism of the modern age, moreover, Ada often generalizes fallaciously from the specific instance. Because "movie-minded children pounced in bands from the alleys," because "the nimble wits and legs of bandits were matched against the sluggish law and the heavy-footed police," and because Dr. Updike on a visit tells of parents who drink and go to the movies while their babies are unattended, Ada spuriously concludes that such behavior is alone representative of the times: "Distraught, chaotic, grotesque, it was an age . . . of cruelty without moral indignation, of catastrophe without courage" (318).

Miss Glasgow's obsessive concentration upon the deficiencies of the 1920's and the 1930's throws the novel badly out of focus. Who is typical of the age, the irresponsible Minna Bergen or her conscientious parents? By attaching too much importance to the irresponsibles of the time and by exhibiting a subjective rather than ironic contempt for them, Miss Glasgow made them loom larger than the fine people with whom her sympathy lay, Ada's neighbors like Mrs. Rawlings, the Hamblens, the elder Bergens, and Mr. Midkiff. In retrospect, Miss Glasgow seems to have been an agitated spectator of the 1920's and the depression instead of a flexible intelligence interpreting the events of these years. When Ada feels that the virtues of the Hamblens, "industry, veracity, self-denial," are antiquated and foreign to the modern age, she underrates the age as mistakenly as she had arbitrarily condemned it for its overt defects.

Dr. Hardenberg's one-sided denunciation of America as "a strange country, with its watered psychology, its vermin-infested fiction, and its sloppy minds that spill over" (365) is likewise factitious. His sweeping condemnation of present-day America as "raw" and "savage" is at variance with Miss Glasgow's celebration of the frontier where life had also been raw and savage. Because Miss Glasgow did not elaborate completely the paradox that the same country might produce an admirable iron race and an irresponsible, sensation-loving one, the novel is confused in conception, and its tone is too sharply divided between elegiac enthusiasm and satiric stridency. It presents, on the whole, a graphic portrayal of the frontier Presbyterians, but it fails to demonstrate the applicability of their virtues to the present because modern life itself is indiscriminately seen as contemptible.

Nor is the characterization of Ada's husband, Ralph McBride, consistently firm. So long as Ralph is the victim of his self-righteous mother and of the other moral Pharisees of Ironside, he is persuasive because his moodiness and recklessness have an adequate cause. When, however, Ralph becomes his own victim, his petulant disillusion so completely exceeds the situations in which he figures that, even as a warped individual, he is not believable. His disgust with war and its aftermath, moreover, is too articulate to have been deeply felt. His psychic wound from the war is too loosely defined through his own protests; its impingement upon the root fibers of his being and upon others is only hinted at. In this outburst, he reveals a narcissistic self-pity which encourages him to assume that he is the only one ever to have suffered from the injustice of the world: " 'Everything flattened out and went dead on me. But I get a lot out of life as long as I take it on the surface. It's only when I punch through the surface that the world seems to go rotten. . . . When I look about me, in spite of all the good times, misery is the only thing that is real. Hunger and cold and disease and physical agony and meanness and rottenness inside and out human nature' " (262).

Missing in the attitudes of the other characters toward Ralph is the use of a controlled irony which might have made more conclusive the objective validity of his spiritual flabbiness. Miss Glasgow herself took Ralph's easily attained cynicism too seriously, without applying to him the standard Ada imagines her grandmother would have applied to his generation, "a puny breed." Although Miss Glasgow no doubt intended to present in Ralph a "lost-generation" character, she did not have sufficient firsthand knowledge of this generation to present it from the inside or, in this novel, the tact to present it in a disinterested manner from the outside, as she had done with comparable figures in *They Stooped to Folly*.

Miss Glasgow's uncertainty in the novel is manifested in a stylistic diffuseness and an intellectual obviousness. There is a steady and proprietary use of words like "joy," "happiness," "ecstasy," "delight," "love," without effort to differentiate the various nuances of these emotional states. This direct, sometimes cloying, expression of feeling represents an unsuccessful attempt to achieve a highly charged atmosphere rather than a definitive rendering of it. For example, the overwrought account of the lovers' reunion after six years lacks precisely the force which Miss Glasgow tried to gain for it: "All the hunger and the thwarted happiness of the last six years were consuming her with his lips. But it was bliss. . . . This is life, this beauty, her thoughts were singing. This is love, this delight" (173). Similarly, when Ada muses over the furnishings in the Queenborough home prior to Ralph's return from the war, there is this same vagueness counterfeiting as intensity: "all these things were swimming in a miraculous fluid, in an extraordinary delight" (239). Notwithstanding the finely wrought natural setting in the Ironside sequences, there is a tendency, even in them, toward the use of the cliché: "the thrilling charm of his mouth," "what a

Miracle love can make of life," "it seemed to Ada that she was stalked by the grim spectre of poverty."

The exhausting of Miss Glasgow's energy is further revealed by interpretative comments in the novel—particularly in Part Five—which, seemingly profound, prove trite in conception and expression. Overelaboration of the obvious occurs when Ada comments upon Mr. Bergen's bringing the news of Ralph's accident: "He put his friendly hand on her arm, and she thought, I always knew he would be a friend in trouble" (280). John Fincastle's sententious reactions to Ranny's fighting with his playmates are, in actuality, pompous and patronizing: "Violence is the spirit of the age, my dear. You wouldn't have him out of touch with his time" (313). Platitudes appear now and then in the novel: for instance, Ada reflects after the family removal to Queenborough from Ironside that "Life may be a pilgrimage . . . but a home is something more than a house" (232). One suspects that Miss Glasgow really had nothing to say after the first half of this novel. At her best as an interpreter of manners and of the ethical problems arising among conflicting individuals, Miss Glasgow did not excel in her more comprehensive attempt—as in the latter part of *Vein of Iron*—at rendering the sociological problems of the modern age. When, however, explicit sociological concern was subordinated to moral preoccupation, her novels gained in substance, as we shall see in *In This Our Life*.

⋄XIII⋄

"A Shocked Atmosphere":
In This Our Life

A more sustained book than *Vein of Iron*, *In This Our Life* has nothing as authentic as the Ironside sequences of its predecessor. As commentary upon the contemporary scene, *In This Our Life* is a more complex work than *Vein of Iron*, and the issues which it explores, however inadequately, are of greater significance. The superiority of Miss Glasgow's intuitions to her definition of them is once more apparent; the book is typical of her mixed accomplishment as a creative artist. It always promises to be better than it is, and its best insights are, all things considered, worthy of a finer vehicle. But these insights justify the book despite its defects, especially as it contains, explicitly or implicitly, Miss Glasgow's most mature views on experience. This novel studies the psychological problems of the Timberlake family, once influential but now alienated especially in Asa, from both the moribund chivalric tradition of the past and from the appalling ugliness of the industrial present. Asa finds some measure of understanding in Kate Oliver, a lifelong friend whose companionship means more to him than sensual satisfaction, and in his daughter Roy, until the loss of her husband Peter Kingsmill to her sister alienates her from Asa's sympathy.

The book is principally concerned with the frustrations of Asa and Roy Timberlake, in whose minds the novel is mainly centered. Asa is defeated by his distasteful marriage to Lavinia and by family obligations; and his daughter Roy is defeated by the selfishness of her sister, Stanley, and by the vacillation of the two men in her life, Peter Kings-

215

mill and Craig Fleming. Craig had been Stanley's fiancé until her elopement with Peter; after a brief engagement to Roy, he is once again impelled irrationally but conclusively into Stanley's orbit. In the end, only
her father gives Roy a sense that life may be meaningful despite all disillusion. Yet even he cannot give her the complete assurance for which
she is seeking. The effectiveness of this last scene in the novel lies in
Asa's tacitly expressed faith that life persists, rather than in Roy's confronting her father directly with her anguished cry that she needs "something to hold by." Her demand is excessively stark and sudden, too
patly externalized, to be an inevitable culmination to her previous sharp
but hitherto elusive agony.

In This Our Life chronicles the maladjustments of modern man to
the world outside him, maladjustments engendered by his sense of outrage at the disproportion between his expectations from life and the
oppressive realities he confronts. The book thus exploits for literary
effect his "compulsive neurosis." This phrase is used to describe the
hypochondriac, Lavinia Timberlake; in her mental sickness she symbolizes, in part, the human condition in the present age. In commenting
upon Roy's loss of her lover for the second time to her sister, her
father—who is often Miss Glasgow's spokesman—succinctly describes
the lives of the people in this novel: "We are living in a shocked atmosphere. Nobody is normal" (433). This sense of general trauma, in
turn, results in an inhibitory sense of isolation: there is little possibility
of meaningful communication between generation and generation, or
between oneself and another.

An apparently unattainable inner security becomes, in effect, the quest
of modern man. Thus Roy continually searches for abiding love, only
to be disappointed with two unworthy lovers, and to suffer with each
loss a nightmare sense of defeat. After Craig's defection at the end of
the novel, Roy rushes out into the night and encounters an embittered
Englishman in a park pavilion where she seeks shelter from a storm.
This Englishman, whose scarred face is an emblem of his distorted
soul, saves her from apathy, since he has suffered far more than she
has. Her own benumbing bitterness is dissolved, then, in the protective
sympathy she now feels toward this stranger who has been completely
adrift since his mother's death.

Despite its fragility and the pain it involves, love is the only meaningful reality, Roy iterates. Miss Glasgow's conclusion, expressed through
Roy, was ambiguous: one must live within the limits imposed by defeated expectations, yet one must still value the transfiguring possibilities of love. Miss Glasgow presumably felt that human affection
can be disabling as well as ennobling. If one denies the affections, he

resigns himself to an inevitable demoralization, like the Englishman's at the end of the story, or else sterility of spirit, like Stanley's, sets in. Yet as Asa concludes, the emotions can become tyrannical. The exasperating thing to Asa is that, though family feeling may be at the base of all our difficulties, there is nothing to put in its place—it has done harm but it has held things together. At the end of the novel, Asa has greater doubts about the family. His own family threatens to shut off once more his chances of escape to a life with Kate, and has, moreover, dishonestly decided to save Stanley at the expense of Parry Clay, her chauffeur and an intellectually aspiring Negro boy.

The distinction of the novel lies in its vital characters whose inner lives are genuine, even if their relationships to their era are either too directly stated or too inconclusively defined. So closely implicated in the passing life of their day, the characters of *In This Our Life,* in retrospect, seem overly preoccupied with problems, personal and sociological, which are less important than Miss Glasgow thought them to be. In part, the situations and issues in the novel lose urgency, because the characters are neurotically engrossed in personal suffering and are surprisingly indifferent to the demands of Necessity. At the unconscious, emotional level, the conflicts in which they are enveloped are genuine; at the rational, conscious level, however, the expression of these conflicts is often ponderous and pretentious, sometimes offhand. Ellen Glasgow's characters in this novel are real to the degree that their inner turmoil or their complete lack of feeling reflect veraciously the confusion or apathy of the world in which they live. To the degree that their somewhat flamboyant emotionalism and self-conscious intellectualism cannot be justified by this external chaos, they are false to the realities which have conditioned them. For this reason the characters who are seen from the outside, such as Stanley Timberlake, Peter Kingsmill, William Fitzroy, Lavinia Timberlake, and Parry Clay, often exert greater pressure upon the imagination than do the more articulate point-of-view characters, Asa Timberlake and his daughter Roy.

The most subtly realized character in the book, Lavinia Timberlake, is seldom in its foreground. She is a selfish hypochondriac whom Asa can hardly tolerate after the enforced intimacy of thirty years of marriage. She is, moreover, a symbol of all those implacable, impersonal forces which have defeated him, uniting as she does a reverence both for fossilized convention and for the materialistic standards imposed by modern industrialism. With Lavinia and all she represents, the aristocratic tradition is played out; and its essential hypocrisy and disregard of the truth become focal points for Miss Glasgow's attack.

Because moral inertia is Lavinia's chief characteristic, Miss Glasgow throughout insisted upon the destructive effects of this woman's passivity. Significantly, by a sort of compensatory fantasy, Lavinia identifies herself with Stanley who is also deficient in sympathy toward others. Lavinia's frigidity is sadistic: since she has had to endure persecution from a younger brother and general neglect from men, she wishes now to make some other man suffer. By his proximity, Asa becomes the principal victim of this "aging Madonna." Lavinia has become his "intimate enemy," undermining his confidence through attrition as effectively as Stanley through overt selfishness despoils Roy. Still it is Lavinia's complexity which imparts vitality to her. Granted that she is a hypocrite, she has a surprising degree of intelligence. The result is that hypocritical evasiveness alternates in her with a sense of reality preternaturally acute. Much as she loves Stanley, for example, Lavinia has no illusions about her selfishness. She has, moreover, a clear cynicism about love and marriage which only a lifetime of disillusion could engender. Acknowledging the familiar Glasgow axiom that love is a primitive rather than an ethical force, she sees that Craig Fleming has been too abjectly devoted to Stanley to hold her love and that, instead, he ought to have instilled in her an admiration of his mastery. Through Lavinia, more effectively than through Asa who is often too closely the author's spokesman, Miss Glasgow expressed her own views of the younger generation. Lavinia is repelled by the rowdiness of the modern; and she feels that the young lack "staying-power," that they run away from life, and that they try to build, without foundations, an impossible happiness.

Just as surely as her husband exemplifies the last faint survivals of the generous Southern chivalry more fully celebrated through General Archbald in *The Sheltered Life,* so Lavinia illustrates the final attenuation of a once vital way of life. As Roy appropriately thinks, her mother now illustrates "the flabbiness of decay" rather than any "delicacy of sentiment." The moral dishonesty of Lavinia's decaying caste is exposed at the time of Stanley's accident. All members of the family except Asa tacitly unite to spare the callous Stanley further distress, and they show no scruples in selecting Parry Clay as their scapegoat. At this crisis the members of the family betray "a collective anxiety," betokening both an individual and a class insecurity and, by extension, the larger insecurity of the contemporary world itself. Their fear of the truth has its parallel, then, in the life-destroying fears which enervate modern society. When Asa bluntly asks Stanley to tell the assembled group the truth about her accident, their pretenses, but not their determination to have their own way, yield to Asa's resolute honesty.

Lavinia, in particular, who resents bitterly any stirring of the calm surfaces of life, is hysterical when her maternal instinct is confronted with her husband's sense of honor.[1] Aunt Charlotte Fitzroy sums up aristocratic casuistry when she rationalizes the situation by maintaining that a colored boy couldn't feel the same way as a white girl. More than for their improbity, Miss Glasgow condemned these people for their inability to evince positive feeling for their fellow men.

Despite Miss Glasgow's view that Stanley was subordinate in importance to Asa and Roy,[2] she is the most forceful person in the novel. She was imagined with greater vehemence than Asa and Roy, and the outline of her character was not blurred, like theirs, by Miss Glasgow's compulsion to have them be her spokesmen. Over and above Stanley's real existence in time, there is something ineffable about her; in her beauty and lack of moral sense, she is, as Roy thinks, a fantasy—"a fantasy clothed in flesh and made living" (168). Except for her effects upon other people, Stanley has no other existence, since her pleasure-seeking and power-loving instincts, like those of Ibsen's Hedda Gabler, must be directed outward. The unintellectual Stanley has, then, nothing to rely upon in a crisis except the blind instincts, the "disconnected sensations" which have brought the crisis on. Her behavior is so largely instinctual that its malignity is, in great part, motiveless; in this sense Stanley is, as Miss Glasgow maintained, "insufficient" rather than actively evil.[3]

But Ellen Glasgow did sense sadistic impulses in Stanley who, like the Undine Spragg of Mrs. Wharton, must out of envy destroy what others possess. The intensity of her drives results in the directionless energy which, like Jenny Blair Archbald's, easily becomes malign. Stanley's fatality thus "lay not in what she had done, but in what she was and would always continue to be; she was not to be blamed that her very imperfections ravished the heart" (297). Thus Asa, the most consciously rational individual in her family, responds with his senses to the fatality of her beauty, even when he is intellectually conscious that her beauty grows more seductive the more havoc it causes. In her, Miss Glasgow epitomized, in microcosm, those perverse forces of unreason in society which erupt in the greater irrationality of war. Accordingly, Miss Glasgow used her to illustrate the fact that "human beings are driven to war by some blind destructive instinct, that the cause of war is deeper than any geographical boundary, and is rooted in the facts of biology, and in primitive impulse."[4]

In her impact upon others, Stanley personifies the forces of death and destruction which Miss Glasgow felt to be at the center of modern life. Stanley's predatory nature, the "innocence that devours," is most accentuated in her relationship with Peter Kingsmill. Resisting her authority over him, Peter at once infuriates and fascinates Stanley, so that the wedded life of the pair becomes an internecine struggle. The final irony resides in Peter's being as effectually destroyed in conflict with Stanley as he would have been, had he abjectly submitted to her in the first place. He is eventually so oppressed by his quandary—he can neither live with Stanley nor without her—that he evades it by committing suicide. Miss Glasgow perhaps most forcefully exposed Stanley's withering touch when, out of caprice and selfishness, the girl brings on a miscarriage. Though she ruins all who come into her sphere, human beings are yet so imperceptive of reality that they flock to console her, even after Asa has divulged her criminal dishonesty. Toward the end of the novel, she becomes, preposterously, the heroine of a drama in which she has incidentally killed a little girl and ruined Parry Clay's career.

Asa Timberlake, like his daughter Roy, is convincing as an individual despite the artificiality which frequently accrues to him as a spokesman for Miss Glasgow's own views. Asa resists, for the most part ineffectively, the insidious effects both of a dead tradition and of disheartening circumstance. Indicative of his deprivation is his life as a worker, without promise of stable employment, in the factory once owned by his grandfather. Just as his father had been defeated by external forces too powerful for him (the monopolistic practices of early twentieth-century business had negated his benevolent feudalism) so Asa never realizes his potentialities.[5] The "age of the individual" passed with Daniel Timberlake; under the new dispensation of an impersonal capitalism, Asa regards himself as an alien.

Furthermore, he has never fully recovered from the trauma induced in him by his father's suicide. His fear of life has been accentuated by his having had to work, as a boy, in his mother's boardinghouse, and by her death. Because he has never completely transcended Oedipal involvement with his mother, he is shut up within himself. Despite his affection for Roy, he is afraid of all women "not maternal and elderly." He is indissolubly married to Lavinia, for as Miss Glasgow cryptically remarked, "Virginia tradition decreed that infidelity should be an expensive pursuit" (15). To the degree that his defeat has been fated he feels an overwhelming futility. Yet his moral integrity organizes his life; and his "ironic amusement" becomes a protective covering for an exacerbated sensitivity, as it did with Ellen Glasgow herself. Asa is the victim, however, except in crises, of his own lack of force and assertiveness. For his vital importance to the novel, Miss Glasgow made him, perhaps inadvertently, overly genteel and passive. To the artistic detriment of her later fiction, the strong man with his aggressive assertiveness too entirely disappeared from it.

Asa repeatedly has the sense that he is existing "between an age that was slipping out and an age that was hastening in," that he is wandering "between two worlds, the one dead, the other powerless to be born." [6] In his isolation, he stands on the ruins of a desiccated past while the inadequate present offers him no refuge. The future, too, seems as unpromising as the chilling present, for Miss Glasgow implied in the epigraph of the book that the new age is a long time in travail:

> Your creeds are dead, your rites are dead,
> Your social order too!
> Where tarries he, the Power who said:
> *See, I make all things new?* [7]

In terms of the plot of the book, Asa senses a final break with the past and with moral order when Stanley runs off with Peter. Since the old restraints of honor and respect for others no longer avail with people who demand at all cost their own gratification, the relentless anarchy inherent in such selfishness now alone determines their actions.

Because Asa feels himself so much a part of a transitional period—as did Miss Glasgow herself—it only follows that his attitudes toward past and present are, like hers, ambiguous and complex. Miss Glasgow's long involvement with the conflicting forces of chivalric tradition and of iconoclastic modernism reaches its ultimate stage in this novel with the projection of Asa's conflicts. We have seen her blunt condemnation of tradition in the person of Lavinia; and in William Fitzroy other features of social convention are satirized, particularly his notion that there is something "unwomanly" about a woman who possesses character and inner strength. Asa himself is critical of "a great tradition," regarding it as "an expensive luxury" which may at moments lend "inspiration," but which inevitably leads, he discerns, "to gradual hardening of the arteries." Certainly, his only sympathetic friend, Kate Oliver, feels that duty, a sense of failure, and "an indomitable tradition" have almost extinguished Asa's identity.

Unsatisfactory as the past may have been, however, in providing a fully valid rationale for living, the present is doubly so. In the past there at least prevailed the belief that spiritual values were important, distorted sometimes as those values may have become. During the terrible days of the Civil War and the Reconstruction, we at least had one compensation, Asa thinks, which the modern age lacks: a belief in ourselves. In the past, order was possible or at least desired, and a certain spaciousness also pervaded the lives of men. Somewhat casually in the effective opening scene, which in essence summarizes his conflicts, Asa expounds this theme in conversation with Jim Maberly's son. The young man is all on the side of "progress" and his chief joy is in "clearing away something old," whereas Asa has an instinctive respect for those old houses and old trees which always seem to get in the way of such progress. Like Willa Cather's Professor St. Peter, Asa feels that such solid homes were meant to last and that they reflect the moral stability of those who lived in them. He is depressed at seeing the wreckers already at work on the fine old house in which he himself had once lived. Now, Asa mournfully muses, the age of standardization has set in and the new houses—he lives in one—possess neither roots nor history nor background. Through Asa Miss Glasgow continued her criticism in her late phase of the New South; he recoils, as she did, from the modern tendency to forego the "graces of life" in favor of a worship of "acceleration."

Modernism, making a fetish of convenience, has not only sacrificed graciousness for efficiency, but has also disfigured all it touches. In a city park where she meets Craig after Stanley's defection, Roy is nauseated by the sight of "all the sordid and disfiguring signs of an overheated humanity." Roy's loathing is in excess of the situation, however, and becomes obtrusive by Miss Glasgow's vehement stress upon unsavory naturalistic detail to indicate her own revulsion from modern life.

Miss Glasgow expressed her attitude toward the younger generation in the 1930's primarily through Asa, an attitude marked generally by querulous complaint. Through him, she asserted that youth is illogical and disorderly. Above all, Asa is chilled by the freedom which stresses privilege and eschews responsibility. Youth can now give full rein to its instincts, whereas at least the forms of beliefs—and some residual faith in life itself—restrained his generation.

Even within the somber context of the novel, however, all of Asa's criticisms are not justified, since they frequently derive from those selected facets of reality which directly supported Miss Glasgow's own ideas. In her strictures upon the modern age there is frequently a sensational fascination with its lurid aspects; in tone her observations become too irritable for the requirements of art. One feels, for example, that the "tough guy" and the widespread imitation of his standards by the young were not so indigenous to America in the 1930's as Miss Glasgow implied in this passage:

I'm in sympathy with them, he said to himself, and added in the next breath: But they haven't learned the first thing about order. They don't know how to reason. They have fine ideas without a string of logic to hold them together. They have made a cult of loose thinking, of disarrangement and rowdiness. Even the dandy of our day, he thought, with his eyes on Craig's rumpled head and limp collar, might have given a lesson in method to the popular tough guy of the present. (210)

Miss Glasgow was, in fact, excessively engrossed in her immediate conviction that the modern temper is "confused, vacillating, uncertain, and distracted from permanent values." [8] The result was an overemphasis upon some superficial qualities in her younger contemporaries in order to prove her point. A disproportion, in short, existed between Miss Glasgow's diagnosis of the age and her overwrought descriptions of its illness. The mistakes in craft were, first, to condemn an age mostly through general comment rather than through its individuals, and also, elsewhere in the book, to look upon neurotics like Lavinia, Stanley, Peter, Craig, even Roy and Asa, as its typical representatives. What disturbs in the novel is not so much Miss Glasgow's contention that modern times are violent and directionless, but the fact that she did not uniformly demonstrate the precise underlying causes for, and the exact symptoms of, contemporary disintegration. Miss Glasgow admired, through Asa, youth's positive search for experience, its "unflinching courage and . . . candid irreverence," even if youth lacks a governing philosophy. Yet this concession to the sincerity of the young does not much mitigate Miss Glasgow's consistently negative approach to the age immediately preceding the second World War.

The positive values which Asa himself exemplifies achieve definition through his omnipresent cynicism that rejects the worthless in his experience. These values are drawn, as Miss Glasgow insisted, from a deeper source than the materialism of the present age. Asa's faith in life originates in his sense of continuity with his past, through his mother, whom he worshipped, to his grandfather who was once benevolently powerful in the industrial life of the Old Dominion. This sense of continuity is not only emotional but moral, and takes compulsive form in a sense of responsibility by which Asa, withstanding the pressures upon him, holds together his identity. His sense of the sanctity of the individual, his conviction that man has an inherent dignity, also derives from the chivalric tradition at its best. He is, then, both an idealist and a rationalist to the extent that he refuses to acknowledge the supremacy of animal instinct and to forego the civilizing advantages of the reason and will. On the other hand, he finds in his attachment for Kate Oliver that the life of instinct—guided by the reason, however—can alone transcend effectively the restrictions imposed by convention.

Despite her desire to make Asa the informing center of the novel, Miss Glasgow displayed some ineptitude in drawing his character. In analyzing his mind, she frequently resorted to embarrassingly direct statements of intent, when, for example, on going to visit Kate Oliver, Asa muses fervently: "I've a whole afternoon. . . . I must taste every drop of it" (174). Like Roy he is given to self-pity in excess of its cause, when he talks to Kate about his life of quiet desperation and declares that he is "damned tired . . . of being sorry for people" (184). Not only are his reflections upon the younger generation self-conscious, but he is too egregious in discussing modern life: "He drew in his breath sharply, while he watched a buzzard sail slowly nearer before it shot down with outspread wings to the earth. 'I wonder what is wrong with the world nowadays' " (186). Thus his expression of self is sometimes stilted, at other times perfunctory.

In Roy are embodied certain other of Miss Glasgow's values—specifically those which, Asa feels, man has always wanted in woman but which he has never consciously sought in her: "courage, truthfulness, a tolerant sense of humor, loyalty to impersonal ends" (21). Except when Roy is too neurotically withdrawn into self to see things as they are, she is notable for her honesty, for her revulsion against hypocrisy, and for her hatred of sentimentality. Her realistic attitude makes her evasive mother uncomfortable; her courage, however, wins her father, especially when she determines to transform her betrayal by Peter and Stanley into a personal victory over emotion. Roy's abrupt dismissal of her father's values—such as duty, responsibility, and the need to act in accordance with a sense of personal integrity—represents a mistake in Miss Glasgow's craft if Roy is to generate the respect which Miss Glasgow obviously felt to be her heroine's due. Miss Glasgow's intrusive anxiety about her also detracts from the objective force of Roy as an aesthetic creation. Miss Glasgow justly sympathized with Roy in her dilemma, but it is difficult to see why Roy must protest so stridently her hardness: "I won't get soft. If I let myself get soft, I'm done for" (147). Generally credible, her courage and self-reliance are difficult at times to reconcile with a querulous self-pity. Such expressions as "I wish . . . there were a war in Spain for me" (249) and "I hate . . . to have to live in a man's world" (265) signify a petulance before life rather than a commanding confrontation of it.

Some of the best-paced scenes in the novel involve the brusque, unlovable business titan, William Fitzroy, Lavinia's uncle. Though something of a stock character, he was created with the same vigor as was Cyrus Treadwell in *Virginia*. William's disagreeable nature provided Miss Glasgow's irony with opportunity for a thorough exposé of social hypocrisy. A "staunch pillar of the Stock Exchange and of St. Luke's Episcopal Church" (10), William is sanctimonious, not kind, and effuses, instead of heartfelt benevolence, the "air of property well applied." Something of a reprobate by instinct under his perfectly respectable exterior, he tempers his "pious hope of future immortality" with a decided preference for young girls in this life. As Stanley becomes to Lavinia a symbol of all the ecstasy she never possessed, so Stanley represents to her Uncle William all his memories of youthful ecstasy. Consequently, it is Stanley whom William turns against in the initial phases of his final illness, since her vitality is in such painful contrast to his own decline. Although Asa cannot sympathize with William when the latter's will to power is deflected by cancer, he comes to admire William, in one of the most forceful scenes in the novel, for his shrewdness in having judged correctly the Timberlake marriage. When he makes possible Asa's freedom by granting Lavinia an annuity, William admits with cynical candor that he admires Lavinia, but that he could never have endured, as a husband, her hypochondriac vagaries.

The most poorly adjusted character in the book, Craig Fleming, is the least firmly conceived. Miss Glasgow's analysis of his conflicts, as they determine his outward conduct, was discerning, but she was less sure in tracing the origin and development of his attitudes. He is the visionary radical, with little of the realist's sense of fact or of the philosopher's compulsion to evolve a firm pattern for living. After his desertion by Stanley, his temperamental weakness and sensitivity are manifested in his apathy; and at the time of his desertion of Roy, they are manifested in his ungovernable instability. Typically, Craig drifts with his emotions instead of radically examining the moral ramifications of what he is doing.

Since he is unable to control his emotions, he is also ineffective in directing his haphazard idealism outward to the social system at large. To this extent, Craig is loosely symbolic of the modern South itself, as Miss Glasgow saw it, in its failure to evince commandingly its inherent sense of nobility. Why his liberalism should be so flabby and why he does not resist identification with an external world in confusion, Miss Glasgow failed to elucidate except to say that his mind is composed less of firmly defined ideas than of immediate impressions and intuitions, and that education has dissolved his foundations instead of providing him with firmness of conviction and critical resiliency.

A more hapless victim of modern life is the Negro, Parry Clay, who is defeated not so much by moral weakness as by implacable forces within and without the self. A mixture of Negro, Indian, and white blood, his nature—recalling that of Faulkner's Sam Fathers—provides its own battleground for forces which he does not fully comprehend. Parry's mixed blood defies classification, makes of him another symbol of chaotic modernism, and induces in his countenance the bewildered anxiety which his intelligence only serves to intensify. In that Parry's active mind seals him from the traditional sphere of the Negro but provides him with no entrée into the life of the white race, he feels a part of neither social world. When he is arrested, the contamination of the prison spreads through his nature like a disease. In essence, the prison represents the disordered world outside the self and epitomizes the evil at work in it. From this sudden initiation into spiritual depravity, Parry, Miss Glasgow implied, will not recover. The half-mad gospel ranter, and the cockroach extinguished by the thumbnail of one of the craps players in the jail, are emblems respectively of the irrationalism and the hidden sordidness of modern life. More pitiably than Asa, Roy, Craig, or Peter, Parry is a sacrificial victim to impersonal powers, and he represents at its most acute the spiritual impuissance of those about him. Even more poignantly than the suicide of Peter Kingsmill, Parry's fate signifies that human beings are often wasted; Asa's view that Peter's end seems deplorable "as a failure of mere human aspiration" applies as well to Parry. At the close of the novel, Asa also sees in the faces of everyone about him the boy's beaten look, his apathetic resignation, and his mute despair. Even the once blustering William Fitzroy has been broken by disease and has lost confidence in his powers.

The only people not thus stricken, the well-adjusted characters in the novel, are, with the exception of the earlier William Fitzroy, minor figures of two sorts: those like Asa's son, Andrew, and his wife Maggie, who have no gifts at all and who represent the passiveness of the ordinary; and those like Kate Oliver and Minerva Clay whose innate wisdom results in a confident serenity lacking in the other characters. Since these "normal" people do not strongly come to life in the novel, Miss Glasgow's picture of the modern age is possibly more one-sided than she had intended it to be. Without an effective counterbalance, the prevailing neuroticism in the novel, significant as it is in emphasizing modern man's spiritual sickness, is ultimately out of proportion to the situations presented. Though Miss Glasgow valued highly Kate Oliver's kindly sympathy and common sense, Kate has hardly a flicker of vitality in her own right. As to Minerva, Miss Glasgow never quite succeeded in recreating her thoughts, though she tried hard to do so by resort to the interior monologue twice in the novel. These attempts to render the idiom of the Negro through the silent stream of the mind are abortive, though Miss Glasgow had unusual success elsewhere in rendering objectively the Negro dialect. For an uneducated and inarticulate Negro, Minerva too coherently defines her own values. Her simplicities are unreal and her sentiments are flat because they reveal neither the urgency of a genuine primitivism nor the wisdom of a genuine sophistication. Her self-reliant endurance so obviously wins Miss Glasgow's approval that Minerva ends by seeming more like one of Miss Glasgow's inner selves than an independently achieved character. Miss Glasgow's grasp of Parry's nature was more firm because she could view the son more distantly than she could the mother.

The vigor of the novel survives its blemishes, and its universe is ultimately authentic, despite many unrealities. Miss Glasgow's psychological acumen was generally keen, and her structural sense fused acceptably the parts of a sprawling organism. The unity of the novel is achieved through a sustained and carefully wrought style, except for those passages wherein lapses of imaginative conception generate a corresponding imprecision of expression. In many instances, the style is actually superior to the ideas it clothes, and in this respect recalls that of *Vein of Iron,* although there are fewer vague generalities in *In This Our Life.* The style is muted rather than brilliant. Miss Glasgow in setting the central mood made skilled use throughout of sunset, autumnal, and neutral tones. In the first pages Asa's walk home through the twilight establishes the wan, elegiac atmosphere of the book: the clouded evening sky frames in Roy's agitated figure when she has her quarrel with Peter; the rain blows in from the window upon Roy after she learns of Peter's defection; the lifeless leaves fall slowly while the Timberlakes wait for Craig to come in when he is courting Roy; the hazy lights of autumn suffuse the various trips to the country; and the heavy storm sweeps down on Roy the night she runs away and encounters the Englishman.

An intermittent reassertion of irony helps preserve the embittered feeling that went into the book. Although Miss Glasgow used an externalized irony of statement to sketch in satiric portraits like those of Lavinia Timberlake and William Fitzroy, she relied mostly upon the irony of circumstance to accentuate the sober quality of her vision. When Peter is about to leave Roy and Roy asserts that freedom does not matter if the two of them love one another, there is the spectacle of a faithful woman whose ardor increases as betrayal comes near. The irony inherent in another betrayal, that of Parry Clay, is intensified, when, in retrospect, William Fitzroy's assertion to Parry is recalled that Negroes do not need to study to become lawyers since white people will always help a Negro in trouble. That the irony in *In This Our Life* emphasizes human futility is seen when Craig states, after the broken engagement to Stanley, that he has always needed a woman like Roy, only to desert her when the destructive Stanley appeals later to his pity. Asa's thought that Parry's scholastic success augurs a new future becomes ominous when it is later called to mind. A failure in justice, and a cynical suggestion that poetic justice is impossible because genuine sympathy for others is too rare, explain the caustic irony with which Miss Glasgow envisioned Stanley's triumph after the accident and Parry's complete defeat. Irony at this point also underlies the alacrity with which Lavinia and Uncle William, who have recently grown critical of Stanley's irresponsibility, rush to defend her.

Several scenes in the novel display Miss Glasgow's depth of feeling and mastery of craft. The family conclave after the accident, in particular, illustrates many of Miss Glasgow's gifts as novelist: her skilled use of characters in contrapuntal fashion to sound the reverberations of a situation, her sense of the antagonisms and attractions at the depths of personality, and her expert externalizing of moral motive into a character's speech—into what he says or fails to say. In particular, the recoil of the family when Asa brings the truth home to them and Stanley's agonized aversion to her father are trenchantly seen. The reconciliation between the sisters after Peter's death ("the modern return of the prodigal daughter") is marked by controlled power, since in counterpoint to the scene is a residual sense of the conflict—never quite resolved at the deepest level—between Roy's surviving love for the now dead Peter and her pity for her sister. The scenes following Peter's desertion of Roy are distinctive for their intense feeling, with the result that Roy's self-conscious musings, then and later, are, for the most part, authentic. As to the scenes between Craig and Roy, a facile exteriorizing of Craig's self-pity and of Roy's romantic restlessness is balanced by the continued presence in Roy's mind of the fear that she may lose Craig's love and be humiliated a second time. The merits of these and other scenes provide a novel whose essential truth is not appreciably diminished by its flaws, and whose over-all scope and vitality attest to the survival of Miss Glasgow's creative force.

Conclusion

"In seeking and in finding there is not ever an end, nor is there an end in seeking and in not finding." These words of Asa Timberlake in *In This Our Life* might have been Ellen Glasgow's own comment upon her intellectual life and her career as writer. Her capacity for spiritual enlargement and growth allowed her to do some of her best work in her fifties. In her sixties, creative force and flexibility of mind diminished with *Vein of Iron* and *In This Our Life;* but these books, along with *A Certain Measure,* do reveal that her ever dissatisfied spirit was still searching for the truth and an adequate form for conveying it. Undoubtedly this same truth-seeking impulse, eager to achieve viable outward expression, led to the writing of *The Woman Within* during these years.

Something of a Jamesian concentration of purpose—or of a Dreiserian persistence—effectively stayed with Miss Glasgow and allowed her to renew herself and do excellent work even after, at various times during her career, she had written one or more relatively inferior novels. Like that of James, her good work is spread over an extended period; and within their somewhat constricted limits, her books reveal a greater range of interest—from the vivaciously witty to the profoundly serious —than do those of most of her contemporaries. Nor did her creative force in fiction spend itself so rapidly as in the case of Sinclair Lewis and Sherwood Anderson. In her combination of irony with the tragic sense, of analytic perceptiveness with emotional depth, of detached satiric intelligence with pervasive human sympathy, she looks back to Henry James and forward to Southern writers as various as Caroline Gordon, Katherine Anne Porter, Eudora Welty, William Faulkner, and Robert Penn Warren. Like practically all these writers whom she foreshadows, Ellen Glasgow was chiefly interested in depicting with candor

229

and sympathy "the dignity of greatness and the pitiable corruption of human nature." [1]

In her early revolt against the sentimental tendency of the South to obscure the social actuality and to avoid the moral implications of such evasion, she analyzed with honesty the inadequacies of Virginia life in the present and the immediate past. Unlike her more genteel predecessors in Southern letters, she saw that, as a writer with genuine artistic aspirations, she could not compromise with present truth in the interest of preserving romantic nostalgia. Still her emancipation from deep feeling with somewhat sentimental overtones was never complete —perhaps fortunately so, if we remember the emotional richness as well as the realistic force of her best novels.

Like most of the realists who immediately preceded her or who were prominent during her early career, she felt that an honest confronting of the facts did not invalidate the reality of the spirit. A modernist and a relativist toward the specific moral issue, she was haunted, too, by the absolutes of the Christian tradition whose relevance she in part rejected: "a few sublime virtues or, more accurately perhaps, a few ideas of sublime virtues . . . called truth, justice, courage, loyalty, compassion." [2] Although she was responsive as a realist to the flux of experience, she found that the pragmatic was by itself insufficient without a philosophy to govern it. The self-within-the-self which resisted change was replete for Ellen Glasgow with a supernal reality outside time, a reality which might impart some deeper meaning to her confrontations with actuality in time. As a result of the fervor with which Miss Glasgow led the detached solitary life of the spirit, she was often able to illuminate profoundly both what she had imagined and what had, in point of fact, happened to her. Like Henry James, she thought that fact as such and its imaginative representation in art were distinct, if related entities.

The spirit in its austere confines could often assign the actual to its most meaningful place in the larger patterns of experience; at other times such dispassionate intelligence might cause a distortion of the actual by failing to apprehend it fully or by applying an inappropriate standard to it. When, therefore, the brooding mind failed to converge precisely upon an empirically defined reality or when a dogmatic version of this reality was insisted upon, sentimentality occurred in Miss Glasgow's fiction. Both kinds of sentimentality are prominent in her last two novels and in the least successful of the early ones, and sometimes they even mar her best work. In *The Ancient Law* Daniel Ordway luxuriates in an ideal world of the suffering spirit, with the result that his struggles are too disembodied to be real. On the other hand, Miss Glasgow's positive views on how things ought to be ordered in actual life resulted in the priggish heroine of *Life and Gabriella,* who determines too expeditiously the exact course of her career. If dispassionate intensity of vision gave rise to the splendid rhythms of the opening chapters of *Barren Ground* and to its intermittent epic grandeur, this same intensity, fastened upon Dorinda Oakley's aspiring spirit, made her too radically competent in achieving her success, too reliably gallant after the advent of adversity, and too complacently certain of her own values.

Another result of Ellen Glasgow's excessive preoccupation with the self within was a recoil from disturbing circumstances without. At times, then, she became defeatist in her own attitude when the actual fell short of ideal expectation and when irony offered an inadequate refuge for her sensitive spirit. As a result, an intermittent exasperation with her aristocratic characters sometimes breaks through the generally maintained objective delineation of their lives, even in such excellent novels as *The Deliverance* or *The Sheltered Life;* and the tableaus from modern life in her last two novels are distorted through jaundiced regret at life's failure to square with her own predilections. An obsessive concern with the personal life within, similar to her own, also marks her self-conscious characters—as various as Christopher Blake, Dorinda Oakley, General Archbald, and Asa Timberlake—who, in their articulate alienation, are tied too closely at some points to Miss Glasgow herself. Some of these figures find reality too much for them as did Miss Glasgow upon occasion. Yet she never gave in to circumstance and admitted defeat when external pressures seemed gratuitously hostile to her. She is at once sympathetic toward, and critical of, such men in her fiction as Oliver Treadwell in *Virginia,* Ralph McBride in *Vein of Iron,* and Craig Fleming in *In This Our Life,* all of whom find that they are unable to order their lives harmoniously and are inclined to drift morally.

Upon occasion, this retreat from actuality in Miss Glasgow or in her central characters led to a false estimate of things as they are. For this reason, Miss Glasgow's struggling central characters often succeed because they ought to, not because they convincingly master circumstances; her somewhat ascetic moral idealism caused her either to dwell excessively upon the beauties of renouncing the love that exists or to be scornful of its deficiencies; and her high valuation of social concord led her to overemphasize the views of her elder spokesmen such as Tucker Corbin, General Archbald, and John Fincastle.

If Miss Glasgow's fiction is at times subservient to the facts or at others nebulously connected with them, it is sometimes pallid in being abstractly intellectual. Too much explicit satire and irony are present in novels like *The Romantic Comedians* and *They Stooped to Folly* for there to be much blood in them. Most of her central characters are in-

terested in ideas, but frequently at an elementary level, the level of
sententious moralizing or of the platitude. Such individuals, while they
perhaps inadequately record Miss Glasgow's own intellectuality, nevertheless demonstrate that her mind is derivative and eclectic rather than
profoundly original. Their lucubrations clog the weaker novels like
The Wheel of Life and *The Builders,* impair the effectiveness of a
potentially fine work like *Vein of Iron,* or detract from the full force of
strong novels like *The Deliverance* and *Barren Ground.* In Miss Glasgow's fiction, philosophical speculation is often only tenuously related
to the psyche of a created character, with the result that the character's
ideas are too easily separable from the depths of his being. Some of the
emotions expressed in her work, especially those deriving from worldly
success, from sexual experience, from inner aspiration or personal fulfillment, and from her own philosophical idealism, also lose vitality
through being too directly intellectualized. This is true even of General
Archbald's deeply felt musings over his existence, which are forceful so
long as they deal with incidents in his past rather than with his "philosophy of life." Miss Glasgow's best insights were intuitive and imaginative rather than intellectual; and she was at her best, therefore,
when realistically and cynically she analyzed characters and social relationships, not ideas. The quality so characteristic of Miss Glasgow herself, the "austerity [which] prolongs the vision of delight," [3] becomes,
in fact, the enemy of delight, and comports more suitably with the
rendition of emotions associated with disenchantment, neurotic indis-
position, psychological antagonism, self-seeking, inner martyrdom, and
spiritual unfulfillment. This austerity was also translated into her high
valuation, too abstractly stated in the fiction, of fortitude. In fact, characters like Abel Revercomb, Gabriella Carr, and Ada Fincastle feel
the need of enduring deprivation more compulsively than their individual
situations warrant.

Inflexible prejudice or overemphatic abstraction might at times prevent Miss Glasgow from perceiving exactly the tangible and intangible
realities; nevertheless, Miss Glasgow's grasp of fact at other times was
strongly pragmatic. This practical sense helped engender her gospel of
fortitude which is, in essence, a provisional philosophy imposed by the
moral obligation to exist without a more dynamic faith and to endure
the worst. Miss Glasgow's novels were written partly out of the Anglo-
Saxon ethical tradition with its emphasis upon the active powers in
man's moral nature. As a result, most of her characters reveal an inability to resign themselves passively to fate, and are driven therefore by an urgent need to impress their own individualities upon hostile

circumstances. Like Thomas Hardy's, Miss Glasgow's central, spiritually perceptive characters strive to maintain a sense of equanimity, even though their personal universe may crumble. Despite a failure at times to see some facts clearly, Miss Glasgow possessed a critical acuity sufficiently strong to distinguish illusion from reality. She possessed, moreover, a well-developed sense of humor which was awake both to the perversities apt to govern the individual's existence and to the absurdities present even in a cosmos governed by natural laws. These two intellectual attributes in Miss Glasgow induced in her a conviction that an absolute pessimism was too pretentious to provide a balanced interpretation of experience. Again, considerations, largely pragmatic, may have determined initially the quality and intensity of her youthful revolt, since she declared that it was easier for the intellectual in the South to break with tradition than to endure it. The only practical alternative to coming to terms with her family was to rebel from it.

When her inner spirit inexorably informed external reality, Miss Glasgow achieved the full perfection of *Virginia* and *The Sheltered Life,* the delicacy and ironic strength of *They Stooped to Folly* and *The Romantic Comedians,* and the bitter intensity and serene detachment of the best parts of *The Deliverance, Barren Ground, In This Our Life,* and *The Miller of Old Church.* In these novels Miss Glasgow was at least partly successful in fusing her artist's fastidious vision with appropriate outer concretions, in reconciling, to the greatest extent possible, the "truth of fiction" and the "truth of life."

An ironic detachment from experience, in conjunction with an idealistic commitment to a flexible but strongly apprehended spiritual principle operating within and outside the self, helped give her books their authentic quality. At the same time, sentimental lapses were also encouraged by this same idealism, and a lack of felt reality by this same detachment. She is at her best when, in *The Deliverance, Virginia, They Stooped to Folly,* and *The Sheltered Life,* the conditions which surround the characters merge with them in their development until inner and outer realities virtually become one and reach full fruition in this interplay. When such full identification of scene with agent is not achieved, a separation occurs between style and subject, with the result that her novels then are either overwritten or wrongly felt. Miss Glasgow's accomplishments and limitations as a writer are best suggested in her own judgment of another Southern writer, Edgar Allan Poe, whose elusive merits she contrasts with his inadequacies:

Poe is, to a large extent, a distillation of the Southern. The formalism of his tone, the classical element in his poetry and in many of his stories, the drift toward rhetoric, the aloof and elusive intensity,—all these qualities are Southern. And in his more serious faults of overwriting, sentimental exaggeration, and lapses, now and then, into a pompous or florid style, he belongs to his epoch and even more to his South.[4]

Miss Glasgow is a transitional figure in the development of our literature, standing as she does between the romanticism of the local color writers and the genteel realism of Howells or Mary Wilkins Freeman on the one hand, and the revolutionary naturalism of Theodore Dreiser and the psychological immediacy of Faulkner on the other hand. Lacking the full vigor of Dreiser and Lewis, the crisp intellectuality of Mrs. Wharton, and the poetic intensity, at their best, of Sherwood Anderson and Willa Cather, she is, in her finest work, distinguished for her mordant sense of social reality and for the precision of her ironic intelligence. Of her nineteen novels, a half dozen are truly distinguished, both for their incidental insights into human nature and for their comprehensive interpretation of human life. The exactness of perception in Henry James at his best was denied to Miss Glasgow, for she never achieved James's command of the self, and consequently of medium; but at her best she explored as deeply as he the subtle relationships existing between personality and environment. The six or seven novels which represent Miss Glasgow at her best are substantial in a way that the achievement of her more erratic contemporaries is not. When all qualifications have been made, Ellen Glasgow emerges as a complex and impressive writer; and one can agree with N. Elizabeth Monroe and Maxwell Geismar that she has been underestimated.[5]

Her talents as a craftsman of fiction are manifold: an ability to envision living characters, a sharp sense of the psychological impact of various individualities upon each other, a skill at fusing her characters with scene, a starkness and concentration of energy in her climactic episodes, an animistic sensitivity toward nature, a gift of witty and exact phrasing and of economy of characterization, and a feeling for structure and narrative pace in the novel. More important still, the creation of a believable universe from out the Virginia past in her best novels, their undeniable insight into the human heart and their pervasive spiritual light and grace, give them a permanent place in our literature. In these novels, one must acknowledge that Ellen Glasgow manifested with ironic lucidity the qualities which she most sought to express as a writer: "Humanity and distinction, reality and art." [6]

NOTES
BIBLIOGRAPHY
and INDEX

Notes

In the chapters which treat individual novels, undocumented quotations are drawn from the novel being discussed. I have documented the longer quotations from the novels in the course of my separate discussions by citing applicable page numbers from the Virginia Edition for the twelve books contained therein (see bibliography below) and from the original editions for the books not found in this collected edition. When Ellen Glasgow's Prefaces to the Virginia Edition are quoted, references will be made to the volume in which they are collected, *A Certain Measure*. Places of publication and publishers for books referred to in the notes will be found in the bibliography or in note 23 of the Introduction.

INTRODUCTION

1 See accounts of her work in Henry Seidel Canby, "Fiction Sums Up a Century," *The Literary History of the United States* (1948); Frederick J. Hoffman, *The Modern Novel in America* (1951); N. Elizabeth Monroe, "Ellen Glasgow: Ironist of Manners," *Fifty Years of the American Novel*, ed. Harold Gardiner (1951); and Maxwell Geismar, *Rebels and Ancestors* (1953).

2 Pp. 20, 22, 33, 65, 71. Her findings were based upon compilations listed in the monthly *Bookman* and *Publisher's Weekly*.

3 *Sewanee Review*, XII (Oct., 1904), 462; *Outlook*, LXXXVIII (Feb. 29, 1908), 511; "No Valid Reason Against Giving Votes to Women," *New York Times Magazine*, Mar. 23, 1913, p. 11; *Nation*, CII (Feb. 17, 1916), 197.

4 "Representative American Story Tellers: Ellen Glasgow," *Bookman*, XXIX (Aug., 1909), 613–18; reprinted in expanded version in *Some American Story-Tellers* (1911), pp. 90–111.

5 Letter to Stark Young, July 28, *Letters,* p. 159. See also her letter to
   Van Wyck Brooks (Nov. 5, 1942) in which she speaks of having "been
   so long acclimatized to the chill air of neglect" and her letter to Signe
   Toksvig (Mar. 26, 1943) in which she asserted that "it has taken me
   more than forty years to win my place in American letters" (*Letters,* pp.
   310, 315).

6 *Prejudices: Second Series* (1920), p. 27; "Two Southern Novels," *Amer-
   ican Mercury,* XVIII (Oct., 1929), 251–53; "A Southern Skeptic,"
   American Mercury, XXIX (Aug., 1933), 504–6. Charles Angoff per-
   haps rightly attributes this change as in part due to Mencken's wife, Sara
   Haardt, who had long been a friend of Ellen Glasgow's (*H. L. Mencken:
   A Portrait from Memory* [1956], p. 106).

7 "The Fighting Edge of Romance," *New York Herald Tribune Books,*
   I (Apr. 19, 1925), 1–3; "Barren Ground," *New Republic,* XLII (Apr.
   29, 1925), 271; "The Last Cry of Romance," *Nation,* CXX (May 6,
   1925), 521–22; "Realism from the Romantic South," *World's Work,* L
   (May, 1925), 99–102; "Soil and Soul," *Saturday Review of Literature,*
   I (July 18, 1925), 907. Sherman as first editor of *New York Herald
   Tribune Books* was in mellower mood than he had been in *On Con-
   temporary Literature* (1917).

8 Preface to *The Voice of the People* (Old Dominion Edition), p. x. Her
   letters to Walter Hines Page, written between 1897 and 1908, indicate
   that she valued greatly his sympathy and understanding.

9 Jacob Zeitlin and Homer Woodbridge, *Life and Letters of Stuart P.
   Sherman,* II, 693, 702; "Barren Ground," *New Republic,* XLII (Apr.
   29, 1925), 271.

10 *Let Me Lie* (1947); *As I Remember It* (1955).

11 Letter to Daniel Longwell, June 22, 1932, *Letters,* p. 117. See also letters
   to Stark Young (July 28, 1934), Bessie Zaban Jones (Feb. 5, 1939) and
   Donald C. Brace (May 4, 1943), *Letters,* pp. 159, 249, 317.

12 Letter, 1935, *Letters,* pp. 190–91.

13 *American Memoir* (1947), p. 305, and *As I Remember It,* p. 224. She
   could be fairer to her contemporaries when there was no question of
   comparative merit involved: see her praise of Willa Cather's *Youth and
   the Bright Medusa* and *Shadows on the Rock,* in *Letters,* pp. 67, 285.

14 Nov. 22, 1897, *Letters,* p. 25.

15 P. 270.

16 *Let Me Lie,* pp. 252–53.

17 Rupert Hart-Davis, *Hugh Walpole* (1952), p. 281.

18 "Ellen Glasgow's Autobiography," *Virginia Quarterly Review,* XXXI
   (Spring, 1955), 297.

19 *Ibid.,* p. 296. See also Isaac F. Marcosson who in 1959 recalled "her
   wit and charm and the grace and ease of her personality" (*Before I Forget* [1959], p. 500).

20 In this connection see Mr. Hardy's letter in *Hopkins Review,* VI (Fall,
   1952), 136–37.

21 *A Certain Measure,* pp. 3, 152.
22 *Ibid.,* p. 68.
23 At appropriate places in my discussions, I take note of Miss Glasgow's achievement as social historian. In establishing the facts of Southern social history, I have found these books the most helpful: Holland Thompson, *The New South* (New Haven: Yale University Press, 1920); William E. Dodd, *The Cotton Kingdom* (New Haven: Yale University Press, 1921); W. T. Couch, ed., *Culture in the South* (Chapel Hill: University of North Carolina Press, 1934); Paul H. Buck, *The Road to Reunion 1865–1900* (Boston: Little, Brown & Co., 1937); Allen W. Moger, *The Rebuilding of the Old Dominion* (Ann Arbor: Edward Brothers, Inc., 1940); W. J. Cash, *The Mind of the South* (New York: Alfred A. Knopf, 1941); E. Merton Coulter, *The South During Reconstruction 1865–1877* (Baton Rouge: Louisiana State University Press, 1947); Francis Butler Simkins, *A History of the South* (New York: Alfred A. Knopf, 1953); C. Vann Woodward, *Origins of the New South 1877–1913* (Baton Rouge: Louisiana State University Press, 1951); C. Vann Woodward, *Reunion and Reaction* (Boston: Little, Brown & Co., 1951); Jay B. Hubbell, *The South in American Literature 1607–1900* (Durham: Duke University Press, 1954); Marshall W. Fishwick, *The Virginia Tradition* (Washington: Public Affairs Press, 1956); Ina Woestemeyer Van Noppen, *The South: A Documentary History* (New York: D. Van Nostrand Co., Inc., 1958); Marshall W. Fishwick, *Virginia: A New Look at the Old Dominion* (New York: Harper & Brothers, 1959); and Henry Savage, Jr., *Seeds of Time: The Background of Southern Thinking* (New York: Henry Holt & Co., 1959).
24 *A Certain Measure,* p. 152.
25 "Ellen Glasgow's Literary Credo," *New York Times Book Review,* Oct. 17, 1943, p. 5. See Ellen Glasgow's comment in *Letters,* p. 334.
26 Letter to Van Wyck Brooks, Nov. 14, 1938, *Letters,* p. 247.
27 Edward F. Harkins and Charles H. Johnston, *Little Pilgrimages among the Women Who Have Written Famous Books* (1901), p. 320.
28 Apr. 18, 1938, *Letters,* p. 238.
29 *A Certain Measure,* p. 208.

CHAPTER I

1 *I Believe,* ed. Clifton Fadiman (1939), p. 94.
2 Sara Haardt, "Ellen Glasgow and the South," *Bookman,* IX (Apr., 1929), 135.
3 *A Certain Measure,* pp. 192–93.
4 Albert F. Wilson, "Can Children Be Taught to Write?" *Good Housekeeping,* LXI (July, 1915), 48.
5 *A Certain Measure,* p. 194. In her later utterances she may have exaggerated somewhat her family's alleged hostility. At least in an early

letter to Horace Traubel she speaks of "my admiring, if evidently demented, family" (May 25, 1899, *Letters,* p. 29).

6   In this connection see *The Descendant,* p. 221, when Rachel Gavin is distressed at Michael's desertion: "She remembered her old childish idea that it [the darkness] was a great black monster with fiery eyes."

7   *A Backward Glance* (New York: D. Appleton-Century Co., 1934), p. 93.

8   *A Certain Measure,* p. 58. It is possibly symbolic that Miss Glasgow visited Westminster Abbey to lay a rose on Darwin's grave rather than on Chaucer's tomb.

9   For the intellectual influences which controlled Miss Glasgow as a young woman and later, see *A Certain Measure, passim.* See also Christine T. Herrick, "The Author of 'The Descendant,' " *Critic,* XXX (June 5, 1897), 383; "New Writer: Ellen Glasgow," *Bookman* (London), XVIII (Sept., 1900), 167–68; Edward F. Harkins and Charles H. Johnston, *Little Pilgrimages among the Women Who Have Written Famous Books* (1901), pp. 315–29; Isaac F. Marcosson, "The Personal Ellen Glasgow," *Bookman,* XXIX (Aug., 1909), 619–21; Sara Haardt, "Ellen Glasgow and the South," *Bookman,* LXXIX (Apr., 1929), 133–39; Ellen Glasgow, "What I Believe," *Nation,* CXXXVI (Apr. 12, 1933), 404–6; and Ellen Glasgow's contribution to *I Believe,* pp. 93–110.

10 Carl Van Vechten, *Fragments from an Unwritten Autobiography,* I (1955), 11.

11 James Southall Wilson, "Ellen Glasgow's Autobiography," *Virginia Quarterly Review,* XXXI (Spring, 1955), 297.

12 *I Believe,* p. 107.

13 *A Certain Measure,* p. 8.

14 *Ibid.,* p. 56.

15 The term "New South" in this book refers to the former Confederate South after 1877. In this year the last Federal troops were withdrawn; and in the years which followed, transition in the South from a predominantly agricultural society to a partially industrialized economy was accelerated.

16 *A Certain Measure,* p. 55.

17 *Ibid.,* p. 108.

18 Nov. 22, 1897, *Letters,* p. 25. In a letter to Page (Dec. 26, 1902) she confessed that his interest in her career had been a profoundly steadying influence, "even when you did not dream that I needed it, when you did not know how bitterly I wanted to throw it all away—and life with it" (*Letters,* p. 40). Another friend and advisor was an associate of Page's after 1903 at Doubleday, Page and Co., Isaac F. Marcosson. Before coming to the firm, he had reviewed favorably *The Voice of the People* (1900) in the *Louisville Times.* After he came to New York, he had many personal and professional contacts with her; he planned the publicity for *The Deliverance* and other works; and he helped her with some of the details of finance in *The Romance of a Plain Man* (1909).

See *Adventures in Interviewing* (1919), pp. 272–73, and *Before I Forget* (1959), pp. 494–500.

19 Dec. 8, 1897, in Burton J. Hendrick, *The Training of an American: The Earlier Life and Letters of Walter H. Page 1855–1913* (1928), p. 337.

20 Letter to Walter Hines Page, Jan. 14, 1902, *Letters*, p. 36.

21 Grant M. Overton, *The Women Who Make Our Novels* (1918), p. 27.

22 *Ibid.*, p. 29.

23 *A Certain Measure*, p. 14.

24 *Criticism and Fiction* (New York: Harper & Brothers, 1891), p. 15.

25 "Evasive Idealism in Literature," *Literature in the Making*, ed. Joyce Kilmer (1917), p. 238.

26 *A Certain Measure*, pp. 14, 16, 28.

27 *Crumbling Idols* (Chicago: Stone and Kimball, 1894), pp. 21, 77. Ellen Glasgow was probably influenced by the earlier Garland. In *The Woman Within*, she praised his "almost savage fidelity to life" in *Main Travelled Roads*, but regretted that later he was "tamed of his wildness" by Howells. Garland reviewed *The Descendant* with enthusiasm (*Book-Buyer*, XI [Aug., 1897], 45–46).

28 *The Responsibilities of the Novelist* (New York: Doubleday, Doran & Co., Inc., 1928), pp. 15, 18, 173.

29 In this connection, see Jay B. Hubbell's discussion (*The South in American Literature* [1954], pp. 732–33) of an anonymous Southern commentator (possibly Walter Hines Page) who in the New York *Evening Post* in 1887 maintained that Northern critics, motivated by nationalistic sentiment, overpraised the writers of the New South and had no adequate standards for judging them. The Southern writer, this critic asserted, should be encouraged to do two things: to seek more comprehensive models than those provided by Northern novelists and to study the great works of world literature. Mr. Hubbell observes that James Branch Cabell and Ellen Glasgow were the first Southern writers after the Civil War to recognize the insufficiencies of current American fiction and to seek guidance from continental sources. The example of Henry James was evidently less potent with Southern writers in the 1880's and 1890's than the requirements of Northern editors and the tastes of a romance-loving public.

30 Letter to Van Wyck Brooks, Oct. 4, 1939, *Letters*, p. 257. See also *A Certain Measure*, p. 18.

31 Quotations are from "The Art of Fiction."

32 *Oeuvres complètes illustrées de Guy de Maupassant* (Paris: Librairie Paul Ollendorff, 1908), VI (*Pierre et Jean*), 11, 9. Translation in text is from *The Life Work of Henry René Guy de Maupassant* (New York and London: W. Walter Dunne, 1903), pp. x, xix, xx.

33 *A Certain Measure*, p. 16.

34 Balzac is mentioned in *A Certain Measure*, pp. 16, 88. In an uncollected essay in 1928 ("Impressions of the Novel," *New York Herald Tribune*

Books, May 20, 1928, p. 6), she called Balzac "the most opulently endowed of all novelists" but felt that his characters are too little developed or capable of development.

35 *Oeuvres complètes de Honoré de Balzac: La Comédie Humaine: Scènes
de la Vie Privée,* I (Paris: Louis Conard, 1912), xxix. Translation in
text is from *Comédie Humaine,* ed. George Saintsbury (London, J. M.
Dent & Co., 1898), VIII, 5.

36 *I Believe,* p. 94.

37 "The Science of Fiction," *Life and Art,* ed. Ernest Brennecke (New
York: Greenberg, 1925), pp. 88, 89.

38 "The Profitable Reading of Fiction," *Life and Art,* p. 61.

39 Christine T. Herrick, "The Author of 'The Descendant,' " *Critic,* XXX
(June 5, 1897), 383.

40 *Roadside Meetings* (1930), p. 350.

41 *A Certain Measure,* p. 30.

42 After 1895 a recrudescence of interest in the historical romance occurred
with the great popularity of Anthony Hope, Rider Haggard, Conan
Doyle, Stevenson, and F. Marion Crawford. See Robert Falk, "The
Literary Criticism of the Genteel Decades: 1870–1900," *The Develop-
ment of American Literary Criticism,* ed. Floyd Stovall (Chapel Hill:
University of North Carolina Press, 1955), pp. 145 ff. In this discussion
I am also indebted to the article by Sheldon Van Auken listed in the
bibliography.

43 Perhaps as a concession to popular taste, Miss Glasgow used as sub-
title for the original editions of the work, "A Romance of the Virginia
Tobacco Fields."

44 Cable's realistic novel of the Reconstruction, *John March, Southerner*
(1894) is briefly discussed in note 3 to Chapter IV below.

45 *A Certain Measure,* p. 121.

46 May 12, 1900, *Letters,* p. 32.

47 Letters to Grant C. Knight, *Letters,* pp. 92–96. See also Grant C.
Knight, *James Lane Allen and the Genteel Tradition* (1935), p. 177.

48 See letters, Mar. 22, 1904, and Feb. 3, 1905, *Letters,* pp. 44, 46.

49 Alice M. Tyler, "Ellen Glasgow," *Book News Monthly,* XXX (Aug.,
1912), 847.

50 Hugh Walpole, "Introduction," *The Romance of a Plain Man* (1926);
Dorothea L. Mann, *Ellen Glasgow* (1927), p. 11. See also *The Woman
Within,* p. 135, and letter to Carl Van Vechten (Aug. 24, 1930), *Let-
ters,* p. 104.

51 Robert H. Elias, *Theodore Dreiser: Apostle of Nature* (1949), p. 201.

52 *Literature in the Making,* ed. Joyce Kilmer, pp. 229–38. For Tarkington's comments, see Grant Overton, *The Women Who Make Our Novels,*
pp. 22–23.

53 "Feminism," *New York Times Book Review,* Nov. 30, 1913, p. 656.
The other article, an interview with Ellen Glasgow, "No Valid Reason

Against Giving Votes to Women," appeared in *Magazine Section*, Mar. 23, 1913, p. 11.

54 "Miss Glasgow at Home," *New York Times Book Review*, July 30, 1922, p. 21.

55 Letter to Mary Johnston, Feb. 3, 1905, *Letters*, p. 46.

56 Letters to Walter Hines Page, Christmas, 1905, and to Mary Johnston, Aug. 15, 1906, *Letters*, pp. 50, 53.

57 Concerning the influence of the *Bhagavad-Gita*, for instance, Miss Glasgow later declared: "I doubt if higher ethical spheres have ever been reached than in that revelation" (letter to Signe Toksvig, Sept. 4, 1943, *Letters*, p. 334).

58 When in 1905 she was in her "mystical" phase, she could speak of her earlier years as her "materialistic and pessimistic days." In spite of her new interest in mysticism, she yet considered herself "a born sceptic" (letter to Walter Hines Page, Christmas, 1905, *Letters*, p. 50).

59 *I Believe*, p. 101.

60 *I Believe*, pp. 103, 110; "What I Believe," *Nation*, CXXXVI (Apr. 12, 1933), 404.

61 That these conflicting approaches to reality were never quite resolved, Miss Glasgow revealed in a late letter to Signe Toksvig (Nov. 1, 1944, *Letters*, p. 360): "What a curious mixture I am! A lover of the Vedanta, of Plotinus, and of the later Mystics, and yet, inherently, a sceptic regarding the evidence of things seen or unseen, or believer or an unbeliever whose only creed holds that it is better to fight on the side of the Eternal . . . for the Eternal, whether we recognize its likeness or not, must be the Good."

62 Harold S—— is to be identified as Henry Watkins Anderson, 1870–1954. He was a prominent Richmond lawyer, railroad executive, and active Republican. President Wilson made him a Lieutenant Colonel, and he was decorated by many European nations for his work with the American Red Cross deputations in the Balkans during the war and afterwards. Subsequent to his return to America, he was a nominee for the vice-presidency in 1920 and unsuccessful in running for governor of Virginia in 1921 on the Republican ticket. He retired from political life until 1936, when he campaigned actively in opposition to Franklin D. Roosevelt. During the Harding and Coolidge administrations, he was from 1921 to 1923 a special assistant to Attorney General Harry Daugherty and later became United States agent on the Mexican Claims Commission and a member of the Wickersham Commission. After he had spent many years as legal counsellor for other railroads, he became counsel for receivers of the Seaboard Airline Railroad in 1929, chairman of its board in 1946, and honorary chairman in 1952. He was also active in the Richmond community, serving as president of the Virginia Museum of Fine Arts. It is likely that Miss Glasgow's revived interest in politics after 1916 may have been due to his influence

(see *The Builders,* 1919, and *One Man in His Time,* 1922). Her relationship with him may also have led her to choose elderly lawyers as central figures in *The Romantic Comedians* (1926) and *They Stooped to Folly* (1929). The satiric and disillusioned tone permeating her presentation of Judge Honeywell in *The Romantic Comedians* also characterizes her account of Harold S—— in *The Woman Within.* Convenient summaries of Anderson's career can be found in *New York Times,* Jan. 8, 1954, p. 21, and in *The National Cyclopaedia of American Biography,* Current Vol. C (New York, James T. White & Co., 1930), 19.

63 James Southall Wilson, "Ellen Glasgow's Autobiography," *Virginia Quarterly Review,* XXXI (Spring, 1955), 295.

64 Letter to Hugh Walpole, Nov. 9, 1920, *Letters,* p. 67.

65 *A Certain Measure,* p. 224.

66 For accounts of this conference see Emily Clark, "A Week-end at Mr. Jefferson's University," *New York Herald Tribune Books,* VIII (Nov. 8, 1931), 1–2; Donald Davidson, "A Meeting of Southern Writers," *Bookman,* LXXIV (Feb., 1932), 494–97; Josephine Pinckney, "Southern Writers' Congress," *Saturday Review of Literature,* VIII (Nov. 7, 1931), 266; and *Letters of Sherwood Anderson,* ed. Howard Mumford Jones and Walter Rideout (1953), pp. 250–54.

67 See item by Emily Clark, preceding note.

68 Virginius Dabney, "A Prophet of the New South," *New York Herald Tribune Magazine,* Aug. 25, 1929, pp. 6, 7, 18.

69 Letters to Stark Young, Jan. 12, 1932, and to Allen Tate, Mar. 6, 1932, *Letters,* pp. 112, 114; Emily Clark, "A Week-end at Mr. Jefferson's University," *New York Herald Tribune Books,* VIII (Nov. 8, 1931), 2.

70 Consult the references in the bibliography. See especially Sherwood Anderson's description of Ellen Glasgow in a letter, probably Oct. 24, 1931, to Laura Lou Copenhaver, *Letters,* p. 250: "Ellen Glasgow took charge. She is charming. She is quite old now, but had tremendous vitality. In some way she reminds me of you, I mean in a kind of mental alertness, eagerness and charm."

71 "Heroes and Monsters," *Saturday Review of Literature,* XII (May 4, 1935), 4.

72 Letter to Frank Morley, May 24, 1944, *Letters,* p. 349.

73 Letter to J. Donald Adams, Apr. 28, 1936, *Letters,* p. 211.

74 Letter, Jan. 12, 1932, *Letters,* p. 112. See also her statement to Stark Young in a letter, July 28, 1934: "if I stopped writing I should probably find a way out of life" (*Letters,* p. 159).

75 Carl Van Vechten, *Fragments from an Unwritten Autobiography,* II, 35.

76 *A Certain Measure,* p. 129. The quotation in next sentence is from the same source.

77 In a perceptive study, one of Miss Glasgow's most recent critics subscribes, I think, too unreservedly to the opinion that her early work "has

relatively little distinction." See Allen W. Becker, "Ellen Glasgow's Social History," *Texas Studies in English*, XXXVI (1957), pp. 12–18.

78 Jan. 30, 1933, *Letters*, p. 127. See also her statements in 1929 to Virginius Dabney in the article in note 68 above.

CHAPTER II

1 *A Certain Measure*, p. 55.
2 *The Woman Within*, p. 98.
3 *Ibid.*, p. 104.
4 *Ibid.*, p. 98.
5 *The Descendant*, pp. 110, 240, 160.
6 In essence, this has been the basic ethical preoccupation of Robert Penn Warren in his fiction.
7 In *McTeague* Norris described the same divided forces struggling for possession of McTeague, as he regards the anesthetized Trina: "Suddenly the animal in the man stirred and woke; the evil instincts that in him were so close to the surface leaped to life, shouting and clamoring. . . . Within him, a certain second self, another better McTeague rose with the brute; both were strong, with the huge crude strength of the man himself. The two were at grapples."

Note also that both men are made what they are by heredity. With Michael "the sins of the fathers" do not pass "in honor the head of the child" (68). With McTeague "the vices and sins of his father and of his father's father, to the third and fourth and five hundredth generation, tainted him" (*McTeague*, Rinehart Edition [1950], pp. 22–24).

8 *A Certain Measure*, p. 121.
9 *Ibid.*, p. 212.
10 *I Believe*, ed. Clifton Fadiman (1939), p. 102.
11 *Ibid.*, p. 94.

CHAPTER III

1 Letters to Walter Hines Page, Mar. 26, 1898, and Dec. 2, 1899, *Letters*, pp. 26, 28.
2 Letter to Walter Hines Page, Dec. 2, 1899, *Letters*, p. 29.
3 As Miss Glasgow indicated in her presentation of the men in the Battle family, this caste was more or less ineffectual immediately after the war. With the Amnesty Act of 1872 and with the end of Reconstruction in 1877 and the development of the New South thereafter, some of these former leaders of the region or their sons became prominent in the new industrialism or else became political leaders in the state and nation. The members of the older caste when it resumed authority were commonly called "Bourbons"; the "Confederate Brigadier" was commonly a power in commerce or politics. The former aristocrats were thus absorbed into the New South or else, like Miss Glasgow's General Battle and Judge Bassett, completely resisted this tendency. In the next generation, aristocrats in the novel such as Ben Galt, Dudley Webb, and Tom

Bassett seek careers in politics and come to terms with their age. The plantation owners often traced their ancestry to colonial times and formed, together with certain urban aristocrats, the first families of Virginia; these families were mostly of English "Cavalier" derivation.

Before the Civil War, a middle class of mercantile or professional origin had existed, especially in the large cities. Many of the leaders of the Old South were drawn from this class, and some of its most prosperous representatives in their turn became plantation owners. This middle class expanded after 1877; and like the more ambitious Bourbons, many of its members also became industrial leaders in the New South. As Miss Glasgow demonstrated in this novel and others, the middle class, with recruits from below, finally became more powerful than the "Bourbon" survivors of the old families. There is some basis for assuming that the two classes eventually tended to merge with one another and to lose the sharpness of caste identity and consciousness. According to one commentator, middle class and Bourbon in the New South came to have much in common: "those indigenously southern tendencies toward a self-contained, well-mannered, restrained, leisurely, non-imitative, assured, complacent, and matured way of life" (Clarence E. Cason, "Middle Class and Bourbon," *Culture in the South,* ed. W. T. Couch [1934], p. 499). There was some cleavage remaining, but class lines became less distinct when white men joined forces to restrict the political enfranchisement of the Negro and to resist radical politics in general. Both classes would, therefore, view with uneasiness the rise to power of a popular leader like Nicholas Burr from the poor white class.

4 This quotation is drawn from the 1900 edition, p. 9, and is part of a passage deleted in the revised form of the novel.

5 Judge Bassett apparently adopted the Conservative (or "Funder") view in the controversy over the "readjustment" of Virginia's debts after the Civil War. The Funders believed that Virginia was in honor bound to repay her obligations; otherwise, the probity of the state would be in question. In the 1900 version of the novel, the Judge is explicit in his condemnation of "Mahonism" (p. 316; the phrase becomes "Readjusters" in revised versions of the novel). It may be that the Judge was more hostile to Mahone than to the question of financial readjustment.

6 This view of the possible contribution by the South to national politics was developed still further in *The Builders* (1919).

7 This quotation is drawn from the 1900 edition, p. 260, and is part of a passage deleted in the revised form of the novel.

8 *The Voice of the People,* p. 116.

9 The book in a fair measure gets beyond the restrictions inherent in the romantic novel, but not so completely as Miss Glasgow thought when she characterized it in a letter to Walter Hines Page as "so unlike the fashionable romantic school" (Dec. 8, 1899, *Letters,* p. 29). Miss Glasgow's strenuous efforts to assemble data to make the novel "real-

istic" are described in the Preface to the novel in *A Certain Measure*. The failure of the novel to be quite "realistic" indicates that realism is, as Miss Glasgow herself later recognized, more an attitude of mind than an assembling of facts (see *A Certain Measure*, pp. 212–13). Some of her subsequent novels, more freely conceived and less factually accurate perhaps, are more true to the life that she was presenting and more convincing to the imagination.

10 This quotation is drawn from the 1900 edition, p. 141, and is part of a passage deleted in the revised form of the novel.

11 See *The Woman Within*, pp. 38 ff., and *A Certain Measure*, pp. 19 ff.

12 Somewhat the same conflict of loyalties characterized the non-slaveholders in the South, who had little to gain from a consolidation of planter power, but who resented military invasion from the North. In Miss Glasgow's only mountaineer in her fiction, Pinetop, this conflict is mirrored. The obscure impulse of local patriotism often led the yeomen and mountaineers to fight in the Confederate armies (though some mountain folk continued to resist military service). At the end of the war, Pinetop realizes that his civilian existence is to be led apart from Dan's, and he resists all urging to return with Dan to Chericoke when they are both sent home on parole. The division between the mountaineer and the former gentry was not closed by the war, especially when the latter reverted to their formerly held Whig principles. See C. Vann Woodward, *Origins of the New South* (1951), pp. 75 ff.

13 *A Certain Measure*, pp. 142–44.

14 A short passage in which this quotation appears was added to the revised form of the novel. Compare Virginia Edition, p. 348, and 1902 edition, p. 458.

15 *Les Misérables* was evidently circulated among the soldiers to the extent that Virginia soldiers regarded themselves with ironic humor as "Lee's Miserables." See Jay B. Hubbell, *The South in American Literature* (1954), p. 455.

16 For the most part the Negroes in these two chronicles illustrate the "local color" tendency which made the Negro quaint and humorous. In these early works of Miss Glasgow the Negro humor is genuine and the rendering of dialect expert, but the emphasis is not greatly different from that found in Joel Chandler Harris. There is in *The Battle-Ground*, however, a fine presentation of a free Negro under slavery, Uncle Levi, who lives in isolation both from his own race and the white. Most effective is the scene in which he gives Betty some eggs when she can find nothing for her starving mother in a ravaged countryside. Dan's servant, Big Abel, is the slave faithful to his master, so popular in the literature of the New South: see "Marse Chan" and other tales by Thomas Nelson Page. One other aspect of the race question is presented in *The Battle-Ground:* fear of another Negro uprising like that of Nat Turner in 1831. This fear haunts Governor Ambler as he guards his home the night following news of the attack on Harpers Ferry.

17   Miss Glasgow's realism had been anticipated earlier in John William de
      Forest's *Miss Ravenel's Conversion from Secession to Loyalty* (1867).
      Miss Glasgow has nothing in her novel to approach the portraits of the
      reprobate Colonel Carter and the demi-mondaine, Mrs. Larue, but her
      rendition of background—the pictorial quality of her imagination and
      her feeling for landscape—is superior to de Forest's. The principals,
      Dan and Betty, though submerged to the requirements of a conventional
      love story, are more interesting and forceful as lovers than Lillie
      Ravenel and Colbourne, possibly because Miss Glasgow's characters
      are more closely implicated in the fate of their native state than are
      de Forest's. Both writers gave pioneering realistic accounts of battle.
      Though de Forest's presentation of the military hospitals is far more
      graphic than anything in *The Battle-Ground,* he lacked Miss Glasgow's
      ability to relate the desolation caused by the war to actual human
      suffering by military and civilians alike.
18   *A Certain Measure,* p. 6.
19   For this aspect of the late nineteenth-century literary scene, especially
      as the fashion was taken up by Northern writers, see Paul H. Buck, "The
      South Begins to Write," and "The North Feels the Power of the Pen,"
      in *The Road to Reunion* (1937), pp. 196–235.
20   *A Certain Measure,* p. 192.

CHAPTER IV

1   Letter to Walter Hines Page, Dec. 26, 1902, *Letters,* p. 41.
2   *Ibid.*
3   Arlin Turner (*George Washington Cable,* Durham: Duke University
      Press, 1956) and Louis D. Rubin, Jr. ("The Road to Yoknapatawpha:
      George W. Cable and 'John March, Southerner,' " *Virginia Quarterly
      Review,* XXXV [Winter, 1959], 118–32) have recently argued that
      George Washington Cable's *John March, Southerner* is the classic
      American novel of the Reconstruction. Both critics are right in feeling
      that the novel has been unfairly estimated as "didactic," and there is
      much in it that is impressive. Ellen Glasgow's novel lacks the scope of
      Cable's, but she conveyed more intensely than he did the psychic
      effects, upon a representative upper-class family, of prolonged depriva-
      tion and of loss of local prestige. Like Miss Glasgow's book, Cable's
      is noteworthy for its honest portrayal of typical Southerners whose
      moral natures are realistically compounded of commendable and ques-
      tionable elements. Cable's novel lacks, I feel, firmness of structure and
      is too clogged with uninteresting details of various land promotion
      schemes. The result is a greater dissipation of force and interest than
      in Miss Glasgow's novel.
4   Radical Reconstruction and carpetbag rule were over in Virginia by
      about 1874, after the election of a conservative governor, a "Con-
      federate Brigadier," General James L. Kemper. In order, therefore, to
      illustrate the prolonged effects of the Reconstruction during the years

1878–90 upon Christopher Blake and his class, Miss Glasgow had to use another object for his hatred than a Northern politician.

5   *The Deliverance,* p. 12. In the 1904 edition (p. 15) the passage reads "that inner spirit which had moulded it into a lasting expression of a racial sentiment."

6   *The Deliverance,* p. 37. In the 1904 edition (p. 50), the last three sentences in this passage are not present, and in place of them there is the following: "Why, I'd rather stick a knife into her heart myself!"

7   *The Deliverance,* p. 307. Maria in the 1904 edition (p. 407) feels that the chief deficiencies of her class are an alienation from the land and the lack of a vital tradition: "our people have always appeared strangers upon the land . . . its very age is a reproach to us, for it shows off our newness—our lack of any past that we may call our own." The members of her class had previously been hired laborers and had lacked a full sense of identity with the land. They neither owned the land nor were happy working upon it.

8   In the 1904 edition, at one point (p. 51) Christopher's "beauty" is described as that "of some ancient ivory carving"; at another point (p. 381), the lines of his profile suggest those "of an ivory carving."

9   This "Gothic" quality seems partly indigenous to the Southern imagination. The influence of the eighteenth-century novel and of Scott, a sometimes flamboyantly displayed individualism, and the tensions resulting from race and class conflict may have helped generate the one-sided intensities in much Southern writing, in the work, for instance, of Simms, Poe, Faulkner, Caldwell, and Warren. In later years Miss Glasgow apparently forgot her own distraught hero of *The Deliverance* when she condemned the work of modern Southern writers because, like Hoffmann's tales, it was often "Gothic" in décor and not "realistic." See letters to Irita Van Doren, Sept. 8, 1933, and to Bessie Zaban Jones, Feb. 7, 1934, *Letters,* pp. 144, 150.

10 James's phrase in "The Art of Fiction."

11 *A Certain Measure,* p. 204.

12 Northrop Frye, *Anatomy of Criticism* (Princeton: Princeton University Press, 1957), p. 40.

13 In this connection see Frye, *Anatomy of Criticism,* p. 213: "Tragedy seems to move up to an *Augenblick* or crucial moment from which point the road to what might have been and the road to what will be can be simultaneously seen."

14 This resort to animal imagery to indicate an untamed ferocity is, of course, one of the conventions of naturalistic fiction. As we have seen, Miss Glasgow had already used it in *The Descendant.*

15 In the 1904 edition at another point (p. 281) Christopher also thinks of his maturing design in similar terms: "the man and the boy would then be held together by blood ties like two snarling hounds in the leash." In the 1904 edition (p. 527), Will becomes a "beast" from liquor rather than a "fool."

16   Quoted in Jay B. Hubbell, *The South in American Literature* (1954), p. 760.

17   *A Certain Measure*, p. 214.

18   This sort of insight links Miss Glasgow with the British "comedy of manners" tradition as it is found, for example, in Fielding, Jane Austen, Thackeray, Meredith, and Galsworthy.

19   *The Deliverance*, pp. 297, 151.

20   *Ibid.*, p. 76. The statement of Mrs. Blake in the 1904 edition (p. 479) is similar in emphasis: "Remember to be a gentleman, and you will find that that embraces all morality and a good deal of religion."

21   Actually, Miss Glasgow presented two kinds of "peasants" in the novel. There are the shiftless "poor whites" represented by the Peterkins and Fred Turner. As Shields McIlwaine has pointed out, Molly Peterkin, in her easy virtue and vanity, anticipates the slatternly and promiscuous poor-white woman in much later fiction. Mr. McIlwaine also observes that Miss Glasgow presented her from the outside as if she were a curiosity (*The Southern Poor-White from Lubberland to Tobacco Road* [1939], pp. 188–89). Sol Peterkin's inability to find a long-lived spouse may anticipate to some extent the sexual difficulties of men from his class, used for comic effect in the work of Caldwell and others. Fred Turner is the boorish, ruffianly man from this class. The Spades are from somewhat higher in the social scale: they run a store and are from the same yeoman stock as the Weatherbys. The sobriety and diligence which make the Weatherbys successful farmers are exaggerated in Mrs. Spade to an obsessive anxiety about human sinfulness. In Mrs. Spade the earnest Protestantism of Presbyterian, Methodist, or Baptist origin, embraced by the yeoman classes in the South before the war and after, gives rise to an inflexible moral code.

The rustics also have dramatic purpose in terms of the story as a whole: Tom Spade, in his disapproval of Christopher's plan of vengeance, serves as a projection of his muffled conscience, and Susan Spade serves as Will Fletcher's nemesis as he starts on the downward path.

CHAPTER V

1   *The Woman Within*, p. 171.

2   *Rebels and Ancestors* (1953), p. 236. Richard Chase also feels that the book has been too often disregarded in criticism of Ellen Glasgow ("Letters to the Establishment," *New Republic*, CXXXVIII [Mar. 10, 1958], 18).

3   Tappahannock is a pseudonymous name for South Boston (see Alice M. Tyler, *Book News Monthly*, XXX [Aug., 1912], 844). In 1897, Miss Glasgow mentioned *Les Misérables*, along with *Anna Karenina* and *Vanity Fair*, as her favorite novels (see Christine T. Herrick, "The Author of 'The Descendant,'" *Critic*, XXX [June 5, 1897], 383).

4   See C. Vann Woodward, *Origins of the New South* (1951), p. 49, and *Reunion and Reaction* (1951), pp. 243–44.

5 Woodward, *Origins of the New South,* p. 4.
6 E. Merton Coulter, *The South During Reconstruction* (1947), p. 255.
7 George is the General's nephew; and Pry is a doctor who prescribes either quinine or camomile for all ailments. Pry is also an enthusiastic Latin scholar and becomes the tutor of George and Ben Starr as boys. The apathy of these men toward industry and finance and the opposition of the Blands to Ben Starr as a husband for their niece may be more than merely personal characteristics, since Virginia appears to have been somewhat less enthusiastic about the New South than were some of the other former Confederate states (see Marshall W. Fishwick, *Virginia: A New Look at the Old Dominion* [1959], pp. 152, 183).
8 See Woodward, *Origins of the New South,* p. 140.
9 The financial panic in the novel was undoubtedly based on that of 1893, although the chronology of events seems to be at variance with this assumption.
10 See Woodward, *Origins of the New South,* p. 4.
11 See Paul H. Buck, *The Road to Reunion* (1937), p. 156.
12 See Woodward, *Origins of the New South,* pp. 120–23, 291–96. This was followed in the 1890's by further consolidation, under Northern control, of Southern railroads. J. P. Morgan bought up the Terminal Company, when it failed in 1893 as a result of gross mismanagement. In 1894 he organized from the Terminal Company the first of the great consolidated railroad empires in the New South, the Southern Railroad.

CHAPTER VI

1 N. Elizabeth Monroe, *The Novel and Society* (1941), p. 165; Edward Wagenknecht, *Cavalcade of the American Novel* (1952), p. 272; John Edward Hardy, "Ellen Glasgow," *Southern Renascence,* ed. Louis D. Rubin, Jr. and Robert D. Jacobs (1953), pp. 242 ff.
2 In *The Deliverance* Miss Glasgow had represented through her yeomen, the Weatherbys, this element of racial continuity. The connection stressed therein had been between past and present; in *The Miller of Old Church* the connection is more between present and future.
3 Although Mrs. Gay has lived off and on at Jordan's Journey for twenty years, she still can say: "I've never known any of the country people about here" (119).
4 *A Certain Measure,* pp. 227 ff.
5 E. Merton Coulter, *The South during Reconstruction* (1947), p. 178.
6 Superficially it seems as if Miss Glasgow had accepted the myth, formulated by the Abolitionists before the Civil War, that Southern society consisted of three classes only, the aristocrats, the Negroes, and the poor whites. This is the contention of Shields McIlwaine in his treatment of this novel (*The Southern Poor-White from Lubberland to Tobacco Road* [1939], pp. 189 ff). Possibly Miss Glasgow did oversimplify sociology in this novel; but it seems to me that her intent was not so much to deny the existence of independent yeomen farmers

before the war as to indicate that they too had proportionately less influence and power then than did the planter caste. In this sense all the lower-class whites were victims of aristocratic domination. Several authorities apparently agree with Miss Glasgow. Paul H. Buck, *The Road to Reunion* (1937), p. 148, contends: "So far as the white farming classes were concerned, the breakup of the plantations destroyed the major force which had repressed their development." Virginius Dabney in *Liberalism in the South* (1932), p. 417, asserts that the yeomanry as well as the poor whites suffered under the plantation economy. A. N. J. Den Hollander in "The Tradition of 'Poor Whites'" (*Culture in the South*, ed. W. T. Couch) presents well-balanced comments on this whole question. He rejects the simplifications of Southern social structure formulated by the Abolitionists, but maintains that the planters were less interested in the poor whites than in their slaves, that the opportunities for advance were limited in a stratified society, and that poor whites and yeomen alike profited from abolition, though not to the extent that has been commonly claimed.

At any rate, the poor white of ability like Abel Revercomb would have found it virtually impossible to improve his status before the war: only in the second generation after the war could Abel emerge from the obscurity of his class. More typical poor-white qualities are found in the shiftlessness of Abel's deceased father, in the unapologetic laziness of Archie Revercomb, and in the moroseness and vindictiveness of Abner Revercomb. In the quarrelsome and senile Revercomb grandparents, who live now only for animal comfort and for the discomfiting of each other, there are elements too of the grotesque comedy which has often been associated with the poor-white tradition in literature.

Mr. McIlwaine rightly feels that Miss Glasgow, in regarding Abel as typical, has overestimated the will and capacity of the poor white to improve himself. In the period immediately following that covered in the novel, Abel might have had a more difficult time in prevailing, since the new Virginia Constitution of 1902 severely limited white as well as Negro suffrage. The triumph of the Democratic political machine in Virginia after 1902 undoubtedly discouraged the social advancement of gifted poor whites like Abel Revercomb.

7 As Edward Wagenknecht has shown ("*Great Expectations* and Ellen Glasgow," *Boston University Studies in English*, III [Spring, 1957], 57–60), Miss Glasgow also made conscious use of *Great Expectations* in the opening sequences of *The Romance of a Plain Man*.

8 *The Miller of Old Church*, p. 80. The class origins of the various rustics are less clearly indicated than in *The Deliverance*. They could be either "poor white" tenants or yeoman farmers and tradesmen. The yeoman class seems to dominate: the Mings are tradesmen in that they run a tavern; and Solomon Hatch and Jim Halloween seem to be relatively prosperous as farmers. Solomon, moreover, speaks with scorn of the

"white trash" when he is describing Abel's family in Chapter I and implies that he is above such people in the social scale. Elsewhere, however, Sarah Revercomb pronounces Hatch to be "particularly thriftless," even though he is apparently an independent farmer. In presenting the rustics in this novel, Miss Glasgow wished only incidentally to be sociologically exact.

9 Under the terms of the will, Molly has to live with the Gays after she is twenty-one and marry only with their consent. Otherwise, she will forfeit most of her inheritance to Chinese missions.

CHAPTER VII

1 *A Certain Measure*, p. 82.

2 *The Woman Within*, p. 192.

3 P. 163.

4 *Virginia*, p. 9. The education of Mary-Cooke Branch corroborates Miss Glasgow's description of education for women in Virginia after the war, when emphasis was placed upon good breeding and polite accomplishments rather than intellectual attainments (see Ina W. Van Noppen, *The South: A Documentary History* [1958], pp. 456–59). Miss Branch also experienced the same frustration as Susan Treadwell did in *Virginia*: both girls wished to attend college, but the polite prejudices of her mother interfered with Miss Branch's ambition, and the social conservativism of her father with Susan Treadwell's. Virginia's child Jenny not only gets to go to Bryn Mawr but evolves in one generation to the point of scorning the older feminine education of Miss Batte and declaring it a "menace." The broadened horizons of Virginia's children thus indicate that considerable progress had been made by the early twentieth century in the emancipation of women.

5 That cultural provinciality was not confined to the South Miss Glasgow recognized in a passage deleted from the revised editions of the novel (1913 ed., p. 128): "In the early eighties profound darkness still hung over the stage, for the intellect of a democracy, which first seeks an outlet in statesmanship, secondly in commerce, and lastly in art and literature, had hardly begun to express itself, with the immaturity of youth, in several of these latter fields."

6 Susan Treadwell is Virginia's best friend and the daughter of Cyrus Treadwell, business leader of Dinwiddie; Mrs. Payson is the wife of the manager of Cyrus's railroad in Matoaca City where Oliver works after his marriage; and Abby Goode is Virginia's good-natured, voluble rival for Oliver's affections when Virginia ceases to be a companion to her husband.

7 W. J. Cash, *The Mind of the South* (1941), p. 82.

8 *Virginia*, p. 241. An interesting parallel to the idea expressed in this passage is provided by Miss Glasgow's contemporaneous ironic description of Fielding's Amelia, who illustrates "the belief that the wor-

ship of a dissolute husband is an exalted occupation for an immortal soul" ("Feminism," *New York Times Book Review*, Nov. 30, 1913, p. 656).

9   Modern Library Edition, p. 338.

10 Part of the pathos of this novel results, as Miss Glasgow remarked, from Virginia's having been "the embodiment of a forsaken ideal" (*A Certain Measure*, p. 82). In a letter to Allen Tate (Apr. 3, 1933, *Letters*, p. 134), she said perceptively: "the irony is directed not at her, but at human nature which creates an ideal only to abandon it when that ideal comes to flower."

11 Distrust of the self-sufficient woman is even voiced by the sensible John Henry Pendleton, until he is able to appreciate the substantial virtues of the Susan Treadwell he finally marries. He had been infatuated with Virginia for many years and had thought of her as an ideal, almost ethereal being. He had then embraced this view: "To demand that a pretty woman should possess the mental responsibility of a human being would have been an affront to his ideas of gallantry" (49). In his un-reconstructed phase he is not much different from the General Boling-broke (*The Romance of a Plain Man*) who had summarily declared: "A strong-minded woman [has] unsexed herself" (143). Thus chivalry, perhaps ironically, encouraged a worship of woman at the same time that it established an undeviating pattern for her behavior and thus de-prived her of freedom. So cloistered was the typical gentlewoman of the early days of the New South that she often was unable to adjust to changed circumstances when her family no longer needed her. What might have mitigated Virginia's loneliness in middle age—participation in community activities—had been frowned upon by her father and other chivalric elders who regarded such activity as vaguely "un-womanly." Thus Susan's efforts to help Virginia when the latter's family is all away from home are unavailing.

12 As Maxwell Geismar has pointed out (*Rebels and Ancestors* [1953], p. 247) Miss Glasgow used to good effect in her presentation of Mandy that aspect of literary naturalism which emphasizes the crude animalistic aspects of the lower social classes in order to suggest how near they still are to the primitive.

13 At one point Miss Glasgow described Cyrus as having gained the world only to lose his soul, as had "all his class" (124). She was aware, here and elsewhere in her fiction, that the South as a traditional society could not welcome all aspects of the new industrialism since some of them went counter to its inherited values. What the Northeastern exploiters of the region and its native redeemers were advocating was not only the new industrialism but a whole new economic philosophy and way of life, that of laissez faire capitalism, with its reliance upon impersonal law in economic matters. See Jay B. Hubbell, *The South in American Literature* (1954), p. 715, and C. Vann Woodward, *Origins of the New South* (1951), p. 148.

14 Gabriel Pendleton's complacent proclaiming of a bowdlerized view of reality thus irritates Oliver more than hostile criticism of his work would have. Gabriel admits no objection "to sweet, clean plays . . . with an elevating moral tone to them" (190). Oliver is essentially right in feeling that the America of his day does not want realism on the stage but "a kind of theatrical wedding-cake" (81).

15 See 1913 edition, pp. 128–29, 404. Through Oliver in the earlier version, Miss Glasgow more directly reflected than she did later her own sense of cultural isolation in the Virginia of the early twentieth century: "Coming a quarter of a century later, he might have made a part of a national emancipation of intellect. Coming when he did, he stood merely for one of the spasmodic reactions against the dominant spirit. Unwritten history is full of such reactions, since it is by the accumulated energy of their revolts that the world moves on its way" (128).

This passage was not deleted from the Old Dominion Edition of the novel, 1929. That Oliver's sense of alienation may have had wider implications and may have reflected the situation of the intellectual in the New South, this comment by Woodward (*Origins of the New South*, p. 163) may indicate: "Withdrawal of the artist or critic sometimes became a secession that was spiritual as well as physical, and resulted not only in the alienation of the writer from his people but in a schism within the spirit of the man himself."

Miss Glasgow was also more critical of Virginia's debilitating influence upon Oliver in the earlier version: "If only in the beginning she had upheld not his inclinations, but his convictions; if only she had sought not to soothe his weakness, but to stimulate his strength; if only she had seen for once the thing as it was, not as it ought to have been—" (404). This passage was deleted from both the Old Dominion and the Virginia Editions of the novel (1929 and 1938).

16 In this connection see Northrop Frye, *Anatomy of Criticism* (1957), p. 39.

17 *A Certain Measure*, pp. 81–82.

CHAPTER VIII

1 Nov. 1, 1914, *Letters*, p. 63.

2 This tendency had reached considerable proportions by the 1880's. See Marshall W. Fishwick, *Virginia: A New Look at the Old Dominion* (1959), p. 151: "Virginia's chief export for a generation was brains."

3 See Ellen Glasgow, in "No Valid Reason Against Giving Votes to Women," *New York Times Magazine Section*, Mar. 23, 1913, p. 11; and Paul H. Buck, *The Road to Reunion* (1937), p. 41.

4 Ellen Glasgow, "Feminism," *New York Times Book Review*, Nov. 30, 1913, p. 657.

5 A minor character in the novel also pungently expresses the traditional viewpoint: "Haven't we got one party already, and doesn't that one have a hard enough time looking after the negroes?" (51).

6   C. Vann Woodward, *Origins of the New South* (1951), p. 65.

7   *The Builders*, p. 115. In her exposition of Blackburn's era, Miss Glasgow
    was less than enthusiastic about the "profound modifications" the Amer-
    ican pioneer stock had recently undergone. In fact, she interpreted
    American reluctance to enter the war in 1916 as being in large part a
    resentment of the new spirit in America toward "any disposition on
    the part of its kindred to dictate or even influence its policy or pur-
    pose" (21).

8   In a letter to Allen Tate (Sept. 22, 1932, *Letters*, p. 125) Miss Glasgow
    spoke of this novel as the worst of those "written simply in the effort to
    escape from too much living."

9   *One Man in His Time*, p. 41. This remark is applied to a minor char-
    acter in the novel, a man of the old school, General Powhatan Plummer.

10 See W. J. Cash, *The Mind of the South* (1941), pp. 346–57.

11 The novel is also occasionally told from Patty Vetch's point of view.
    Three chapters out of twenty-four and parts of three others reflect the
    action through her mind.

12 In an interview with Grant Overton (*The Women Who Make Our
    Novels* [1918], p. 26), Ellen Glasgow declared: "I cannot write short
    stories. They bore me excruciatingly. The whole technique of the short
    story and the novel is different. All the best of the short stories must
    be painfully condensed with slight regard for the evolutionary causes
    bringing about this or that effect. Everything that I see, I see in the form
    of a novel—as a large canvas. I want to trace the process of cause and
    effect; and that is why both *Virginia* and *Gabriella* were a joy in the
    writing."

13 *The Shadowy Third*, p. 79. Corinna Page had similarly speculated:
    "And what was life . . . except a complex and intricate blend of hu-
    man relations?" (278).

14 This story first appeared in *Harper's Magazine* for 1899. The other
    stories in *The Shadowy Third* first appeared in periodicals from 1916
    to 1923 (see bibliography).

CHAPTER IX

1   See letter to William H. F. Lamont, Feb. 9, 1928, *Letters*, p. 90.

2   Aug. 23, 1923, *Letters*, p. 69.

3   Feb. 4, 1944, *Letters*, p. 341.

4   See *The Woman Within*, p. 270.

5   The foremost present-day historian of Virginia, Marshall W. Fishwick,
    insists that this agrarian sentiment is a particularly Virginian char-
    acteristic: "The soul is wedded to the soil; no one can or would separate
    them" (*The Virginia Tradition* [1956], p. 2). Through Dorinda Oakley's
    involvement with the land in *Barren Ground*, Miss Glasgow was thus ex-
    pressing local sentiment as well as regional Southern feeling. Her place in
    the wider "agrarian" tradition in the South has been suggestively defined
    by Allen W. Becker ("The Period 1865–1925" in "Agrarianism as a

Theme in Southern Literature," *Georgia Review,* XI [Summer, 1957], pp. 150–54). Mr. Becker sees Miss Glasgow as the heir of those Southern authors who expressed directly or by implication a love of the soil: Jefferson, Legaré, Simms, Kennedy, Caruthers, Johnston, Page, Harris, John Esten Cooke, and most strikingly, Lanier whose opposition of agriculture and industrialism in a poem like "Corn" is one dominant aspect of present-day agrarianism. She was also the connecting link between these writers and later Southern writers.

As Mr. Becker has shown, Miss Glasgow's emphasis in *Barren Ground* upon a "mystique of the land" puts her squarely in the Southern agrarian tradition. Her distinctive contribution was to express this sentiment in a realistic framework. Dorinda Oakley loves the fields but has to slave on her farm to win mastery over them. This combination of realism and a poetic identification with the land marks the fiction of Miss Glasgow's exact contemporary, Elizabeth Madox Roberts (whose *The Time of Man,* 1926, appeared almost simultaneously with *Barren Ground*) and the work of succeeding writers such as Faulkner (*Absalom, Absalom!,* 1936, and *Go Down Moses,* 1942), Caroline Gordon (*The Garden of Adonis,* 1937, and *The Women on the Porch,* 1944), Robert Penn Warren (*Night Rider,* 1939), and Eudora Welty ("The Whistle" and "A Curtain of Green," *A Curtain of Green,* 1941). This juxtaposition of concrete, realistic detail with impassioned feeling for locale also suffuses most of the best recent Southern poetry, particularly that of the Nashville group. It is no coincidence that Miss Glasgow was enthusiastic about Allen Tate's "Ode to the Confederate Dead" (see letters to Allen Tate, Mar. 6, 1932; July 18, 1932; and Nov. 6, 1937, *Letters,* pp. 114, 119, 229).

6 *Barren Ground,* pp. 9, 48, 99, 112, 217, 322.

7 For discussions of Southern agriculture after the Civil War and later, see C. Vann Woodward, *Origins of the New South* (1951), pp. 175 ff. and pp. 406–16; Clarence Poe, "The Farmer and His Future," *Culture in the South,* ed. W. T. Couch (1934), pp. 319–43; Allen W. Moger, *The Rebuilding of the Old Dominion* (1940), pp. 43–63; and Henry Savage, Jr., *Seeds of Time* (1959), pp. 211 ff.

8 In the early nineteenth century, John Calvin Abernathy moved from the Valley of Virginia where the Scotch-Irish predominated to the lowlands where Presbyterianism did not so completely dominate. A canny, practical streak in his personality had enabled him to look beyond all facts disturbing to his conscience and to square his theology with morally dubious economics. Like certain other scrupulous believers, Abernathy had "reconciled divine grace with a peculiar institution," and had rationalized the resale of fifty slaves by using the money for "the redemption of black souls in the Congo."

9 *Barren Ground,* p. 360. Dorinda is too secular in outlook to feel the typical Calvinist sense of abasement before personal transgression. When she is jilted, she feels more anger at Jason than remorse for her own

"sin." At a deeper level, her austere religious inheritance may have induced her excessive recoil from physical love after Jason leaves her, an aversion which in its long duration is unnatural, possibly psychopathic.

10 "The Last Cry of Romance," *Nation*, CXX (May 6, 1925), 522.

11 *Barren Ground*, p. 434. That Dorinda's cheerless view of life derives from her sober Calvinist inheritance is implied when Mrs. Oakley at her death looks back over the waste of her life only to say: "It doesn't seem just right that we have to be born. It ain't worth all the trouble we go through" (291).

12 In Dorinda survives Miss Glasgow's earlier preoccupation with the personality of Nietzschean strength who commands circumstance through assertion of the will.

13 Letter to Signe Toksvig, Feb. 4, 1944, *Letters*, p. 341.

14 *Barren Ground*, pp. 79, 81, 418. The Prydes represent the poor white in an all but degenerate aspect. Pryde is a laborer who dislikes work, has a weakness for alcohol, and is regarded by his neighbors as mentally deficient; Almira is slatternly, lacking in energy, and serenely indifferent to the birth each year of a new child.

CHAPTER X

1 *A Certain Measure*, p. 213.

2 Clarence E. Cason, "Middle Class and Bourbon," *Culture in the South*, ed. W. T. Couch (1934), p. 491.

3 *A Certain Measure*, p. 213.

4 *Ibid.*, p. 211.

5 *Ibid.*, p. 218.

6 In his disturbing relationship with Annabel, the Judge undoubtedly experiences the same misgivings felt toward love in New York society by Laura Wilde in *The Wheel of Life* (1906): "Was love, when all was said, merely a subjection to the flesh instead of an enlargement of the spirit?" (109).

7 *The Cycle of American Literature* (1955), p. 220.

8 *The Woman Within*, p. 276.

9 *Ibid.*, p. 140. In the novel Miss Glasgow described the gracious society of Queenborough as never having passed beyond "an early stage of arrested development" (4).

10 Edmonia Bredalbane caustically criticizes the unwritten "code" for women in the South. She maintains that Virginia in the 1880's persecuted the woman who was original in any way, whether she was, according to conventional standards, a "sinner" or merely an unsettling influence. Posterity might view the socially dedicated woman as a "saint," but her contemporaries would typically regard with hostility her departure from racial norms for feminine behavior. Edmonia was harshly treated in her fall from sexual purity; no less severely treated was Johanna Goodwin, the suffragist. Late nineteenth-century America

valued the intellectual timorousness and the moral dissimulation of Amanda Lightfoot, and discouraged women from any display of individualism. Thus, in her attitudes and ideas, Amanda never ventures beyond those countenanced "by the feelings of a lady and the Episcopal Church" (101). If the Judge—at least ostensibly—reverences woman, he is also contemptuous of her intellectual powers and characteristically assigns her "some misty area between inspiration and lunacy" (153).

11 *Anatomy of Criticism* (1957), p. 169.

12 Curle is satirically presented and his portrait indicates that Miss Glasgow had become critical of the values of those who sponsored the New South. Virginius thinks that his son would "make the world a desert and call it progress" (222); and Martin Welding, who is antipathetic to his brother-in-law, criticizes "this mass production of mediocrity you call progress" (268).

13 *A Certain Measure*, p. 244.

14 *They Stooped to Folly*, p. 26. In his father's time a Southern gentleman could not, with impunity, compromise a woman from his own class. In "the ages of gallantry," he often sought diversion not only outside of class but outside of race, since he did not especially fear "the perils of miscegenation" (60). In her description of the elder Littlepage Miss Glasgow revealed the consummate hypocrisy of the Victorian age. As his wife said, he may have "lived loosely" but he was always truly "religious," and his daughter-in-law respects his "high"—and somewhat too vocal—ideals.

15 I am indebted here to Alfred Kazin's account of Ellen Glasgow in *On Native Grounds* (1942), p. 262.

16 *The Novel and Society* (1941), p. 172.

17 She is disdainful of Mrs. Dalrymple and patronizingly priggish toward her rival for Martin Welding's affection, Milly Burden.

18 See C. Vann Woodward, *Origins of the New South* (1951), pp. 447 ff. See also Marshall W. Fishwick, *Virginia: A New Look at the Old Dominion* (1959), pp. 170–71.

19 A recent critic of the novel notes convincing parallels between its physical and intellectual milieu and that found in the earlier "wasteland" poetry of T. S. Eliot. See Robert Holland, "Miss Glasgow's Prufrock," *American Quarterly*, IX (Winter, 1957), 435–40.

20 See Frye, *Anatomy of Criticism*, p. 41.

21 *They Stooped to Folly*, pp. 143, 167, 200.

22 E. Merton Coulter, *The South During Reconstruction* (1947), p. 200.

23 "A Memorable Novel of the Old Deep South," *New York Herald Tribune Books*, X (July 22, 1934), 1.

24 "George Santayana Writes a 'Novel,'" *New York Herald Tribune Books*, XII (Feb. 2, 1936), 1.

25 Fishwick, *Virginia: A New Look at the Old Dominion*, p. 167.

26 In this connection see Northrop Frye's formulation of the essentials of satire: "one is wit or humor founded on fantasy or a sense of the

grotesque or absurd, the other is an object of attack" (*Anatomy of Criticism*, p. 224). The object of attack is, of course, the inflexible older morality; its most absurd manifestations, all equally "fantastic," are the figures of Mary Victoria, Aunt Agatha, and Mrs. Burden.

CHAPTER XI

1 *A Certain Measure*, p. 202.

2 Letter to James Southall Wilson, Dec. 14, 1929, *Letters*, p. 99.

3 In this connection see also Miss Glasgow's utterance in 1913: "For love, which would be so easy a solution of life's problems if it existed as a pure essence, may become sometimes, through its strange interminglings, as morally destructive as hatred" ("Feminism," *New York Times Book Review*, Nov. 30, 1913, p. 657).

4 *The Modern Novel in America* (1951), p. 69.

5 P. 154.

6 Eva during her illness after her operation has the same look of "defeat" which the General had frequently seen on Southern faces after the war and during the Reconstruction.

7 As a sensitive boy with literary ambitions in poetry, the General was scorned by his virile grandfather as a "milksop." The grandfather paints the boy's face with fox's blood when he has shown a disinclination for the hunt. Yet the grandfather is generous and hospitable. In him are blended two contrary tendencies in the Old South: the enjoyment of the graces of life and the impulsive resort to violence and cruelty. For the collocation of these two elements in the Old South, see C. Vann Woodward, *Origins of the New South* (1951), p. 160. That these opposing tendencies survived into the New South may be seen in the contrast in *The Sheltered Life* between what Eva ideally represents and the violence of what happens to her.

8 Modern Library Edition, p. 12.

9 *On Native Grounds* (1942), p. 263.

10 *Anatomy of Criticism* (1957), p. 39.

11 *Rebels and Ancestors* (1953), p. 271.

12 Modern Library Edition, p. 40. John Welch aptly thinks of Jenny Blair as a typical product of "the sheltered life" in that she has been taught only to think of self and to disregard the world outside her own limited sphere. One result of this training, he sees, is to induce an imagination which becomes "a hothouse for sensation."

13 *Rebels and Ancestors*, p. 272.

14 *The Sheltered Life*, p. 209. Even the "progressive" John Welch who embraces, sometimes too uncritically, many modernistic tendencies, finds that Southern life is perhaps preferable to American civilization at large in that it is less "noisy."

15 *A Certain Measure*, p. 204.

16 She is distressed by the fact that Isabella would marry a man in overalls, but once the marriage has taken place, she resolves, with high-

minded hypocrisy, to improve the situation. She now finds that the Crockers are "quiet" rather than "plain" and she is mollified when Joseph exchanges the Baptist Communion for the Episcopal Church. She hires expert genealogists to give her the information she desires. Accordingly, they find that Joseph's first American ancestor settled in James City County in 1635; on the "distaff" side, they trace Joseph's ancestry to the Barons of Runnemede. For this general tendency of ancestor hunting in the South, see Francis B. Simkins, *A History of the South* (1953), p. 378, and Woodward, *Origins of the New South,* p. 157.

17 These visitations of instinct, apparently incapable of being controlled by the will, are indications of a strain of decadence in the Archbald family. This strain may be partly accounted for through the insanity of Archbald's grandmother: emotional instability and a tendency toward melancholy and depression thus entered the Archbald line. These qualities come out most forcibly in the General's daughter Etta, and there is some hint of the ancestral waywardness in both Isabella and Jenny Blair.

18 "Impressions of the Novel," *New York Herald Tribune Books,* IV (May 20, 1928), 5.

19 "Portrait of a Famous and Much Loved Dog," *New York Herald Tribune Books,* X (Oct. 8, 1933), 3.

20 "Impressions of the Novel," *New York Herald Tribune Books,* IV (May 20, 1928), 1.

21 *A Certain Measure,* p. 204.

CHAPTER XII

1 In this connection see J. Wesley Hatcher, "Appalachian America," *Culture in the South,* ed. W. T. Couch (1934), pp. 381 ff. This commentator distinguishes three classes among the mountain inhabitants. The most prosperous live in the valleys, a less prosperous people are found further up in the hills, and the degenerate and the oppressed are higher up still, in the least favorable surroundings. In *Vein of Iron* Miss Glasgow describes the "half-wit" inhabitants high in the mountains whom Grandmother Fincastle has sometimes been called upon to succor in illness. There is also Toby Waters (the village idiot) and his harlot mother. But all such references to the degenerate were subordinate to Miss Glasgow's interest in the sober descendants of the pioneers of Presbyterian persuasion who inhabit the lowland portion of the lower Great Valley (the upper Valley is inhabited chiefly by descendants of German origin). For discussions of these settlers and their descendants, see Marshall W. Fishwick, *The Virginia Tradition* (1956), pp. 55–61, and *Virginia: A New Look at the Old Dominion* (1959), pp. 38–51, 109–20.

2 "Ellen Glasgow's New Book," *New Republic,* LXXXIV (Sept. 11, 1935), 133.

3 *Vein of Iron,* p. 219. That Grandmother's morality is too strongly

prescriptive and does not allow for the specific contingency is seen in her unyielding view of Ada's "sin." Grandmother finds it inexplicable that Ada does not repent her act, that she considers it fulfillment rather than degradation, and that she is not moved by the family "disgrace" she has caused. In this novel we have a tragic rendition, therefore, of the moral conflict between generations, a theme treated comically in *They Stooped to Folly*. In the earlier novel Mrs. Burden cannot bring Milly Burden to repent her passion for Martin Welding.

4   Miss Glasgow also perceptively caught, not only in Grandmother Fincastle but in Mrs. McBride, the militant aspects of the strongly Calvinistic temperament. Despite her sincere anxiety about Ralph when he goes to war, Mrs. McBride finds in the war a convenient justification for the strong but negative feelings characteristic of her morbid nature. Her patriotism is rooted in the same hatred as her piety and in the same domineering assertiveness as her affection for her son. Mr. Black's sermons now touch her deeply, since they are "fiery with the wrath of God"; and like Grandmother Fincastle's, but still more joylessly, her Calvinism finds in war its most viable sublimation.

5   *The Woman Within*, p. v.

CHAPTER XIII

1   Lavinia has no fellow feeling for the members of an alien race, even for Minerva Clay and her boy Parry (Minerva had been governess to the Timberlake children). Lavinia distrusts Parry's intellectual aspirations and his desire to borrow books from Asa. She believes that "the colored race (especially when it has profited so freely by white blood) should be held firmly down to its proper station" (26).

2   *A Certain Measure*, p. 259.

3   *Ibid.*

4   Letter to Bessie Zaban Jones, Sept. 27, 1938, *Letters*, p. 245.

5   His father committed suicide when the Standard Tobacco Company forced him out of business. In his father's day, employer and workers had formed a single social unit with at least some common aims and ideas and some mutual feeling and respect for one another. Workers were human beings, not a list of printed names; and employers knew their men. The heads of the Standard Tobacco Company live in New York and spend the winter in Florida, and are thus absentee proprietors of enterprise. Asa is insecure in his job, because at fifty-nine he is in danger of being replaced by a younger man. In evaluating a worker's performance, no allowance is made under an impersonal regime for his loyalty, length of service, or personal qualities. Mechanization of the tobacco industry, which Miss Glasgow thus referred to in passing, was accelerated after 1885. The twentieth century saw the rise of the large scale entrepreneur in the tobacco business and the founding of corporations in this industry in Virginia and North Caro-

lina. See C. Vann Woodward, *Origins of the New South* (1951), pp. 128–31.

6 Marshall W. Fishwick (*Virginia: A New Look at the Old Dominion* [1959], p. 181) independently used this same phrase from Matthew Arnold ("Stanzas from the Grande Chartreuse") to describe the civilization of present-day Virginia, with its perhaps excessive involvement in the past and its understandable reluctance to accept completely the values of New South industrialism. In its somewhat ineffectual present-day restlessness, Asa might then be loosely symbolic of the Virginia civilization which produced him.

7 From Matthew Arnold's "Obermann Once More."

8 *A Certain Measure*, p. 249.

CONCLUSION

1 Letter to Van Wyck Brooks, Sept. 7, 1944, *Letters*, p. 353. In a recent stimulating essay, C. Hugh Holman indicates those qualities in Ellen Glasgow's mind and art which are in their essence Southern and which anticipated the work of major present-day Southern writers: "a sense of evil, a pessimism about man's potential, a tragic sense of life, a deep-rooted sense of the interplay of past and present, a peculiar sensitivity to time as a complex element in narrative art, a sense of place as a dramatic dimension, and a thorough-going belief in the intrinsic value of art as an end in itself, with an attendant Aristotelian concern with forms and techniques" ("Ellen Glasgow and the Southern Literary Tradition," *Virginia in History and Tradition*, ed. R. C. Simonini, Jr. [1958], p. 102).

2 "What I Believe," *Nation*, CXXXVI (Apr. 12, 1933), p. 406.

3 "Mr. Cabell as a Moralist," *New York Herald Tribune Books*, I (Nov. 2, 1924), p. 2.

4 *A Certain Measure*, p. 132.

5 "Ellen Glasgow: Ironist of Manners," *Fifty Years of the American Novel*, ed. Harold C. Gardiner, S.J. (1951); "Ellen Glasgow's Private History," *Nation*, CLXXIX (Nov. 13, 1954), 425.

6 Letter to Bessie Z. Jones, May 9, 1938, *Letters*, p. 240.

Bibliography

ELLEN GLASGOW'S PUBLISHED WORK

NOVELS

The Descendant. New York: Harper & Brothers, 1897.
Phases of an Inferior Planet. New York: Harper & Brothers, 1898.
The Voice of the People. New York: Doubleday, Page & Co., 1900.
The Battle-Ground. New York: Doubleday, Page & Co., 1902.
The Deliverance. New York: Doubleday, Page & Co., 1904.
The Wheel of Life. New York: Doubleday, Page & Co., 1906.
The Ancient Law. New York: Doubleday, Page & Co., 1908.
The Romance of a Plain Man. New York: The Macmillan Co., 1909.
The Miller of Old Church. Garden City: Doubleday, Page & Co., 1911.
Virginia. Garden City: Doubleday, Page & Co., 1913.
Life and Gabriella. Garden City: Doubleday, Page & Co., 1916.
The Builders. Garden City: Doubleday, Page & Co., 1919.
One Man In His Time. Garden City: Doubleday, Page & Co., 1922.
Barren Ground. Garden City: Doubleday, Page & Co., 1925.
The Romantic Comedians. Garden City: Doubleday, Page & Co., 1926.
They Stooped to Folly. Garden City: Doubleday, Doran & Co., 1929.
The Sheltered Life. Garden City: Doubleday, Doran & Co., 1932.
Vein of Iron. New York: Harcourt, Brace & Co., 1935.
In This Our Life. New York: Harcourt, Brace & Co., 1941.

COLLECTED EDITIONS

The Old Dominion Edition of the Works of Ellen Glasgow. Garden City: Doubleday, Doran & Co. The following novels appeared in 1929: *The Battle-Ground, The Deliverance, They Stooped to Folly,* and *Virginia*.

The following novels appeared in 1933: *Barren Ground, The Miller of Old Church, The Romantic Comedians,* and *The Voice of the People.* All except *They Stooped to Folly* appeared with Prefaces, which in most cases were revised for the Virginia Edition.

The Virginia Edition of the Works of Ellen Glasgow. New York: Charles Scribner's Sons, 1938. The following novels appeared in this edition: *The Voice of the People, The Battle-Ground, The Deliverance, The Romance of a Plain Man, The Miller of Old Church, Virginia, Life and Gabriella, Barren Ground, The Romantic Comedians, They Stooped to Folly, The Sheltered Life,* and *Vein of Iron.*

SHORT STORIES

"Between Two Shores," *McClure's Magazine,* XII (Feb., 1899), 345–52.

"A Point in Morals," *Harper's Magazine,* XCVIII (May, 1899), 976–82.

"The Shadowy Third," *Scribner's Magazine,* LX (Dec., 1916), 658–71.

"Thinking Makes It So," *Good Housekeeping,* LXIV (Feb., 1917), 18–22.

"Dare's Gift," *Harper's Magazine,* CXXXIV (Feb., Mar., 1917), 322–30, 515–24.

"The Past," *Good Housekeeping,* LXXI (Oct., 1920), 64–66.

"Whispering Leaves," *Harper's Magazine,* CXLVI (Jan., Feb., 1923), 147–57, 334–43.

"The Difference," *Harper's Magazine,* CXLVII (June, 1923), 28–42.

"The Artless Age," *Saturday Evening Post,* CXCVI (Aug. 25, 1923), 10–11, 89, 91, 93.

"Romance and Sally Byrd," *Woman's Home Companion,* LI (Dec., 1924), 10–13.

The Shadowy Third and Other Stories. Garden City: Doubleday, Page & Co., 1923. Includes "The Shadowy Third," "Dare's Gift," "The Past," "A Point in Morals," "Whispering Leaves," "The Difference," and "Jordan's End."

OTHER BOOKS

The Freeman and Other Poems. New York: Doubleday, Page & Co., 1902.

A Certain Measure: An Interpretation of Prose Fiction. New York: Harcourt, Brace & Co., 1943. Reprints Prefaces from novels in Virginia Edition and a Preface for *In This Our Life.*

The Woman Within. New York: Harcourt, Brace & Co., 1954.

Letters of Ellen Glasgow, ed. Blair H. Rouse. New York: Harcourt, Brace & Co., 1958.

UNCOLLECTED ESSAYS

"Feminism," *New York Times Book Review,* Nov. 30, 1913, pp. 656–57.

"The Dynamic Past," *Reviewer,* I (Mar. 15, 1921), 73–80.

"Mr. Cabell as a Moralist," *New York Herald Tribune Books,* I (Nov. 2, 1924), 1–2. Review of James Branch Cabell's *Straws and Prayer-Books.*

"Van Doren on Cabell," *New York Herald Tribune Books,* II (Apr. 5, 1925), 3–4. Review of Carl Van Doren's *James Branch Cabell.*

"The Soul of Harlem," *Bookman,* LXIV (Dec., 1926), 509–10. Review of Carl Van Vechten's *Nigger Heaven.*

"Preferences of Four Critics," *New York Herald Tribune Books,* IV (Apr. 15, 1928), 2.

"Impressions of the Novel," *New York Herald Tribune Books,* IV (May 20, 1928), 1, 5–6.

"Some Literary Woman Myths," *New York Herald Tribune Books,* IV (May 27, 1928), 1, 5–6. Most of this article in revised form became the Preface to *They Stooped to Folly,* reprinted in *A Certain Measure,* 1943.

"The Novel in the South," *Harper's Magazine,* CLXIII (Dec. 1928), 93–100. Reprinted in revised form as the Preface to *The Miller of Old Church* for Old Dominion and Virginia Editions of the novel, 1933 and 1938. Again revised for *A Certain Measure,* 1943.

Introduction, *A Memorial Volume of Virginia Historical Portraiture, 1585–1830,* ed. Alexander Wilbourne Weddell (Richmond, 1930), pp. xxv–xxx.

"The Biography of Manuel," *Saturday Review of Literature,* VI (June 7, 1930), 1108–9. Review of Storisende Edition of the works of James Branch Cabell.

"An Experiment in the South," *New York Herald Tribune Books,* VII (Mar. 22, 1931), 1, 6. Review of Emily Clark's *Innocence Abroad.*

"Modern in Tempo and American in Spirit," *New York Herald Tribune Books,* IX (Jan. 8, 1933), 3. Review of Isabel Paterson's *Never Ask the End.*

"Portrait of a Famous and Much Loved Dog," *New York Herald Tribune Books,* X (Oct. 8, 1933), 3, 21. Review of Virginia Woolf's *Flush: A Biography.*

"A Memorable Novel of the Old Deep South," *New York Herald Tribune Books,* X (July 22, 1934), 1–2. Review of Stark Young's *So Red the Rose.*

"One Way to Write Novels," *Saturday Review of Literature,* XI (Dec. 8, 1934), 335, 344, 350. Reprinted in *The Saturday Review Treasury,* ed. Jon Haverstick, New York: Simon & Schuster, Inc., 1957, pp. 44–53. An enlarged version of this essay formed the Preface to *The Sheltered Life,* reprinted in *A Certain Measure,* 1943.

"What I Believe," *Nation,* CXXXVI (Apr. 12, 1933), 404–6. Reprinted in *America Through Women's Eyes,* ed. Mary R. Beard, New York: The Macmillan Co., 1934, pp. 538–46; and in *1934 Essay Annual,* ed. Erich A. Walter, New York: Scott, Foresman & Co., 1934, pp. 123–31.

"Heroes and Monsters," *Saturday Review of Literature,* XII (May 4, 1935), 3–4. Reprinted in *What Is A Book?* ed. Dale Warren, Boston: Houghton Mifflin Co., 1935, pp. 15–20; and in *How Writers Write,* ed. Nettie Sue Tillett, New York: Thomas Y. Crowell Co., 1939, pp. 109–15.

"Branch Cabell Still Clings to His Unbelief," *New York Herald Tribune*

Books, XII (Oct. 6, 1935), 7. Review of Cabell's *Smith: A Sylvan Interlude*.

"George Santayana Writes a 'Novel,'" *New York Herald Tribune Books*, XII (Feb. 2, 1936), 1–2. Review of Santayana's *The Last Puritan*.

"Elder and Younger Brother," *Saturday Review of Literature*, XV (Jan. 23, 1937), 3–5.

"The Inscription," *Of Ellen Glasgow: An Inscribed Portrait*. New York: The Maverick Press, 1938.

"Ellen Glasgow," *I Believe: The Personal Philosophies of Certain Eminent Men and Women of Our Time*, ed. Clifton Fadiman. New York: Simon & Schuster, 1939. Pp. 93–110.

CRITICAL AND BIOGRAPHICAL
ACCOUNTS OF ELLEN GLASGOW

The following critical accounts I have found of value in writing this study. I have listed some works in which only incidental mention is made of Ellen Glasgow, but which are important for establishing facts about her life and career and for determining her place in modern literature. I have included some of the more significant reviews of her work, especially when they seemed general in scope. Some accounts which seemed either unimportant or untrustworthy I have not included; and I have not mentioned materials which I have not been able to examine. As for anthologies of American literature, I have included only those which deal with the South or with the literature of the 1920's. My compilation should be supplemented by the bibliographies of Egly and Quesenbery, listed below. There are some items in my compilation which will not be found elsewhere. I have given important articles on Ellen Glasgow which appeared in 1959 or early 1960, even though I have not been able to make use of them in my book. I have listed reprintings of the items below only if significant revisions were made or if the item has thereby been made more generally available.

Adams, J. Donald. "The Novels of Ellen Glasgow," *New York Times Book Review*, Dec. 18, 1938, pp. 1, 14. Review of the *Virginia Edition*.

Adams, J. Donald. "A New Novel by Ellen Glasgow," *New York Times Book Review*, Mar. 30, 1941, p. 1. Review of *In This Our Life*.

Adams, J. Donald. *The Shape of Books to Come*. New York: The Viking Press, 1944. Pp. 30, 32, 89, 114–19, 124, 141, 163.

Adams, J. Donald. "Speaking of Books," *New York Times Book Review*, Dec. 2, 1945, p. 2.

Anderson, Sherwood. *Letters of Sherwood Anderson*, ed. Howard Mumford Jones and Walter Rideout. Boston: Little, Brown & Co., 1953. Pp. xv, 250–54.

Angoff, Charles. *H. L. Mencken: A Portrait from Memory*. New York: Thomas Yoseloff Inc., 1956. P. 106.

Anonymous. "New Writer: Ellen Glasgow," *Bookman* (London), XVIII (Sept., 1900), 167–68.

Anonymous. "Miss Glasgow's Novels and Poems," *World's Work*, V (Nov., 1902), 2790–92.

Anonymous. "No Valid Reason Against Giving Votes to Women," *New York Times Magazine Section*, Mar. 23, 1913, p. 11.

Arnavon, Cyrille. *Histoire Littéraire des États-Unis*. Paris: Librairie Hachette, 1953. Pp. 312, 314.

Baird, Newton. "Leadership in Ideal Proportions: Ellen Glasgow's *The Voice of the People*," *Talisman*, No. 10 (Winter-Spring, 1956), 30–40.

Baldwin, Alice. "Ellen Glasgow," *South Atlantic Quarterly*, LIV (July, 1955), 394–404. Review of *The Woman Within*.

Basso, Hamilton. "Ellen Glasgow's Literary Credo," *New York Times Book Review,* Oct. 17, 1943, pp. 5, 37. Review of *A Certain Measure.*

Beatty, Richard Croom, Floyd C. Watkins, and Thomas Daniel Young, eds. *The Literature of the South.* New York: Scott, Foresman and Co., 1952. Pp. xviii, xxi, 815–33. Reprints "The Deep Past" from *The Sheltered Life.*

Becker, Allen W. "Ellen Glasgow's Social History," *Texas Studies in English,* XXXVI (1957), 12–18.

Becker, Allen W. "Agrarianism as a Theme in Southern Literature: The Period 1865–1925," *Georgia Review,* XI (Summer, 1957), 150–54.

Becker, Allen W. "Ellen Glasgow and the Southern Literary Tradition," *Modern Fiction Studies,* V (Winter, 1959–60), 295–303.

Benet, Stephen Vincent and Rosemary. "Miss Ellen: A Rebel Against Regimentation," *New York Herald Tribune Books,* XVII (Nov. 17, 1940), 7.

Bernard, Harry. *Le Roman Régionaliste aux États-Unis (1913–1940).* Montreal: Fides, 1949. Pp. 72, 75–76, 77, 78, 347, 351.

Brande, Dorothea. "Four Novels of the Month," *Bookman,* LXXV (Aug., 1932), 405–6. Discussion of *The Sheltered Life.*

Brewer, Frances J. *James Branch Cabell: A Bibliography of His Writings, Biography and Criticism.* Charlottesville: University of Virginia Press, 1957. Pp. 6, 7, 39, 44, 68, 71, 84, 94, 114, 121, 127, 135, 139.

Brickell, Herschell. "The Literary Awakening in the South," *Bookman,* LXVI (Oct., 1927), 138–43.

Brickell, Herschell. "Miss Glasgow and Mr. Marquand," *Virginia Quarterly Review,* XVII (Summer, 1941), 405–17.

Brodin, Pierre. *Le Roman Régionaliste Américain.* Paris: Librairie G. P. Maisonneuve, 1937. Pp. 97–98.

Brodin, Pierre. *Les Écrivains Américains du Vingtième Siècle.* Paris: Horizons de France, 1947. Pp. 81–94.

Brooks, Van Wyck. *The Confident Years: 1885–1915.* New York: E. P. Dutton & Co., 1952. Pp. 43, 50, 51, 339, 342–52, 455, 515, 546, 560.

Brooks, Van Wyck and Otto L. Bettmann. *Our Literary Heritage: A Pictorial History of the Writer in America.* New York: E. P. Dutton & Co., 1956. Pp. 216–17.

Bruccoli, Matthew J. *James Branch Cabell: A Bibliography, Part II: Notes on the Cabell Collections at the University of Virginia.* Charlottesville: University of Virginia Press, 1957. Pp. 90, 95, 99, 130, 136, 137, 138, 141, 142, 151, 152, 154–68.

Burnett, Whit, ed. *This Is My Best.* Cleveland and New York: The World Publishing Co., 1945. Pp. 372–92. Reprints "The Deep Past" from *The Sheltered Life,* with Ellen Glasgow's comment.

Butcher, Margaret J. *The Negro in American Literature.* New York: Alfred A. Knopf, 1956. Pp. 127–28, 163, 166, 168.

Cabell, James Branch. "The Last Cry of Romance," *Nation,* CXX (May 6, 1925), 521–22. Review of *Barren Ground.*

Cabell, James Branch. "Two Sides of the Shielded: A Note as to Ellen Glasgow," *Some of Us*. New York: Robert M. McBride and Co., 1930. Pp. 45–58.

Cabell, James Branch. "The Portrait," *Of Ellen Glasgow: An Inscribed Portrait*. New York: The Maverick Press, 1938.

Cabell, James Branch. "Miss Glasgow of Virginia," *Let Me Lie*. New York: Farrar, Strauss & Co., 1947. Pp. 229–67. In part, reprints in revised form Mr. Cabell's earlier articles on Ellen Glasgow.

Cabell, James Branch. "Speaks with Candor of a Great Lady," *As I Remember It*. New York: The McBride Co., 1955. Pp. 217–33; also pp. 57, 64, 93, 163, 242.

Cabell, James Branch. Foreword, *James Branch Cabell: A Bibliography of His Writings, Biography and Criticism*, ed. Frances J. Brewer. Charlottesville: University of Virginia Press, 1957. Pp. 6–7.

Canby, Henry Seidel. "The Moth and the Flame," *Saturday Review of Literature*, III (Sept. 25, 1926), 133. Review of *The Romantic Comedians*.

Canby, Henry Seidel. "Youth and Age," *Saturday Review of Literature*, IX (Aug. 27, 1932), 63. Review of *The Sheltered Life*.

Canby, Henry Seidel. *Seven Years' Harvest*. New York: Farrar & Rinehart, Inc., 1936. Pp. 5, 87, 273.

Canby, Henry Seidel. "Ellen Glasgow: Ironic Tragedian," *Saturday Review of Literature*, XVIII (Sept. 10, 1938), 3–4. Review of the *Virginia Edition*.

Canby, Henry Seidel. *American Memoir*. Boston: Houghton Mifflin Co., 1947. Pp. 266, 288, 304–6.

Canby, Henry Seidel. "Fiction Sums Up a Century," *Literary History of the United States*, ed. Robert E. Spiller *et al.* New York: The Macmillan Co., 1948. Vol. II, 1216–19; also 1197, 1210, 1211, 1227, 1236, 1296, 1314.

Cash, W. J. *The Mind of the South*. New York: Alfred A. Knopf, 1941. Pp. 144, 325, 374–75.

Chamberlayne, Lewis P. "Virginia," *Sewanee Review*, XXI (Oct., 1913), 500–503. Review of *Virginia*.

Chase, Richard. *The American Novel and Its Tradition*. New York: Doubleday & Co., Inc., 1957. Pp. 158, 159, 160, 161.

Chase, Richard. "Letters to the Establishment," *New Republic*, CXXXVIII (Mar. 10, 1958), 18–19. Review of the *Letters*.

Clark, Emily. "Appreciation of Ellen Glasgow and Her Work," *Virginia Quarterly Review*, V (Apr., 1929), 182–91. Reprinted in revised form in Emily Clark, "Ellen Glasgow," *Innocence Abroad*. New York: Alfred A. Knopf, 1931. Pp. 55–69; also pp. 5, 6, 20, 31.

Clark, Emily. "A Week-end at Mr. Jefferson's University," *New York Herald Tribune Books*, VIII (Nov. 8, 1931), 1, 2.

Collins, Joseph T. *Taking the Literary Pulse: Psychological Studies of Life and Letters*. New York: George H. Doran & Co., 1924. Pp. 68–72.

Collins, Joseph T. "Realism in a Southern Novel," *Ellen Glasgow*, ed.

Dorothea L. Mann. Garden City: Doubleday Doran & Co., Inc., 1927. Pp. 32–38. Discussion of *Barren Ground.*

Commager, Henry Steele. *The American Mind: An Interpretation of American Thought and Character since the 1880's.* New Haven: Yale University Press, 1950. Pp. 56, 65–66, 145–47.

Cooper, Anice P. "Ellen Glasgow: Her Jeremy Looks at Life," *Authors and Others.* Garden City: Doubleday, Page & Co., 1927. Pp. 23–27.

Cooper, Frederic Taber. "Representative American Story Tellers: Ellen Glasgow," *Bookman,* XXIX (Aug., 1909), 613–18. Reprinted in expanded version as "Ellen Glasgow" in *Some American Story-Tellers.* New York: Henry Holt & Co., 1911. Pp. 90–111.

Cowley, Malcolm. "Miss Glasgow's 'Purgatorio,'" *New Republic,* CIV (Mar. 31, 1941), 441. Review of *In This Our Life.*

Cowley, Malcolm. "Promise Paid," *New Republic,* CXIII (Dec. 10, 1945), 805.

Dabney, Virginius. "A Prophet of the New South," *New York Herald Tribune Magazine,* Aug. 25, 1929, pp. 6, 7, 18.

Dabney, Virginius. *Liberalism in the South.* Chapel Hill: University of North Carolina Press, 1932. Pp. 361, 382–84, 386, 389.

Davidson, Donald. "A Mirror for Artists," *I'll Take My Stand: The South and the Agrarian Tradition, by Twelve Southerners.* New York: Harper & Brothers, 1930. P. 58.

Davidson, Donald. "A Meeting of Southern Writers," *Bookman,* LXXIV (Feb., 1932), 494–97.

Davidson, Donald. *The Attack on Leviathan.* Chapel Hill: University of North Carolina Press, 1938. Pp. 92, 100.

Davidson, Donald. "The Trend of Literature," *Culture in the South,* ed. W. T. Couch. Chapel Hill: University of North Carolina Press, 1934. Pp. 181, 188, 191, 193, 199–201; also pp. 172, 177, 627.

Davidson, Donald. "Another Woman Within," *New York Times Book Review,* Jan. 19, 1958, pp. 7, 14. Review of *Letters.*

Edel, Leon. "Miss Glasgow's Private World," *New Republic,* CXXXI (Nov. 15, 1954), 20–21. Review of *The Woman Within.*

Edel, Leon. "Postal Portrait," *Saturday Review,* XLI (Jan. 18, 1958), 17. Review of *Letters.*

Egly, William. "Ellen Glasgow, the Social Thinker," *Social Science,* XVI (Apr., 1940), 144–49.

Egly, William. "Bibliography of Ellen Anderson Gholson Glasgow," *Bulletin of Bibliography,* XVII (Sept.–Dec., 1940), 47–50.

Elias, Robert H. *Theodore Dreiser: Apostle of Nature.* New York: Alfred A. Knopf, 1949. P. 201.

Ewing, Majl. "The Civilized Uses of Irony: Ellen Glasgow," *English Studies in Honor of James Southall Wilson,* ed. Fredson Bowers. Charlottesville: University of Virginia Studies, IV, 1951. Pp. 81–91.

Fadiman, Clifton. "Miss Glasgow," *New Yorker,* XIX (Oct. 16, 1943), 92, 94. Review of *A Certain Measure.*

Field, Louise M. "Miss Glasgow at Home," *New York Times Book Review,*
July 30, 1922, p. 21.

Field, Louise M. *Ellen Glasgow: Novelist of the Old and the New South:
An Appreciation.* Garden City: Doubleday Page & Co., 1923.

Fishwick, Marshall W. "Ellen Glasgow and American Letters," *Common-
wealth,* XVII (Jan., 1950), 13–14.

Fishwick, Marshall W. *The Virginia Tradition.* Washington, D.C.: Public
Affairs Press, 1956. Pp. 2, 13, 20, 21, 36, 40–46, 71.

Fishwick, Marshall W. "Cabell and Glasgow: Tradition in Search of Meaning," *Shenandoah,* VIII (Summer, 1957), 24–35.

Fishwick, Marshall W. *Virginia: A New Look at the Old Dominion.* New
York: Harper & Brothers, 1959. Pp. 124, 139, 156, 165, 178, 183,
185–95, 216.

Freeman, Douglas. "Ellen Glasgow: Idealist," *Saturday Review of Literature,* XII (Aug. 31, 1935), 11–12.

Garland, Hamlin. " 'The Descendant' and Its Author," *Book Buyer,* XI
(Aug., 1897), 45–46.

Garland, Hamlin. *Roadside Meetings.* New York: The Macmillan Co.,
1930. Pp. 349–50.

Garland, Hamlin. *My Friendly Contemporaries.* New York: The Macmillan
Co., 1932. P. 378.

Geismar, Maxwell. "The Armor of the Legend," *Rebels and Ancestors: The
American Novel, 1890–1915.* Boston: Houghton Mifflin Co., 1953. Pp.
219–86, *et passim.*

Geismar, Maxwell. "Ellen Glasgow's Private History," *Nation,* CLXXIX
(Nov. 13, 1954), 425. Review of *The Woman Within.*

Geismar, Maxwell. *American Moderns: From Rebellion to Conformity.*
New York: Hill and Wang, 1958. Pp. 13, 15, 23, 25, 27, 100, 101, 147,
163, 192.

Giles, Barbara. "Character and Fate: The Novels of Ellen Glasgow,"
Mainstream, IX (Sept., 1956), 20–31.

Haardt, Sara. "Ellen Glasgow and the South," *Bookman,* LXXIX (Apr.,
1929), 133–39.

Hackett, Alice Payne. *Fifty Years of Best Sellers.* New York: R. R.
Bowker Co., 1945. Pp. 20, 22, 33, 65, 71.

Haines, Helen E. *What's in a Novel.* New York: Columbia University Press,
1942. Pp. 3, 21, 46, 93.

Hardy, John Edward. "Ellen Glasgow," *Hopkins Review,* V (Summer,
1952), 22–36. Reprinted in *Southern Renascence: The Literature of the
Modern South,* ed. Louis D. Rubin, Jr. and Robert D. Jacobs. Baltimore:
The Johns Hopkins Press, 1953. Pp. 236–50.

Hardy, John Edward. Letter to Editor, *Hopkins Review,* VI (Fall, 1952),
136–37.

Harkins, Edward F. and Charles H. Johnston. "Ellen Anderson G. Glasgow,"
Little Pilgrimages among the Women Who Have Written Famous Books.
Boston: L. C. Page & Co., 1901. Pp. 315–29.

Hart-Davis, Rupert. *Hugh Walpole.* New York: The Macmillan Co., 1952. Pp. 193, 228, 274, 281.

Hatcher, Harlan. *Creating the Modern American Novel.* New York: Farrar and Rinehart, 1935. Pp. 21, 26, 28, 94–98, 132.

Heiney, Donald. *Recent American Literature.* Great Neck, New York: Barron's Educational Series, Inc., 1958. Pp. 179, 182–89, 256, 581.

Henderson, Archibald. "Recent Novels of Note," *Sewanee Review,* XII Oct., 1904), 456–64. Review of *The Deliverance.*

Henderson, Archibald. "Fiction and Social Ethics," *South Atlantic Quarterly,* V (July, 1906), 254–63. Written under pseudonym of Erskine Steele; a review based on *The Wheel of Life.*

Henderson, Archibald. "Soil and Soul," *Saturday Review of Literature,* I (July 18, 1925), 907. Review of *Barren Ground.*

Hendrick, Burton J. *The Training of an American: The Earlier Life and Letters of Walter H. Page, 1855–1913.* Boston and New York: Houghton Mifflin Co., 1928. Pp. 335–37.

Herrick, Christine Terhune. "The Author of 'The Descendant,' " *Critic,* XXX (June 5, 1897), 383.

Herrick, Robert. "The Romantic Comedians," *New Republic,* XLIX (Dec. 8, 1926), 91–93. Review of *The Romantic Comedians.*

Herron, Ima Honaker. *The Small Town in American Literature.* Durham: Duke University Press, 1939. Pp. 129, 217, 288, 330–33, 334, 353, 431.

Hicks, Granville. *The Great Tradition.* New York: The Macmillan Co., 1935. Pp. 226, 227.

Hoffman, Frederick J. *The Modern Novel in America, 1900–1950.* Chicago: Henry Regnery Co., 1951. Pp. 17, 18, 63, 65–75, 105, 201.

Holland, Robert. "Miss Glasgow's Prufrock," *American Quarterly,* IX (Winter, 1957), 435–40.

Holman, C. Hugh. "Ellen Glasgow and the Southern Literary Tradition," *Virginia in History and Tradition,* ed. R. C. Simonini, Jr. Farmville, Virginia: Publications of Longwood College, 1958. Pp. 85–105.

Hoskins, Katherine. "The Time of Ellen Glasgow," *Nation,* CLXXXVI (Feb. 15, 1958), 143–44. Review of *Letters.*

Hubbell, Jay B. *Virginia Life in Fiction.* Dallas: 1922. Pp. 33–36, 39.

Hubbell, Jay B. "Ellen Glasgow," *The South in American Literature: 1607–1900.* Durham: Duke University Press, 1954. Pp. 842–45; also pp. 542, 686, 688, 691, 740, 743, 769, 804, 846, 850, 868, 879.

Hubbell, Jay B. [Review of *Letters of Ellen Glasgow*], *American Literature,* XXXI (March 5, 1959), 87–89.

Hutchens, John K. *The American Twenties: a Literary Panorama.* Philadelphia and New York: J. B. Lippincott Co., 1952. Pp. 12, 15, 22–23, 25–27, 32. Also contains selection from *They Stooped to Folly.*

Jarrell, Randall. "Ten Books," *Southern Review,* I (Autumn, 1935), 397–401. Review of *Vein of Iron.*

Jessup, Josephine L. *The Faith of Our Feminists: A Study in the Novels of Edith Wharton, Ellen Glasgow, Willa Cather.* New York: Richard R.

Smith, 1950. Pp. 9–13, 33, 34–53, 54, 56, 76–118, 122–123.

Jones, Howard Mumford. "Battalions of Women," *Virginia Quarterly Review*, VIII (Oct., 1932), 591–94. Review of *The Sheltered Life*.

Jones, Howard Mumford. "Ellen Glasgow, Witty, Wise and Civilized," *New York Herald Tribune Books*, XIV (July 24, 1938), 1–2. Review of the *Virginia Edition*.

Jones, Howard Mumford. "Product of the Tragic Muse," *Saturday Review of Literature*, XXIII (Mar. 29, 1941), 5. Review of *In This Our Life*.

Jones, Howard Mumford. "The Regional Eminence of Ellen Glasgow," *Saturday Review of Literature*, XXVI (Oct. 16, 1943), 20. Review of *A Certain Measure*.

Kazin, Alfred. *On Native Grounds*. New York: Reynal & Hitchcock, 1942. Pp. 247–49, 257–64, 428, 443.

Kazin, Alfred. "The Lost Rebel," *New Yorker*, XXX (Oct. 30, 1954), 114–19. Reprinted in *The Inmost Leaf*. New York: Harcourt, Brace & Co., 1955. Pp. 136–41.

Kilmer, Joyce. " 'Evasive Idealism' Handicaps Our Literature," *New York Times Magazine*, Mar. 5, 1916, p. 10. Reprinted as "Evasive Idealism in Literature," *Literature in the Making*, ed. Joyce Kilmer. New York: Harper & Brothers, 1917. Pp. 229–38.

Knight, Grant C. *American Literature and Culture*. New York: Ray Long and Richard R. Smith, Inc., 1932. Pp. 349, 356, 433–34.

Knight, Grant C. *James Lane Allen and the Genteel Tradition*. Chapel Hill: University of North Carolina Press, 1935. Pp. 78, 119, 176, 177, 186, 208, 213, 221, 226.

Knight, Grant C. *The Strenuous Age in American Literature*. Chapel Hill: University of North Carolina Press, 1954. Pp. 28, 62, 159, 187, 221, 225.

Kohler, Dayton. "Recognition of Ellen Glasgow," *English Journal*, XXI (Sept., 1942), 523–29.

Kronenberger, Louis. "Family Feeling," *Nation*, CLII (Mar. 28, 1941), 382–83. Review of *In This Our Life*.

Krutch, Joseph Wood. "A Novelist's Faith," *Nation*, CLVII (Oct. 16, 1943), 442, 444. Review of *A Certain Measure*.

Kunitz, Stanley J. and Howard Haycraft, eds. *Twentieth Century Authors: a Biographical Dictionary of Modern Literature*. New York: The H. W. Wilson Co., 1942. P. 540.

Lawrence, Margaret. *The School of Femininity*. New York: Frederick A. Stokes Co., 1936. Pp. 290–93.

Leisy, Ernest E. *The American Historical Novel*. Norman: University of Oklahoma Press, 1950. Pp. 15–16, 162, 185–86, 189.

Lewis, Sinclair. "Fools, Liars and Mr. de Voto," *Saturday Review of Literature*, XXVII (Apr. 15, 1944), 9–12.

Lively, Robert A. *Fiction Fights the Civil War*. Chapel Hill: University of North Carolina Press, 1957. Pp. 12, 25, 33–35, 63, 128, 167, 171–72, 191.

Loggins, Vernon. "Manners: Ellen Glasgow," *I Hear America: Literature in the United States since 1900.* New York: Thomas Y. Crowell Co., 1937. Pp. 188–94.

Loveman, Amy. "Ellen Glasgow, a Tribute," *Saturday Review of Literature,* XXVIII (Dec. 1, 1945), 26.

Luccock, Halford E. *Contemporary American Literature and Religion.* New York: Willet Clark & Co., 1934. Pp. 28, 32, 59, 106–10, 175, 277.

Luccock, Halford E. *American Mirror: Social, Ethical and Religious Aspects of American Literature, 1930–1940.* New York: The Macmillan Co., 1941. Pp. 64, 70, 86, 90.

Manchester, William. *Disturber of the Peace: The Life of H. L. Mencken.* New York, Harper & Brothers, 1951. Pp. 132, 234, 279.

Mann, Dorothea L. "Ellen Glasgow, Citizen of the World," *Bookman,* LXIV (Nov., 1926), 265–71.

Mann, Dorothea L. "Ellen Glasgow," *Ellen Glasgow,* ed. Dorothea L. Mann. Garden City: Doubleday, Page & Co., 1927. Pp. 1–25.

Marble, Annie R. *A Study of the Modern Novel, British and American since 1900.* New York and London: D. Appleton & Co., 1928. Pp. 314–16.

Marcosson, Isaac F. "The Personal Ellen Glasgow," *Bookman,* XXIX (Aug., 1909), 619–21.

Marcosson, Isaac F. *Adventures in Interviewing.* New York: Dodd, Mead & Co., 1919. Pp. 36–37, 272–73.

Marcosson, Isaac F. *Before I Forget: A Pilgrimage to the Past.* New York: Dodd, Mead & Co., 1959. Pp. 48, 53, 66, 71, 494–500, 504.

Marshall, George O., Jr. "Hardy's 'Tess' and Ellen Glasgow's 'Barren Ground,'" *Texas Studies in Literature and Language,* I (Winter, 1960), 517–21.

Matthiessen, F. O. *Theodore Dreiser.* New York: William Sloane Associates, 1951. Pp. 110–11.

May, Henry F. *The End of American Innocence.* New York: Alfred A. Knopf, 1959. Pp. 79, 85–86.

McDowell, Frederick P. W. "Ellen Glasgow and the Art of the Novel," *Philological Quarterly,* XXX (July, 1951), 328–47.

McDowell, Frederick P. W. " 'The Old Pagan Scorn of Everlasting Mercy'— Ellen Glasgow's *The Deliverance,*" *Twentieth Century Literature,* IV (Jan., 1959), 135–42. An earlier version of discussion in this book.

McDowell, Frederick P. W. "Theme and Artistry in Ellen Glasgow's *The Sheltered Life,*" *Texas Studies in Literature and Language,* I (Winter, 1960), 502–16. An earlier version of discussion in this book.

McIlwaine, Shields. *The Southern Poor-White from Lubberland to Tobacco Road.* Norman: University of Oklahoma Press, 1939. Pp. 172, 184–93, 195, 198, 217, 231–32.

Meade, Julian R. "Ellen Glasgow, a True Genius," *Writer,* XLII (Oct., 1930), 239–41.

Meade, Julian R. *I Live in Virginia.* New York: Longmans, Green & Co., 1935. Pp. 181–90, 193, 194.

Mencken, H. L. *Prejudices: Second Series.* New York: Alfred A. Knopf, 1920. P. 27.

Mencken, H. L. "New Fiction," *American Mercury,* V (July, 1925), 382–83. Review comments on *Barren Ground.*

Mencken, H. L. "Two Southern Novels," *American Mercury,* XVIII (Oct., 1929), 251–53. Review comments on *They Stooped to Folly.*

Mencken, H. L. "A Southern Skeptic," *American Mercury,* XXIX (Aug., 1933), 504–6. Review of the *Old Dominion Edition.*

Mencken, H. L. "The South Astir," *Virginia Quarterly Review,* XI (Jan., 1935), 46–60.

Mencken, H. L., ed. *Southern Album* by Sara Haardt. Garden City: Doubleday, Doran & Co. Inc., 1936. Pp. xviii, xix.

Millett, Fred B. Introduction, *Contemporary American Literature,* ed. John Matthews Manly and Edith Rickert. Rev. ed. New York: Harcourt, Brace & Co., 1929. Pp. 19–20.

Millett, Fred B. *Contemporary American Authors.* New York: Harcourt, Brace & Co., 1940. Pp. 42–43, 59, 63, 374–76.

Mims, Edwin. *History of Southern Fiction, The South in the Building of the Nation* (VIII). Richmond: The Southern Historical Publication Society, 1909. Pp. xlix, lxii, 359–79. Reprints selections from *The Voice of the People* and *The Battle-Ground.*

Mims, Edwin. "The Social Philosophy of Ellen Glasgow," *Social Forces,* IV (Mar., 1926), 495–503. Reprinted in revised form in Edwin Mims, "From Romance to Realism," *The Advancing South.* Garden City: Doubleday, Page & Co., 1926. Pp. 202–4, 214–26; also pp. 10, 50–51, 255.

Moger, Allen Wesley. *The Rebuilding of the Old Dominion: A Study in Economic, Social, and Political Transition from 1880–1902.* Ann Arbor, Edwards Brothers, Inc., 1940. Pp. v, 1, 43, 44, 47, 48, 49, 53, 54, 61.

Monroe, N. Elizabeth. "Contemplation of Manners in Ellen Glasgow," *The Novel and Society.* Chapel Hill: University of North Carolina Press, 1941. Pp. 139–87; also pp. 5–6, 32–33, 35, 111, 116, 196, 255–56.

Monroe, N. Elizabeth. "Ellen Glasgow: Ironist of Manners," *Fifty Years of the American Novel: A Christian Appraisal,* ed. Harold C. Gardiner, S.J. New York: Charles Scribner's Sons, 1951. Pp. 49–68.

Moore, Virginia. *Virginia Is a State of Mind.* New York: E. P. Dutton & Co., 1943. Pp. 293, 301–3, 306.

Morison, Samuel Eliot and Henry Steele Commager. *The Growth of the American Republic.* New York: Oxford University Press, 1942. Vol. II, 286, 573.

Moses, Montrose J. *The Literature of the South.* New York: Thomas Y. Crowell & Co., 1910. Pp. 462–63.

Murdock, Kenneth B. "Folly and the Ironist," *Virginia Quarterly Review,* V (Oct., 1929), 596–600. Review of *They Stooped to Folly.*

The National Cyclopaedia of American Biography. New York: James T. White & Co., Vol. XIII (1906), 103; Current C (1930), 348; XXXV (1949), 200–201.

Nevius, Blake. *Edith Wharton: A Study of Her Fiction.* Berkeley and Los Angeles: University of California Press, 1953. Pp. 85, 139, 217.

Overton, Grant M. "Ellen Glasgow," *The Women Who Make Our Novels.* New York: Moffat, Yard & Co., 1918. Pp. 20–40. Rev. ed. New York: Dodd Mead & Co., 1928. Pp. 157–66.

Overton, Grant M. "Ellen Glasgow's Arrow," *Bookman,* LXI (May, 1925), 291–96.

Overton, Grant M. *An Hour of the American Novel.* Philadelphia and London: J. B. Lippincott Co., 1929. Pp. 115–18.

Page, Rosewell. "Ellen Anderson Gholson Glasgow," *Library of Southern Literature,* eds. Edwin A. Alderman, Joel Chandler Harris, and Charles W. Kent. Atlanta: The Martin and Hoyt Co., 1909. Vol. IV, 1847–72. Reprints portions of *The Battle-Ground* and *The Deliverance,* "The Freeman," and "A Creed."

Paine, Gregory, ed. *Southern Prose Writers.* American Writers Series. New York: American Book Co., 1947. Pp. cix, cxi, cxii, cxv, cxvi.

Parker, William R. "Ellen Glasgow: A Gentle Rebel," *English Journal,* XX (Mar., 1931), 187–94.

Paterson, Isabel. "Rue with a Difference," *New York Herald Tribune Books,* V (Aug. 4, 1929), 1, 5–6. Review of *They Stooped to Folly.*

Pattee, Fred Lewis. *The New American Literature, 1890–1930.* New York: The Century Co., 1930. Pp. 10, 91, 256–60, 267, 350.

Patterson, Daniel W. "Ellen Glasgow's Plan for a Social History of Virginia," *Modern Fiction Studies,* V (Winter, 1959–60), 353–60.

Perkins, Maxwell E. *Editor to Author: The Letters of Maxwell Perkins,* ed. John Hall Wheelock. Charles Scribner's Sons, 1950. Pp. 151, 251, 298.

Pinckney, Josephine. "Southern Writers' Congress," *Saturday Review of Literature,* VIII (Nov. 7, 1931), 266.

Quesenbery, W. D., Jr. "Ellen Glasgow: A Critical Bibliography," *Bulletin of Bibliography,* XXII (May–Aug. and Sept.–Dec., 1959), 201–6, 230–36.

Quinn, Arthur H. "Ellen Glasgow and the New South," *American Fiction: an Historical and Critical Survey.* New York: D. Appleton-Century Co., 1936. Pp. 670–82; also pp. 507, 720.

Ransom, John Crowe. "Modern with the Southern Accent," *Virginia Quarterly Review,* XI (Apr., 1935), 184–200.

Rascoe, Burton. *We Were Interrupted.* New York: Doubleday & Co., 1947. Pp. 303–6.

Rawlings, Marjorie K. "Regional Literature of the South," *College English,* I (Feb., 1940), 381–89.

Richardson, Eudora Ramsay. "Richmond and Its Writers," *Bookman,* LXVIII (Dec., 1928), 449–53.

Richardson, Eudora Ramsay. "The South Grows Up," *Bookman,* LXX (Jan., 1930), 545–50.

Richardson, Eudora Ramsay. "Those Queer People Who Write," *Bookman,* LXXIV (Sept., 1931), 61–67.

Rogers, Cameron. "Realism from the Romantic South," *World's Work,* L (May, 1925), pp. 99–102. Review of *Barren Ground.*

Rosenberger, Francis Coleman, ed. *Virginia Reader: A Treasury of Writings from the First Voyages to the Present.* New York: E. P. Dutton & Co., 1948. Pp. 495–504. Contains selection from *Barren Ground.*

Rouse, H. Blair. "Ellen Glasgow in Retrospect," *Emory University Quarterly,* VI (Mar., 1950), 30–40.

Rouse, H. Blair. "Time and Place in Southern Fiction," *Hopkins Review,* VI (Fall, 1952), 37–61. Reprinted in *Southern Renascence: The Literature of the Modern South,* ed. Louis D. Rubin, Jr. and Robert D. Jacobs. Baltimore: The Johns Hopkins Press, 1953. Pp. 126–50.

Rouse, H. Blair. Letter to Editor, *Hopkins Review,* VI (Fall, 1952), 134, 136.

Rouse, H. Blair. Introduction, *Letters of Ellen Glasgow.* New York: Harcourt, Brace & Co., 1958. Pp. 11–20.

Rubin, Louis D., Jr. "The Image of an Army: Southern Novelists and the Civil War," *Texas Quarterly,* I (Spring, 1958), 17–34.

Rubin, Louis D., Jr. "The Road to Yoknapatawpha: George W. Cable and 'John March, Southerner,' " *Virginia Quarterly Review,* XXXV (Winter, 1959), 118–32.

Rubin, Louis D., Jr. "Miss Ellen," *No Place on Earth: Ellen Glasgow, James Branch Cabell and Richmond-in-Virginia,* *Texas Quarterly,* II (Autumn, 1959), 3–49.

Savage, Henry, Jr. *Seeds of Time: The Background of Southern Thinking.* New York: Henry Holt & Co., 1959. P. 269.

Sherman, Stuart P. "Ellen Glasgow: The Fighting Edge of Romance," *New York Herald Tribune Books,* I (Apr. 19, 1925), 1–3. Reprinted in *Critical Woodcuts.* New York: Charles Scribner's Sons, 1926. Pp. 73–82.

Simkins, Francis Butler. *A History of the South.* New York: Alfred A. Knopf, 1953. Pp. 7, 385, 437, 438, 440–43, 445, 449–51, 453–54.

Simkins, Francis Butler. "The Education That Doesn't Educate: the Persistence of Virginia Folkways," *Virginia in History and Tradition,* ed. R. C. Simonini, Jr. Farmville, Virginia: Publication of Longwood College, 1958. Pp. 8, 14, 17.

Snelling, Paula. "Ellen Glasgow and Her South," *North Georgia Review,* IV (Winter, 1941), 26–27. Review of *In This Our Life.*

Spencer, Benjamin T. "Regionalism in American Literature," *Regionalism in America,* ed. Merrill Jensen. Madison: University of Wisconsin Press, 1951. Pp. 239, 240.

Spiller, Robert E. *The Cycle of American Literature: An Essay in Historical Criticism.* New York: The Macmillan Co., 1955. Pp. 219–24.

Stewart, Randall. "The Outlook for Southern Writing: Diagnosis and Prognosis," *Virginia Quarterly Review,* XXXI (Spring, 1955), 252–63.

Stewart, Randall. *American Literature and Christian Doctrine.* Baton Rouge: Louisiana State University Press, 1958. P. 20.

Stone, Grace Z. "Ellen Glasgow and Her Novels," *Sewanee Review,* L (July–Sept., 1942), 289–301.

Stovall, Floyd. *American Idealism*. Norman: University of Oklahoma Press, 1943. P. 138.

Strode, Hudson. "The Secret Places of a Heart," *New York Times Book Review*, LIX (Oct. 31, 1954), 1, 42. Review of *The Woman Within*.

Tate, Allen. "The New Provincialism: With an Epilogue on the Southern Novel," *Virginia Quarterly Review*, XXI (Spring, 1945), 262–72. Reprinted in *Collected Essays*. Denver: Alan Swallow, 1959. Pp. 282–304.

Tate, Allen. "A Southern Mode of the Imagination," *Collected Essays*. Denver: Alan Swallow, 1959. Pp. 554–68.

Thorp, Willard. *American Writing in the Twentieth Century*. (The Library of Congress Series in American Civilization). Cambridge: Harvard University Press, 1960. Pp. 234, 235, 237–39, 258.

Tyler, Alice M. "Ellen Glasgow," *Book News Monthly*, XXX (Aug., 1912), 843–48.

Van Auken, Sheldon. "The Southern Historical Novel in the Early Twentieth Century," *Journal of Southern History*, XIV (May, 1948), 157–91.

Van Doren, Carl. *Contemporary American Novelists*. New York: The Macmillan Co., 1923. Pp. 132–34.

Van Doren, Carl. "Barren Ground," *New Republic*, XLII (Apr. 29, 1925), 271. Review of *Barren Ground*.

Van Doren, Carl. *The American Novel, 1789–1939*. Rev. ed. New York: The Macmillan Co., 1940. Pp. 214, 216, 217, 264–66.

Van Gelder, Robert. "An Interview with Miss Ellen Glasgow," *New York Times Book Review*, Oct., 18, 1942, p. 2. Reprinted in Robert Van Gelder, *Writer and Writers*. New York: Charles Scribner's Sons, 1946. Pp. 319–23.

Van Noppen, Ina Woestemeyer, ed. *The South: A Documentary History*. New York: D. Van Nostrand Co., 1958. Pp. 457, 504–8. Contains selection from *Barren Ground*.

Van Vechten, Carl. "A Virginia Lady Dissects a Virginia Gentleman," *New York Herald Tribune Books*, II (Sept. 12, 1926), 1, 2. Review of *The Romantic Comedians*.

Van Vechten, Carl. *Fragments from an Unwritten Autobiography*. New Haven: Yale University Library, 1955. Vol. II, 29–35; also Vol. I, 10–12, 29, 32–34.

Villard, Léonie. "L'Oeuvre d'Ellen Glasgow, romancière américaine," *Revue Anglo-Américaine*, XI (Dec., 1933), 97–111.

Wagenknecht, Edward. "Ellen Glasgow: Triumph and Despair," *The Cavalcade of the American Novel*. New York: Henry Holt & Co., 1952. Pp. 267–80; also pp. 302, 391.

Wagenknecht, Edward. "*Great Expectations* and Ellen Glasgow," *Boston University Studies in English*, III (Spring, 1957), 57–60.

Walpole, Hugh. Introduction, *The Romance of a Plain Man*. Lambskin Library Edition, Garden City: Doubleday, Page & Co., 1926.

Wellington, Amy. "Militancy and Ellen Glasgow," *Women Have Told: Studies in the Feminist Tradition*. Boston: Little, Brown & Co., 1930. Pp. 157–73.

Whicher, George. "Resurgent South," *The Literature of the American People: An Historical and Critical Survey,* ed. Arthur Hobson Quinn. New York: Appleton-Century-Crofts, Inc., 1951. Pp. 915–17; also pp. 660, 665, 772.

Williams, Harold. *Modern English Writers: Being a Study of Imaginative Literature 1890–1914.* New York: Alfred A. Knopf, 1919. P. 473.

Wilson, Albert F. "Can Children Be Taught to Write?" *Good Housekeeping,* LXI (July, 1915), 48.

Wilson, James Southall. "Ellen Glasgow's Novels," *Virginia Quarterly Review,* IX (Oct., 1933), 595–600. Review of the *Old Dominion Edition.*

Wilson, James Southall. "Two American Novels," *Virginia Quarterly Review,* XI (Oct., 1935), 620–26. Review of *Vein of Iron.*

Wilson, James Southall. "Ellen Glasgow: Ironic Idealist," *Virginia Quarterly Review,* XV (Winter, 1939), 121–26. Review of the *Virginia Edition.*

Wilson, James Southall. "Ellen Glasgow: 1941," *Virginia Quarterly Review,* XVII (Winter, 1941), 317–20. Review of *In This Our Life.*

Wilson, James Southall. "Ellen Glasgow's Autobiography," *Virginia Quarterly Review,* XXXI (Spring, 1955), 292–98. Review of *The Woman Within.*

Wilson, James Southall. "Ellen Glasgow's Letters," *Virginia Quarterly Review,* XXXIV (Summer, 1958), 455–59. Review of *Letters.*

Wish, Harvey. *Society and Thought in Modern America: A Social and Intellectual History of the American People from 1865.* New York: Longmans, Green & Co., 1952. Vol. II, 61–62, 472.

Wolfe, Don M. *The Image of Man in America.* Dallas: Southern Methodist University Press, 1957. P. 224.

Wolfe, Thomas. *The Letters of Thomas Wolfe,* ed. Elizabeth Nowell. New York: Charles Scribner's Sons, 1956. Pp. 512, 513, 568.

Woodress, James. *Booth Tarkington: Gentleman from Indiana.* Philadelphia and New York: J. B. Lippincott Co., 1954. Pp. 244, 249.

Woodward, C. Vann. *Origins of the New South, 1877–1913.* (*A History of the South,* Vol. IX, ed. Wendell Holmes Stephenson and E. Merton Coulter.) Baton Rouge: Louisiana State University Press, 1951. Pp. 161, 431, 432, 434–36.

Young, Stark. "Deep South Notes VI: At Sheltered Valley," *New Republic,* LXXII (Sept. 7, 1932), 100–102. A discussion of *The Sheltered Life.*

Young, Stark. "Prefaces to Distinction," *New Republic,* LXXV (June 7, 1933), 101–2. Article on the *Old Dominion Edition.*

Young, Stark. "Ellen Glasgow's New Book," *New Republic,* LXXXIV (Sept. 11, 1935), 133. Review of *Vein of Iron.*

Young, Stark, ed. *Southern Treasury of Life and Literature.* New York: Charles Scribner's Sons, 1937. Pp. 721–34. Contains selections from *The Romantic Comedians* and *The Sheltered Life.*

Young, Stark. "Beautiful Apologia," *New Republic,* CIX (Oct. 25, 1943), 588–91. Review of *A Certain Measure.*

Zeitlin, Jacob and Homer Woodbridge. *Life and Letters of Stuart P. Sherman.* New York: Farrar & Rinehart, Inc., 1929. Vol. II, 693, 702.

Index

— philosophy of fiction, 19–24, 144, 230–31, 233

— comedy and tragedy, views on, 32, 77, 78–79, 105–7, 123, 151, 152, 155, 161–62, 167, 170, 177–78, 179, 180–81, 181–82, 187, 188, 192, 195–97, 204, 205–6, 215–16, 219–20, 225–26, 229, 233. *See also* Ellen Glasgow: Intellectual Life and Attitudes, "ironic and comic view of experience"; and Ellen Glasgow: Artistry, "humor and comedy," "irony and satire," and "tragedy"

— dedication to art of writing, 5–6, 18–19, 25, 37, 229

— historical romance, relation to, 24–25, 60, 65, 67, 78–79

— modernism in literature, ambiguous attitude toward, 17–18, 19–24, 26, 32–34, 35–36, 39. *See also* Ellen Glasgow: Intellectual Life and Attitudes, "modernism"; and Ellen Glasgow: Principal Themes and Subjects, "modernism"

— naturalism in the novel, 21–23, 26, 39, 43–44, 53, 71, 75, 101–2, 133, 222, 233

— realism in the novel, 17–18, 19–24, 25, 26, 36, 40–41, 53, 60–61, 65, 67–68, 75, 91, 92, 96, 101–5, 111, 121–22, 145, 151–54, 158, 162, 173, 177, 179, 180–81, 184, 201, 203, 207, 208–9, 219–20, 227–28, 230–31, 233, 234

— universality of the artist, belief in, 8, 9, 19–20, 21, 23, 229–30, 233, 234

GLASGOW, ELLEN: PRINCIPAL THEMES AND SUBJECTS

— determinism, 22–23, 45, 59–60, 67, 71, 72, 73, 77, 86, 92, 101–4, 109, 118, 122, 123, 128, 137, 140, 142, 147, 149–51, 153, 154, 155–56, 165, 170, 171, 174, 176, 177–79, 185, 186, 187–88, 189–93, 195, 204–6, 211, 212–13, 219–23, 224, 225, 226, 230–31

— disenchantment, 42, 50–51, 53, 68–69, 77, 78–80, 83–85, 103–4, 111, 115, 121–23, 124, 129, 134, 142, 145, 152, 153, 155, 163, 165, 168, 175, 177–80, 183, 184, 193, 204–6, 209, 210–11, 213, 216–20, 224, 226–27. *See also* Ellen Glasgow: Intellectual Life and Attitudes, "disenchantment"; and Ellen Glasgow: Life and Personality, "internal conflicts and alienation"

— evil, recognition of, 43–44, 47–48, 59, 63, 70, 73–77, 86, 98–100, 103–4, 117, 132–33, 135, 148, 150–51, 179–80, 189, 190, 195–97, 209, 219–20, 225–26, 230

— heredity and environment, relative influence of, 22–23, 44, 55–56, 57, 58–60, 70–73, 89, 92–94, 101–4, 112–14, 115, 116, 118–19, 127–28, 130–33, 135, 139–40, 142–43, 149, 155–56, 167, 175, 176, 187, 189–90, 193, 195–97, 206, 208–9, 211, 212–13, 218–26

— isolation and alienation, 16–17, 44, 50–51, 55–56, 58–59, 70–71, 73, 77, 86–87, 92, 100–101, 119–20, 121, 123, 124, 128, 132, 140, 142–43, 145–49, 155–56, 160, 162, 165, 169–70, 177–81, 187–89, 191–92, 193, 195–97, 204–6, 209–11, 212–13, 215–17, 220–22, 224, 225

— land, mystical identification with, 67, 75, 96–98, 145, 147–54, 158–59, 206

— love: 18, 42, 52, 57–58, 67, 77–78, 84, 94, 97–98, 102–4, 112, 120–21, 123, 124, 130, 131, 132–35, 142, 145, 152–55, 160, 162–65, 174, 175, 179, 181–82, 185–89, 191, 194–97, 200, 204, 206, 209, 211, 215–20, 224, 228, 231. *See also* Ellen Glasgow: Social History, "sexual morality"

— "modernism," criticism of, 47–48, 119–20, 140–42, 167–68, 177–80, 191–92, 210–13, 221–23, 225–27. *See also* Ellen Glasgow: Intellectual Life and Attitudes, "modernism"; and Ellen Glasgow: Literary Philosophy, "modernism in literature"

— moral and philosophical idealism, 44–45, 49, 50–51, 58–59, 63, 66, 77, 78, 82–84, 86, 87, 88, 94, 97, 110,

Murfree, Mary N. ("Charles Egbert Craddock"), 17, 24
Musset, Alfred de, 99

Nashville Group, 33
New England, 36
New Freedom, the, 35
Newman, Frances, 33
"New South, The," 18, 34, 38, 41, 56, 89, 90, 91, 94, 95, 118, 126, 129, 136, 191, 222. *See also* Ellen Glasgow: Social History, "Post-Reconstruction Virginia" and "industrialism and the 'New South'"
New York, 15, 16, 17, 27, 30, 31, 40, 41, 48, 50, 52, 53, 64, 82, 91, 115, 118, 121, 124, 130, 131, 133, 150, 151, 152, 156, 157. *See also* Ellen Glasgow: Social History, "city life"
Nietzsche, Friedrich Wilhelm, 15, 18, 43, 50, 51, 59, 74, 137
Norris, Frank, 4, 20, 43, 45, 91
Novalis (Friedrich Leopold von Hardenberg), 23
"Novel in the South, The" (Eilen Glasgow), 34

Old Dominion Edition, 10, 11, 20
"Old South, The," 38, 56, 57, 63, 67, 69–71, 79, 94, 101, 114, 118, 126, 131, 187, 191, 193. *See also* Ellen Glasgow: Social History, "pre-Civil War Virginia"
One Man in His Time, 5, 31, 127, *139–44*
"Only a Daisy in a Garden of Roses" (Ellen Glasgow), 14
Orient (literature and religion), 28, 83, 204. *See also* Ellen Glasgow: Social History, "religion"; and Ellen Glasgow: Intellectual Life and Attitudes, "religion"

Page, Thomas Nelson, 17, 24
Page, Walter Hines, 6, 18, 25
Paris, France, 17, 170
Pascal, Blaise, 28
Peterkin, Julia, 33
Petersburg ("Dinwiddie"), 112–22, 124–25

Phases of an Inferior Planet, 6, 40, *48–53*
Phillips, Ulrich B., 34
Piedmont (rural Virginia), 147
Pinckney, Josephine, 33
Plato, 28, 83
Plotinus, 28, 29, 209
Poe, Edgar Allan, 114, 233
"Point in Morals, A" (Ellen Glasgow), 144–45
Populism, 56, 60
Porter, Jane, *Thaddeus of Warsaw,* 65, 113
Porter, Katherine Anne, 187, 193, 229
Presbyterian Church. *See* Ellen Glasgow: Social History, "religion, Calvinism"
Proctor, Adelaide Ann, 113
"Progressives," the Southern, 136, 137, 139, 141
Proust, Marcel, 200
Pulitzer Prize (1941), 37
Puritanism. *See* Ellen Glasgow: Social History, "religion, Calvinism"

Queenborough. *See* Ellen Glasgow: Social History, "city life"

Radicals, Northern, 57, 70
Railroads, development of Southern, 89–91
Ransom, John Crowe, 34
Rascoe, Burton, 33, 34
Rawlings, Marjorie K., 32, 34
Readjuster Movement, 57
Reconstruction: 13, 17, 18, 57, 69–81 *passim,* 93, 100, 113, 118, 128. *See also* Ellen Glasgow: Social History, "Reconstruction Period"
"Redeemers," the Southern, 89, 91
Republican Party, 135. *See also* Ellen Glasgow: Social History, "politics in Virginia and the South"
Rhett, Robert Barnwell, 63
Ricardo, David, 15
Rice, Alice Hegan, 34
Rice, Cale Young, 34
Richardson, Samuel, 24
Richmond, Virginia, 12, 13, 18, 30, 36,